ALASKA

A·L·A·S·K·A

AN AMERICAN COLONY

SECOND
EDITION

STEPHEN W. HAYCOX

UNIVERSITY OF WASHINGTON PRESS
Seattle

12371 A

Design by Katrina Noble
Composed in Arno Pro, typeface designed by Robert Slimbach

24   23   22   21   20   5   4   3   2   1

Printed and bound in the United States of America

UNIVERSITY OF WASHINGTON PRESS
uwapress.uw.edu

LIBRARY OF CONGRESS CATALOGING-IN-PUBLICATION DATA
LC record available at https://lccn.loc.gov/2019041057
LC ebook record available at https://lccn.loc.gov/2019041058

ISBN 978-0-295-74686-9 (hardcover), ISBN 978-0-295-74685-2 (paperback), ISBN 978-0-295-74687-6 (ebook)

COVER DESIGN: Katrina Noble
COVER AND TITLE PAGE PHOTOGRAPHS: (*cover, top*) St. George Island, Alaska. © Nathaniel Wilder. (*cover, bottom; and title page*) Mountains from Alaska aerial surveys, National Archives 95-GP-5351-12371.

The paper used in this publication is acid free and meets the minimum requirements of American National Standard for Information Sciences—Permanence of Paper for Printed Library Materials, ANSI z39.48–1984.∞

For Dagmar

CONTENTS

PROLOGUE

Alaska is a vast, rugged, beautiful land. Most people who have lived there have seen little of the state, but what they have seen has left an indelible impression and has suggested the wonder of the rest of Alaska. This is true wherever one has lived in the state—in the extraordinary rain forest and mountain country of the coastal Panhandle, in the frigid, silent reaches of the Interior, or in the urban-oriented but remarkably diverse and magnificent south-central region. Whether Native or non-Native, those who have lived out of reach of Alaska's meager road system, in the southwest Kuskokwim-Yukon lake and delta country, or in the remote villages along the Bering and Arctic sea coasts, have experienced one of America's truly unique natural habitats and ways of life.

Alaska stands as an icon of wilderness in the American mind. Those who have lived in the territory and those who have only read of it, possibly dreamed of it, visualize the state as an unpeopled or sparsely populated land dominated by nature, a pristine environment that is untamed and untrammeled. Indigenous people—Alaska Natives—have inhabited the region for fourteen thousand years; many still live in remote, roadless villages. Through much of the twentieth century, Alaska was also viewed as a last frontier, a land where men and women might yet prove themselves capable and worthy through the work and sacrifice of homesteading and building new settlements, where they could live freely by and with the fruit of their own labor, relying on only themselves for success or failure. But the rise of environmental consciousness in American culture, particularly strong in the 1960s and 1970s, has diminished Alaska's role as the last settlement and has shifted the national consciousness to the region's role as the last forest, the last wild, the last natural place. In mid-century the government advertised Alaska as an opportunity for a new

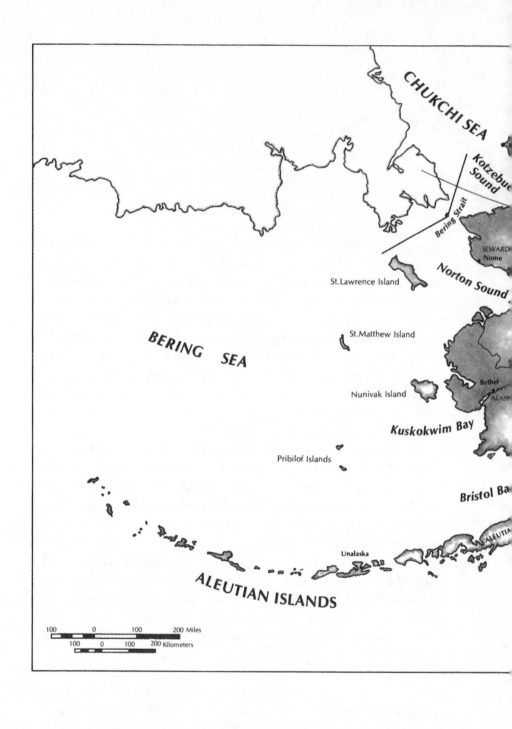

CHUKCHI SEA

Kotzebue Sound

Bering Strait

SEWARD
Nome

Norton Sound

St.Lawrence Island

St.Matthew Island

BERING SEA

Nunivak Island

Bethel

ALASK

Kuskokwim Bay

Pribilof Islands

Bristol Ba

ALEUTIA

Unalaska

ALEUTIAN ISLANDS

100   0   100   200 Miles

100   0   100   200 Kilometers

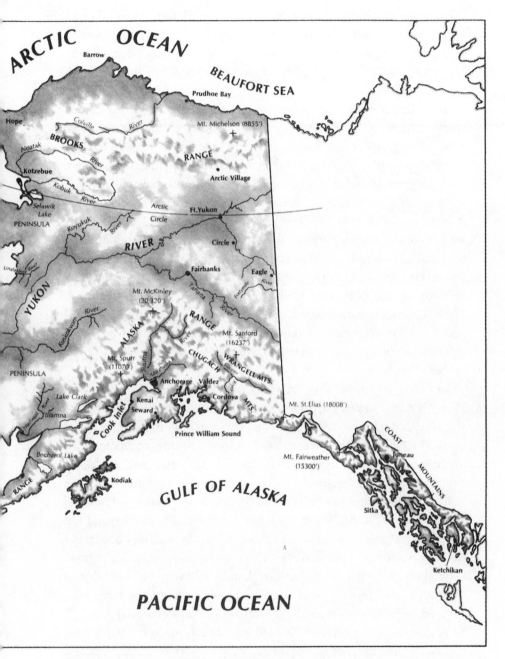

Alaska. From Antonson and Hanable, *Alaska's Heritage*, 586–87, by permission of the State of Alaska, courtesy of the Alaska Historical Commission.

life, and journalists celebrated its growth and development toward traditional forms of western culture. By the end of the century most writers celebrated Alaska's wilderness attributes nearly exclusively, decrying the continuing and potential inroads into a land increasingly imagined as a natural preserve.[1]

The reality of Alaska has seldom matched the Alaska of the imagination, however. Although there is vast wilderness in the state, little of it is untrammeled. Today, guides operating from tourist lodges fly visitors for hunting and fishing to ostensibly remote lakes and rivers throughout the territory, while government and private biologists and environmentalists hike, camp, and photograph almost everywhere. There are but 780,000 residents in the state, 115,000 of them Native, and nearly none of them lives in isolation or without most of the amenities of modern civilization, unless they do so by conscious choice and by considerable effort. Although villages off the road system may have mail delivery only a few times a week, and then only by light airplane, all villages and towns are connected to the mainstream culture by internet access, satellite television and radio, and long-distance telephone and fax machines. By the end of their teens most Native village children have made numerous trips to Alaska's urban centers and to cities in the lower states.

In addition, there is little in Alaska that resembles frontier settlement. Most Alaskans (70 percent, in fact) live in the state's urban centers.[2] Nearly 300,000 people live in Anchorage or its environs, and 150,000 live in the nearby Matanuska Valley, which has become a bedroom community for Anchorage. Together these residents represent more than half of Alaska's population. Twenty-five thousand live in the coastal communities of the Kenai Peninsula and Prince William Sound: in the towns of Cordova, Valdez, Seward, Kenai/Soldotna, Homer, and Kodiak, just beyond the end of the Kenai Peninsula. Sixty thousand urban residents live in the coastal rain forest communities of Southeast Alaska, in Ketchikan, Petersburg, Wrangell, Sitka, Juneau, Haines, Skagway, and a number of smaller places. These towns are easily supplied by barge and ferry from Tacoma, Washington, typically a two- or two-and-a-half-day journey. More than 100,000 people live in Fairbanks and its environs, North Pole, Salcha, Harding Lake, and along the rail corridor between Anchorage and Fairbanks. It has been estimated that only about 50,000 non-Natives live in rural Alaska. Although many of the 115,000 Natives live in the state's more than 227 Native villages, many spend at least some years living in

Fairbanks, Anchorage, or the towns in the Southeast. Anchorage's population includes more than 20,000 Alaska Natives—8 percent of the city's residents and 20 percent of the state's Native population.

Life in Alaska's urban centers is nearly indistinguishable from life in the cities and towns that dot the landscape across the rest of the United States. People are not self-sufficient; they work at traditional jobs for regular wages; their work places are as likely to be glass monoliths with central heating and indoor-outdoor carpet as in any other part of America, or if in a smaller town, the framed, more cozy structures of the American hinterland. Most Alaskans drive ordinary cars on asphalt streets to platted subdivisions of framed houses with unruly grass and unruly children. They shop for groceries in modern supermarkets and for fashionable clothing in typical variety stores, and in the larger towns Alaskans have their choice of warehouse stores or upscale clothing shops. Their lives and lifestyles are the same as those of mainstream America, for as consumers and developers they have imported the culture they know and with which they are comfortable. Few people have come to Alaska to live an alternative lifestyle of hunting their own food, hewing their own wood, and carrying their own water. Rather, most have come with prearranged jobs, having been assured first of adequate housing, good schools, and a favorable tax climate. Many would not have come at all without the guarantee of job security and the opportunity to recreate and perpetuate the familiar American culture they know and take for granted.

Perhaps more significant is the fact that most of the non-Native population—and all of the Tlingit, Haida, and Tsimshian Indians—live either on the coast, directly accessible by water-borne transportation two or three days from Seattle, or along the railbelt corridor linking Seward, Anchorage, and Fairbanks, the southern terminus of which is on the coast just three or four days from Seattle. Access to water-borne freight, either directly or by way of the railbelt corridor (which is basically identical to the road system), is the central fact of settlement in Alaska. Almost all of the people along the southern coast and in the railbelt corridor live an imitative lifestyle that is made feasible only because the cost of shipping goods fifteen hundred miles to the North can be kept within reasonable limits.[3] Low freight rates facilitate settlement in Alaska, for few would live there if they could not enjoy the amenities of mainstream U.S. culture, and few could afford to live there in that lifestyle in any location substantially distant from the coastal-railbelt axis. Even a nominal distance from the coast and rail corridor dramatically inflates the cost of living, limiting settlement and population accordingly. The farther one goes from the habitation axis, the fewer non-Natives there are, and the more the population is composed of Natives depending to some degree on subsistence for their livelihood.

It is appropriate to call the narrow habitation axis a "replication corridor," lying lightly along the southeastern coast and thrust deep into Alaska's interior mainland. Together, residents along this axis from Ketchikan to Fairbanks account for about 80 percent of the state's total population, or 625,000 people. Alaskans living here have always been able to realize their commitment to the recreation of mainstream American capitalist consumer culture. From clothing, toiletries, and household furniture to automobiles, nights out complete with restaurant meals, alcohol, and entertainment to newspapers and magazines, non-Native settlers in Alaska have from the beginning demanded enough discretionary income and leisure time to act like other Americans. They have always been able to do so because there have been jobs to supply the necessary income. But the jobs have been provided only by absentee capital investment in Alaska's natural resources, because there is no other way to build an economy in Alaska. Manufacturing would require the expensive import of raw materials, service, investment; nonmanufacturing jobs would require conditions that could attract and hold the necessary highly technically skilled labor force. Economies of scale have so far defeated all such attempts in Alaska, however, and seem likely to do so into the foreseeable future.

Of the 115,000 Alaska Natives in the state—Northern (Inupiat) and Southern (Yuit) Inuit, Aleut, Athabaskan (in the Interior), and Pacific Northwest Coast (Tlingit, Haida, and one village of Tsimshian Indians)— approximately 40,000 are permanent urban residents. The rest live on lands that sustained aboriginal people and their ancestors for thousands of years before European contact, near the mid-eighteenth century.[4] Most Natives today live in remote villages of 50 to 150 persons that are not connected to American civilization by road. Cash income in the villages is scarce, because there are few jobs and few prospects for economic development. All villages have a satellite dish for communication, though, and nearly all have an elementary school. Yet seventy of these villages have no indoor plumbing. All have landing strips for small aircraft, and many retain a village safety officer who works with the state trooper (police) office. Most have a village health aide who is in touch with a public health service doctor in the larger cities of Bethel, Nome, or Fairbanks. Many villages have high schools, the result of a court agreement and major building program by the state in the late 1970s.

In Southeast Alaska the villages are larger, the climate is less severe, and all the villages are accessible by water-borne transport. The Tlingit and Haida have more high school and college graduates than other Alaska Native groups. Subsistence plays a much less significant role in these villages than in the Yupik villages of the Yukon-Kuskokwim delta country and the Athabaskan villages along the Yukon River, where most seasonal activity is still tied to subsistence, using modern technologies. As a result of the Alaska Native Claims Settlement Act of 1971 (ANCSA), Alaska Natives became stockholders in economic development corporations that generate annual dividends,[5] but for many Natives these annual dividends are not yet substantial, although their significance is growing. Education still lags in most Alaska Native villages, many of which are plagued by high unemployment, high rates of teenage suicide, alcoholism, spousal and child abuse, and youth drug use.

Regarded as a great victory by most Native groups when it passed in 1971, ANCSA has been criticized in recent years as an act of cultural genocide: it has forced Natives to learn to think in terms of profit capitalism because they are stockholders in development corporations, and it has compelled the leadership cadre to become corporate and portfolio managers. But some commentators argue that the act's benefits, which include economic and political empowerment, outweigh the costs. As culture change is a constant in human society, the anxiety and frustration about, and resentment toward, change felt by Native village Alaskans tends to focus on the western agents of change as much as on the changes themselves. The sense of forced change, change without choice, has elicited the most criticism in village Alaska and has given rise to a strong Native sovereignty movement, sovereignty that would give villagers substantially greater control over their daily lives. Recent scholarship on Native American history has focused on resilience, including the growing capability of Indigenous groups to gain increasing control over their own affairs and to make accommodations that empower them in the modern world. Alaska Natives are fully in stride with this understanding and evolution of Native culture.[6]

As a prelude to this pluralist, mobile, and technologically literate contemporary society, Alaska has a complex and varied history, much of which is little known and dimly appreciated, even by long-term residents. Alaska has a very high transiency rate, and new residents have little opportunity or occasion to learn the state's history. Further, much of the history on television or in tourist videos romanticizes the past, presenting heroic and triumphalist interpretations of the gold rush sourdoughs, the Matanuska Valley colonists, the successful statehood campaign, and the pipeline construction engineers and laborers. Such representations of the past tend to present a history of mythic proportions. Of course there was heroism in Alaska's past, and previous residents of this northern clime, Native and non-Native, deserve to be celebrated for their perseverance, ingenuity, and determination. But as in most societies past realities are much more complex, rich, and meaningful than simple morality tales.

In a real sense Alaska has two post-contact histories: one of Russian America, the other of American Alaska. The history of Russian America is part of the saga of European exploration of the New World, the capitalist exploitation and colonization of its resources, and the bringing of the Native populations into the European Enlightenment and the world market stream. The legacy of that history in Alaska today is thin, because the Russians made little commitment to establishing a new society in North America. They understood their American experience almost exclusively in economic terms; their chief objective was exploitation of the available resources, mostly furs, on the least costly terms possible. Reflective of their concept of colonization in Alaska, the largest number of Russians ever in America at one time was a mere 823![7] Only at Sitka did the Russians attempt to create a permanent community.

Perhaps Russian America's most tangible bequests to modern Alaska are the national boundary, drawn in the Anglo-Russian Treaty of 1825, and the congregations of the Russian Orthodox Church, a strong faith today among the Aleut people and in some Tlingit, Yupik, and Athabaskan villages. There are other less visible and recognized legacies, however. Most significant, the Russians never solved the problem of supplying their personnel in North America; inadequate transportation and resources left the colony dependent on the Natives, on American Yankee traders, and later on the Hudson's Bay Company.[8] Supply in the American period was less a problem but only because resource extraction attracted (and continues to attract) substantial absentee investment capital and the federal government has continually supported development with extraordinary levels of spending; such private and public investment in Alaska has generated levels of settlement never contemplated by the Russians.

What links these two periods of Alaska's history, Russian America and American Alaska, is colonialism. The Russians always viewed Alaska as a resource for exploitation on the least costly terms, using the smallest material and personnel investment possible. Never adequately solving the challenge of supply, the Russian colony was always dependent on external sustenance, from Russia itself, and more economically from American and British trade. Russian America never attained self-sufficiency. American Alaska has been similarly dependent because the capital necessary to develop its natural resources has never resided in the territory. This is typical of colonial enterprises: they must be sustained from without, creating dependencies that inevitably diminish the capability of the Native people to maintain their aboriginal culture and self-determination and that render the non-Native (and later the acculturated Native) colonial population subject to the economic and political judgments made by the absentee investors in pursuit of their own objectives.

Alaska is no more economically self-sufficient today than it was in the Russian period; outside support is still necessary to sustain settlement in the region. In fact, some have characterized Alaska as an economic appendage of Seattle. Present day politicians routinely call for economic diversity to lessen dependence on taxation of petroleum production for state general fund revenues. When "petrodollars" began to flow in Alaska at an unprecedented rate in the 1970s with the construction and operation of the Trans-Alaska Pipeline, state government sponsored several initiatives that were designed to generate internal economies, especially self-sustaining agriculture. But such attempts at economic independence have failed in Alaska and are unrealistic in the context of today's globally organized capitalism. The challenge of maintaining economic enterprise in Alaska, a challenge the area shares with other high-latitude regions, is an essential aspect of Alaska's history, a theme that unites the Russian and American phases of the territory's history.

Another theme common to the Russian and American periods of Alaska history and central to understanding its meaning is the broader context in which that history has taken place. Alaska has not evolved in a vacuum. Rather, it has been part of larger stories, of the movement of Native peoples and their contact and accommodation with Western culture and their criticism of colonialism, of the spread of the European political economy to the New World, and of the expansion of American capitalism and culture. Decisions made in New York and Washington, D.C., affect conditions and development in Alaska almost daily. Because Alaskans seek to avail themselves of the amenities of U.S. culture, they are dependent on the forces, circumstances, and mechanisms that make the importation of that culture possible. Such dependence has been a constant factor in Alaska history. What follows is an attempt to describe and explain Alaska's relationship to that broader world, particularly the influence of Alaska's internal evolution.

ACKNOWLEDGMENTS

Many people contributed in many ways to this new history of Alaska. It is not possible to thank them all individually. I am particularly grateful to my many students through the years; they have helped me to explore, understand, and articulate the themes manifest here. Also, my thanks to the small community of Alaska historians, some of whom generously critiqued my work, and my many friends and colleagues at the University of Alaska Anchorage and in the Alaska Historical Society. I am grateful to Morgan Sherwood and Terrence Cole, who read early versions of the manuscript, and to John Whitehead, Jim Ducker, and Mike Dunning. Bill Robbins of Corvallis, Oregon, has been a special colleague and friend; Patricia Limerick first suggested that I write this book in 1990. I thank them both for their encouragement. Finally, to my wife, Dagmar, without whose counsel and expectation this book would have been much less, my love and gratitude.

ALASKA

Introduction

Alaska Geography and the Anthropology of Its Native Peoples

A HISTORY OF ALASKA must appropriately begin with a discussion of the region's geography and aboriginal populations that have inhabited that geography since the end of the last mass glaciation of the Northern Hemisphere, the last ice age, more than ten thousand years ago.[1] In analyzing the events that constitute Alaska's human history, it is important to know where these developments occurred. This is important not just in terms of macrogeography, the relationship of broad regions with one another, but also with respect to the biotic character of the land, the natural environment. All human history is conditioned by the environment in which it takes place; the evolution of people and culture does not take place in a vacuum but in the very real context of the natural landscape and how the people who live in that environment relate to it. The people who inhabit a particular area develop an identity with it, one that helps form their view of themselves. In fact, a profound sense of place is a part of the fundamental identity of both people and cultures. To ignore the physical geography, the landscape in which cultural evolution takes place, would lead to a false understanding of that process and of the people who manifest it. Thus the role of place, and how people express their relationship to it, is a recurring focus of this book.

At 375 million acres (586,000 square miles), Alaska is so large, its size almost defies comprehension. Although its shape as rendered on a map becomes familiar to those who live in the state and repeatedly see it depicted, that shape hardly conveys real meaning, particularly when it is cut off at 141 west longitude and along the crest of the coastal mountains adjacent to the Alexander Archipelago, as if there were nothing but a white vacuum to the east. Irritating too is the frequent placement of the Aleutian Islands on maps in a box in the Gulf of Alaska, another problem that highlights the impossibility of meaningfully assimilating the region's vast size. Alaska's shape and size are results of judgments made in the early nineteenth century by European and American diplomats, and today these dimensions are readily recognized by only a few Alaskans; the focus of most Alaskans is on their immediate local geography, not on where they are in a broader context.

State administrators, somewhat optimistically, divide the state into supposedly more manageable regions: the southeast Panhandle, with Juneau as the administrative center; the south-central coastal area, focused on Anchorage; the interior and Fairbanks; the Seward Peninsula and Nome; and the Arctic Coast (the North Slope), with Utqiagvik (formerly Barrow).[2] But such divisions compound rather than simplify. Alaska is more than twice the size of Texas. It is nearly four times as large as California, which has 101 million acres. By way of comparison, Oregon is 62 million acres, Washington 45 million.

Alaska is a large peninsula at the continent's extreme northwest extremity. All of North America's Pacific Coast—from Baja California to the Aleutian Islands—has been pressed onto the continent proper over the past two hundred million years, having been transported northward by the Kula Plate (now all but completely subducted) and the Pacific Plate (currently subducting under the massive North American Plate). The western edge of the much older (one to two billion years) North American craton (the continental mass) is roughly along the line of the Mackenzie River in Canada. Thus much of Alaska is mountainous, characterized by rugged, forested terrain. There are large areas of reasonably flat land as well, in the Yukon-Kuskokwim delta region in western Alaska and on the Arctic coastal plain north of the Brooks Range.

The relatively new theory of plate tectonics offers a fresh understanding of the composition of the earth's crust and its relationship to the dynamic and volatile geography of the land areas around the Pacific Ocean. In the 1920s when Alfred H. Brooks, longtime head of the Alaska Division of the U.S. Geological Survey, outlined the region's major geographic sections and their relation to North American geography, the theory had not yet been conceived. Brooks's otherwise excellent observations, made over more than two decades of fieldwork in Alaska, therefore appear quite uninformed and quaint today, even though the surface evidence he surveyed is nearly unchanged.[3] A dozen huge plates float on the mantle of the planet, a semiliquid mass beneath the earth's crust. The plates are in constant motion. Heat from deep within the earth, perhaps generated by radioactive material, flows in currents caused by convection. At some places these convection currents rise through the mantle, usually along rift zones on the ocean floor, and the plates move with the convection currents. The oceanic plates are denser than the continental plates, and when the two collide, the more dense plate "dives" or is subducted under the less dense, more buoyant continental plate. That is how all of Alaska was formed from crustal pieces transported by Pacific plates and grafted onto the material already there. Those pieces were too buoyant to be subducted and so were scraped off onto the continental margin. The subducted material heats as it descends, partly melting and generating magma that rises and erupts on the earth's surface as volcanoes. Earthquakes are frequent along the lines where the plates collide and grind along each other, as the major quakes recorded in Alaska testify.

Alaska's major mountain systems are related to the systems of western North America. The coastal mountains of California, the Pacific Northwest, and Canada are matched in Alaska as the Coast Mountains, the St. Elias Mountains, the Chugach Mountains, and the Kenai Mountains; the Rocky Mountains of the western United States and Canada continue in Alaska as the Alaska Range, which includes Mount McKinley (located in Denali National Park), the highest peak on the continent at 20,300 feet (and still growing as crustal material continues to be mashed onto the continental margin). The Alaska Range continues westward as the Alaska Peninsula. All of coastal Alaska is a portion of the so-called ring of fire around the Pacific Rim, where subduction of the Pacific plates generates earthquakes and volcanic activity. The Brooks Range south of the Arctic Coast is independent from the Rocky Mountains. The Wrangell Mountains lie in between the coastal ranges and the Rocky Mountain Alaska Range.

One of Alaska's major geographic regions is the North or Arctic Slope, the northern flank of the Brooks Range, which slopes to the Arctic Ocean. This area includes Prudhoe Bay, the site of the largest oil discovery in North America in 1968 (fifteen billion barrels), which lies about 150 miles west of Hershel Island (near the mouth of the Mackenzie River in Canada's Yukon Territory), and Utqiagvik (pop. about 4,000 in 2018), which lies near Point Barrow, the farthest north point in the mainland United States. Villages along the Arctic Coast west of Barrow include Wainwright, Point Hope, and Kivalina, among others. The Seward Peninsula is mainland North America's farthest west point. Cape Prince of Wales, the site of the Inuit village of Wales (pop. 150), is just fifty-six miles from Cape Dezhnev, Asia's farthest east point. Kotzebue Sound lies north of the Seward Peninsula; the long Baldwin Peninsula lies along the mainland coast across Kotzebue Sound from the Seward Peninsula. Situated at the northern end of the Baldwin Peninsula is the town of Kotzebue (pop. 3,300). The chief town of Nome (pop. 3,850) is on the Seward Peninsula, which is bordered on the south by Norton Sound of the Bering Sea. Unalakleet (pop. 750), a Yuit village on Norton Sound, marks the boundary between the Inupiat and Yuit people.

An extension of the Alaska Range, the Alaska Peninsula is a long, mountainous peninsula jutting southwestward from the south-central mainland of Alaska, southwest of Cook Inlet. Bordered on the north by Bristol Bay, the most prolific salmon fishing area in the world, the Alaska Peninsula's extreme western tip was where the Russian fur trappers first discovered the mainland of North America—a discovery that, when understood by Spain and other European nations, initiated a heated contest for sovereignty on the Northwest Coast. Kodiak Island lies southeast of the head of the Alaska Peninsula, separated from the mainland by the Shelikof Strait. The town of Kodiak (pop. 6,000) is the island's only major town.

The Aleutian Islands stretch about a thousand miles westward from the Alaska Peninsula's western tip, between 54° and 52° north latitude and between 165° west longitude and 172° east longitude. The distance from Anchorage to Attu at the far west end of the island chain is fifteen hundred miles, the same distance as from Anchorage to Seattle. All of the Aleutian Islands lie south of Alaska's southern mainland boundary, 54° 40' north latitude in Dixon Entrance. The Aleutian Islands comprise four principal island groups: the Fox Islands, the chief islands there being Unalaska and Umnak and the main service center at Unalaska (pop. 3,500); the Andreanof Islands, the main islands being Atka and Adak; the Rat Islands, the primary islands being Amchitka and Kiska; and the Near Islands, the chief islands being Attu and Agattu. The Japanese captured Attu and Kiska Islands during World War II and held them for a year. The Atomic Energy Commission exploded three test shots on Amchitka Island in the late 1960s and early 1970s (known as Long Shot, Millrow, and Cannikin), the last of which in 1971 was a megakiloton underground device. The Rat Islands and the Near Islands lie east of 180° longitude; technically they are in the Eastern Hemisphere. However, the International Date Line has been drawn to respect the natural physical geography: it is moved eastward beyond 170° west longitude to include the Chukchi Peninsula to the west and then west beyond 172° east longitude to include the Rat and Near Islands to the east.

The south-central coast is punctuated by the Kenai Peninsula, a mountainous peninsula characterized by glaciers and wilderness streams and rivers; it is accessible by road from Anchorage. The peninsula is bordered on the west by a hundred-mile estuary, Cook Inlet, and on the east by Prince William Sound. Cook Inlet divides into two arms, the Knik Arm and the Turnagain Arm at its head, each about fifty miles in length. Portage Glacier, at the head of the Turnagain Arm, covers a twelve-mile land connection between Cook Inlet and Prince William Sound. Katchemak Bay on the west shore of the Kenai Peninsula is a well-protected scenic bay rich in marine life. Homer (pop. 5,700), on Homer Spit on the bay's north shore, is a popular summer recreation area as well as the home for a significant fishing fleet. Halibut Cove and Seldovia on the southern shore are popular summer tourist destinations. Anchorage, at the head of Cook Inlet on a bench of land between the Chugach Mountains and the Knik and Turnagain Arms, is the state's principal political, economic, and administrative center. It is also the state's primary population center with nearly 300,000 people, almost ten times the population of the state's next largest town. As of 2019, half of Alaska's population of 740,000 lived in Anchorage and its environs, including the Matanuska Valley to the east and Girdwood and Whittier to the south.

Prince William Sound is a large, spectacular inland bay bordered by islands; it is considerably larger than Puget Sound. The towns of Cordova (pop. 2,200) and Valdez (pop. 4,000) are on the north side of the sound, Valdez being the southern terminus of the Trans-Alaska (hot oil) Pipeline, which runs 789 miles from Prudhoe Bay on the North Slope. Bligh Island off the Valdez Arm was the site of the wreck of the *Exxon Valdez* oil tanker in 1989, spilling at least 11 million gallons of oil into the sound's pristine waters, the largest oil spill in North America, after the 2010 *Deepwater Horizon* spill in the Gulf of Mexico (nearly 210 million gallons). The Gulf of Alaska coast south of Prince William Sound and the Copper River delta is indented by only a few bays, Icy Bay and Yakutat Bay, between which is the Malaspina Glacier, as large in area as the state of Rhode Island, and Lituya Bay.

The Alexander Archipelago is an extensive island archipelago adjacent to the coast. Together with Vancouver Island and the Queen Charlotte Archipelago off the coast of southern British Columbia, these islands constitute a thousand-mile inland waterway from Puget Sound and the Strait of Juan de Fuca to the head of Lynn Canal and to Glacier Bay on Icy Strait.

The principal islands of the Alexander Archipelago are Prince of Wales Island (the largest island in the United States), on which are located the Tlingit villages of Klawock and Craig and the Haida village of Hydaburg; Admiralty Island, on which is located the Tlingit village of Angoon and which supports the world's largest concentration of brown (grizzly) bears; Baranof Island, on which is situated the town of Sitka; and a number of lesser islands. Major channels include Icy Strait, Lynn Canal, Stephens Passage, Clarence Strait, Chatham Strait, Sumner Strait, and Frederick Sound. Glacier Bay, off the northern side of Icy Strait, is a national monument into which pour numerous significant glaciers. Dixon Entrance is a major sound separating the Alexander and Queen Charlotte Archipelagos, off the mouth of the Skeena River.

Alaska's southern boundary, 54° 40' north latitude, is an international border between Canada and the United States. All of the Alexander Archipelago is bordered by a twelve-to thirty-mile-wide coastal strip of U.S. territory, the western flank of the Coast Mountains. This strip is bordered by northern British Columbia, and had history proceeded logically, the English almost certainly would have acquired the Alexander Archipelago as well as the North American mainland in this region. But the wars of the French Revolution and the Napoleonic Wars interrupted the logic of history. As Britain's resources and energies were consumed in Europe, Russia took advantage of the temporary absence of the British from the coast to establish themselves firmly where the British otherwise might have been.

The Yukon is the major river of interior Alaska. It rises in Canada's lakes east of the southeastern Alaska Panhandle, flowing northwesterly to the Yukon Flats area (Fort Yukon) of the eastern Interior before turning to flow southwesterly toward the coast, where it empties into the Bering Sea in an unusually large, expanding delta. It is about twenty-three hundred miles in length over its entire course. One of its sources is Lake Bennett, about thirty miles from the coast across the Coast Mountains from the head of Lynn Canal. This proximity made the river a natural Indian trade corridor and later a natural route from the coast to the Interior, particularly to the Klondike gold rush. The Klondike is a tributary of the Yukon at about 140°

west longitude. For a time at the end of the eighteenth century it was thought that the Colville River, which flows northward into the Arctic Ocean from the Brooks Range in northern Alaska, was the outlet of the Yukon River, and the Yukon flowing southwesterly through mainland Alaska was regarded as a separate river; the Russians called the river the Kvikpak.

Major tributaries of the Yukon in Alaska include the Porcupine, which joins the Yukon in the Yukon Flats areas; the Tanana, which joins the Yukon still farther to the west (Fairbanks is located on the Tanana River, area pop. 32,000; the village of Tanana is at the confluence of the Yukon and the Tanana); and the Koyukuk, still farther west (about five hundred miles from the mouth of the Yukon). The villages of Wiseman, Bettles, Allakaket, Huslia, and Hughes are on the Koyukuk; the village of Koyukuk is at the confluence of the Koyukuk and the Yukon, and the village of Galena is just upriver from the confluence. In the vicinity of the village of Rampart, downriver from the Porcupine confluence, the Yukon flows through a significant canyon, Rampart Canyon, which in the 1950s was thought suitable for damming the river. South of the Koyukuk confluence on the Yukon are located the villages of Nulato, Anvik, Kaltag, Holy Cross, Marshall, and Mountain Village, among others. The huge delta of the Yukon is so unstable that no villages are located permanently on any of the many outlet channels. In 1833 the Russians established Redoubt St. Michael about fifty miles northward along the Bering Sea (Norton Sound) coast from the mouth of the Yukon River.

Both the Kobuk and Noatak Rivers flow from the south flanks of the Brooks Range near its western extremity. The Kobuk flows into Hotham Inlet east of the Baldwin Peninsula. The Noatak flows into the entrance to Hotham Inlet, across the mouth of the inlet from the village of Kotzebue (pop. about 2,900), located on the extreme north point of the Baldwin Peninsula. The village of Kotzebue lies nearly at the northwestern extent of the Baldwin Peninsula, which encloses Hotham Inlet. West of Baldwin Peninsula, Kotzebue Sound and Goodhope Bay are defined by Cape Espenberg. Before the impact of global climate change became apparent, this area was usually frozen nine months of the year. Before contact, Kotzebue was only a summer fishing camp. It became a permanent village when the government established a reindeer station at the site in 1897.

The Kuskokwim River flows southwesterly from the flanks of the Alaska Range in western Alaska. McGrath is located on the upper river; Aniak,

Kalskag, and Akiak are on the lower river. The principal town along the lower river is Bethel (pop. about 6,500). It is the main service center for southwestern Alaska, including such coastal villages as Tuntutuliak, Tununuk, and Scammon Bay. There are about fifty villages in the Yukon-Kuskokwim delta region. The Nushagak River also flows southerly from the flanks of the Alaska Range into Bristol Bay. Dillingham, near the mouth of the Nushagak, is a village of about 2,500.

In south-central Alaska the major rivers are the Matanuska, the Susitna, and the Copper. The Susitna flows southerly from the Alaska Range into upper Cook Inlet, west of Anchorage. A significant tributary of the Susitna is the Chulitna. The Matanuska flows southwesterly into Knik Arm at the extreme head of Cook Inlet. The Matanuska rises from the Matanuska Glacier on the northern flank of the Chugach (coastal) Range. The Copper River flows into the Gulf of Alaska south of Prince William Sound. It rises on the northern flank of the Wrangell Mountains. With a significant rate of fall over its course, the Copper is a fast-moving river. The Matanuska Valley lies east of Anchorage and north of the Matanuska River. The principal towns in the valley are Wasilla (pop. 10,000), founded about 1915, and Palmer (pop. 7,000), founded in 1935 as the headquarters for the Alaska Rural Rehabilitation Corporation (Matanuska Colony) Project. The valley's total population is about 50,000. Although the valley's land is suitable for agriculture, economies of scale mitigate against successful mass marketing of valley crops and produce. The town of Glennallen (named for U.S. Army explorers Lieutenant Henry Tureman Allen and Lieutenant Edwin Fitch Glenn, who crossed the region in 1885 and 1898 respectively) lies close to the Copper River in the shadow of the Wrangell Mountains, at the junction of the Richardson and Glenn Highways. It is a highway village rather than a river village (and predominantly white rather than Native), having been founded on the site of a construction camp at the time of construction of the Alaska and Glenn Highways.

On the Kenai Peninsula between Prince William Sound and Cook Inlet, the Kenai River flows westerly into Cook Inlet. Soldotna (pop. 4,700) lies fifteen miles inland from the mouth of the river, the town of Kenai (pop. 8,000) lies at the river's mouth. Total population on the Kenai Peninsula, including Homer (pop. 5,700) at the neck of Homer Spit, Seward (pop. 2,800) at the head of Resurrection Bay, and Cooper Landing (pop. 250) fifty miles upriver from the Kenai River mouth, is about 20,000.

In Southeast Alaska life is dominated by the inland waters of the Alexander Archipelago. Juneau (area pop. about 32,000), the state capital, is located on Gastineau Channel at the head of Stephens Passage. Haines (pop. 1,200) and Skagway (pop. 750) lie at the head of Lynn Canal. Sitka (pop. 9,000) is situated on the west coast of Baranof Island, on Japonski Bay. In the southern region of the Panhandle, Ketchikan (pop. 8,200) is situated on Revillagegedo Island north of Dixon Entrance; Wrangell (pop. 2,500) is on Wrangell Island off of Clarence Strait. Wrangell lies adjacent to the mouth of the Stikine River, a major artery cutting through the coast range, rising in British Columbia on the slopes of the Cassiar Range. The town was founded as a British trading port during Alaska's Russian period. Petersburg (pop. 2,800), a Norwegian community, lies at the eastern end of Frederick Sound. The Chilkat River flows into the head of Lynn Canal west of the Chilkat Peninsula. Each year from October to January large numbers of eagles gather along the river to feed on salmon returning late to spawn in the warmer river water. The Skeena River flows into Hecate Strait, south of Dixon Entrance. While the river is wholly in British Columbia, it is important to Alaska because of the proximity of Prince Rupert, British Columbia, which lies at the mouth of the Skeena, and the close relationship between the area's Tsimshian Indians to the Alaska Tsimshian village of Metlakatla on Annette Island near Ketchikan, and with the Haida and Tlingit Indians of Southeast Alaska.

Alaska is surrounded on three sides by three distinct oceans: on the north the Arctic Ocean, to the west the Bering Sea, and to the south the Gulf of Alaska of the Pacific Ocean. Each of these has its own particular characteristics. The Arctic Ocean is host to the gigantic polar ice cap that floats within its boundaries. Manifesting the phenomenon of rapid climate change, the Fifth United Nations Intergovernmental Panel on Climate Change (2014) concluded that the Arctic ice mass has declined more than 5 percent since 1979, and it continues to decline rapidly, affecting human, animal, and plant populations. Regular ship voyages through the Northwest Passage along the North American Arctic Coast may become a reality within a decade. There is a general east-to-west current in the ocean, which fills from the Atlantic and empties into the Pacific, so there is a circum-polar drift of the ice pack from east to west. The ice cap is not smooth, at least not around its edges, which are in constant motion because of local currents and the fact that in the deepest cold of the Arctic winter the ice often reaches the land around its edge (in summer it retreats with the summer sun). All around the edge of the pack there are leads of open water where the ice has been torn into large pans and sections. There are also long, high ridges of jagged ice around the pack's edge resulting from large pans and sections being jammed against each other with great force. Although these ridges are normally ten or twenty feet high, they can reach sixty or eighty feet. The chaotic character of the pack edge mitigates against migration across the ice and even greatly complicates occasional expeditions, by ski, by snow machine, or by dog sled.

The Gulf of Alaska is subject to severe winter storms that sweep down from the Arctic and out of Siberia. The weather can change almost instantly, and ships often get into difficulty as a result. The container vessels that sail a regular schedule to Anchorage and Kodiak from Tacoma, Washington, across the Gulf often encounter such storms and may arrive in Anchorage encrusted with ice on the exposed superstructure. Shipwreck due to these Gulf storms is not unheard of, and it is not uncommon for containers to be swept overboard—a major inconvenience to those to whom goods have been consigned.

The Bering Sea is a particularly shallow sea. Beneath it is a shelf that, like the land itself, has been welded to the continental margin by the subducting Pacific Plate. The shelf has been exposed several times: about forty thousand years ago, again about twenty-eight thousand years ago, and most recently between ten thousand and fourteen thousand years ago. The sea's shallowness explains a remarkable phenomenon: the peopling of North America. Although hominids have been walking the earth for one or more million years, there were none in North or South America until about fourteen thousand years ago. The exposure of the Bering Sea shelf, or floor, was caused by major glaciations in the Northern Hemisphere, ice ages reflecting temperature changes the reasons for which are not clear.

The glaciations interrupted the normal hydrologic cycle in which water evaporates from the oceans, which cover 70 percent of the earth's surface, and is carried to the land where it precipitates, only to run off as rivulets, streams, and rivers back into the oceans. In the North about 20 percent of the water was trapped as ice—enough to completely deplete the Bering Sea. The process was probably very gradual, so much so that it was not noticeable, although there might have been an oral tradition through which stories of the sea survived. Recent climate change, however, suggests that the draining of the Bering Sea may have occurred more quickly, also the melting of the ice and refilling of the sea. The Paleolithic people who lived in the region did not have a transcendent view of world geography; they had no idea of the placement of the continents on the planet or of their size or relation to one another. These people knew their own local geography intimately of course, for they depended on it for food and survival. But they would not have known the concept "continent," nor that they were living on the edge of one. Their movements, like those of all aboriginal peoples, were directed by their annual hunting or food-gathering cycle. They would have used whatever resources they had the technology and experience to exploit. They would have used any lands available to them.

Paleolithic people would not have known from the evidence around them of a growing shoreline that they lived on the edge of a continent, and that when the sea was completely gone, that their land was now connected to another continent. Their interest would have been in using whatever lands they felt safe in for whatever resources the land might produce. The most dramatic food source in their environment was the woolly mammoth, and they would have hunted that large and dangerous beast on the tundra before them, which is now called Beringia, or more commonly the Bering land bridge. Over a very long period, perhaps more than three thousand years, Paleolithic people would have roamed freely back and forth across Beringia. When the glaciation receded to its current extent, about ten thousand years ago, significant numbers of Paleolithics were living on the North American side of the land bridge.

Although the glaciation was extensive, not all the land in the Northern Hemisphere was covered with ice. In fact, very little of present-day Alaska was glaciated. Thus there would have been abundant habitable land even though the phenomenon that caused the exposure of Beringia in the first place was glaciation of the lands. Peoples living on the North American mainland, after the recession of the glaciation and the refilling of the Bering Sea, eventually migrated southward along land corridors that opened in the glaciated areas. Eventually they reached the present-day contiguous United States and Central and South America. There are major American Indian groups in southwestern North America, the Navajo and the Apache, who speak a language, Diné, which is of the same language family spoken by Athabaskan Indians in Alaska and western Canada.

The notion of migration has sometimes been used to explain the movement of people into the Americas from Siberia, but that is a misleading idea. Even if the climate changes were sudden and dramatic, which is not confirmed, it would not have been so sudden as to alter traditional hunting patterns so rapidly that people could think in terms of new lands. Rather, there would simply have been less pressure on the populations adjacent to Beringia and more land available for hunting as the people near the sea moved with its shoreline. Anthropologists agree that the primary peopling of the Americas came through Beringia. Certainly there were occasional boats or ships that reached the Americas from across the Pacific, or the Atlantic, usually by accident but perhaps even by design.

Recent confirmed discoveries of artifacts in Peru indicate habitation there about fourteen thousand years ago, nearly coincident with movement through Beringia. People could have arrived there by boat across the Pacific or by moving along the coast. In fact, Paleolithics may have gradually extended a marine culture all along the coast of the Americas from Beringia to southern South America. Further research in this field, where basic assumptions are constantly being challenged, will likely alter understanding of the Beringia phenomenon. There is some controversy among anthropologists regarding the dating of the inruption of populations into the Americas, however. Some artifactual evidence has been found and studied that might suggest habitation in the Americas twenty-eight thousand years ago, a date consistent with the last hemispheric glaciation, the Wisconsin. But to date the evidence is inconclusive, although it may eventually prove to be sufficient.

Alaska's weather systems are not related in the same way as the mountain systems are related. There are a number of major influences on basic weather patterns. Two of the most important are Siberian and Arctic cold air masses that sweep southeasterly across the Interior and warm, moist coastal air masses partly warmed by the Japan Current that flow in a northeasterly direction through the North Pacific and across the Gulf of Alaska. The Interior has higher mean summer temperatures and lower mean winter temperatures than does the coast, including south-central Alaska, which is protected from the cold air masses that affect the Interior by the Alaska Range (including Denali, the highest mountain in North America). It is also influenced by weather that reflects the warming trend of the Japan Current. The occlusions resulting from cold air moving southeasterly from the Arctic meeting the warmer weather associated with the Japan Current passing south of the Aleutian Islands results in extremely wet weather along the island chain. Some of the far western islands have recorded as few as fifty days of sun or partial sun in a calendar year.

The continental cordillera (mountain barrier) along the West Coast is the predominant influence on the weather in Southeast Alaska. All along the cordillera (from Alaska to Tierra del Fuego) weather blown by the prevailing westerly winds across the Pacific is forced to rise, losing its ability to hold moisture as it cools. The resulting precipitation can be substantial, typically in excess of 180 inches of rain annually at Ketchikan (compared with Anchorage's annual 15 inches). The dense and lush rain forest of the southeastern coast reflects this annual precipitation.

Much of Siberia—that part of Asia within Russia lying between the Ural Mountains to the west, the Pacific Ocean to the east, China and Mongolia to the south, and the Arctic Ocean to the north—resembles Alaska in climate, although it is vastly larger. Most of the population in Siberia is situated farther south than most of Alaska's population. As in Alaska, non-Native immigrants comprise about 80 percent of the current population, and the Native population less than 20 percent. There are more similarities than differences to places in Alaska to spots at the same latitude in Siberia.

To appreciate the relationship between Siberia and North America, it is necessary to know some basic geographic features of eastern Siberia. The Ob (with its major tributary the Irtysh), the Yenesy, and the Lena are major north-flowing rivers that rise in southern Siberia and flow to the Arctic Ocean. The Kolyma rises in central far east Siberia and also flows north to the Arctic. The Chukotsk or Chukchi Peninsula is Siberia's easternmost part; it lies north of 65° north latitude. Along the southern coast of the Chukchi Peninsula is the Gulf of Anadyr and the mouth of the east-flowing Anadyr River, which rises on the southern flanks of the peninsula's mountainous spine. Jutting southward from below far east Siberia is the Kamchatka Peninsula, running along a north-south axis between 50° and 60° north latitude. It was from Kamchatka that the Russians would push eastward to the Eastern (Aleutian) Islands and eventually to the North American mainland in the mid-eighteenth century.

Petropavlovsk on the eastern Kamchatka shore and Bolsheresk on the western shore were important towns in the Russian American period. An island archipelago stretches southwesterly from the Kamchatka Peninsula to the northernmost Japanese Island, Hokkaido; these are the Kuril Islands (under Russian sovereignty since World War II). West of the Kamchatka Peninsula and northwest of the Kuril Islands lies the Sea of Okhotsk. The village of Okhotsk on the sea's western shore was the eastern terminus of the overland supply route from European Russia to Russian America, north of Hokkaido and west of the Kurils is Sakhalin Island, also under Russian sovereignty. On the Siberian mainland north of the mouth of the Amur River is the port of Aian, established by the Russian American Company (RAC) in the early nineteenth century.

In southeastern Siberia, near the China border, lies the city of Irkutsk, near the south end of Lake Baikal, the world's largest (by volume) freshwater lake, and also near the headwaters of the Lena River. Irkutsk was the principal administrative seat of far east Siberia in the Russian American period. From here travelers would descend the Lena to the village of Yakutsk (at about 62° north latitude) and would then trek over the rugged Stanovoi Mountains to Okhotsk village, where they would embark for Bolsheresk or Petropavlovsk on Kamchatka and then to the Eastern Islands and Russian America. South of Irkutsk in the mountains on the China border is the town of Kiakhta, site of the trading station where agents of the RAC traded Russian American sea otter and fur seals to the Chinese for tea and other goods. Rising east of Irkutsk on the eastern flank of the Yablonovy Mountains are the headwaters of the great Amur River, the modern-day boundary between China and Siberian Russia. The Amur flows eastward to the Sea of Okhotsk. After the 1850s it would become a major tradeway for the Russians. The port of Aian is north, across the Udshaya Gulf north from the mouth of the Amur. Aian marked the Russia-China border until 1858.

In the Russian period of Alaska's history, Siberian and North American geography flow together: the Russians came from the west and the RAC's jurisdiction after 1799 included Kamchatka and Okhotsk, the Kuril Islands, and the port of Aian. In the American period Russian geography was quickly lost from view, except for occasional glimpses, as with the importation of Siberian reindeer to Alaskan Inuit villages at the end of the nineteenth century by the missionary-educator Sheldon Jackson. Only in the 1950s, with the maturity of the Cold War, would Siberian geography affect American and Alaskan psyches and then as a fearsome, foreboding, and threatening presence. That threat was largely erased with the collapse of the Russian Soviet state in 1990. Since 1989 large numbers of Russian immigrants have arrived in Alaska as permanent residents and as university students. And in the 1990s Alaskans undertook numerous campaigns to deliver material aid to Siberian towns and cities suffering material privation as a result of the fallen Russian economy. In addition, there were a number of visits by Alaskan Natives to Siberian villages and towns to renew relationships, share histories, and look for long-lost relatives.

Before the arrival of modern culture, the natural environment—primarily the biology and topography of Alaska's major geographic provinces—determined the material culture of the aboriginal populations there. All of the Natives in Alaska followed a cyclical pattern of hunting and gathering, moving at different seasons of the year to where food resources were most available.[4] For many Natives, particularly Eskimos in the Arctic and Athabaskan Indians along the interior rivers, late winter sometimes brought a great scarcity of resources as winter supplies were exhausted before spring "break-up" and the reappearance of summer animals. But wherever they lived, Natives used the environment's flora and fauna to construct the material culture with which they made their lives.

In the Arctic, Natives made fur garments from such furbearing mammals as polar bear and wolf; they wore furs because their environment contained furbearers, and they needed the warmth of animal skins. They relied also on fur seals, which provided not only useful pelts, but which with other seals were an almost perfect food, supplying all of the essential nutrients to sustain life. The Inuit hunted other marine mammals, including walrus, sea lion, and whale. Because of the size of whales, the danger in hunting them, and the amount of food they provided for a village, extensive rituals developed around the hunt. Inuits and Indians of the region also hunted caribou, which provided meat and tough hides for shelter and clothing. Interior Athabaskan Indians used caribou as well, and moose, which are not common in the Arctic. They also took significant numbers of migrating salmon from the Interior rivers. They made fine birch canoes because their environment contained an abundance of birch trees, and they needed reusable river transport. Most Athabaskans lived in the Subarctic, characterized by northern forests of birch and spruce. Thus they made habitations using a frame of cut trees covered over with animal skins.

In Southeast Alaska, in the Alexander Archipelago, Tlingit Indians enjoyed one of the richest biotic provinces in North America, generously supplied with ample resources. They made clothing of spruce bark and houses of split cedar planking. So abundant were food resources that the ability of a clan to amass food and other materials, such as bentwood boxes and animal skins, became the culture's primary measure of prestige, a phenomenon not unfamiliar in modern western culture. Tlingit Indians living in exogamous clans developed the potlatch as their principal ceremonial ritual: clan leaders could distribute large quantities of dried salmon, berries, animal skins, and other goods because these goods could be replaced within a reasonable number of months by the concerted and organized effort of the clan.

Only through the development of modern technologies have humans broken the link between an environment's natural resources and the material culture those resources can be made to produce. Today in Alaska most people enjoy a rich and diverse material culture. The sophisticated technologies of Western culture permit much greater independence from the environment, although no culture escapes environmental limitations completely. The framed houses of modern Western culture can be sufficiently insulated and heated at such a reasonable cost that within them inhabitants can ignore even the coldest temperatures and most violent storms, dressing in garments more naturally appropriate to tropical climes. Automobiles with studded snow tires, together with motorized snow plows and a highly ordered dispatch regime for them, permit modern life to be carried on nearly without reference to inclement winter weather. The regional headquarters buildings of the large oil companies located in Anchorage are versions of large glass monoliths hung on steel skeletons that are more suited to Texas or California; on a cold, crisp winter day the heat can been seen exuding from the sleek, dark glass exteriors of these buildings. They are not architecturally adapted to the northern environment, but they are feasible structures for Alaska because they can be heated and the air in them filtered to create an artificial environment not dissimilar from that inside identical buildings in Houston or Los Angeles, all at a cost their owners can tolerate. The insulated, heated dwellings common in urban Alaska are made of wood from the Pacific Northwest, the automobiles fueled by petroleum refined in Washington, the produce, meat, and other goods grown in Washington and California, and the clothing produced in any number of states and countries, made of cotton, wool, and synthetics. All of these material goods characterize a material environment that essentially ignores any limitations place might impose.

So used to such transcendence have humans become that many expect it and make it a condition of living. It becomes second nature to have modern homes, automobiles, and the latest in entertainment, food, and clothing. Without such products many people would feel deprived, and few would live where they could not have them. Seldom if ever do people focus on how the natural environment, which one might call "first nature," gets transformed into all the material aspects of modern culture that people often take for granted, which one might collectively call "second nature."[5] These abilities to transcend the natural environment and to transform it are profound ones that represent a substantive change in human history, one that has taken place most markedly just in the past two hundred years.

A full understanding of human history also demands careful consideration of the sociopolitical environment. Political geography differs from physical geography; it deals with the power that individuals and groups exert over others and over the land. Its origins can only be understood in historical context. In terms of the physical geography, most political geography is artificial; it dissects natural boundaries willy-nilly, without regard to natural physiographic features, integral ecosystems, or perhaps most significant, cultural units. Alaska provides a graphic representation of this phenomenon. Its political boundaries often ignore natural geography and, in several instances, cultural groups (the Gwitchin-Han Indians, for example).

Political geography is generated by historical realities that represent potent imperial and enlightening forces. It also represents assumptions of a right of priority, perhaps even technological superiority. In any case its cultural context—that is, the cultural assumptions of those who devised it—is very different from that of the people who lived on the land and whose cultures were "natural" rather than "artificial." Indigenous cultures were characterized by adherence to such natural rhythms as hunting and gathering cycles and sun time. The Euro-American cultures that affected the aborigines and came to dominate their landscape, with the imposition of new boundaries, were characterized by clock-watching and the organization of life by abstract goals and objectives, by the organized, cooperative labor of large numbers of people over long periods of time, by the regular distribution of time, and by the development of writing for record-keeping.

If longevity of use and occupation are the guides, Alaska's Native peoples clearly have first claim on Alaska's land and its resources. The history of their introduction to Alaska and of their evolution through more than ten thousand years of living in and on the land are properly the subject of Alaska anthropology, but there are several reasons for including some elemental information about Alaska Natives and their cultures here. First, Alaska Natives are today a significant part of contemporary Alaskan society. About

75,000 Natives live in more than 170 Native villages spread across the vast reaches of the territory, all of them retaining some aspects of their traditional cultures and all of them active, full participants in the state's political and social life.[6] Another 40,000 live in Alaska's urban centers. Many Native men and women are leaders in Native communities and organizations as well as in positions in Alaska's broader political, economic, and administrative life. In addition, interaction between Alaska's Native peoples and the non-Native population that migrated to Alaska has been a constant aspect of Alaska's human history for more than a century. The technology and political force of the non-Natives have come to dominate Alaska, as they dominated almost all other environments where Euro-Americans migrated.

The history of the interaction between Natives and the dominant, immigrant, non-Native culture that supplanted Native centers and modes of control in Alaska has in broad scope been little different from the history of interaction between aborigines and Euro-Americans in the contiguous United States or elsewhere in the world. The Europeans imposed a colonial model on the aborigines of the New World and elsewhere, for the most part disregarding the sovereignty and rights of Native people and relegating to them the roles of laborer, slave, or enemy. The Russians and to a lesser degree the Americans imposed that same colonial model in Alaska. Today, however, Alaska Natives are constitutionally equal partners in Alaska's evolution, although the survival of Native cultures is severely threatened by a lack of sustainable development in many Native villages. In reviewing the history of Alaska, the development of Native cultures and peoples is an integral element in the story, the absence of which would render that story incomplete at best and prejudicial at worst. Moreover, it is important to know who the Native people are and what the nature of their cultures were at the time of contact so that it is possible to judge the character of non-Native impact on them. The following passages examine the evolution of Native peoples and their cultures in Alaska.

It is probably not possible to demonstrate the superiority of various ways of organizing life, the natural or the abstract (some would say artificial, while others might say civilized). Suffice it to say that many Natives and non-Natives alike today struggle with the problem of reconciling the two systems and with the basic questions of identity that accompany the problem. The imperial character of culture represented by the capability to draw artificial lines across the landscape and make them count for something is profound. It represents the difference between the natural and the manipulated world, between precontact and historical culture.

It is not likely that most precontact cultures practiced a "natural" conservation of resources, although they did identify with specific objects and aspects of nature.[7] Most precontact cultures in the Americas were naturalistic, that is, people did not think of themselves as separate from nature, as in the Christian ideological tradition, but as a part of it. Just as people had spirit, so did fauna and even flora. When an aboriginal hunter prepared to take game or fish, for example, he acknowledged the sacrifice being made by the prey and he expressed his gratitude, carefully observing rituals that had developed for just that purpose that symbolized humankind's unity with nature. Among those Indian groups that depended on salmon, the first salmon caught was shared with the group, and the washing, preparation, and sharing rituals were observed meticulously.[8] Many environmental historians have argued for an aboriginal environmentalism, but the subject is quite controversial. Nearly all aboriginal people altered the landscape in which they lived to make it more productive; among other methods, they did this through burning, planting, irrigation, and the herding of animals. Their use of the environment was practical, not ideal.

Few precontact cultures accorded women as significant a status as they hold today in most industrial Western democracies (which, lamentably, is not yet equality). Even in cultures in which kinship was traced matrilineally, women still were regarded as property for most purposes and were treated as such. In Inuit culture a woman performed such critical tasks as chewing her mate's mukluks (skin boots) every morning to make them supple so he could go out to hunt food. Athabaskan women often tended fish weirs set for salmon on the rivers while the men of the group hunted land mammals. Tlingit women often set the terms for trading goods between groups. European explorers and traders often noted the role of Tlingit women in the trade, which was conducted by the men but governed by the women of the clan. In some Tlingit clans, when a male heir proved incapable or unworthy, the women controlled the selection of the successor, which was critical to the prestige of the clan.

Acculturation of the Native populations would become the policy of the Euro-Americans, although in the beginning the aborigines were held at bay rather than expected to become assimilated. This is reflected in American Indian policy, which from the earliest days of American national government was based on the principle of removal. Once the Americans broached the plains in significant numbers, after the 1820s, policy moved in the direction of acculturation, that is, the imposition of Western culture in place of Native cultures. Acculturation is an extremely complex phenomenon. Natives quickly recognized the value of Western technologies and thus adopted many of them. Their adoption of Western ideologies was much slower, however, and undoubtedly had the more profound long-term impact.

For much of the twentieth century, Indians were seen in the dominant culture as a vanishing people, doomed to extinction if they did not assimilate (or acculturate, to become integrated into the dominant culture). However, recent scholarship has suggested that Native populations were successful at selective adaptation of Western technologies and mores, finding those that could be adapted into Native life and that would permit survival in an imperial context. Indeed, Natives did not disappear, as progressive thinkers in the late nineteenth and early twentieth century thought they would. However persecuted, and persecuted they were, Native peoples survived these centuries and today continue to struggle for dignity and equal opportunity.[9] Organized to pursue their claims to the land in Alaska they traditionally lived on and harvested, Alaska Native leaders worked with the state and federal governments to craft the landmark Alaska Native Claims Settlement Act of 1971. In the first decades of the twenty-first century, Native leaders and organizations have called for greater recognition of both their equal place in multicultural and diverse populations such as Alaska's, and their capability and persistence in surviving the colonialism that sought to obliterate their collective identities.

At the time of contact, the mid-eighteenth century, there were about 80,000 Natives living in what is now Alaska. Although the ancestors of the Indians, Athabaskans, and Pacific Northwest Coast peoples entered the Americas by way of Beringia, almost certainly the Inuit and Aleut did not. No recovered artifacts that might be associated with Inuits or Aleuts date back to the last hemispheric glaciation, the Wisconsin. The Inuit and Aleut probably have a common origin—a people called the Eskaleut, who entered Alaska six thousand or seven thousand years ago, probably coming by boat across the Bering Strait and then migrating over time to their present locations. The distinct nature of Aleut culture most likely is a function of insular (island) isolation.

Of the major groups of aborigines in North America, perhaps the Inuit intrigued Europeans most because of their ability to survive in an environment Europeans considered uninhabitable. As a consequence the Northern (Arctic) Inuit, the Inupiat people, have been much studied and written about. They are a short, heavy-boned, and muscular people but taller than the Yuit. Their heads are large and their faces somewhat flat. Over the centuries they probably developed some genetic adaptations to the Arctic environment, including the retention of baby fat into adulthood and better circulation in their hands and feet. Although the Inuit inhabited the least supportive environment in Alaska, they developed technologies and behaviors that ensured their survival. For example, the Inuit routinely hunted seals and other sea mammals that contain nearly all of the nutrients necessary to sustain human life. It is said that the Inuit used everything in their environment that could be used to sustain life—and used it very efficiently (in most cases, 100 percent).[10]

There are four major groups of Inupiat: Bering Straits, Kotzebue Sound, North Coast, and Interior. At the time of contact the Inupiat probably numbered about 10,000 altogether. They survived by hunting marine mammals, by fishing, and by taking caribou from the great herds that still continue to roam the coastal plains. Although all the Inupiat groups hunted whales from time to time, these largest of mammals (especially the bowhead whale) played a larger role in the culture of the Bering Straits people. The technology used in whale hunting included a toggle-headed harpoon (i.e., a harpoon from which the head could be detached from the spear or lance by means of a line pulled by the hunter), seal bladder floats with lines attached, and the *atlatl* or spearthrower. The Interior Inupiat, who relied more heavily on caribou, constructed long, funnel-shaped game fences to herd the animals to lakes or corrals where they could be killed more easily. The coastal Eskimo also constructed large, open skin boats called *umiaks*. These were usually about twenty feet long and carried six or eight people, although larger versions were known. The kayak, a closed skin boat typically with a single hatch, was also common. Snowshoes and flat sledges were used for overland travel in winter. Dogs and dogsleds were not used for transportation.

The Inuit normally lived in dwellings that were partly subterranean and partly sod blocks or skins covering a conical driftwood frame above ground. These were twelve to fifteen feet long by eight to ten feet wide. They had a separate underground tunnel entrance that served as a cold trap. Eight or more people could live quite comfortably in such a house, which would have perhaps five hundred or six hundred cubic feet of living space. With their own body heat and a small seal oil lamp (a wick in a shallow bowl of seal oil), the temperature could be kept more than adequate for winter survival even in severe storms. The Inuit did not live in igloos, although sometimes hunters might construct temporary shelters made of snow blocks for protection from storms while on long hunting trips.

Most villages, numbering perhaps 50 to 100 people, all an extended family group, were sedentary, at least through the winter cold. Spring might mean movement to better fishing areas and to areas adjacent to favored sea-hunting regions. The Interior Inupiat likely moved their villages as the caribou changed migration patterns. Kinship was central to the social organization of the Inupiat. In fact, individuals who could not verify kinship with members of a group they might encounter were often killed, strangers being perceived at first view as a threat to the group's survival, probably because of the ever-present potential for a scarcity of food. Unlike some other Alaska Native peoples, Inupiat kinship lines were understood to be bilateral, that is, both parents were regarded equally. In lieu of verifiable kinship, the Inupiat used several methods for adopting a nonthreatening stranger into a community. Men from different communities established trading partnerships, sometimes including an exchange of spouses as a sign of the closeness of the friendship. People with the same name recognized a relationship among themselves, and any special friendship could lead to adoption from one family into another. Although egalitarian relationships characterized Inupiat society, wealth and leadership did distinguish some individuals. Whaling captains accumulated and bequeathed substantial property, particularly umiaks and hunting tools. They also played central roles in ceremonies and trading expeditions, as well as in the hunt itself.

The Inupiat apparently believed in the reincarnation of spirits, both human and (other) animal. Newborns often were given the names of the recently deceased. Reincarnation was tied to the need for future food resources. If the spirit did not regenerate, the food necessary for survival might not be available. Thus much ceremonial activity involved appeasing members of the spirit world lest they withhold their favors.

The Yuit or Southern Inuit are usually classified in two large groups, the Bering Sea Yuit and the Pacific Yuit. Included in the Bering Sea Yuit are people of the Bristol Bay area, the Yukon-Kuskokwim delta, Nunivak Island, and the people of St. Lawrence Island, who were distinct from the other three groups. The Pacific Yuit include people from the southern

Alaska Peninsula and Kodiak Island (Koniags), the southern and eastern portions of the Kenai Peninsula (Unegkurmiut), and Prince William Sound (Chugach). Yuit villages tended to be larger than Inupiat, 100 to 300 people, who traced their lineage matrilineally, save for the St. Lawrence Island people, who traced kinship patrilineally. The St. Lawrence Island people relied heavily on walrus, which migrate past the island annually. The delta people hunted caribou in addition to sea mammals. The Bristol Bay people used salmon as well as the smaller sea mammals. The Pacific Yuit villages relied mostly on smaller sea mammals, although salmon also played a significant role in their diet.

All Bering Sea Yuit lived in house pits surrounded by a wood frame covered with sod. Among the Pacific Yuit plank houses were not uncommon, reflecting the region's forests and the Tlingits' influence on the southern coast. Yuit villages also contained a larger structure, perhaps thirty by thirty feet, called the *kashim* (men's house), where interrelated groups of men who owned the house lived. Hunting gear was stowed there, and the structure was used also for sweat or steam baths, the steam generated by pouring water over heated rocks. The village women brought food to the men in the kashim.

There were some social distinctions among the Pacific Yuit, including slaves. The Bering Sea Yuit were more egalitarian. The Yuit believed in the necessity of maintaining a positive relationship between hunters and the spirits of their prey. Special amulets and ceremonies were used to address that relationship and to appease the spirits of the hunted. The Yuit also believed in reincarnation, and special naming ceremonies were used for the newborn. Souls not reborn lived underground and were regarded with suspicion and unease. The Yuit believed that such souls could appear above ground and harm people. Ceremonials were highly developed among the Bering Sea Yuit, with several important community-wide celebrations and exchanges of visits by whole villages.

The Aleut inhabit the far west portion of the Alaska Peninsula and the Aleutian Islands. Their adaptation to the maritime environment was quite remarkable and characterized by highly specialized technologies developed for hunting such marine mammals as sea lions, seals, and sea otters. The sea lion was the Aleut's most important diet staple and also provided material for clothing (the hide, the stomach, and the intestines). They also hunted whales (like the Eskimo) and developed complex rituals around that major enterprise. Whales were hunted by lone hunters operating from a single kayak (called a *baidarka*, a Russian word, after contact), relying primarily on poison (made from the aconite plant) painted on the harpoon tip. The poison was slow-acting, so many whales that were struck were not ultimately recovered or might beach far from where they were initially struck. The skill of the Aleut hunters in their baidarka became legendary after contact, as Europeans were amazed at the boat's engineering and the hunters' ability to maneuver it in the open sea.

Although there are actually nine subgroups of the Aleut, based on language these are classified collectively as the Eastern, Central, and Western Aleut. The total Aleut population at the time of contact was probably about 20,000. The eastern population was greater than the western. The term "Aleut" was first introduced by the Russians, based on a word from the Koryak or Chukchi Native languages from far northeastern Siberia. The Eastern Aleut lived on the Alaska Peninsula and in the Shumagin Islands. The Central Aleut inhabited the Fox and Andreanov Islands, and the Western Aleuts the Rat and Near Island groups.

Aleut villages were larger than Inuit villages, numbering about 200 inhabitants. They were inhabited year-round, although seasonal summer camps were not uncommon. The basic house structure was the *barabara*, a pit house constructed of sod laid over a wooden frame. These were thirty-five or forty feet long and twenty or thirty feet wide. Entrance was through a hole in the roof, reached by a pole ladder. Aleut kinship was traced matrilineally, and children were raised by the mother's brother. A woman usually owned the barabara, whose primary inhabitants were her brothers and their families. There was no political leadership; the house was the central social unit. Villages, consisting of several houses, were characterized by three classes: wealthy, common, and slaves. Whale hunters inherited their position.

Raids on distant villages were not uncommon, but good relations among villages were maintained through a winter feast that involved a head of household, one of the men, from one village inviting a headman from another village. Wooden masks were used in dancing at these feasts to invoke the presence of powerful spirits. Many of these, collected by European explorers and anthropologists, have been returned in recent years under the provisions of the 1990 Native American Graves Protection and Repatriation Act. The Aleut apparently believed in a creator who was related to the sun and who could be instrumental in hunting success. They also believed in the reincarnation of souls and their migration between earth and the worlds above and below it. In the animal world there were good and evil spirits, and hunters wore amulets and charms to appease spirits and guarantee hunting success.

The Athabaskan Indians were mainly riverine people, with the exception of the Tanaina, who lived along the shores of upper Cook Inlet, and those classified as upland. The precontact population was probably about 10,000. There are nine subdivisions. The riverine groups included the Ingalik, who lived along the lower Yukon and the Kuskokwim, the Koyukon on the middle Yukon and Koyukuk, the Tanana on the lower Tanana, and the Holikachuk on the lower-middle Yukon and the Innoko River. Upland groups included the Gwitchin on the upper Yukon and the Porcupine River, the Han on the upper Yukon, and the Upper Tanana on the upper Tanana River. The Pacific groups included the Ahtna on the Copper River and the Tanaina on upper Cook Inlet, the Susitna, and the upper Kuskokwim Rivers.

Generally, the Athabaskans were divided into regional bands, which were further divided into local bands of between fifteen and seventy-five people. Marriage partners were taken within the regional band. Local bands were divided again into household units of one to three families living together. Among the Ahtna, the Tanaina, and the Ingalik, whose villages were more sedentary than those of the others, the village had a permanent, recognized territory. The riverine and Pacific groups relied on summer salmon fishing supplemented by fall caribou and moose hunting. They also gathered berries in the fall and small land mammals throughout the winter. Not all groups were able to put up enough dried salmon to last through the winter, and they sometimes experienced significant deprivation in the last part of the winter.

There were a variety of house types among the Athabaskan, depending on climate and proximity to other Native groups. The Ingalik lived in covered house pits, similar to their Yuit neighbors. Ten or twelve such pits constituted a village, which also had a kashim. The Koyukon and the Tanana used semisubterranean log dwellings. The Tanaina built house pits with log walls and tunnel entrances. Some Ahtnas built plank houses similar to the Tlingit, a manifestation of their contact with these coastal Indians, but other Ahtnas lived in small bark-covered houses similar to the dwellings of the upper Tanana. The Gwitchin used a portable dome tent of caribou or moose skin over a frame of saplings. In winter these were covered with conifer boughs and snow to provide insulation.

Among the highlights of Athabaskan material culture were birch bark canoes and snowshoes of diverse designs. Dogs were used only as pack animals. Athabaskan clothing was unique and highly prized by other Native groups. Men wore a tanned caribou skin that covered to midthigh. A single legging piece included boots and pants as one. Winter wear included parkas with the fur turned inward.

Kinship ties among the Athabaskan were traced matrilineally. Social organization was based on the clan. The Ahtna and the Tanaina also identified moieties, the Raven and the Seagull. Social stratification was most pronounced among the Ahtna, the Tanaina, and the Ingalik. There was some slavery, but it was apparently essentially incidental. Warfare (constant skirmishing) was common among the Koyukon, the Gwitchin, and the Tanaina. The Gwitchin fought with the Koyukon and the Inupiat; the Tanaina fought with the Koniag, the Chugach, and even the Ingalik. The potlatch was the principal Athabaskan ceremony, one group hosting another for the distribution of gifts. The most important potlatches were held as mortuary feasts, although they also commemorated births, marriages, and successful first hunts and sometimes were used to resolve interpersonal conflict. The stick dance, a marathon dance ritual using a central pole, also was important.

Athabaskan belief structure included the notion that humans and animals were indistinguishable in spirit. The Raven as trickster represented the caprice of life, and continually disrupted ideal morality through deception. Stories about Raven were used to teach children the moral order. Among the Koyukon a malevolent spirit, *nahani*, inhabited the forest and captured the unwary. Among the Pacific Athabaskan the shaman was important, having both magical and medical qualities and either a positive or negative reputation.

The Tlingit and Haida Pacific Northwest Coast Indians were the most sophisticated Natives in Alaska and among the most sophisticated aborigines in North America in terms of their social and economic structure and artistic achievement. Both groups share many characteristics with other Pacific Northwest Coast people to the south, including the Coast Tsimshian, the Kwakiutl (Kwakwaka'wakw), the Bella Coola, the Nootka (Nuu-chah-nulth), the Coast Salish, the Makah, the Quileute, the Tillamook, and others. The Tlingit occupied the coast from Yakutat Bay south to Portland Canal, including most of the Alexander Archipelago. The Kaigani Haida occupied the southern part of Prince of Wales Island, although most Haidas lived in the Queen Charlotte Archipelago to the south (as they still do). At the time of contact there were about 50,000 Tlingits divided into thirteen subunits, called *kwans* (not tribes); there were about 1,800 Kaigani Haidas. The Tlingit and the Haida lived in villages, although the village was merely a loose assemblage of distinct clan houses without any transcending political leadership. The villages were occupied during the winter, from October to March.

Salmon was an important part of the coastal diet, as was eulachon (candlefish) oil. Clans had specific summer salmon-fishing sites that were partly occupied most of the summer months. Clams and other shellfish were gathered routinely. Bird eggs were also important, as were halibut, moose, deer, and other land mammals. The Tlingit fashioned elaborate stone and wood weirs for salmon fishing and complex, heavy cedar and yew hooks for halibut fishing. They used heavy, carved cedar canoes for transportation.

Tlingit and Haida houses were large structures, sometimes as large as forty by sixty feet, made of split cedar planks with vertical end posts supporting a central horizontal ridge pole. As many as four families comprising twenty to thirty people lived in the house. These Northwest Coast Indians traced kinship matrilineally. People were divided into two moieties—Raven and Wolf—with a third, Eagle, in some locations. The principal social unit was the clan; at contact there were perhaps seventy or eighty Tlingit clans. Each had a totemic animal symbol that was used on clothing, houses, and ceremonial implements. Clans owned houses, fishing sites, and other property. The head of the clan house, the clan leader (*hitsati*), was responsible for the well-being of the residents of the house. The society was rigidly stratified into three classes: aristocracy, commoners, and slaves. Uncles, mothers' brothers, had the principal responsibility for childrearing. The position of hitsati was inherited.

The principal ceremony among the Northwest Coast people was the potlatch, a feast held to honor the deceased.[11] It was also used to proclaim the social status of the host. Funerals were handled by members of the opposite moiety, and the potlatch was held to reward them for their services. Goods accumulated during the time (usually at least a year) between the funeral and the potlatch were distributed by the host, given to the guests, and ceremonial robes, boxes, blankets, bowls, spoons, and the like were displayed to show the clan's wealth and prestige. Pieces of carved copper were particularly prized as clan property and were sometimes broken and given away as a special honor. Often a mortuary pole would be com-missioned (or if completed, raised) at a potlatch. In a sense the potlatch was the raison d'être of Tlingit life; the hitsati directed clan activity and the accumulation of wealth, which was used to demonstrate the clan's power and position in the community. Competition among the clans was sharp, and feuds were common. Reciprocity was the basic principle of justice, social injuries and slights were compensated materially. The Tlingit believed in the soul's immortality and in reincarnation. The Raven was a supernatural trickster who was responsible for creation of most of the material world. The shaman, the *ixt*, communicated with the spirits and could cure maladies and predict the future. Witches were often identi-fied and persecuted.

Today Alaska's Native peoples are an integral, vibrant, and central factor in state affairs, intimately involved and represented politically and admin-istratively at every level. But as in every other place where western Euro-American culture has dominated earlier aboriginal cultures, Natives have paid a heavy price for such integration.

Diseases brought by the Europeans—virgin soil epidemics, as historian of ecology Alfred Crosby has called them—decimated the population of the Americas. In Alaska smallpox in the 1830s and influenza in 1918 and 1919 took a terrible toll.[12] Even more significant, forced acculturation—whatever its attributes—disrupted Native culture dramatically, leaving people sus-pended between two cultures, the traditional and the modern. Some Natives made a near complete transition to modern culture; others stayed as firmly rooted in traditional culture as it was possible to do. Still others functioned easily in both worlds, often serving as cultural brokers between the two. And some Natives have found comfort in either culture, not want-ing to turn their backs on their cultural roots or to deny themselves and their children the full panoply of goods, services, and concepts of modern culture. But whatever the nature of their individual accommodation, Alaska Natives have dealt with externally imposed, rapid change, changes so sweeping that they threaten the survival of traditional culture.

Recovery and retention of traditional values and mores is a matter of grave concern in contemporary Alaska Native cultures, especially among elders and leaders. Nearly all the Native regions have established some sort of summer "culture camp" for young people, and in many villages classes in Native culture are now a mandatory part of the school curriculum. But the pressure on traditional culture remains, exacerbated by the challenge of economic sustainability in the remote villages, a challenge few of the villages have been able to meet with much success. Most Alaska Natives today enjoy almost all the material opportunities of rural residents in the rest of America, even though significant numbers rely on subsistence hunting, fishing, and gathering in their family economies. For these activities they use the latest technologies, from snow machines and modern rifles to chain saws and motorized watercraft. But because many of the villages are not economically viable, they must rely heavily on employment with the regional or village corporations, on government transfer payments, on various government grants (many obtained through village nonprofit entities), and on distributions from regional corporate dividends and the annual Alaska Permanent Fund distribution. Such dependence has generated uncertainty, and with it, misunderstanding and mistrust, particularly as the state legislature, pressed with fiscal challenges of its own, has made choices not always beneficial to Native peoples, and as state government has grappled with jurisdictional questions relating to Native sovereignty claimed by tribal governments and other Native bodies.

How to surmount such mistrust, and how to achieve economic sustainability in Native Alaska, is one of the state's greatest continuing challenges today. The history of the interaction between Alaska's Native and non-Native peoples, which has brought Alaska to its current challenge, is one of the major themes of this book.

With a broader understanding of Alaska's geography and its Native people, the text now begins the story of Alaska's colonial history, its internal development, and its relationship to the broader world that has influenced its development so profoundly.

PART I

RUSSIAN AMERICA

1

Russian America, an Introduction

THE HISTORY OF Russian America begins with the expansion of Russian fur trappers, known as *promyshlenniki* in Russian, across the steppes of Siberia to the Sea of Okhotsk, the Amur River valley, and the lower Lena River basin. Not until near the end of Peter the Great's reign in 1725 did the government undertake exploration of Siberia and the North Pacific Ocean. The problem of North Pacific geography, determining the shape and size of the continents, complicated the leap across the Pacific to America, which did not come until nearly a century after Russians reached Okhotsk. The saga of Russian expansion forms a prelude to settlement in America.[1]

Russian development in North America falls into several fairly well-defined chronological periods. The first, from Bering's discovery of the North American mainland in 1741 to the tsar's first charter for the Russian American Company (RAC) in 1799, encompasses the movement of the promyshlenniki, organized by private investors, through the Aleutian Islands to the Alaska Peninsula and Kodiak Island, and their subjugation of the Aleut people. After the accession of Catherine the Great in 1762 and the inconclusive Krenitsyn/Lazarev expedition of 1768, the greater distances and costs forced some consolidation of this activity into the hands of a smaller number of investors, highlighted by the government's charter of Grigorii Shelikhov's company and his successful founding in 1784 on Kodiak Island of the first permanent Russian settlement in North America.

Three elements combined to produce the creation of the monopoly company by Tsar Paul: Aleksandr Baranov's aggressive organization of

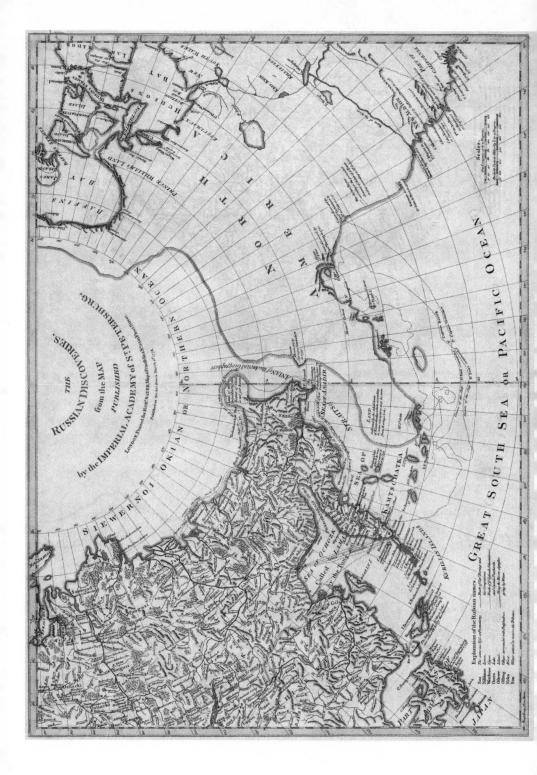

activity in North America, the determination of Shelikhov's widow, Natal'ia, to keep his partners united in one group, and the diplomacy and competence of her son-in-law Nikolai Rezanov lobbying in St. Petersburg among the nobility and in the imperial court. The contest among European powers for sovereignty along the Northwest Coast of North America began in this period as well, after the findings of the Krenitsyn expedition circulated among the St. Petersburg intelligentsia and quickly beyond, exciting Spain particularly. Baranov's extension of Russian occupation of the coast was coincident with the creation of the monopoly.

The second period circumscribes Baranov's tenure as the first manager of the RAC and the first governor of Russian America, from 1799 through 1819. England, which had the strongest navy at the time and therefore logically perhaps ought to have occupied the coast north of the Spanish outpost at San Francisco, became embroiled in the French wars and was thus unable to attend to the Northwest Coast. Both Spain and Russia attempted to capitalize on the "vacuum" left by Britain's distraction, but only the Russians had success. Baranov not only recaptured his post at Sitka from the Tlingit, but he established a post in California ninety miles north of San Francisco. In this period Baranov came to understand what the board of directors in St. Petersburg would grasp only after the tsar and the navy had reorganized the RAC, the magnitude of the problem of adequately supplying Russian America. His failure to gain a foothold in Hawai'i, together with Rezanov's failure to force the Japanese to open their ports to Russia, forced Baranov to purchase supplies from Yankee maritime traders, a decision that created great unease back in Russia.

The third period of Russian colonial history in America focuses on the mature RAC. Eleven naval governors brought able administration to the colony through the mid-nineteenth century, beginning with Matvei Murav'ev in 1820 and culminating with Prince Dmitri Maksutov, who presided over the liquidation of company holdings in 1867. Successive governors eased conditions for the Natives somewhat, encouraged scientific and geographic exploration, supported the activities of the Orthodox mission, and explored opportunities for economic diversification. By the 1840s Sitka had become the "Paris of the Pacific," a remote colonial

(*opposite*) Coast of northwest America and northeast Siberia, 1758, showing the fictitious Gamaland. University of Alaska Fairbanks, Elmer E. Rasmuson Library G9236 S12 1775 J431.

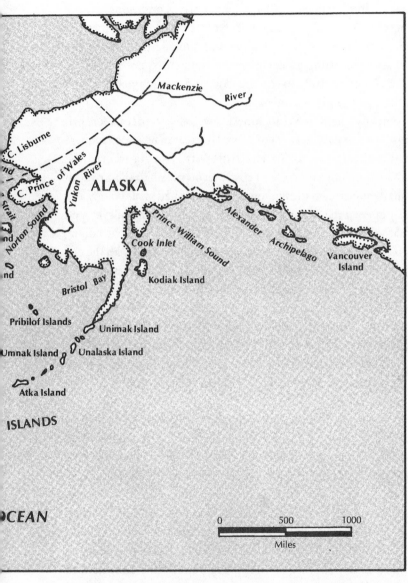

Mackenzie River

C. Lisburne

C. Prince of Wales

Yukon River

ALASKA

Norton Sound

Strait

Prince William Sound

Cook Inlet

Alexander Archipelago

Vancouver Island

Bristol Bay

Kodiak Island

Pribilof Islands

Unimak Island

Umnak Island

Unalaska Island

Atka Island

ISLANDS

OCEAN

0   500   1000
Miles

The Bering Sea, with Siberia and Alaska. From Antonson and Hanable, *Alaska's Heritage*, 114, by permission of the State of Alaska, courtesy of the Alaska Historical Commission.

outpost of European civilization where there were trade goods from around the world and frequent formal entertainments for Europe's military, commercial, and diplomatic elite. At the same time, however, the RAC's labor force lived in deplorable and exploitative conditions, the sea otter were nearly extinguished, and the Aleut Natives, despite somewhat better conditions, continued to be subjugated. During this period the Russians became increasingly dependent on both the supplies and the goodwill of the Tlingit Indians of the Alexander Archipelago, who fiercely maintained their independence.

But the company's hold in North America was always precarious, primarily because the Russians never determined to create a new society there and provided no incentives for its citizens to stay. Russia wanted the resources of North America on the least costly terms possible. The Crimean War (1854–56) demonstrated the tenuous hold Russia had on its colony and coincidentally opened the Amur River valley, an area rich in undeveloped resources that was easier to supply and defend. This rendered the colony vulnerable to a crisis of stockholder confidence that occurred with the circulation of information about a false "sale" of the RAC to the United States during the war. Circulation of Russian naval captain Pavel Nikolaevich Golovin's report on colonial conditions in 1862 exacerbated the crisis, leading ultimately to the decision to sell the colony. By 1867 the Russians knew all of Russian America's potential, and they knew also that they did not have the will to commit the human and material resources necessary to develop it. American expansionism during this period provided Russia with a welcome solution to that dilemma.

As it would be in the future, during the Russian period of its history Alaska was a colony, although a very limited one. Only at Sitka did the Russians establish a substantial post with schools, a library, ship repair facilities, an administrative corps, and other marks of colonial organization. As the Canadian geographer James R. Gibson pointed out several decades ago, the Russians never adequately solved the challenge of colonial self-sufficiency.[2] Moreover, Gibson has argued, the Russians would not have been able to colonize North America to the limited degree that they did without comprehensive reliance on the Native population.[3] In American Alaska developers would learn some of the same lessons painstakingly learned by the Russians: that distance acts as a tyranny to defeat supply, that remoteness and harshness of climate complicate the challenges of administration and drive up its costs, and that those same circumstances inhibit self-sufficiency. They would also learn that the Native people of Alaska are resilient and adaptable, and long before the Russians arrived, Natives had learned to fulfill their own needs to prosper and had created cultures rich in resources, art, and wisdom.

2

Russian Eastward Expansion and the Kamchatka Expeditions

RUSSIA IS PRIMARILY a European nation. The seat of Russian political, economic, and cultural life and development is now and has historically been in Europe, in Moscow and St. Petersburg, and before that in Kiev and Novgorod.[1] As Spain colonized South and Central America and Britain colonized the Atlantic littoral (coastal plain) of North America, so Russia colonized Siberia and later the Northwest Coast of North America. But for Russia, Siberian development was tangential; Russia's face has historically been turned to the West.[2] Today Alaska's non-Native population (as well as that of northern Norway, Sweden, and Finland) is about 85 percent of the total population. In Siberia it is also about 85 percent. But Russia's first forays into Siberia were tentative and inconclusive.

Siberia is a vast and varied land comprising all of northern Asia between the Ural Mountains (the natural physical boundary between Europe and Asia) on the west and the Pacific Ocean on the east, a distance of roughly four thousand miles (by comparison, it is about three thousand miles from Los Angeles to New York City), and stretching southward from the Arctic Ocean to the hills of north-central Kazakhstan and the mountain border with Mongolia and China. The most northern reaches of Siberia are north of 70° north latitude (as is Barrow, Alaska). Most Siberian cities lie south of 60° north latitude (Anchorage lies just north of 60° north latitude). Siberia falls into three, very large major regions. In the west, abutting the Ural Mountains, is the West Siberian plain, drained by the Ob and Yenisey

Rivers, varying little in relief and containing huge tracts of wetlands. East of the Yenisey is the Central Siberian Plateau, which rises above five thousand feet in the northwest. Farther east the valley of the Lena River separates the plateau from a complex series of mountains and basins that make up the Siberian Far East. Other mountain ranges extend south and east along the Mongolian border. The major river basins of the Far East are the Amur, opening eastward to the Pacific, and the Indigirka, Yana, and Kolyma, opening to the Arctic.

Russian occupation of Siberia began in 1581, when the Cossack Timofeyevich Yermak (also spelled Ermak) led an expedition across the Ural Mountains from European Russia, conquering the capital of Sibir, or Kashlyk, on the Irtysh River. The expedition was a response to raids of Siberian tribesmen westward across the mountains into properties of the wealthy Stroganov family, who owned mines, salt works, granaries, and fur-trapping operations along the west flanks of the Urals. Strengthened with troops sent by the tsar, Yermak was successful at first but was eventually forced out of the area, back westward across the Urals.

But the Russians recognized the potential for wealth in the abundant furs of western Siberia, particularly sable. With others, they quickly followed this first incursion into Siberia, and by the 1590s the Russian conquest of Siberia was well engaged. Russian free entrepreneurs, the promyshlenniki, moved successively into the major river basins, trapping out the easily accessible furs and collecting tribute (*iasak*) from the Native tribes. Traders found the market for sable almost inexhaustible, and because the tsar collected a substantial tax on the peltry, the government encouraged the trappers. In addition, the tsar implemented a monopoly on fur exports. By the end of the century, income from furs may have contributed 10 percent of all government revenue, a return that provided the incentive for a more focused and concerted expansion eastward.[3]

In 1607, the same year the English founded Jamestown in North America, the Russians established a post on the Yenisey River, and in 1632 they had reached the Lena. There they founded Irkutsk, and in 1639 the first Russians arrived at the Pacific Ocean on the Sea of Okhotsk, west of Kamchatka. The *ostrog* (a crude fort) at Okhotsk dates from 1648. This was the first European settlement on the Pacific Coast north of Mexico. The lack of natural barriers between the Urals and the mountains east of the Lena facilitated the promyshlenniki advance. Although most trappers were uneducated and social or political outcasts, others were highly capable leaders who provided the guidance and direction that allowed rapid advance across the vast distance, circumstances that would be repeated later when the Russians began to advance on the Aleutian Islands.[4]

With other Europeans the Russians carried with them assumptions of superiority as they moved out from their centers of power and supply.

Based initially on technology, these presuppositions easily and early developed into firm cultural and ideological convictions as well. Europeans were neither unaware nor unwitting in their impositions on the aboriginal populations they encountered. Debating before the Spanish Council of the Indies, the cleric-historian Bartolome de Las Casas's plea that Americans are human beings equal to the Europeans went unheeded; the theologian Juan Gines de Sepulveda gave articulation in 1550 to what by then had become axiomatic: that the aborigines of the Americas had no rights that the Europeans did not wish to accord them because the Indians did not have the capacity to understand rights.[5] Among the promyshlenniki, brutalization of Siberian Natives was routine. It did not proceed from any immediate philosophical considerations, of course, but in the context of business as usual. The trappers had the technological capacity to overwhelm the Native population, and they did, although from time to time not without debilitating attacks by their victims. But these were mere temporary setbacks that ultimately did not impede the relentless progress of the promyshlenniki across the land.

By 1650 there were fifty thousand Russians in Siberia and by the end of the century, twice that number. The Russians routinely took hostages of the Native populations they encountered—Voguls, Ostiaks, Tungus, Iakuts, Lamuts, Iukagirs, Koriaks, Chukchi, Kamchadals, and others. Hostages helped to ensure the safety of the oppressors, provided needed knowledge of the land and its resources, and performed much of the labor of trapping Siberian furs. The toll on Siberia's Natives was severe, both through outright subjugation and from disease, the virgin soil epidemics that greatly reduced the Native populations. In this the Russians differed little from the Spanish, French, English, Dutch, Portuguese, and other Europeans who spread across the world in the sixteenth century.

Russian expansion into Siberia and eventually into North America differed from other European colonization on the new American continents in at least one respect. The Spanish government was directly involved in the establishment and exploitation of New Spain. France attempted to keep restrictive controls on the development of New France, although the

Montreal fur traders did resist the bonds that Paris meant to impose. Although the British government did not pay for the colonial enterprises of its subjects, it monitored them closely, failing to understand until it was too late that it had provided them with too much self-direction. The promyshlenniki and Cossacks in Siberia often proceeded without much government insight or, at times, even awareness. The territory was so vast and so distant from St. Petersburg that a thorough monitoring of the promyshlenniki's activities would have been problematic under any circumstances.

When they reached the Sea of Okhotsk, the Russians turned both north and south. To the south lay the rich Amur, one of Asia's great rivers, flowing twenty-seven hundred miles from the Yablonovyy Mountains east of Baikal through alpine valleys and plateaus to the Pacific near the north end of Sakhalin, its basin rich in furs. The Ch'ing dynasty of China had secured the loyalty of Native tribes living along the river, and when the Russians coming from the north raided their villages, the Natives appealed to the court at Beijing. At first the Chinese did not realize that the raiders had come from Europe by land; they thought they were adventurers who had come upriver from the Pacific. When some of the tribesmen defected to the Russians, however, the Chinese learned who they were, and began a determined negotiation with the Russian tsar, Ivan the Terrible.

The Chinese greatly feared the Russians; if the tsar could send raiders across Asia from Europe, the Ch'ing leaders reasoned, his resources must be mighty. At the same time the Russians understood that a protracted war to secure the Amur would be costly and difficult to maintain and in the end probably futile. Therefore, the two forces began negotiations that produced the Treaty of Nerchinsk in 1689, which, with some later additions, would govern Russian-Chinese relations for more than 150 years and would profoundly affect the nature of Russia's North American fur trade. By its terms Russia withdrew from the Amur, which along most of its length would be recognized as the international border. To underscore their determination to protect their frontier, however, the Chinese insisted that the border's eastern portion go far north of the river, reaching the ocean on the Sea of Okhotsk, thus securing the mouth of the Amur. As a concession to the tsar, the Ch'ing court licensed Russian merchants to cross the border to trade. This led to merchant caravans traveling to Beijing with European goods, although they brought mostly furs because that was the resource Siberia had to offer. Later, in 1728, the Chinese would place severe restrictions on the trade, limiting most exchanges to the border town of Kyakhta in the mountains south of Irkutsk. When Russian trappers began to bring furs from North America, Kyakhta was their principal marketplace.

At the Sea of Okhotsk the Russians also turned north. In 1648 a commercial agent named Fedor Alekseev Popov organized an expedition of ninety promyshlenniki and several Cossacks to proceed eastward along the Arctic Coast to search for the Anadyr River, reportedly rich in sable. The Cossack Semen Dezhnev was assigned to collect *iasak*, or tribute, from the Natives. The party debarked from the mouth of the Kolyma River in seven *koches*, small boats of about forty feet with a single mast and one square-rigged sail. The route was quite dangerous, and four of the boats were lost to storm and heavy seas before reaching the tip of the Chukotsk Peninsula. A fifth boat was lost on the peninsula. The remaining two boats, captained by Dezhnev and a subordinate named Alekseev, rounded the peninsula, Asia's farthest east point, and worked their way south before being thrown on the shore south of the Anadyr during yet another storm.[6]

The survivors of this epic voyage trekked overland toward the Anadyr, but Natives killed Alekseev's party. Dezhnev with twenty-four survivors continued overland, but half the men were lost in a snowstorm. Dezhnev finally reached the river and established an Anadyr outpost, from which he sent reports of the expedition's fate back to officials at Iakutsk (Yakutsk). Dezhnev's was an extraordinary voyage of 1,450 miles in fairly primitive vessels in the face of extremely difficult conditions. Although he may not have realized its implications, geographers later would: he had rounded northeastern Asia through what would later be named the Bering Strait. Asia and North America, the geographers would realize, were not connected. In addition, Dezhnev demonstrated that the Arctic Coast was navigable. He also heard from the Natives tales of a "great land" to the east, a land that was not an island, a land somehow different in character from Asia. In fact, Siberian and Alaska Natives had long engaged in cross-strait trade, which would later be interrupted with the beginning of the Bering Sea whale fishery in the early nineteenth century.[7] Although accounts of the journey filtered through official circles in far east Siberia, apparently they were vaguely understood at the time. Only later would the implications become clear.

Dezhnev's voyage did not carry the Russians beyond the limits of Asia. For three-quarters of a century the Siberian coast confined Russian expansion. When they would finally gather themselves for a leap beyond Siberia, the initial impetus came not from the promyshlenniki but from one of Russia's most remarkable historical figures. His motivation was the same as the promyshlenniki: economic profit.[8] Peter the Great (1672–1725), who ruled from 1682 to 1725 (without regency from 1696), was one of the most significant and accomplished leaders in Russian history.[9] He was a reformer. Extremely intelligent and raised in a progressive atmosphere, Peter toured Europe in 1697 and 1698, sometimes incognito, to learn technologies and methodologies as yet unfamiliar in Russia, especially ship construction and navigation. After his return he moved the Russian capital to St. Petersburg on the Baltic, introduced many Western ideas and processes, overhauled the Russian military and government, and increased the monarchy's power. In 1721 he was named emperor. In foreign policy Peter pursued access to the sea in the Baltic and the south, engaging in war with Sweden, with Turkey, and with Persia. Upon his death Russia was more secure and advanced than it had been before his reign.

It was Peter who initiated Russia's interest in and search for America. At the end of the seventeenth century, the geography of the North Pacific was unknown. The Spanish had established ports on the west coasts of South America and Mexico, but their colonization of North America had been by way of the Rio Grande and the land between the upper Rio Grande and the Mississippi River. They had also crossed the Pacific to colonize in the East Indies, but although they knew vaguely of California (San Diego Bay had been discovered near the end of the sixteenth century), they did not direct their activities there. The North Pacific region was a vacuum in terms of geographic understanding. The Russians would make great strides in solving the puzzles of North Pacific geography. For a time they would be distracted by false leads, however. Their commitment to trace out those leads and pursue the question of North Pacific geography constitutes a substantial contribution to the saga of world exploration, even as it was motivated primarily by the search for new economic resources to exploit.

While in Amsterdam in 1697, Peter learned that a Dutch scholar interested in Russia, Nicholas Witsen, believed there was a close connection between Kamchatka and America by way of a large island or American peninsula; he imagined it to be located where today we know the Bering Sea and the Aleutian Islands actually lie. This great peninsula, bulbous in shape, was thought to project westward in the area north of the Aleutian

Islands, on its western edge approaching within several hundred miles of the Kamchatka Peninsula. Some Russian geographers produced maps showing the peninsula even closer to Kamchatka. On the basis of all the geographers' suppositions, Peter thought the distance from Kamchatka to this North American peninsula would be quite short. Stories of a "great land" to their east, brought by the promyshlenniki from Siberian Natives, seemed to confirm the geographers' conclusions. So did tales from Spanish mariners who used the Japan Current to cross the North Pacific Ocean on their return from the Philippines and the East Indies back to the western coast of Mexico. Sometimes the Spanish ships were driven north by storms, and the mariners thought they caught sight of land to the north. This fictitious land was given various names; one was Gamaland, named after the Portuguese navigator Juan de Gama, one of the first to report the possibility of some large land in the area. Much Russian energy would be directed toward the search for Gamaland.

Peter's attention was occupied with Russia's relation to Europe during most of his reign, but in 1719, wanting to extend Russian territory to new lands and resources, he directed two navigators in eastern Siberia, Ivan Evreinov and Fedor Luzhin, to describe the region of Kamchatka and to determine if Asia and North America were connected, a question about which world geographers were very curious. From Kamchatka the Russians might colonize southward to Japan and the Philippines and eastward to America and California. Evreinov and Luzhin explored both coasts of Kamchatka and the northern Kuril Islands and, using accounts from Russians already familiar with the Anadyr and Chukotsk coasts, reported to Peter that there was no land connection.[10]

In January 1725, just before his death, Peter the Great drafted instructions for an expedition to Kamchatka and beyond. He selected the Danish mariner Vitus Bering, then in Russian service, to head the expedition. Bering led a group of eighty men across vast Siberia, exploring the river valleys and expanses of plateau as they went. They reached the Sea of Okhotsk in 1728. From there Peter's instructions ordered the party to sail "along the land which goes to the north, and according to expectations (because its end is not known) that appears to be part of America."[11] Bering was also instructed to find where this land was connected to North America, to proceed to the first European settlement, to explore and map the land in between, and to return to Kamchatka. The late historian Raymond Fisher of UCLA argued that the land that best fit the description of "the land which goes to the north" was the fictitious Gamaland, the bulbous peninsula or subcontinent of North America extending westward nearly to Kamchatka. Bering carried a map that showed Gamaland quite close to Kamchatka.[12] Fisher's interpretation fits well with Peter's instruction to find "where this land is connected to North America." From the Evreinov and Luzhin voyage, Peter knew that Kamchatka was not connected to America, and Fisher argued that from their decades-long association with the Chukchi Natives, the Russians knew northern Siberia was not connected to North America either.

Sometime on his trip across Siberia, however, Bering became convinced that there was no Gamaland, probably from reviewing Russian and Spanish sources. Upon reaching the Sea of Okhotsk, he had a small ship constructed, the *Fortuna*, which his crew sailed across to the western shore of Kamchatka. Unsure of the geography south of the peninsula, despite the information reported by Evreinov and Luzhin, they dismantled the boat and carried its hardware and rigging across Kamchatka. From the peninsula's eastern coast they could set out to fulfill Peter's instructions. Because Bering now concluded there was no land to the east close to Siberia, to "sail along the land that goes to the north" he now interpreted to mean sailing northward along the Siberian coast. He reasoned that if there was a land connection to America, it would have to be in the north; he felt his obligation was to prove its nonexistence. Accordingly, Bering constructed a ship, the *Sv. Gavril* (St. Gabriel), and charted the coast northward along Kamchatka, around the Gulf of Anadyr, and through the strait that now bears his name.

The *Sv. Gavril* was not a large vessel capable of ocean voyaging. Because in the design of the expedition, before Bering left St. Petersburg, believing that Gamaland lay close to Kamchatka, the plans called only for a vessel capable of sailing along the coast. Thus Bering did not sail eastward toward Gamaland, which he had decided did not exist, or was not close enough to sail to, but instead he chose to sail northward along the east Siberian coast.[13] He did not expect to find a land connection in the north, which he did not. But because of fog and weather, neither did he see the North American mainland while transiting Bering Strait, even though the strait is only fifty-six miles wide. Bering continued to sail northward, and above 67° north latitude he sailed back and forth east and west to see if there was land that far north. He concluded there was not and returned to Kamchatka and then to St. Petersburg.

Although Bering failed to pursue the intent of Peter's instructions, the voyage was nonetheless significant. Bering filled in and corrected the charts of the Siberian coast, he effectively disproved any land connection between Asia and America for those who needed further evidence on that point, and he confirmed that the seas south of the Kamchatka Peninsula were navigable for entry into the Sea of Okhotsk. Peter's motivation for this voyage bears reflection. It was not primarily to make contributions to science or to geography. Rather, he sought new resources for Russia, including land, Natives, furs, minerals, and anything else that might be of value. In addition, whatever new lands could be added to the empire represented not only new opportunities for Russia, but in the best mercantilist thinking of the day, it also meant that those lands and their resources would be denied any other nation. Obviously, geographic knowledge was necessary for expansion, but it was not the primary objective of expansion; resources were.

Not long after Bering had passed his way, the governor of Siberia, in Tobol'sk on the Irtysh River in the West Siberian Plain, ordered a captain of dragoons, Dmitrii Pavlutskii, to take a company of four hundred men and proceed to Chukotsk in 1727 to subdue the Chukchi Natives there. As part of the same effort, in 1730 a Cossack from Iakutsk named Afanasii Shestakov took a force of nearly one thousand men to attack the Chukchi from the land of the Koriaks, in the region just north of the neck of the Kamchatka Peninsula. But the Chukchi wiped out Shestakov and his force. Pavlutskii ordered navigator Ivan Fedorov and geodesist (surveyor) Mikhail Gvozdev in 1732 to take Bering's vessel, the *Sv. Gavril*, which had been left at Okhotsk, and sail to the mouth of the Anadyr. From there the vessel was to sail eastward to the great land, which the Chukchi continued to tell the Russians lay nearby. In July of that year Fedorov and Gvozdev with a junior officer, four sailors, thirty-two Cossacks, and an interpreter sailed from the Anadyr. Striking northeast they came upon the two Diomede Islands, where they found Natives who refused to pay tribute. They then proceeded to Cape Prince of Wales, North America's farthest west point on the east side of the Bering Strait, and then southeast along the Seward Peninsula to an inhabited village, most likely Wales. They were unable to land because of shallow water and adverse winds. They continued on to King Island but again could not land because of contrary winds. The party then returned to the Siberian coast.[14]

The Gvozdev voyage made remarkably little impact. Shestakov and Pavlutskii had organized the voyage, not Gvozdev, making the assignment of responsibility complicated. In addition, command communication ran from Okhotsk to Iakutsk (far up the Lena River), then through Irkutsk to Tobol'sk, two thousand miles away, and finally to St. Petersburg. Thus neither Tobol'sk nor St. Petersburg had much control over their field captains Shestakov and Pavlutskii. The reports submitted by Fedorov and Gvozdev were filed at Iakutsk, and information about the voyage did not reach St. Petersburg until 1738. Moreover, it is not clear that Fedorov and Gvozdev understood exactly where they were. Although they clearly had found Natives and villages, they had no way of knowing whether these were on islands or part of the mainland of North America. On the map that Gvozdev subsequently made of the voyage, he labeled the land southeast of the Cape as the "great land," but his notion of its shape and extent or its relationship to known lands was unclear and conjectural.

Subsequently, the Russian government planned a second exploratory enterprise, called the Great Northern expedition. This was a massive undertaking unlike any exploratory expedition ever conceived within Russia or beyond. Siberia's major rivers were to be surveyed all along their courses to the Arctic Ocean. The Arctic Coast was to be charted from the mouth of the Ob to the mouth of the Lena. The entire coast of the Sea of Okhotsk was to be charted, as was Sakhalin Island and Hokkaido in Japan. Finally, a voyage was to be made southeasterly from Kamchatka in search of Gamaland and beyond to find its connection with America. The last part of the enterprise, directed by Bering and Alexii Chirikov, is usually called the second Kamchatka expedition. Although not all the sections of this extraordinary undertaking were completed, enough were to make the undertaking highly significant.

It is noteworthy that unlike the later maritime explorations of James Cook, Alessandro Malaspina, or the other major European investigators of the North Pacific, Bering's and Chirikov's transpacific voyages were not planned and organized as scientific explorations. Rather, their purpose was political and economic. Bering and Chirikov were to claim unoccupied areas of the North American coast for Russia, thus laying the basis for Russian sovereignty there and excluding the sovereignty of other European nations.[15] In addition, they were to identify resources that the Russians could exploit, including Native populations from whom iasak could be collected. The German naturalist Georg Wilhelm Steller accompanied Bering, but he was included on the expedition not as a scientist but as a mineralogist and assayer.

After crossing Siberia with the main body of the expedition between 1738 and 1741, Bering and Chirikov set out from Petropavlovsk (City of Peter and Paul) on the eastern coast of Kamchatka on 4 June. By that time Bering had knowledge of Gvozdev's voyage in the north. But the focus of the second Kamchatka expedition was in the south. In two ships, the *Sv. Petr* and the *Sv. Pavel*, the two captains headed southeasterly in search of Gamaland. That they proceeded as far south as 46° north latitude (the latitude of Astoria, Oregon) before abandoning the effort shows the extent of their commitment to find Gamaland. Separated by a storm on 20 June, the two ships proceeded independently. On 14 June, Bering in the *Sv. Petr* sighted Mount St. Elias on the North American mainland north of the Alexander Archipelago. The next day Chirikov, now out of touch with Bering and unaware of his whereabouts, made a landfall on the North American coast far to the south. Or rather, he attempted to make a landfall, probably on Baker Island, off Bucareli Bay on Prince of Wales Island in the southern portion of the archipelago (or it may have been Cape Addington on nearby Noyes Island). At this time the ships were more than three hundred miles apart.

Neither captain spent much time on the coast. Both crews needed fresh water, and they were beginning to show some early signs of scurvy, the great limiter of the time ships could stay at sea.[16] Moreover, neither captain knew the disposition of the North American Natives. The story of Chirikov's visit is particularly tragic. Sailing northwesterly along the coast, on 18 July he sent eleven men in a longboat to Iakobii Island for fresh water. The crew were to signal if in difficulty. Although the ship's company waited expectantly for six days, the men did not return and there was no signal. Chirikov then dispatched a second longboat, his last, this time with a crew of four. Again the boat did not return, and there was no signal. But after two days a large Native canoe with a dozen men emerged from behind a promontory. The canoe approached to within several hundred yards of the ship, and the Natives performed a chanting and gesturing ritual and then rowed back from where they had come. The fate of Chirikov's men has never been determined. Unwilling to risk further misadventure, Chirikov set sail for Kamchatka. On the return voyage the ship sighted the Kenai Peninsula (1–3 August) and Afognak and Kodiak Islands. On 5 September they were off Umnak Island and on 10 September they were near Adak, where they first met Aleut Islanders. On 22 September Chirikov and his crew passed Agattu and Attu Islands.

In the meantime Bering made his landfall on Kayak Island, just off Cape Suckling on the coast south of Prince William Sound. While the crew fetched fresh water and made minor ship repairs, Bering permitted the naturalist Georg Steller to survey the island. He had just seven hours. Steller could not walk the whole island in that time, but working frantically he noted characteristic features of climate and soil and collected numerous examples of resident flora and fauna, some previously unknown, and some rock samples. He also discovered a Native encampment, probably temporary, with the coals of the campfire still warm. Feeling that he was being watched, Steller collected some Native artifacts and left in their place some iron implements.

Bering set sail immediately and on his return passed some of the Aleutian Islands, where the crew obtained fresh water. By the time the ship reached a small island group lying in the four-hundred-mile expanse between Attu, the farthest west island of the Aleutians, and the Kamchatka Peninsula, many of the crew were very ill with scurvy, and it was a hardship to find sufficient men to sail the vessel. Without the capability to compute longitude, which was developed only later in the mid-eighteenth century, the crew did not know if they were yet far enough west to be off the Kamchatka coast or among islands still far from the mainland. After a debate First Officer Sven Waxell landed the ship where they were and the crew disembarked. Soon after, a violent storm wrecked the ship. Nineteen men died during the ensuing winter, including Captain-Commander Bering, who succumbed on 8 December.[17] Steller had worked out the recipe for some antiscorbutic broths that constituted a symptomatic treatment for scurvy, and his ministrations are credited with keeping a number of the men alive. The following summer forty-six survivors constructed a longboat from the planking of the *Sv. Petr* and sailed on to Kamchatka.[18]

For all of its efforts and the tragedy associated with it, the second Kamchatka expedition accomplished little directly. Although both Chirikov and Bering did in fact touch on the North American mainland, they brought back little information about its resources or inhabitants, despite Steller's desperate attempts. Most important, the geographical results were mixed. Although they did generally disprove the existence of Gamaland, the relation of their two separate landfalls to each other, to Gvozdev's, and to Siberia was not clear. The Northwest Coast of North America had yet to be charted, and the continent's shape and location in that quarter had yet to be divined and understood. Yet it is probably not inappropriate to accord Bering the "discovery" of North America in the latitudes in which the two ships sailed, for subsequent explorations and hunting expeditions would lead to Russian discovery of all the Aleutian Islands and the mainland in the vicinity of the Alaska Peninsula and Kodiak Island, even though the full understanding of continental geography would await the scientific voyages of James Cook in 1778 and 1779.

The greatest significance of Bering's voyage was not in geography but in fur peltry, which the survivors of the winter in the Commander Islands brought back with them. These included a variety of fox and seal skins and more than fifteen hundred sea otter pelts, more luxurious and lustrous than any pelts yet seen in Siberia. In these lay Russia's future in North America, and the future of the Aleutian Islanders, for they brought forty times the price Chinese merchants paid for Siberia sable belts, the staple of the trade between Russia and China. This was an opportunity the promyshlenniki could not ignore.[19]

3

Exploitation and the Origins of the Contest for Sovereignty

BEGINNING IN 1743, successive expeditions of Russian fur trappers voyaged to the Aleutian Islands, known to the Russians as the Eastern Islands, to hunt furs. Between then and the end of the century, when the Russian American Company (RAC) was founded, there were about one hundred such voyages that garnered more than eight million silver rubles.[1] Each year the promyshlenniki (fur trappers) pushed farther east, exploiting the resources of one island after another in their quest for profits. By the 1760s they had reached the Fox Island group and soon after, the mainland on the tip of the Alaska Peninsula.

Such voyages required capital. A ship had to be built and outfitted, and food and other supplies procured. Even though the ships were of crude construction and supplies were kept to a minimum, few of the promyshlenniki had the finances for such ventures. Enterprising merchants from Siberian and Russian cities stepped in to outfit these expeditions and to seize the opportunity they represented. Merchants from Irkutsk, Tobol'sk, and other Siberian cities, as well as from European Russia, became the principal investors, and a number traveled on the voyages to the islands. In fact, the merchant investors who sailed in the islands constitute a separate class of promyshlenniki, a number of whom were important leaders in the expansion through the Eastern Islands. They are distinguished from the much larger group of hunters that made up the crews of the expeditions and performed the labor associated with exploitation of the islands.

The latter, to whom the term *promyshlenniki* is more broadly and famil-
iarly applied, were largely illiterate, were often social outcasts, and typically
lived their lives in poverty, many in debt servitude to the investors who
financed the voyages. Some very few promyshlenniki acquired the capital
and experience to lead expeditions.

There were significant differences for the promyshlenniki as they left
Siberia and Kamchatka and ventured eastward across the ocean. Their
object was the same as it had been in Siberia: the "soft gold" of the furbearers. Their method of taking the peltry was much the same: demanding
iasak (tribute) from the Natives and holding women and children villagers
as hostages while forcing the male hunters to go out under Russian direction to bring in a sufficient number of pelts. But taking animals from the
sea was vastly different from taking them on land, and managing an enterprise flung across hundreds of miles of islands required much different
organization and techniques than moving systematically up Siberia's vast
river valleys. In the Eastern Islands the government was much less involved
in the expansion of promyshlenniki enterprise than it had been in Siberia.
As a result, exploitation of the Aleutian Islands proceeded almost exclusively through the initiative and leadership of the merchant voyagers. The
government sent Cossacks to ensure the collection of iasak, sent an expedition in the 1760s to monitor promyshlenniki activity and perhaps acquire
more territory, and recorded the departure and arrival of ships and cargoes
at Petropavlovsk and Okhotsk. But the primary energy for expansion and
development of the enterprise was private.

In Siberia the hunters had actively participated in collecting furs, traveling with Native hunters, and sometimes hunting exclusively on their own.
In the islands, however, because they did not know and did not master
the technology of marine harvesting, nearly all of the hunting was done
by the Natives, under Russian leadership and coercion.[2] Partly for this
reason, in the islands and later on the mainland, the Russians encountered continuing, sometimes violent resistance, unlike their experience in
Siberia, where the less populous, disunited, and technologically inferior
Native cultures posed little problem. In addition, there had been no European competitors in Siberia, but in America the promyshlenniki encountered vigorous foreign competition for occupancy of the territory and for
control of the fur trade with coastal Natives.

Siberian furs were sold in European Russia and in western Europe; Russian American furs, however, were marketed mostly in China. The more

dense pelt and longer hairs of the sea otter produced a luxuriant garment with a "rich and magnificent" appearance; customers regarded it as among the finest. Because the fur turned hard when cold, however, the Chinese used it most often for trim. Nonetheless, desire for sea otter trim was very high and the market nearly insatiable. In the 1820s, when the American and European beaver markets were still strong and a full beaver pelt brought $4.50, a sea otter tail alone sold for $5 in Canton while a full sea otter pelt fetched $40. A complete sea otter robe, trimmed, might bring $500 or even $1,000 in North China.[3] The Russian merchants sought to capitalize on this market. Each year one or more vessels left Okhotsk or Petropavlovsk on Kamchatka for hunting trips to the islands. Typically, the ships would sail to the Commander Islands, where they would spend some time in slaughtering and preserving the meat of Steller's rhytina (a sea cow), a large, defenseless sea mammal that lived throughout those islands. The expeditions would then proceed to whichever of the islands seemed likely to yield a sufficient cargo of peltry.[4]

Most of the promyshlenniki were wilderness dwellers. In Siberia they lived in the forests among the Native populations and were at home in primitive conditions that required a thorough knowledge of survival skills and considerable personal courage. A typical expedition to America might include thirty to fifty experienced promyshlenniki in one vessel. The profits from the voyages would be divided into as many shares as there were Russian hunters, plus a few extra shares. The government took one-tenth of all profits. Signing with an "X," the trappers accepted contracts that gave them each one half-share of the remaining profits, a sum that could be quite substantial. The investors took the other half of each remaining share, or 50 percent of the profits. As many as half the crew might be Kamchadal Natives from Kamchatka. They were paid a pittance from the investors' shares. One full share went to the ship's navigator, and a share was usually given to charity. In addition, the Russians collected iasak from the Natives, which went to the government treasury. Few of the Russian hunter/ laborers actually became rich, however. Few had the financial experience to capitalize on their opportunities, and the investors charged all possible expenses against their accounts. As a result, the promyshlenniki saw very little of the eight million rubles the investors earned before formation of the RAC in 1799.[5]

Europeans commonly took hostages among the aboriginal peoples they encountered to guarantee "trouble-free" relations. The Russians continued this in the Aleutians. Usually the voyagers would take as hostage some or even all of the women and children of an island village, holding them until the able-bodied hunters accompanying the Russians brought in enough pelts to make up a cargo. In fact, the Russians became increasingly and widely dependent on the Aleut people.[6] Not only did the Aleuts constitute the hunting force, but they performed nearly all other labor as well. They also supplied the Russians with food and other supplies. In addition, the Russians relied on Aleut women for sex and companionship. No aspect of Aleut life was untouched by the Russians, and little that the Russians did in the islands existed without Aleut support. Even after the founding of the RAC, the Russians continued to rely on the Aleuts, although under changed circumstances.[7]

Appreciation of this phenomenon of dependence emerges more clearly when measured against the small number of Russians involved. In the 1970s the Russian scholar Svetlana Fedorova documented that the largest number of Russians ever in Russian America at one time was 823; typically there were not more than about 600.[8] It is not surprising then that Russian dependence on the Native population was critical to Russian occupation of the Northwest Coast. These 823 Russians seem a very small number to manage such a far-flung commercial empire; obviously only the barest colonial edifice could be erected with so few people. But if the Russians did not intend to establish in America a colony that would become self-sustaining and would take on a life of its own through population growth and trade, if instead they intended only to exploit the furs on the cheapest and most efficient terms possible, then 823 people was probably too many. Sir George Simpson of the Hudson's Bay Company (HBC) thought the Russians wasteful in their commitment of material and personnel in America; the HBC managed a vast interior fur empire in the years 1821 through 1858 with far fewer personnel.[9] The Russians would continue to develop a philosophy for exploitation of their American holdings only over time and not always consistently.

The impact of Russian occupation on the Aleut population was devastating. Disease, the great scourge of contact, probably reduced the precontact Aleut population from twenty thousand to fewer than five thousand people.[10] In addition, many of the Aleuts were resettled to meet Russian demands for labor, compensating for depopulation in areas where labor needs were persistent. A number of villages apparently disappeared entirely. There were important changes in daily life as well. Aleut hunters were often taken away from their villages for long periods of time to hunt furbearers for the Russians. Their absence meant the procreation of fewer offspring; food-gathering patterns were significantly altered; and women had to supply most of the food, which probably meant a greater reliance on fish and shellfish. There were other changes in daily life. Aboveground structures replaced traditional underground houses known as *barabaras*. The design and nature of clothing, implements, and utensils changed when the hunters no longer could supply needed materials.

Scholars have recently focused on the accommodations and adaptations aboriginal populations made as they coped with the Euro-Americans who came to dominate their cultures, accommodations that permitted not only their survival as a people but also the survival of significant aspects of traditional culture. The Aleut made many such adaptations.[11] But overall, the occupation of their islands by the Russians can only have been disruptive, particularly in the early period of contact, before they felt the mitigating effects of policies of the Russian Orthodox mission and some of the colony's more enlightened governors. Several analysts have disputed this interpretation of "selective assimilation" and accommodation, insisting that the period was characterized primarily by destruction and an overwhelming loss of human life.[12] The latter interpretation seems to fit the eighteenth century better than the nineteenth, however.

There is ample evidence of early Aleut resistance to the Russian occupation of their islands. The chronicler Vasilii N. Berkh has reported that in 1745 the navigator Mikhail Nevodchikov had to pass up landing on at least one island because a hundred islanders gathered on a beach to oppose him. In 1753 navigator Petr Bashmakov sailed farther eastward than most voyagers, probably to the Andreanov Islands, where he and his crew were attacked after their ship wrecked. In the same year the Natives killed several promyshlenniki who were with Fedor Kholodilov in the Andreanovs because the hunters had been guilty of "improper conduct" with the wives of some of the islanders. In 1757 a party of Aleuts attacked the crew of the ship *Kapiton*, commanded by Ignati Studentsov, probably in the western Fox Islands. There were many other incidents of violence between Russians and Aleuts, and finally in 1762 the Fox Island Aleuts staged a coordinated attack on four vessels and several shore parties in the islands, killing more than three hundred Russians.[13]

The promyshlenniki exacted a severe revenge for the 1762 attack. Ivan Maksimovich Solov'ev, a Tobol'sk merchant with a reputation as an exceptional navigator, sailed on the vessel *Petr i Pavel* in 1764 to Unalaska Island. Attacked while building a winter encampment, he repulsed the islanders, killing more than one hundred. He then sent out companies of Russians on punitive expeditions. Solov'ev became known among the promyshlenniki as "the deadly nightingale," a pun on his name (*solovei* is Russian for nightingale), for his harsh measures. In one instance, for example, he was said to have lined up a number of Aleut men, one behind the other, and fired a musket into the chest of the first to see how many it would penetrate, as an example of his authority. Solov'ev's and others' punishment for the Fox Island revolt effectively ended Aleut resistance to the Russians.

The investors who employed the promyshlenniki undertook their ventures in the Eastern Islands on their own initiative; the expeditions were private ventures, financed by merchants from cities across Siberia and Russia. The government monitored the activity but did not fund or initiate it. Each voyage was a separate venture. Different combinations of i vestors formed as many as forty different companies to engage in the hunting between 1743 and 1799, when the government granted the Russian American Company monopoly.[14] In the process the promyshlenniki successively discovered and charted the major Aleutian Island groups, and eventually the Alaska Peninsula of the mainland, although for many years after its discovery that peninsula was believed to be an island. Between 1746 and 1765, Andreian Tolstykh, a merchant from Selenginsk, discovered the Rat Island and Andreanov Island groups, the latter being named for him. In 1759, Stepan Gavrilovich Glotov of Iarensk discovered Umnak Island and in 1763, Kodiak Island.

At just this time an important change occurred in the Russian monarchy. Catherine II, the wife of Peter's grandson, ascended to the throne. Known to historians as one of the "enlightened despots" of eighteenth-century Europe (because of her understanding of liberal thought), Catherine was exceptionally astute and energetic. She set out to complete much of the work of Peter the Great. Revolution in Poland, acquisitions in the south, in the Crimea and Danubia, and the Pugachev rebellion in the Ukraine occupied much of her reign, but she took a limited interest in the Eastern Islands and in the potential resources of North America. Catherine wanted accurate and complete information on which to construct her policy for the Eastern Islands. Accordingly, military and court officials designed several expeditions to assess fully promyshlenniki activity

Catherine II (Catherine the Great), empress of Russia, 1762–1796. Alaska State Library P20.005.

and the condition of the Native people and to survey possibilities for future development. The first of these, known as the Tobol'sk Secret Expedition, was to include occupation of the Amur Basin and development of agricultural lands on the Sea of Okhotsk in the Nerchinsk region. However, when Russia became entangled in the Seven Years' War after 1764, the tsarina scrapped the plan. A smaller expedition sailed in 1764, led by Lieutenant Ivan Sindt, a Baltic German who had sailed on Bering's second expedition. Sindt was supposed to survey all the islands between Kamchatka and America. He was incompetent, however, and accomplished little beyond confirming the location of the Commander Islands.

The most significant of these early expeditions was led by two young naval officers, Captain Petr Krenitsyn and Lieutenant Mikhail Levashev. Inauspiciously, three of the four ships they started with were wrecked while crossing from Okhotsk to Kamchatka in 1766. Reorganized, they sailed in two vessels from Kamchatka in 1768. Unfortunately they encountered violent weather and were forced to winter over, Krenitsyn on Unimak Island and Levashev on Unalaska. There they learned that the promyshlenniki had reached the mainland on the long peninsula the Aleuts called Alaska, meaning "a land which is not an island."[15] Short of supplies and constantly attacked by Natives, they returned to Kamchatka the next year, where, remarkably, Krenitsyn drowned in the Kamchatka River. The expedition made some notable geographical discoveries, primarily along the north shore of the Alaska Peninsula, but far short of what the tsarina had anticipated. Nonetheless, all of the information gained by these enterprises, however meager, was added to the maps of the time, the Russians working consistently to develop an accurate picture of North Pacific geography, which was still incomplete and error prone. At the same time the Russians hoped to keep exact details of the Krenitsyn voyage a state secret.

But this was not to be. Reports of the voyage circulated among the Russian aristocracy in St. Petersburg and inevitably reached the ears of European diplomats serving there. Although the Krenitsyn expedition meant little in terms of new geographic knowledge, it set off alarm bells throughout Europe, for it signaled an impending change in the balance of power. When they learned the full extent of Russia's activity in the North Pacific, all of Europe was excited, no country more than Spain. The Spanish had long claimed the Northwest Coast as its own, based on the ancient Treaties of Tordesillas of 1494 and 1496, in which the papacy had divided the unknown world between Spain and Portugal. The Spanish also based their claim on occupation of the west coasts of South and Central America. Spain had colonized along the upper Rio Grande in the 1580s and had discovered San Diego Bay at about the same time. But Spanish administration had yet to reach California; accommodation with the interior Indians had been a long process, and in El Norte Spanish resources were stretched precariously thin. This mitigated against expansion toward California. The information supplied by the Krenitsyn expedition, however, forced a change in Spain's California policy.

In 1761 the Spanish government sent the Marques de Almodovar to Russia as a special envoy to gather information about Russian promyshlenniki activity. After a seven-month stay, mostly in St. Petersburg, Almodovar reported that distance, weather, navigation, and supply diminished the Russian threat in the North Pacific but that the activity there was worrisome nevertheless, and he recommended close monitoring of future Russian efforts. In 1762, Catherine II's ascension signaled the renewal of Russian interest in North America; she enthusiastically endorsed the plans for the Krenitsyn–Levashev expedition. Almodovar's successor in St. Petersburg, Vizconde de la Herreria, sent disturbing reports of the renewed Russian imperial interest, together with detailed accounts of Russian progress in the Aleutians. The Russians, he advised, had apparently reached the mainland of North America and had battled with the Natives, resulting in the death of three hundred Russians.[16] Jóse de Gálvez, newly appointed as the crown's representative in Mexico, judged the Pacific situation to be serious and decided to pursue the Russian challenge. At the government's direction, he established a new naval post on the Mexican western coast just below Baja California at San Blas.

Spain's anxiety about the Northwest Coast was not abstract. The mercantilist economic theory of the day held that gaining control of new resources strengthened a country and weakened its rivals, by denying them those same resources and whatever use the controlling country might make of them. The Spanish knew of sea otter from their presence along the California coast. They had taken some to the Philippines; the pelts had sold there and in Canton very handsomely. San Blas was to be the base for a new, concerted Spanish effort to control the North American coast, to keep out the Russians and any other interlopers who might have designs on a resource Spain considered within its exclusive right.

In 1769, as the Krenitsyn expedition was concluding, Gálvez, together with the viceroy of Mexico, Antonio Maria de Bucareli Ursúa, dispatched five separate expeditions to Alta California, two overland and three by sea. Gaspar de Portolá founded San Diego presidio in 1769, and over the next seven years presidios were established in Monterey and San Francisco (1776) and a series of mission stations were founded along the coast between San Diego and San Francisco Bay. In the meantime the maritime expeditions reached Cape Mendocino, Nootka Sound on Vancouver Island, and Dixon Entrance, between the Alexander and Queen Charlotte Archipelagos (1774).

In 1775, Bruno de Hezeta and Francisco Mourelle in the *Santiago* and the *Sonora* sailed to Vancouver Island and then southward along the coast. South of the Quinault River on the Washington coast seven men from the *Santiago* were killed by Indians when they went ashore to get fresh water. Mourelle, with Juan Francisco de la Bodega y Quadra, continued northward in the *Sonora* and reached the southern islands of the Alexander Archipelago before turning back. Mourelle kept a journal of the voyage that he later submitted to the crown, along with the other expedition papers. Mourelle's was the first Spanish expedition to sail in waters of what would eventually become Alaska.

The Spanish continued sending expeditions northward after the founding of San Francisco in 1776. In 1779, Ignacio de Arteaga in *La Princesa* entered a large sound on the west shore of Prince of Wales Island, which he named Bucareli Bay in honor of the Mexican viceroy. He spent a month among the Tlingit of the region, trading, surveying, and, though not by intention, exchanging hostages. The same year Gonzalo López de Haro in the *San Carlos* sailed to Prince William Sound and Cook Inlet, passed by Kodiak and Umnak Islands, and visited the Shumagin Islands and Unalaska, where he met and exchanged information with the Russian fur trappers.

Little came of these and subsequent Spanish voyages, although they obtained important ethnographic information. During their weeks in Bucareli Bay, for example, Arteaga and his crew learned a great deal about the material culture, social structure, and trading practices of the Tlingit of the west coast of Prince of Wales Island. Among others things, for example, it was clear to the Spanish that Tlingit women determined what prices would be charged for Indian items offered in trade and exercised approval power over trade terms negotiated by the men. Arteaga reported that the Tlingit were a highly organized, sophisticated people who would challenge European assertions of sovereignty in their area. But in 1779, Spain already was stretched beyond the limit of its capabilities in North America. Some of the crews of the northern voyages had been gathered from among mine laborers in Mexico because there were not enough experienced seamen available. Supplies for the ships were inadequate. In addition, there was internal competition between the land-based and the maritime initiatives, and later, concern about American and British threats to Spanish interests in eastern North America.

In the meantime the Russian promyshlenniki continued their exploitation of the Eastern Islands and the mainland, despite Spanish mobilization and expressions of concern to Tsarina Catherine by Spanish diplomats. In 1784, Grigorii Shelikhov founded a post on Kodiak Island and other investors would establish operations in Cook Inlet. Shelikhov's achievement was highly significant and will be discussed further in chapter 4. It seemed that the Russians and the Spanish must eventually clash somewhere on the coast. But even as the Russians pushed farther east, new powers turned their attention to the Northwest Coast—Great Britain and then the United States. And when it came, the clash would not be between Russia and Spain, but between Spain and Great Britain.

Driven by the mercantilist paradigm and their ethnocentric convictions, the Europeans, and with them the Americans, ignored the question of the Native people's sovereignty, or at least did not address it effectively. Generally, although they were not incognizant of the issue of Native rights, they subordinated such concerns to their economic motivation. In practice they viewed the continent as a vacuum to be claimed and appropriated by whichever country could make their claim tangible by acts of possession and eventual occupation. The Natives were considered a valuable resource; they provided the furs that motivated the increasingly sharp competition for sovereignty on the coast, and they provided needed supplies, alliances, and companionship.

Somehow, copies of Mourelle's journal of his 1775 expedition to the southern islands of the Alexander Archipelago surfaced in England, likely through clandestine means. At the time the English Admiralty was assiduously pursuing the question of a passage through the North American continent, which would eliminate that barrier to world trade. In 1774 the English Parliament passed a bill authorizing a prize of twenty thousand pounds sterling to the first ship to traverse such a passage, which was assumed to lie in the northern latitudes because it had not been found farther south; naval vessels were eligible. In the navy, admiralty officials chose James Cook to sail to the North Pacific to search for the passage from the west. Cook was one of the great navigators of all time. Learning his seamanship on colliers (coal ships) along the English coast, during the Seven Years' War he had mapped difficult areas of the St. Lawrence estuary in northeast North America, facilitating the English conquest of Quebec in 1759.

Engraved portrait of Captain James Cook, 1728. Cook's third global circumnavigation provided the first accurate representation of the geography of North America and far-east Siberia. Alaska State Library P20.007.

In 1768, commissioned a lieutenant, he was chosen to command a scientific expedition to the Pacific. After observation of a transit of Venus across the sun from Tahiti, Cook sailed west, looking for a southern continent that geographers were convinced must lie in the southern latitudes. Cook did not find it, but he did discover and chart the islands of New Zealand and then Australia's two-thousand-mile east coast, navigating the Great Barrier Reef, one of the greatest navigational feats ever accomplished. Because of his use of watercress, sauerkraut, and a kind of orange extract, no one died of scurvy on his voyage. Presented to King George III upon his return, Cook was promoted to commander, and between 1772 and 1775 he made one of the most remarkable voyages in the annals of the sea. Sent again to find the southern continent, again he did not, even though he circumnavigated the planet in the high southern latitudes, sailing as far south as 70° south latitude. But he did find and chart Tonga and Easter Island, and New Caledonia, as well as the South Sandwich Islands and South Georgia Island in the South Atlantic. Again, no one died of scurvy. Upon his return to England he was hailed as a hero and promoted to captain.

Little wonder then that the admiralty entrusted the search for a northwest passage to Cook. The landings of Bering and Chirikov on the Northwest Coast had been known in England for many decades, so historians suggest that it was the new Spanish interest in the coast that motivated the British Admiralty to send the third Cook expedition.[17] Despite the Russian and Spanish voyages of 1774 and 1775, the outline of North America above 55° north latitude was as yet unknown. Despite Bering's work, the notion of a peninsula or land mass attached to or a part of America extending westward toward Kamchatka still was not definitively disproved.

Cook sailed from Plymouth, England, with two vessels, the *Discovery* and the *Resolution*, on 2 July 1776, despite hostilities in North America.[18] Not only was William Bligh the sailing master of Cook's companion vessel, but the roster for the voyage also included George Vancouver, Joseph Billings, Nathaniel Portlock, George Dixon—all destined to become famous navigators—as well as the American adventurer John Ledyard. After considerable time in the South Pacific, Cook headed north, turning eastward at 45° north latitude. On this course he discovered the previously unsuspected Hawaiian Islands. Continuing on, he struck the North American mainland near present-day Newport, Oregon. From there, Cook's vessels made a general reconnaissance northward along the continent to the far Arctic ice pack. The expedition stopped for a time at Nootka Sound on Vancouver Island, which was familiar to the Spanish. Nootka well protected the site of several Indian villages. At one of these Cook purchased two silver spoons the Indians had stolen from Estaban Martinez on the 1774 Spanish expedition. Cook also obtained fifteen hundred sea otter pelts, not realizing their full value because most had been sewn up as clothing and many were badly deteriorated. In subsequent years independent maritime fur traders would favor Nootka for trade and refitting their vessels.

When Cook sailed from Plymouth, he took with him a much improved map of the North Pacific, one produced in London in 1774 that included information brought back from the Krenitsyn (Russian) expedition. Instead of the bulbous Gamaland peninsula jutting out from North America's West Coast into the Bering Sea, the new map showed the Bering Sea full of islands.[19] Although it was not accurate (it showed a break in the continent at about 75° north latitude, for example), it suggested to the British Admiralty that there Cook might find the much sought Northwest Passage through the North American continent.

When Cook approached the entrance to the long inlet that would eventually be named for him, at about 60° north latitude, there was considerable excitement aboard his ships, for this might be the fabled passage. Soon, however, Cook and his senior officers realized that Cook Inlet (named by George Vancouver in 1794) was not the passage but a mountain-bound estuary. Nonetheless, here the English captain made his first ceremonial act of possession, at Point Possession, the Kenai Peninsula's farthest north point (within sight of present-day Anchorage, Alaska). While there the crew also obtained more sea otter pelts. The Natives of the point selected the land for ownership under the Alaska Native Claims Settlement Act of 1971 but in 2002 sold it to the federal government for $3.3 million. Today Point Possession is part of the Kenai National Wildlife Refuge.[20]

Upon leaving Cook Inlet, the ships continued along the coast past Kodiak to the Aleutians and then northward, traversing the Bering Strait. In a later visit to the Keniatze Indians at the newly named Point Possession, one of Cook's lieutenants secreted in a rocky hillock a brandy bottle in which had been placed a parchment proclaiming English possession. It has never been found, doubtless recovered by the Natives once their English visitors were out of sight.

It is significant that Cook waited until he was in the high latitudes to make a formal act of possession. He knew that the Spanish had planned another expedition to the northern coast at about the same time he antici-pated being there, and although the maritime powers had acknowledged the inoffensive nature of his enterprise, Cook did not want to risk an encounter with the Spanish, then emerging as an ally of the American col-onists in the developing war. The inlet where he did finally take possession of the coast was farther north than he imagined the Spanish would probe. Acts of possession on this remote coast were tangible manifestations of del-icate diplomatic maneuvering designed to signal intentions. Published accounts of them warned other nations of the risk they might be taking in treading on territory already claimed by another. Whether they were hon-ored or not depended on the political circumstances of the moment and on a realistic assessment of national strength—one's own and one's foes.

On the return from the Bering Strait the vessels stopped at Unalaska (Samganoodha or English Bay), where Cook had meetings for two days with Gerasim Grigorevich Izmailov, a promyshlenniki navigator com-manding the *St. Paul*, sent out by the merchants A. Orekhov, I. Lapin, and V. Shilov. Although Izmailov shared no language in common with any of Cook's company, he shared considerable information with the English, and they with him. Cook told Izmailov of Nootka Sound, and Izmailov assured Cook that the Russians had no outposts east of Unalaska. Cook entrusted to the Russian a letter to the British Admiralty and a chart of the North-west Coast; Izmailov in turn gave Cook his own letters for Major Behm, governor of Kamchatka at Bol'sheretsk (on the west coast) and another for the commanding officer at Petropavlovsk.

From Unalaska, Cook went to Hawai'i to winter. In an altercation with Natives at Kealakekua Bay on the island of Hawai'i, Cook was killed, one of the grand tragedies of the era of maritime exploration. Recent scholars have questioned Cook's treatment of Natives.[21] His instructions from the British Admiralty were to treat the Natives with civility and courtesy, but also with firmness. He was to take possession of lands undiscovered by Europeans only with the permission of the inhabitants. Generally, Cook honored these instructions and dealt with Native leaders on equal terms. But he interpreted firmness to mean he should not allow humiliation or abuse. On the island of Hawai'i, Cook took captive a chieftain, Kalani'opu'u, as hostage against the return of a long gun that had been stolen. It was a fatal error that led to Cook's death, as the Natives refused Cook's terms.

Captain Charles Clerke took the expedition vessels north to the Bering Strait again, and charted the eastern coast of Kamchatka, dying himself of tuberculosis before the ships reached Petropavlovsk. John Gore and James King continued the voyage. The vessels stopped at Canton, China, on the homeward voyage, where the peltry, most particularly those sea otter skins that were in good condition, sold for substantial profit, $120 each, perhaps an eighteen hundred percent return, considering the trifles that had been traded for them. This caused a near mutiny among the crew, who wanted to return to Nootka for more before the vessels made their way back to England. More scientific heads prevailed, however, and the expedition made its way home via Good Hope.

With publication of the journals of Cook's third voyage in 1784, the world finally learned the geography of Northwest North America and its relation to Siberia and Kamchatka. The fiction of Gamaland was revealed: there was no such place. The "great land to the east" that Chukchi Natives had told of was indeed very near Cape Dezhnev, a mere fifty-six miles. Mikhail Gvozdev had likely visited there in 1732, without quite knowing it. The land that Spanish galleon navigators had seen in the north was the Aleutian Island chain; discovery of the furs there had led the Russians across the Pacific along the chain successively to the Near Islands, the Rat Islands, the Andreanov Islands, the Fox Islands, and ultimately to Alaska itself (the Alaska Peninsula) and Umnak and Kodiak Islands. Bering's and Chirikov's landfalls were along a mainland coast, the shape and relation of which to Gvozdev's landfall had been unknown until the Cook expedition. This was the principal significance of Cook's voyage for the history of Russian America, the solution to the geographic puzzle that Peter the Great and the navigator Vitus Bering had sought earlier in the century. Although overland explorers would continue to hunt for diminutive versions of it (including Meriwether Lewis and William Clark in 1803 through 1806), Cook effectively disproved the notion of a Northwest Passage. Not until 1903 and 1904 would Roald Amundsen make a successful passage along the north coast of North America, a feat repeated in 1970 by the oil tanker S.S. *Manhattan*, both voyages demonstrating the impracticality of the route for any economic advantage.

The great profit gained from the Northwest sea otter pelts that Cook's crew sold in Macao excited the commercial world. The British Admiralty had attempted to keep information about the voyage secret until the conclusion of the American Revolutionary War; official publication of Cook's journals came the year after the American peace treaty was signed. But pirate publishers got out two accounts in 1781 (one anonymous, another by

John Rickman) and another in 1782 (by William Ellis). Private investors immediately moved to take advantage of potential profits in the furs the expedition had found on the Northwest Coast. The maritime fur trade on the southern part of that coast began in 1785 with the arrival of British merchantman James Hanna, who captained the *Harmon*. The next year Hanna returned in the *Sea Otter*. He was taking a considerable chance, for by then the English government had chartered two firms, the British East India Company and the South Sea Company, with exclusive British trading rights on the American West Coast. Ships trading there needed licenses from both companies, a stipulation that the companies were able to implement after the first years of the trade.

Also in 1786, Captain James Strange headed a trading expedition with two vessels, the *Captain Cook* and the *Experiment*, to the coast. The next year four British vessels visited the coast. One, the *Imperial Eagle*, captained by Charles William Barkley, brought the first white woman to visit the Pacific Northwest, Barkley's seventeen-year-old new bride. She would sail with her husband for ten years, visiting the ports of the seven seas, before the two settled on land. But the exclusive grants inhibited other British traders. Then they were challenged by American trading ships coming from Boston, Salem, Martha's Vineyard, Nantucket, Portsmouth, and other New England ports. In the 1790s the Americans would completely dominate the trade as the British found themselves embroiled in the wars of the French Revolution.

France reacted to the publication of Cook's journals and the end of the American Revolutionary War by outfitting its own scientific and reconnoitering expedition to the Northwest Coast. Headed by Jean Francois Galaup, Comte de la Perouse, and planned partly by Louis XVI, the French intended to circumnavigate the globe. Soon after leaving France in 1785, the expedition's two vessels called at Talcahuano, the port for the Spanish town of Concepción in Chile. There Perouse's scientists told Spanish officials all they knew of Russian activity in the north, indicating that the Russians already had posts in four places: Unalaska, the Trinity Islands west of Kodiak, Prince William Sound, and Nootka Sound on Vancouver Island. The information regarding Nootka was false, but the rest was true, and in any case there was every reason for the Spanish to expect that the Russians would press as far south as they could.

At the Spanish court word was that the Russians hoped to expand southward to all the land north of where the Spanish were, that is, San

Francisco. For their part the Russians did nothing to dissuade such thinking; quite the contrary, they encouraged it, for expansion continued to be Russian policy, so long as it could be done without international conflict. At Talcahuano the French also indicated that they expected the British would challenge the Russians in that effort. Because clashes at sea could easily embroil their countries in war, commanders of maritime expeditions took care not to incite hostilities among themselves. But the Northwest Coast was quickly becoming a sensitive and potentially volatile area of conflict for European sovereignty. Following Perouse's visit, for example, the Spanish intendente at Concepción wrote to José de Gálvez recommending that the Spanish establish a post in Cook Inlet (Alaska) to impede the Russian advance.

From Chile, Perouse sailed on to the Northwest Coast. His orders were to take possession of some spot north of Bucareli Bay, which was conceded to the Spanish by virtue of Arteaga's act of possession there in 1779. Landing at Lituya Bay, the only bay along the coast apparently not yet visited by any Europeans, Perouse performed his own act of possession. He then sailed back south to Monterey, where the Spanish now had a substantial supply base. Perouse's expedition was accompanied by great tragedy. At Lituya Bay, which he named Port des Francais, he lost twenty-one officers and men in breakers at the bay's entrance when a tidal bore swept into the narrow opening while they were taking soundings. Then, after leaving Monterey, the expedition voyaged to Asia and visited a number of ports, including Botany Bay, Australia. After leaving there, however, they were never heard from again. Not until 1827 did a British sea captain learn that the French ships wrecked near Vanikoro in the Solomon Islands, where apparently about thirty men were massacred by Natives. Others who escaped to distant islands also apparently were killed and eaten by Natives.

Publication of Cook's journals also generated great consternation in Russia, an alarm exacerbated by news of France's planned Perouse enterprise. In 1785, Tsarina Catherine made plans for a new Russian expedition to the Eastern Islands and North America, partly to anticipate Perouse's arrival. Although supposedly secret, details of the mission quickly spread to Madrid, London, and Paris. The new venture was entrusted to Captain Joseph Billings, an Englishman who had sailed with Cook from 1776 through 1779 but now served in Catherine's navy. Billings was to investigate the promyshlenniki's activities and to chart islands and territories tributary to Russia, particularly areas frequented by European fur traders. If

Idealized view of Shelikhov's establishment at Three Saints Bay, 1790. Engraving by Luka Voronin in G. Sarychev, *Atlas* (St. Petersburg, 1802). University of Alaska Fairbanks, Elmer E. Rasmuson Library 0015.057.

possible, he was to sail as far south as the north end of Vancouver Island, 51° north latitude, but no farther. The Russians knew that both the Spanish and the English had visited Nootka, and Catherine had no intention of being caught between the two. This was quite wise judgment.

The initial Russian plan called for Billings to sail along the Siberian Arctic Coast from Archangel to the Bering Strait. The expedition found this route impractical, however, and Billings made his way to the Sea of Okhotsk by the normal route overland, that is, to Irkutsk, down the Lena to Iakutsk, and then across the mountains to the coast. At Iakutsk he met John Ledyard, the American adventurer who had sailed with Cook. The voyage to find the Northwest Passage had fired Ledyard with the idea of finding a water route across North America that would facilitate American trade with the Orient. He had entered Russia from Europe and had crossed Siberia heading for Kamchatka, hoping there to secure passage across the Pacific to the Northwest Coast, where he would undertake a land crossing of North America. At Iakutsk, Russian officials suspicious of Ledyard's motives arrested him. He was transported quickly back westward to St. Petersburg and expelled from Russia at the Polish border.

The Billings expedition was a grand undertaking, known as the Northeastern Secret Geographical and Astronomical Expedition. Assistants included Lieutenant G. A. Sarychev, Lieutenant Christian Bering, grandson of the great explorer Vitus Bering, and Martin Sauer. But the results were less than expected. In 1790, Billings sailed from Kamchatka in the *Slava Rossii* (Glory of Russia), passing through the Aleutians to Unalaska. The ship then went on to Kodiak Island, where Billings visited Gregorii Shelikhov's newly founded settlement. Billings then went on to Prince William Sound and south along the coast. After sighting Kayak Island (Bering's 1741 landfall) and Mount St. Elias, however, he turned back because of scurvy among the crew. The ship wintered in Petropavlovsk. The next season Billings went again to Unalaska and then sailed north, sighting King Island, landing at Cape Rodney and the Diomede Islands, and landing again at St. Lawrence Bay on the Chukotka Peninsula. From there, Billings and a party crossed the peninsula by foot and trekked along the Arctic Coast to the mouth of the Kolyma River. Meanwhile, Sarychev took the *Slava Rossii* back to Unalaska, where he passed another winter, sailing to Petropavlovsk in the spring.

Catherine had planned a second expedition in conjunction with Billings's. Grigorii Ivanovich Mulovskii was to have headed Russia's first round-the-world voyage, commanding four ships that would go to Hawai'i, where they would divide, two exploring the Kuril Islands south from Petropavlovsk and opening talks with the Japanese, while the other two explored the North American coast north from Nootka Sound to the point in the Alexander Archipelago visited by Chirikov in 1741. The principal aim of the expedition's North American section was to confirm Russian interest in and occupation of the Northwest Coast. It was this information that led Perouse to tell the intendente at Concepción, Chile, that the Russians already had people at Nootka. The four ships were ready to depart in 1787 when Russia went to war with Turkey, a war that Sweden soon entered. Mulovskii's ships were immediately committed to the European war and did not make their North American voyage. The history of the coast might have developed considerably differently if they had.

The Cook and Perouse expeditions greatly excited Spain, leading to further expeditions into the north. In 1790 the Billings expedition nearly crossed paths with one of these. In 1789, Alejandro Malaspina di Mulazzo undertook an important scientific circumnavigation, meticulously planned in the highest circles of Spanish society and government. Stopping at San Blas, two ships sailed north as far as Prince William Sound and Cook Inlet, searching still for a northwest passage (which they hoped Cook had missed). The expedition sighted and named the great Malaspina ice field and explored in Yakutat Bay before turning southward to visit Nootka, Monterey, and again San Blas before crossing the Pacific. In 1790 yet another expedition, headed by Salvador Fidalgo, went to Prince William Sound, where they took possession of a bay they called Cordova and visited an arm of the sound they called Valdez. The ship, again the *San Carlos*, entered Cook Inlet where the explorers found a Russian post with Catherine's coat of arms over the gate, two blockhouses, and a palisade with a catwalk where sentries kept watch. This was Pavlovskaia, the Pavel Lebedev-Lastochkin Company post at the mouth of the Kenai River. The crew of the *San Carlos* already had spotted a small Russian fishing station at the mouth of the Kasilof River in the Inlet. Fidalgo did not stop at either location but sailed back out of the inlet. First, however, he landed at a point somewhat south of the Kasilof River for a secret ceremonial act of possession.

Remarkably, the Billings expedition was nearby when Fidalgo exited the inlet. Billings sent Fidalgo a letter by way of a longboat, inviting the Spanish captain to a rendezvous in Prince William Sound. However, Fidalgo thought better of the opportunity. It was obvious that he was in territory that the Russians frequented and regarded as their own. Billings had two ships to Fidalgo's one, and his vessels were outfitted as warships. More important, however, a clash so deep in an area impossible to defend could not end positively for the Spanish. While Billings waited for two weeks at Prince William Sound, Fidalgo sailed on to Kodiak, where he noted the position of Shelikhov's post and then returned to Monterey and San Blas. Fidalgo's caution foretold Spain's position in the competition for sovereignty of the coast.

4

Grigorii Shelikhov and the Russian American Company

T HE EXPEDITION OF Joseph Billings and the aborted expedition of Grigorii Ivanovich Mulovskii were of grave concern to the Spanish, because they represented a strong threat to Spain's intention to take control of the entire Northwest Coast. Spain would shortly attempt to dislodge its competitors. But the Spanish were equally dismayed by the expansionist activity of Grigorii Shelikhov, for this unusually capable merchant had succeeded where others had failed and had accomplished what others had only talked about: he established the first permanent Russian post in North America. This chapter first details Shelikhov's enterprises and then follows Spain's reactions to Russia, England, and America, which culminated in confrontation in Nootka Sound in 1789.

Shelikhov was born in Ryl'sk in European Russia. In 1772 at about age twenty-five he went to Irkutsk as an agent of Ivan Golokov, another Ryl'sk merchant who had settled there. Shelikhov went to Okhotsk in 1774 and over the next eight years was involved in ten companies engaged in the fur trade. Realizing that the competition among investors was wasteful, inefficient, and increasingly costly as promyshlenniki (fur trapper) voyages took more and more time to go farther and farther east, Shelikhov advocated the creation of a monopoly for the trade. His idea would develop in time, but for the moment after 1780 he formed a company with Golokov and Golokov's nephew, Mikhail, to hunt furs in North America and in the Kuril Islands. Unlike the other promyshlenniki ventures, which were ad hoc investments (i.e., intended only for the life of a particular voyage and its cargo), Shelikhov's new company was chartered by the government for ten years.

His vision far surpassed simply sailing to the islands and bringing back to market a collection of raw furs. He planned a continuing, coordinated capitalist development involving, among other things, establishing settlements as well as collecting furs. This was a new departure in Russia's approach to North America and represented Tsarina Catherine's growing appreciation of the significance of what the promyshlenniki had accomplished. They had done what the Krenitsyn expedition of 1768 had not: gathered an impressive store of information about the geography and the Natives of the region and demonstrated to foreign powers Russia's ability, and by implication its intention, to occupy at least a portion of the Northwest Coast. Yet these achievements had not resulted from government direction or even clear design; rather, they were the result of private investors and adventurers seizing the opportunity for profit represented by resources—sea otter peltry.

Acting on his new charter, in 1781 and 1782, Shelikhov invested in several different voyages with a number of different partners. One of these was Pavel Sergeevich Lebedev-Lastochkin, who later would become one of Shelikhov's chief rivals. Another was Gavriil Pribylov, who discovered the islands now named for him (the Pribilof Islands). Still others went to Cook Inlet (Kenai Bay) and Prince William Sound (Chugach Bay), the first penetration by the Russians beyond the Alaska Peninsula. Then, in 1783, Shelikhov undertook his grand enterprise. Having hired workers and purchased the necessary supplies and equipment, he left from near Okhotsk with three ships on a voyage of fur-gathering and settlement planting. The expedition, which carried 192 officers and crew, also included Shelikhov's wife, Natal'ia. They proceeded to the Kuril Islands, where one vessel was lost in a storm, and then to Bering Island for the winter. The next year they went to Unalaska and then to Kodiak Island, where Shelikhov established a post at Three Saints Bay on the southwestern coast. This was the first permanent Russian post in North America. It was also the beginning of a new phase of Russian trade and trapping in America, for Shelikhov organized his new American venture as a permanent enterprise. He organized his venture as the North East Company, and he would conduct his American affairs under that title for the next fifteen years.

Lebedev-Lastochkin also had attempted to establish a permanent post in America and thus became Shelikhov's principal rival. From 1784 until 1797 the two would compete in exploiting the fur resources of Cook Inlet, called Kenai Bay by the Russians, and Chugach Bay, the Russians' Prince William Sound. Shelikhov's hunters had reached Kachemak Bay in Cook Inlet by 1786. The next year a Lebedev-Lastochkin party headed by Stepan Zaikov established a post at the mouth of the Kenai River; they called it Pavlovskaia.[1] Shelikhov eventually would best Lebedev-Lastochkin in the Cook Inlet rivalry and later in Prince William Sound. But for a decade Levedev-Lastochkin's men thoroughly exploited the furs in Cook Inlet.

In the meantime, in a report he submitted when he returned to Siberia, Shelikhov told of fierce resistance to his efforts to subdue the Natives, forcing them to pay tribute and to trade with the Russians. At one point, he said, he had fought off four thousand Koniag warriors on Sahklidak Island. The actual number was probably not more than four hundred. These and other exaggerations, as well as his heavy-handed treatment of islanders, combined to diminish Shelikhov's stature among analysts and some historians, but his achievement was nonetheless extraordinary. Staying two winters on the island, he dispatched hunting parties along the Alaska Peninsula's south shore and made preparation for sending them routinely into Kenai Bay and Chugach Bay.

This first permanent settlement, and the ensuing rivalry with Lebedev-Lastochkin, both advanced Russian occupation of America and confirmed for the other European powers Russian intentions to possess the coast north of Nootka. It also extended greatly the range of Russian fur trappers in North America. Yet both Shelikhov's and Lebedev-Lastochkin's were private ventures, albeit monitored and sanctioned by the government. In 1786, Shelikhov returned to Okhotsk for additional supplies and reinforcements. Leaving the Yenesy merchant and promyshlenniki Konstantin Samoilov in charge, Shelikhov allowed that upon his return he wanted to send hunting parties southward along the coast toward California to latitude 40 (the Oregon-California border is at 42° north latitude), that is, just north of where the Spanish were at San Francisco.

In Irkutsk, Shelikhov made his report and described his plans for expansion. He hoped a monopoly company could develop trade with Japan, Korea, China, the Philippines, and India and at the same time with the English, the Spanish, and the American Indians along the North American coast. He wanted a government ship, a hundred soldiers, and a loan of five hundred thousand rubles for twenty years. Shelikhov also requested priests and talked of founding schools for the Native people. These requests were not outlandish for the project of developing the trading potential of eastern Siberia and North America. They were endorsed by Ivan Iakobi, the governor-general of Siberia. Tsarina Catherine was committed to the principle of free trade, however, and in any case not ready to support such an ambitious design. Because of the impending war with Turkey and Sweden, she could afford neither money nor soldiers. Among other things, she awaited reports from the Billings expedition, then preparing for its survey of the Northwest Coast islands. Thus, although Catherine did not feel the same urgency about America's Northwest Coast as did the Spanish, she nonetheless was not blind to the need for a stronger and more official Russian presence than that represented by the promyshlenniki, as her commitment to the Billings expedition demonstrated.

In the end, Catherine rejected nearly all of Shelikhov's requests, and with them the notion of a major Russian engagement in North America. She agreed to send Orthodox priests but otherwise left the merchants essentially on their own, with token government oversight. This was the beginning of what would develop into Russia's approach to North America throughout its presence there: minimum investment in the enterprise, never a commitment to establishing a true colony on the English, Dutch, or Spanish model. Catherine's decision prefigures the resolution of the tsar and his advisors a century later to sell their North American enterprise to the United States, though no one at the time, in the 1760s, saw that far ahead.

Needing to replace Samoilov, who wished to return to Siberia, Shelikhov hired Evstratii Delarov, who went to Three Saints Bay in 1787. An able manager, Delarov sent hunting parties into Kenai Bay and had crests of Russian possession nailed to trees there and along the Alaska Peninsula. His hunting parties founded a post, Aleksandrovskaia, at modern-day Seldovia on the south shore of Kachemak Bay. Lebedev-Lastochkin had already established additional posts farther up Kenai Bay (Cook Inlet), however, and for a number of years monopolized the fur trade there. Partly for this reason, and partly to pursue his broader vision of Russia's opportunity in America, Shelikhov ordered Delarov in 1788 to send Dmitrii Bocharov and Gerasim Izmailov, who had parlayed with Cook at Unalaska in 1778, to reconnoiter the coast south to 45° north latitude, the Oregon of today. The two captains explored along the shore from Chugach Bay to Yakutat Bay and Lituya Bay (the Frenchman Comte de la Perouse's Port de Francais). The next year Izmailov explored all of the coast of the Kenai Peninsula.

During this time the Spanish continued their reconnaissance of the Northwest Coast, although they had not yet formulated clear plans for how to meet the growing challenges to their claims of exclusivity on the continent. In 1788, Gonzalo López de Haro in the *San Carlos* and Estaban Martinez in *La Princesa* sailed north from San Blas to Prince William Sound to look for evidence of Russian activity. There, in a cove on Montague Island, they found a dwelling of wood and reed, probably from one of Shelikhov's ships from 1783 and 1784; it is not clear that de Haro and Martinez recognized it as Russian. De Haro continued westward, and off the south shore of the Kenai Peninsula he encountered Natives who had small scraps of paper carrying Russian writing. He bartered for five of these and was given also a letter in English (which no one on the ship could read). Continuing further, de Haro came upon Shelikhov's settlement at Three Saints Bay on Kodiak Island. Delarov came out in a launch to meet the ship, and he and de Haro conversed at length. Delarov told de Haro there were seven Russian posts on the coast between Unalaska and Prince William Sound and that there was a Russian sloop in the sound with forty promyshlenniki who traded along the coast each year as far south as Nootka. This latter piece was surely a fabrication intended to intimidate the Spanish, and it probably had the desired effect.

In the meantime Martinez also sailed westward, eventually to Unalaska at today's Dutch Harbor, where he found Potap Zaikov, a Shelikhov veteran. Zaikov told Martinez that although the Russians had not yet gotten farther south than Cape St. Elias, two frigates were on their way from Kamchatka; with one other vessel they would head for Nootka to establish a post to block English trading. Zaikov was referring, of course, to the Billings expedition, although he exaggerated its mission. Russia was taking this action, Zaikov said, because of English captain James Hanna's 1785 trading voyage that had taken Nootka furs to Canton at a high profit.

The Spanish knew the Russians were exaggerating their strength on the coast, for Delarov had told de Haro that there were 120 Russians at Unalaska when in fact they discovered that Zaikov was the only one, working with a large party of Aleuts. Nonetheless, it was obvious from the information gathered at the Kenai Peninsula and at Three Saints Bay that the Russians were well established. When out of sight of Zaikov, the Spaniards performed an abbreviated act of possession before departing for Monterey and San

Blas. In Mexico and Madrid, Spanish officials were undecided about how to deal with the Russian and English threats to their assertions of sovereignty over the Northwest Coast. They were particularly concerned about Nootka Sound, for it was obvious that the English favored the long estuary not only as a trading site but as an ideal location for wintering on the coast and refitting their vessels as well. The English trader John Meares would later claim to have erected a fort at Nootka, though he undoubtedly exaggerated the scope of his post and his activity there. In fact, the Spanish did not know the full extent of foreign interloping.

In addition to the English, American traders also had reached the coast (the first American voyage was in 1788), and they favored Nootka as well. Robert Gray in the *Lady Washington* and John Kendrick in the *Columbia Rediviva*, both private trading vessels, had wintered in the sound and intended to spend the 1789 season collecting furs there and farther north. Soon the Englishmen William Douglas and Robert Funter in the *Ifigenia* and the *Northwest America* would arrive at Nootka as well. They had been sent from Macao by John Meares. James Colnett and Thomas Hudson were also on their way in the *Argonaut* and the *Princess Royal*, also sent by Meares. The *Eleanora* and the *Fair American*, American vessels captained respectively by Simon Metcalfe and his eighteen-year-old son, Thomas, were also en route.

The scene shortly became the setting for a major international incident and a clash of singular significance for the contest for European sovereignty on the Northwest Coast, for in Mexico a new viceroy, Manuel Antonio Flores, greatly alarmed at all the evidence accumulating of unbridled competition, decided to act. In 1789 he dispatched a new expedition north, specifically to Nootka, to make a show of Spanish force and intention. Though ostensibly the law of sovereignty rested on claims and acts of possession, in fact, occupation increasingly was coming to be recognized as the practical, necessary confirmation of possession. The Spanish themselves had implicitly acknowledged this in not attempting to dislodge the Russians from the coast in the north, in Prince William Sound, Cook Inlet, Kodiak, and Unalaska. However, Bucareli Bay in the Alexander Archipelago and particularly Nootka Sound on Vancouver Island were close enough to San Francisco that they represented more than a contest for sovereignty; they constituted threats to actual Spanish occupation, stations from which Spain's competitors might easily launch forays of aggression and conquest of their own. Viceroy Flores determined that Spain had to take a stand.

Again Estaban Martinez and Gonzalo López de Haro in *La Princesa* and the *San Carlos* were chosen for the mission. Martinez was to "take such measures" as he could and as seemed "convenient" to him. He had separate instructions for dealing with the Russians, the English, and the Americans. Spain had been America's ally in the recent war against England, and the Americans thought they had little to fear. Gray and Kendrick, and later Metcalfe, treated the Spanish with respect and deference, though not with subservience. The English traders, however, very much objected to Spanish blandishments of exclusivity. Already Meares had made substantial profits from Northwest peltry, and he anticipated considerably more. Moreover, the English had a long history of enmity with Spain dating from before the Spanish Armada of 1588. Meares had obtained papers in Macao identifying his vessels as Portuguese, a ruse intended to guarantee their security. But even though Douglas on the *Ifigenia* carried a Portuguese "captain," it was obvious that Douglas was the real captain; the crew were all English, and the instructions written in English were substantially more detailed than the brief cover written in Portuguese. Even at that, though, the Portuguese orders directed Douglas to resist any Spanish ship inferior to his own with all the force at his disposal.

Martinez was probably the wrong man for Spain to have at the center of the contest for sovereignty on the coast. The activities of the several nations had pushed the Europeans inexorably closer and closer to confrontation, and superior ability and careful judgment would be required if war were to be avoided. But Martinez was impetuous and a tippler. He was quick to take offense at slights to his competence or to his country. His performance on the 1788 voyage to Unalaska had raised questions about his character, but he was the only man available when Flores decided he must respond quickly to the Russian and English encroachments in the North. Martinez arrived at Nootka a few weeks after leaving San Blas. His primary concern was the Russian (Mulovskii) expedition of three or four ships, supposed to sail via Cape Horn for Nootka and which Martinez expected to arrive at any time, not knowing Catherine had decided to keep them in Russia. Martinez was surprised to find instead that Nootka Sound was overflowing with English and American traders. He acted quickly and somewhat impulsively. Soon after arriving, he arrested Douglas and impounded the *Ifigenia*, its crew, and cargo. Later he allowed the ship to proceed to Macao, where its worth, vessel and cargo, would be determined and appropriate payment made to Spanish agents. Once clear of the sound, Douglas violated this agreement, thereby putting his ship and crew at considerable risk.

Next, Martinez approached the Americans. Although he questioned them closely and concluded that they intended to trade for furs along the coast, he did not attempt to detain them, although he warned them that the coast was under Spanish protection. Soon the English captains arrived, one after the other. When the small *Northwest America* arrived, Martinez quickly arrested Funter and his crew and confiscated the ship. Needing a vessel for exploring the island's coast, he rechristened the ship *Santa Gertrudis la Magna*. Not long after, the unsuspecting Hudson brought in the *Princess Royal*. He too was arrested and sent to Macao under the same bond as Douglas. Just as Hudson cleared Nootka Sound, Colnett appeared in the *Argonaut*, also to be ensnared in Martinez's lair. Not realizing the situation, Colnett allowed his ship to be towed, and the Spaniards put the vessel right in line with guns from a fort they had built on an island in the sound.

But in Colnett, Martinez had his match for impetuosity and quick offense. Invited to Martinez's cabin to explain himself, Colnett ranted and stormed and at one point pulled his sword. Martinez had him arrested and confined, and his stores confiscated. Cowed, Colnett first became angry, then despondent; he attempted to drown himself by jumping out a porthole. Martinez determined to take him to San Blas. Then, just as Martinez had settled himself regarding Colnett, Hudson reappeared in the *Princess Royal*. Disregarding his bond to proceed to Macao, he had instead traded along the coast and had returned to Nootka expecting Martinez would already be gone. Hudson had not intended to enter the sound, but his ship was becalmed on an incoming tide. He was taken captive in a Spanish longboat, and his ship towed in. Shortly afterward, Martinez sent Colnett's *Argonaut* to San Blas, manned by a Spanish crew, carrying Colnett and a group of English sailors as prisoners. The American boats the *Fair American*, the *Columbia*, and the *Lady Washington*, witnesses to the entire series of events, sailed from the sound soon afterward, ostensibly for Hawai'i and Macao but in reality to resume trading along the coast.

But Martinez had badly miscalculated. Soon to emerge as master of the seven seas, England was not disposed to accept Spain's rigid and likely empty assertion of sovereignty so far from its American centers of power in Mexico and Peru. Garbled, highly prejudicial accounts of the high drama at Nootka soon reached London and the British press. Parliament debated the matter amid repeated calls to punish Spain for its insults to British honor. The coast was now too populated with Europeans and Americans for the doctrine of sovereignty by acts of possession to prevail any longer. Now occupation and the capacity to defend it would replace the older regime of burying possession plaques and parchments and publicly warning other countries away. The Spanish would have to recognize this changed circumstance, and many voices in Parliament called for the point to be made by sword and cannon. Britain was on the verge of formally declaring hostilities when the Spanish backed away, recognizing how ill prepared they were for a new war and how vulnerable they would be on the Northwest Coast.

Diplomats of the two countries signed an agreement, the Nootka Convention of 1790, in which they agreed to send negotiators to Nootka to decide upon conditions for future interaction and activity on the coast. Although some general principles were articulated, the details were left to the negotiators, and there was considerable confusion about what was intended. The British understood that they should have unmolested access to the coast anywhere north of San Francisco. The Spanish, however, understood that they were to cede to the English Nootka property that Meares claimed to have acquired and also cede any place where the English had landed and performed acts of possession.

The negotiators, Juan Francisco de la Bodega y Quadra for Spain and George Vancouver for England, met at Nootka in 1792. Even though at the time the Spanish had seven vessels on the coast, the two captains found themselves drawn to each other and put aside their countries' ambitions for a season of exploration and conversation. What emerged from their encounter was the doctrine that in future the coast would be open to whoever could occupy it. As it happened, that might be a lot of people, for quite by coincidence nearly all of the Spanish, English, and American voyagers who had ever been to Nootka visited there in 1792, either as part of official expeditions of their governments or as traders seeking more furs from the Indians along the coast. Martinez and Kendrick did not visit, Hudson had been lost at sea, and the Metcalfes (Simon and his son Thomas) were dead. But everyone else paid a visit, although not necessarily because the negotiators were there, and most provided official or informal testimony for history about circumstances on the coast.

The conclusion of the Nootka incident was highly significant. Although the Spanish would continue to send expeditions north for several years, their inability to enforce their ancient and keenly felt claim to the northwest quadrant of North America would become plain and unmistakable. English and American fur merchants had traded with the Indians with impunity and would continue to do so as long as the market for their American furs sustained. In terms of European claims of sovereignty, the coast was now open to whichever country could possess it. And possess they must, for the lesson of Nootka established the methodology of claims for the Northwest Coast afterward: brass plaques nailed to trees and buried bottles would no longer suffice. But Nootka did not generate a land rush to the Northwest Coast. Its fate would be decided largely in Europe, not America, as France and England and their allies began to mobilize for the final chapter in their contest for supremacy of the seven seas, and with it, control of world commerce.

Meanwhile, at the Strait of Juan de Fuca, Quadra and Vancouver set about exploring. Together they discovered that the land on which Nootka was situated was in fact a very large island, and the official name they gave it was Quadra and Vancouver's Island. The Spanish had missed, but Vancouver did not, the remarkable inland maze of islands and waterways that the Englishman named Puget Sound, after one of his lieutenants. An island there was named Whidbey after another lieutenant. Remarkably, in the same season the American Robert Gray discovered the mouth of a great river the Europeans had learned of from the Indians, but that no one had yet located. In 1775, Quadra and Bruno de Hezeta had sighted the large bay at the mouth of the river, but the outflowing current had been so strong that they could not make headway against it from seaward, and they had been forced to sail on. Cook and the various Spanish expeditions and several of the American traders had searched for the river since that time, but fog, weather, and the combination of currents had defeated them all. But in May 1792, Gray not only found the bay twice but crossed the treacherous entry bar and ascended the river twenty-five miles, naming it for his ship *Columbia*. This gave the Americans a strong claim to some part of the coast. Gray claimed for the United States all the land drained by the river and its tributaries; that would eventually give America a strong claim to all the land west of the Continental Divide between Puget Sound and California.

In the meantime Vancouver carried out an extensive survey of the coast of North America, from the Juan de Fuca Strait to Cook Inlet in Alaska. While in 1792 and 1793 the work ran from south to north, in the 1794 season Vancouver began surveying southward from Cook Inlet. The ship anchored off the mouth of Eagle River, northeast of where the city of

Anchorage is today, and Knik Arm was the beginning point of the season's investigations. Peter Puget and Joseph Whidbey did many of the actual descriptions, working from longboats.

Following Vancouver's extensive work, the English probably would have established themselves in the Alexander Archipelago, for the Russians had yet to occupy any site south of Yakutat Bay. Vancouver would visit the Russian posts in Cook Inlet, and the English were willing to concede Russian presence in the Far North. But Britain quickly became deeply embroiled in the war with France that developed out of the French Revolution of 1789, which became a contest for world dominance and would last until 1815, when Napoleon would be defeated once and for all and Britain's supremacy on the world's seas would be unchallenged and complete. But by then, the Russians had occupied the southern islands and had their sights set on the regions still farther south, to at least the Queen Charlottes and, if possible, all the way to San Francisco.

The Russians were not unaware of developments at Nootka, and had the Mulovskii expedition sailed, the Russians most likely would have become fully enmeshed in the controversy there. Moreover, had Billings gotten farther south than Yakutat on his 1790 voyage, the Russians might have been drawn into the fray from that quarter as well. But Russia's official attention at the time was distracted by the war with Turkey and Sweden, and its resources in the Pacific were stretched to their limit.[2]

In the meantime Shelikhov, who had traveled to St. Petersburg to present his vision of North Pacific development to the court, returned to Irkutsk. While wintering there in 1789 through 1790, he persuaded a merchant from Kargopol, Aleksandr Andreevich Baranov, a veteran of the Siberian fur trade, to go to America as manager of Shelikhov's activities. Baranov had been in Siberia since 1780. He had a glass factory and a distillery in Irkutsk and with his brother had established a fortified post on the Anadyr River in 1788. However, he had recently suffered a number of reverses. Shelikhov had twice before asked Baranov to be his manager, and the renewal of the request was probably opportune for Baranov. Baranov sailed from Okhotsk in August 1790. He would remain in America twenty-eight years.

Shelikhov also renewed his requests to the crown and solicited support in St. Petersburg and in Siberia. The new governor-general of Siberia, Ivan Pil, was enthusiastic. Shelikhov apparently arranged for a commitment of Russian troops in Siberia to the American enterprise, although these were never dispatched. He sent an English shipwright in Russian service, James Shields, to Kodiak to work with Baranov. At the same time he sent an expedition to the Kuril Islands to establish a post on the island of Urup. In 1793 the government granted his request for laborers to be sent to America as colonists and in the same year approved his request for a group of missionaries. In 1794 fifty-two craftsmen and peasants and their families, with ten clergymen, were sent from Okhotsk to Kodiak.

Baranov's introduction to America was perhaps fitting, given the difficult conditions with which he would have to contend. On his voyage from Okhotsk in 1790 the ship wrecked leaving Unalaska, and he and the crew and passengers wintered on the island. During the winter he had three *baidaras* (large open skin boats used by the Aleut Natives) built, and in the spring he sent two to seek new hunting areas while he set out for Kodiak in the other. After a dangerous voyage Baranov reached Shelikhov's settlement in June. Baranov proved an exceptionally able manager for the Russian posts in America. He was well organized, tough, even ruthless at times, and determined. He also had a vision of what could be accomplished. One of his first tasks was to move the post from Three Saints Bay, which he considered a poor site because it was too indefensible. He chose instead St. Paul Harbor on Chiniak Bay, the current location of the town of Kodiak. From there he sent hunting parties to the Alaska Peninsula and to Kenai and Chugach Bays. In 1793 he established a post on Resurrection Bay where the town of Seward is today and had a three-masted vessel, the *Phoenix*, built there by the shipwright Shields. In 1794 he sent his chief lieutenant, Egor Putrov, with a party of Russians and a fleet of five hundred *baidarkas* (kayaks) along the coast to Yakutat, Lituya, and Icy Bays. The Russians had seen Vancouver that year surveying in Cook Inlet, and Putrov's group met Vancouver's companion vessel, the *Chatham*, near Yakutat. Vancouver wanted to meet with Baranov, but the Russian thought the better course was to remain incommunicado, probably not wishing to reveal nor have to refuse to reveal Shelikhov's plans. Baranov failed to keep three appointments made for him by Vancouver through letters carried by Russian hunting parties Vancouver met while surveying. Returning to Kodiak, Baranov arrived in time to welcome Archimandrite Ioasaf and the ten clerics arriving from Okhotsk. Not long after, another ship with 130 promyshlenniki laborers and thirty settlers and their families arrived. These groups had been sent by the government at Shelikhov's urging.

On their return from Yakutat, Putrov and his party had been harassed by hunters working for Lebedev-Lastochkin, who now had a temporary post at Nuchek in Chugach Bay. Shelikhov and Lebedev-Lastochkin still were co-investors in some voyages, but Shelikhov seemed to favor his alliance with the Golokovs, and his rivalry with Lebedev-Lastochkin grew. Over the next several years Baranov, on behalf of Shelikhov's company, fought a running battle of sorts with Lebedev-Lastochkin's company. One of the latter's foremen at the Kenai River post caused considerable trouble, maltreating the Natives and some Shelikhov hunting parties, prompting another of the Lebedev-Lastochkin foremen to join Baranov. Shelikhov was fortunate to have Baranov to do his fighting for him since Shelikhov was still a sometime investor with Lebedev-Lastochkin. Baranov effectively outmaneuvered his competition, partly because he was better supplied, having a well-stocked post at Kodiak Island. Lebedev-Lastochkin was overextended, and his relations with the Natives were apparently harsher than even Baranov's.

Because they lived on the mainland, the Natives of Cook Inlet, the Kenaitzy Tanaina (Athabaskan Dena'ina), were better able to escape Russian domination than were the Aleut. In typical promyshlenniki fashion, Lebedev-Lastochkin's manager, Piotr Kolomin, took Native hostages. He had brought with him a number of Kamchadals as well. But the Natives remained independent, nonetheless, and the Russians had to trade with them to obtain most of their furs. Bartering with the Indians depleted the Russians' supplies, and no new goods arrived from Okhotsk, Lebedev-Lastochkin's headquarters. Finally, in August 1791 a Lebedev-Lastochkin vessel arrived at Pavlovskaia with sixty-two Russians, but instead of solving Kolomin's difficulties, it multiplied them. The ship's captain, Grigorii Konovalov, refused to cooperate with Kolomin and eventually drove him from the post. According to historians Katerina Solovjova and Aleksandra Vovnyanko, Konovalov's men terrorized the local Natives, seized their food supplies, and destroyed their baidarkas.[3] Not surprisingly, during the winter the Kenaitzy retaliated throughout the region, killing ten Shelikhov men and four Lebedev-Lastochkin hunters. Kolomin and his men sought refuge at Shelikhov's post, Aleksandrovskaia, but Baranov had ordered his men not to cooperate. Angered, Kolomin besieged the post for a time.

Lebedev-Lastochkin's lieutenant, Stepan Zaikov, arrived in the midst of this imbroglio. He arrested Konovalov and sent him to Okhotsk in irons on a Shelikhov vessel. He then set about reestablishing positive relations with the Indians. He was apparently successful, for when George Vancouver visited the post on his 1794 reconnaissance of the inlet, Natives were living alongside the Russians inside the post, which contained two dozen structures. Some of the buildings were used as schools for teaching the Indians Russian language and Orthodox Christianity. One object of such schooling was to train the Natives better to serve as hunters and attendants to the Russians. Vancouver also observed Russians and Natives living together in apparent harmony at a Lebedev-Lastochkin post at the modern location of Tyonek and at other locations in Cook Inlet.

Relations did not stay amicable, however. In 1796 Indians killed all members of a party of Lebedev-Lastochkin hunters that had traveled from Pavlovskaia over the pass between the Matanuska and Copper River drainages. Two years later Indians attacked Lebedev-Lastochkin's posts at Iliamna Lake and on Kodiak Island. Shelikhov's posts fared better, probably because Baranov was ruthless in his dealings with the Natives and his policy was not confused by inconsistency. Baranov counseled "peace and tenderness" toward the Natives, but the first Orthodox missionary in the region, the Hieromonk Makarii, reported that Baranov's men treated Natives "in the most barbaric manner. . . . They take the wives and young daughters as their sexual partners. They kill any who refuse to hunt sea otters."[4]

When Lebedev-Lastochkin's men had exhausted the sea otters in Kenai Bay, they moved to Chugach Bay (Prince William Sound). There they had to compete more directly with Shelikhov's people and again were often set upon by Natives. By the time of Vancouver's visit, Natives in the sound had guns, with which they were better able to equalize their position. Baranov was able eventually to dislodge Lebedev-Lastochkin. After 1792, Lebedev-Lastochkin sent no new supplies. Baranov capitalized on the deprivation in which Lebedev-Lastochkin left his men, offering better wages and living conditions, and his greater success with the Natives. Then, in 1795, Shelikhov finally obtained some limited support from the government in the form of a limited monopoly that prohibited competitors from operating near his American posts. Thereafter Lebedev-Lastochkin's time in America was short.

In the meantime Shelikhov, at the height of his power and influence, continued to envision a broader, more expansive role for Russia in North America. But he would not see it come to fruition. In the midst of planning still another major expedition, again to the Kurils, he died in July 1795. The cause of his death is unknown, although there were rumors that his wife and her lover had poisoned him. In addition, his investments were failing, although with time they might well have recovered. His contribution to Russian occupation in North America had been remarkable, which is acknowledged in the accolade accorded him by some modern Russian historians: the Columbus of Russian America. Following Shelikhov's death, Lebedev-Lastochkin attempted to organize a group of the principal merchants against Shelikhov's widow, Natal'ia, to break up her husband's company. Nikolai Myl'nikov, a sometime Shelikhov partner, and Myl'nikov's sons and others participated in this effort. The collapse of Shelikhov's company would have been no surprise. But the rivals had not counted on the strength of Natal'ia Shelikhova. An able, intelligent woman of great will, she held most of the investors together, successfully fending off the conspirators' efforts to usurp Shelikhov's enterprise, his monument.

Shelikhova was greatly aided in her success by two important developments. First, Baranov continued his consolidation and aggressive tactics in the colony. Realizing that Lebedev-Lastochkin could not adequately supply his posts in Kenai Bay, Baranov completed his rescue of the rival company's hunters at posts there, bringing them comfortably within the Shelikhov orbit. The Lebedev-Lastochkin promyshlenniki greatly strengthened Baranov's operations, for they were already familiar with the country, and they were all experienced hunters. In addition, the shipbuilder Shields completed two smaller vessels at Spruce Island near Kodiak, and in 1796 Baranov sent Purtov and others to Yakutat, where they founded the settlement Novorossisk (New Russia). In 1797, returning from a voyage of his own to Yakutat, Baranov stopped at Nuchek and persuaded most of the remaining Lebedev-Lastochkin employees there to join him in Shelikhov's company.

Second, Shelikhova had a powerful ally in the highest circles of the Russian government, in the inner circle at court. Not long before Shelikhov's death, his daughter, Anna, had married Nikolai Petrovich Rezanov, at thirty years old a chamberlain in Empress Catherine's court, not titled but a member of the lesser nobility. Although born in St. Petersburg, Rezanov may have lived some time in Irkutsk. Through a family friend, the poet Derzhavin, Rezanov secured the position of secretary for senate reports after he had written important legislation and tax regulations for the government. In that position he executed special assignments for the empress and her courtier, Prince Zubov. In Irkutsk on a court mission in 1794 or 1795, he met with Shelikhov, whom he may have known earlier, and became enthused with the latter's plans for America and the Kurils. It was there that he married Anna Shelikhov, then about fifteen years old.

Rezanov became the chief protector of the family interests because of his connections at court and in 1795 persuaded the tsarina to grant Shelikhov's company a limited monopoly: her decree prohibited competitors from approaching within sixty-six miles of a Shelikhov post. This was a grand concession for Rezanov and Shelikhova, although it was little enough from the tsarina's point of view, for Baranov had effectively created the limited monopoly in the colony: competitors already had learned not to provoke the tenacious manager.

Nikolai Rezanov, who persuaded Tsar Paul I to form the Russian American Company to exploit the resources of North America. Alaska State Library P20.082.

In 1796, Catherine II died at age sixty-seven. She had stamped her character and her name on Russia during the generation of her reign. During the brief ascendancy of her son, Emperor Paul (Paul I), Rezanov rose still higher in the court, becoming secretary of the senate in 1797. He apparently had the tsar's ear, perhaps because of his relationship with Paul's mother's regime. As part of their conspiracy, Myl'nikov and his group brought charges against Shelikhov's widow, contesting her claims to her husband's enterprises by virtue of their sometime partnerships with him. But at the same time Rezanov worked at court to gain support for the company. Rezanov was the more successful, and in 1797, Paul approved a merger of Shelikhov's and Myl'nikov's companies into a new, larger group called the United American Company. This was a substantial victory for Rezanov and Shelikhova, as the new group included the Golokov interests. Thus those who had become Shelikhova's enemies in an attempt to gain control of her husband's many interests wound up subordinated to her and to her son-in-law in St. Petersburg. Lebedev-Lastochkin refused to join the new company. Rezanov received considerable help in his effort to protect Shelikhov's assets from Mikhail Matfeevich Buldakov, a merchant from Velikii-Ustiug in northern Russia. In 1797, Buldakov married another Shelikhov daughter, Avdot'ia.

Initially the company's headquarters were in Irkutsk. Myl'nikov and the others continued to make mischief, but Rezanov pressed his advantage in St. Petersburg. He understood the potential of North America for Russia, and he embraced Shelikhov's vision of a comprehensive, integrated Russian commercial enterprise there. More important, Rezanov realized that without government support, Russia's hold in North America would likely be lost to European competitors for North American furs. In addition, the Russian investors would not have the resources necessary to maintain profitability in light of growing costs associated with greater distances. Rezanov undertook as his mission to persuade the tsar and the imperial senate of the necessity and wisdom of a fully developed colonial enterprise.

Finally in 1799 he succeeded, convincing the tsar to embrace a fully imperial vision in America by establishing a monopoly, a joint-stock company modeled on the British East Indian Company and the Hudson's Bay Company. It would be called the Russian American Company (RAC). Henceforth all Russian enterprise in America would come under the direction of this company, to which the tsar granted the exclusive right to exploitation of any and all resources in the Eastern Islands and North America. This was a landmark development, bringing all activity in America under one administration and at the same time creating a civil entity, the colony of Russian America. It was even more remarkable considering that Catherine had opposed monopolies, being herself a confirmed advocate of free trade. At the same time that the Tsar Paul approved the creation of the RAC, he appointed Buldakov as one of the original four directors. He was to represent directly the Shelikhov family and their interests. Buldakov would remain one of the four principal directors until 1825.

The creation of the RAC was the culmination not just of Rezanov's campaign at court but of more than a half century of promyshlenniki expansion across the Pacific. It also represented a bold declaration by the Russian government of its intentions to take firm control of a portion of the Northwest Coast. Whether that step would be successful would depend much on the determination of Aleksandr Baranov.

5

Aleksandr Baranov

CATHERINE THE GREAT never intended that her son Paul—weak, mentally unbalanced, and ineffectual—should succeed her. Instead, she favored her grandchildren, particularly Alexander (Aleksandr), who was both bright and competent and shared her understanding of and commitment to rational government. In March 1801, Alexander authorized a palace coup in which he replaced the tsar, who was murdered a short time later. The change in government had no effect on the organization of the new Russian American Company (RAC). Alexander I approved establishing the RAC headquarters in St. Petersburg, which kept it completely under Nikolai Rezanov's protection and direction. Among other things, Rezanov urged members of the court and the aristocracy in St. Petersburg to invest in the new entity, which they did readily, including the tsar. With that expression of confidence, by the end of 1802 the number of shareholders had risen from seventeen to four hundred.

ORGANIZING THE RUSSIAN AMERICAN COMPANY

Starting from the collection of posts and caches established by the persistent but uncoordinated drive of the merchants and promyshlenniki (fur trappers), the RAC worked steadfastly as a colonial enterprise to develop the commercial potential of fur and other resources of the Northwest Coast north of the Queen Charlotte Archipelago until the government's sale of its American territory to the United States in 1867. The RAC was granted extraordinary rights and privileges for a commercial enterprise, and while its principal pursuit was economic, the company was in fact, if not in name, an arm of the imperial government and a fundamental aspect of its mission was to take control of the northern part of the Northwest Coast in America.

Mercantilist capitalism played a central role in this motivation. But while the RAC was modeled somewhat on the Hudson's Bay Company and the Dutch East India Company—and in this sense was a classic colonial exploiter of distant resources solely for economic enrichment of the investors; and through tax revenue, benefit to the government—there were significant differences from those two ventures. The government was more directly involved in RAC administration, allowing the company much less freedom of decision. Government direction would become more comprehensive when the second twenty-year charter was granted in 1821.[1]

The company also played a role in international politics. The Billings and aborted Mulovskii expeditions of the late 1780s were directed at securing Russian occupation of the coast north from the Spanish possessions. The Russians would continue to pursue this objective after 1799 through the RAC. Sovereignty over the coast would both extend and protect Russia's eastern frontier. The company's quasi-private nature was politically helpful. It protected the government from potential conflict with foreign powers while at the same time relieving some of the financial burden of administering a distant colony directly. But the government always maintained control of the company, for the tsar and his family as well as a number of important court ministers were shareholders in the RAC. In addition, after Alexander Baranov's retirement in 1818 the chief administrators were naval officers and enjoyed all the ranks and perquisites of government employees. Furthermore, the government closely monitored the company's revenues and expenditures and its capabilities. In the end the decision to liquidate the RAC's North American theater was a government decision.

There were elemental inhibiting factors in this Russian enterprise in the faraway American North. After all, Russia was a European country; its culture and focus were European not Asian, Western not Eastern. While the RAC became well acquainted with the resources of Russian America and the Pacific North, and investigated the development of most of them, neither the government nor the company ever committed the personnel and material resources that would have been necessary to fully exploit the region's potential. This is manifest in the fact that the surprisingly small number of Russians and others that were ever in the Russian American colony at any one time was 823.[2] It is remarkable that so few people could organize and control such a vast area, reaching ultimately from the mouth of the Amur River and Sakhalin Island through the Kurils to the Sea of Okhotsk and Kamchatka, across the Aleutian chain to the Alaska Peninsula and Kodiak, down the American coast from Cook Inlet and Prince William Sound to the Alexander Archipelago, with a post north of Bodega Bay in California, and from the 1820s posts along the north shore of Bristol Bay, at the mouth of the Kvikpak (Yukon) River and five hundred miles upstream at Nulato. They could only do so with the labor of the approximately fifteen hundred Creoles in the colony and the several thousand Aleuts they subjugated.[3] In fact, the Russian vision was limited to viewing North America as a fur warehouse and an imperial outpost. Russia had neither the will nor the capacity to do more with it.

Neither did the RAC ever successfully solve the challenge of supplying Russian America. Although Native populations in Northwest America had been self-sufficient for millennia, the Russians never became so, despite both Gregorii Shelikhov's and Nikolai Rezanov's understanding that the colony could not long be prosperous without self-sustaining resources. From the early 1760s when they reached the mainland, the Russians were unable to subdue other Native peoples as they had the Aleut. On the islands the Aleut could not escape from their oppressors but on the Alaska Peninsula and in Cook Inlet and Prince William Sound, the Alutiq, the upper Inlet Athabaska, and the various groups in the sound could simply abandon their accustomed places of habitation and flee into the wilderness where the Russians were too few to follow effectively. In the Alexander Archipelago the Tlingit had a tradition of ferocity and were tightly organized socially. Not only could the promyshlenniki not subdue them, but they were forced into an uneasy and dependent truce.

The Russians enticed the Natives into a trading relationship, using a variety of goods the Natives found both useful and attractive, including cooking pots and utensils, knives, animal traps, European clothing, especially heavy woolen coats, as well as decorative items such as beads and calico. All of these items had to be brought from Europe. In addition, the Russians needed a wide variety of manufactured goods for their own purposes, mainly to maintain their few colonial stations. These included, among other items, guns, building tools, axes and adzes, brick-making molds, structural iron and decorative copper materials, clothing, business items such as writing paper, account books, and pens, and not least, candles. Food was also a constant, pressing Russian need in the colony. The Russians needed flour for bread, tea, butter, dried meat, salt, beans, barley and other grains for food for the laborers and the few draft animals, rice, vodka, sugar, chocolate, and a variety of other foodstuffs. Again, these all had to be brought from Europe.

The trip from European Russia was long, arduous, and dangerous. Because of the treacherous waters around Tierra del Fuego at Cape Horn and contrary winds along the central North American West Coast, the preferred route was down the coast of Africa and around the Cape of Good Hope, across the Indian Ocean and through Indonesia and northward through the South China Sea and past Japan to Petropavlovsk in Kamchatka before trying the unforgiving passage along the islands between the unpredictable, cold Bering Sea and the North Pacific, warmed by the Japan Current. When sea storms did not threaten and delay such voyages, often ships became becalmed in the waters east of Good Hope. A typical voyage could easily take as long as a year. But the RAC did not have the means to finance annual voyages, so most goods did not come by sea at all; rather, they were shipped overland to Okhotsk and then loaded on company vessels for the trip to America. That journey was even more arduous and took much longer, sometimes as long as two years. In addition to pilferage and spoilage, freight rates were high and progress unpredictable. By the time the goods arrived in the colony, most of the butter was rancid, the flour filled with worms and lice, and the rice desiccated. Supply was a constant worry, playing a significant role in colonial management throughout Russia's tenure in America. A continuing challenge to all high-latitude colonization and economic development, self-sufficiency would eventually defeat the Russians in America.

But the full realization of the magnitude of that challenge would become clear only in time. Even as it did become clearer, the Russians kept their focus on the purpose of their colonial effort: capitalist profit. In its three successive twenty-year charters (1799, 1821, 1844) the government granted the RAC the exclusive right to establish and profit from all current and future economic ventures in the Aleutian, Kuril, and other islands of the North Pacific and along the coast of North America above 55° north latitude. This grant included the right to establish permanent settlements, hire essential personnel, run its colonial possessions, and build company ships. The RAC had the right to purchase arms and ammunition from government stores. It also had the right to trade throughout the Russian empire, and with China, Japan, and all other countries of the North Pacific, as they might permit such trade. In times of need, Russian military and civil officials were obligated to aid and protect the company. The RAC had the right to employ male Natives between the ages of eighteen and fifty and, a provision that manifested the colonial assault on Native freedom, to insist that all Natives in North America sell their furs only to the RAC, at the prices it should set.[4]

The RAC had significant obligations of its own. It would protect the areas under its control and avoid entanglements with foreign powers. It would also spread Russian Orthodox Christianity throughout its possessions and construct churches and pay for their maintenance. The company would provide its employees with proper living quarters, clothing, food, and medical care and would treat the Natives humanely and pay them reasonable wages for their work and offer them educational opportunities. In addition, the charters mandated that the RAC would provide education for employees' children and would support the Orthodox missionaries. To help the company meet these obligations, the government administered important aspects of its activity: the Ministry of Foreign Affairs handled the company's relations with foreign powers; the Ministry of Finance supervised RAC finances; the Ministry of the Navy defended the company at sea and transported mail and supplies (after 1818 naval personnel served in a variety of RAC posts in addition to colonial governor and chief manager); the Ministry of Internal Affairs handled criminal matters; the Holy Synod had jurisdiction over religious matters; and a special Permanent Council addressed political items.

Four directors in St. Petersburg established company policy. In addition to Buldakov, the original directors were V. V. Kramer, A. I. Severin, and I. O. Zelensskii. These men were responsible for the RAC's financial health; they negotiated promyshlenniki contracts, hired agents and other personnel, issued instructions for hunting and trade, and represented the company in all legal and civil matters. Minor company officials managed the activities of legal counselors, secretaries, specialists, copyists, appraisers, and others in branches at Moscow, Irkutsk, Kiakhta, Iakutsk, Okhotsk, and at Kazan, Tiumen, Tomsk, Gizhiga, and Kamchatka. In North America all affairs were administered by the chief administrator or chief manager (*glavnyi pravitel*), whose authority was tantamount to that of a civil governor as well as a chief commercial manager; his staff was extensive. In the Pacific region the manager had branches at Sitka, Kodiak, St. Michael (after 1833), Unalaska, Atkha, the Kuril Islands, and Fort Ross, California (after 1812). Throughout each branch were a number of separate posts, either fortified redoubts or one-man *odinochkas*. In addition to *prekashchiks* (assistants) at such posts, the company identified and employed Native headmen (*toions*) to organize hunting parties, to distribute food to needy Natives, to keep peace and order in the Native villages, to resolve conflicts, and to see that all Natives were engaged in constructive activity for the RAC. The manager was to ensure that all company personnel and all Natives were protected and treated humanely.

In reality, however, the company followed through on few of these stipulations. Posts were established in all the places authorized, but conditions in them were deplorable. The RAC employed Russians, Creoles, and Natives, the latter classified as dependent (those under more or less complete Russian control: Kurils, Aleuts, Koniags), partially dependent (Kenais, Chugach), and independent (Tlingits, Athabaskans, Yupik, and Eskimo). The company mistreated almost all its subjects. While officers in the colony lived reasonably well, and "semi-distinguished" persons, such as prekashchiks and navigators, fared better than most, common laborers often found themselves in near serfdom. The difficulty of attracting and keeping a sufficient supply of labor was another relentless lesson of high-latitude development, and many laborers were shanghaied or bribed into contracts to serve in America, usually for seven years. All expenses incurred in their employment were deducted from their wages, and nearly everything they used was charged against them, including food and lodging. The company set usurious prices on all goods imported, which was nearly everything, leading to debt servitude (i.e., earning less wages than obligated expenses), which was common; repayment of debt was a condition of severance. What the laborers got for the charges was barely tolerable. In fact, lodging was often inadequate, damp, unsanitary, and pest-ridden. Food for the workers came from whatever resources were available: fish, whale meat, and blubber.[5] Medical services were paltry; scurvy and pneumonia were common ailments, and malnutrition and exposure endemic. Critics were punished severely. Company officials in St. Petersburg probably did not know the full extent of this colonial hardship. In 1850, however, they began to classify Russian employees in company employ as "colonial citizens" and provided each with a plot of land for growing vegetables and the like and granted to each an annual pension.

Creoles had a status below Russians. All were obligated to work for the RAC, and those who performed well could claim education at company expense, for which they were expected to work for the company for ten years. Many welcomed that opportunity, however, and a number became significant prekashchiks and navigators and Church clergy and leaders. Many Creoles traveled to Siberia for advanced training. The Natives certainly suffered the worst, an ironic circumstance given the fact that the Russians could not have existed in the colony without their labor, supplies, and companionship. Although the RAC ceased the collection of tribute (*iasak*), all Natives were nonetheless required to hunt and perform other labor. The Aleuts in particular continued to be subjugated. Although paid for their labor, the sum was a pittance, inadequate to secure necessary food and clothing that could not be obtained in the traditional manner. Natives were moved about at the will and need of the company; often the barracks in which they lived were crowded and little more than animal sheds. The women were in a state of effective perpetual concubinage. The RAC moved to correct some of these conditions after 1821, and some Natives were able to obtain education, and some rose to positions of significance in the company.[6]

Despite some policies that might be viewed as enlightened, the RAC was a thoroughly exploitative, capitalist enterprise. Its motivation was profit and its early directors, whatever their ideological sympathies with the European Enlightenment may have been, were part of a feudal system that treated all peoples not born to the aristocracy as inferiors, the only object of whose existence was to serve the needs and desires of that same aristocracy. Tsar Alexander approved the coup against his father Paul partly on the grounds that he was an unreconstructed feudal monarch. But in the American colony liberal policies had no force or hearing, and the business of the protected monopoly was conducted on the most exacting terms enforceable. Only the Orthodox Church mitigated the company's ruthlessness, and not always effectively.

In 1793, following the results of the Billings expedition, Empress Catherine had approved an Orthodox mission for Gregorii Shelikhov's operations in America. The ten members of the mission who reached Kodiak with Archimandrite Ioasaf in 1794 included eight clerics and two servitors (lay aides). Their objective was to convert the Natives to Christianity and to provide pastoral care for the Russians in the colony. Initially they reported many conversions, perhaps as many as seven thousand in the areas they were able to reach around Kodiak in their first year. Many of these likely were superficial, and many may have been the solemnizing of baptisms already performed by laymen (the organized churches of Christendom have always accepted lay baptism under appropriate circumstances).[7]

The company ostensibly supported the mission, but the priests and monks quickly came into conflict with Baranov and his assistants. Conversion reduced common-law relations and promiscuity. In addition, the missionaries protested the brutal treatment meted out to Natives, complaining that the aborigines were held in virtual bondage and effectively persecuted by the RAC. Orthodox liturgy was flexible and culturally adaptive. A number of priests, for example, set about to learn the Native languages. Many clergy were yet illiterate themselves, however, and particularly in the early years not always conscientious in their duties.[8] Nonetheless, the Church became a powerful if not always effective antidote to the brutality that was the norm in company treatment of both Natives and common laborers. In 1796, for example, the Hieromonk Makarii left Unalaska with six Aleuts to travel to St. Petersburg to protest the treatment of the Aleut people; they took with them a letter of grievance signed by a number of Aleut headmen. One of the Aleuts died when the group reached the Kurils, and two others had to turn back because of illness; another died when they got to Moscow. Emperor Paul formally received the remaining two and Makarii. However, the court did almost nothing to ameliorate the Natives' complaints, an inertia all too common among Western governments when apprised firsthand of the effects of their policies on aboriginal populations in distant places.

Makarii and the two Aleuts started their return across Siberia, but the Natives died upon the trio's departure from Irkutsk. Writing in the 1930s, Soviet historian Semen B. Okun suggested the deaths might have been deliberate to forestall Aleut rebellion upon learning that nothing had been accomplished, but most historians discount this speculation. Makarii also died before reaching the colony; the ship carrying him from Okhotsk was lost en route. Ioasaf died with him: the archimandrite had been recalled to Irkutsk to be consecrated the first bishop of Kodiak and was returning to the islands on the same ship. Their deaths temporarily drove the mission into quiescence.[9]

There was at least one extraordinary individual associated with the original mission, however: the monk known as German or Herman (anglicized). Pious from his early years, German worked in Kodiak from his arrival in America until word of the deaths of Makarii and Ioasaf. He then moved to Spruce Island off St. Paul Harbor (Kodiak), where he lived a life of prayer and contemplation until his death in 1836, achieving a reputation of sanctity. Visitors from within the colony and from Europe commented on his solitary and pious life. Over time Native boys were sent to him for training in agriculture, and from them German learned of conditions for Natives in all the company's posts. Lieutenant Ivanovich Ianovskii visited German in 1820, coincident with the outbreak of an epidemic at Kodiak; he reported favorably on the monk's work with the sick and dying, and helped to raise funds for him in the colony. After German's death his reputation for piety increased, and several extraordinary events were attributed to his intervention. In 1970 he was canonized as the first American saint of the Orthodox Church. Iuvenalii, another monk from the original mission, died while missionizing among the people of the Lake Iliamna region; he was canonized in 1994, the mission's bicentennial year.

In 1804 the Metropolitan of the Church in St. Petersburg sent the Hieromonk Gedeon to revitalize the colonial mission. Based in Kodiak, his pastoral work was extensive, but he was steadfastly opposed by Ivan Banner, Baranov's assistant at Kodiak, and by the lesser company officers there. In 1805, when Rezanov stopped at the post on his way to Kodiak, he asked Gedeon for a list of materials the monk needed. But when Gedeon's list grew long (he requested tools and building materials, provisions, cloth, and items he could use as rewards with the local Natives), Rezanov refused to consider anything. Later Baranov prohibited Gedeon from taking three of his best pupils with him for a pastoral reconnaissance of Kamchatka. Such circumstances limited the work the hieromonk could do to reinvigorate the missionary effort and had an intimidating effect on his colleagues, an effect doubtless much intended. Other remarkable individuals served the Church in the colony. The story of the Orthodox mission is discussed later in chapter 6.

BARANOV'S ALASKA

Part of the rationale for creating the Russian American Company in 1799 was to rationalize, advertise, and secure the areas of North America under Russian control and, if possible, to extend those areas. When the government promulgated the tsar's *ukase* (official imperial decree) establishing the RAC, the board of directors named Baranov to the position of chief manager. Acknowledging his great success in organizing the colony's various operations, but also to denote his new authority and position, the tsar awarded him the Order of St. Vladimir, effectively making Baranov a member of the lesser nobility. Secretly, the company ordered him to extend the colony southward as far as possible without confrontation with foreign powers.

Baranov already had undertaken just such an extension. In 1799 with a huge flotilla of several hundred baidarkas and one Russian ship, a force of one hundred Russians, seven hundred Aleuts, and three hundred Koniags, he voyaged from Kodiak across the entrance to Kenai Bay to the Kenai Peninsula, to Chugach Bay, and then southward along the coast to Yakutat, and finally to Icy Strait, an extraordinary voyage by any standards and nearly unimaginable in a kayak today. Surviving a harrowing passage through Peril Strait, the force came eventually to the major Tlingit village at Sitka. Negotiating with one of the clan chiefs there, Katlean (a Kiksaddy Raven), Baranov secured permission to establish a post. He built a substantial fort on the west shore of (later named) Baranov Island, naming the place Mikhailovsk. From there he sent hunting parties throughout the archipelago and southward toward California.

After more than a year Baranov returned to Kodiak. Not long after his return, American and British traders brought word that Tlingits had attacked the new post, burning it and killing all but forty-two of four hundred and fifty people there, including perhaps eighty Russians. The Tlingits erected poles around the post surmounted by the severed heads of many of the Russians. English trader Henry Barber happened into Sitka harbor in his ship *Unicorn* the day after the attack, and with the help of American John Ebbetts, he rescued the survivors, using force to free some of them. Barber took them to Kodiak, where he ransomed them to Baranov for ten thousand rubles worth of furs.

Why the Tlingits attacked the fort is not clear; there may have been disagreement among the clan heads, or the Russians may not have understood the terms the Tlingits had established, or the Russians may have maltreated the Tlingits. Kirill Khlebnikov, a company clerk who lived at Sitka for several years in the 1820s, wrote that it was the climax of an inter-clan, intertribal, concerted campaign to oust the Russians from the archipelago.[10] In any case Baranov immediately determined that he must

reestablish the post. This was a momentous decision, and one fully representative of Baranov's personality and his managerial policy. He could easily have conceded Tlingit control of the archipelago, but he apparently did
not consider such a course. In 1804, with a fleet of three hundred baidarka
and several Russian sloops, he sailed again along the coast. Arriving at
Yakutat, he learned that Tlingits had attacked there at the same time they
razed Mikhailovsk, but the post had been saved by advance information
brought by a friendly Tlingit. Baranov continued on. When he arrived at
Sitka, he was surprised to find there the *Neva*, a Russian ship of the line
captained by Iuri Lisianskii. Lisianskii and Ivan Krusenstern had brought
the *Neva* and the *Nedezhda* from Khronstadt with Rezanov on board.
Upon reaching Hawai'i they had learned of Mikhailovsk's destruction,
and while Krusenstern proceeded on to Petropavlovsk, Lisianskii hurried
to Kodiak, only to learn that Baranov had already left for Sitka. The *Neva*
then hastened to Sitka, where Lisianskii waited for a month for Baranov,
who was hunting along the coast.

Knowing the Russians would return in large numbers, soon after the
successful attack in 1802 the Indians had erected a new fortification six
miles south of the original Russian post, atop a hill overlooking Indian
River. It was a substantial and well-fortified stockade defended with several cannons taken in the raid on Mikhailovsk; the Tlingits were well armed
with American guns for which they had traded furs over the years. The
battle to retake Sitka began on 28 September and lasted into the early days
of October. Baranov tried to lead an infantry assault with a few Russians
and several hundred Aleuts but was beaten off, taking a bullet in the arm.
Lisianskii then reduced the Native post with his ship's guns, and the Tlingit evacuated the site. Baranov established a new post, Novo Arkangel'sk
(New Archangel), on the site, placing his own house on the same hill the
Indians had fortified.

The retaking of Sitka was highly significant, for without a demonstrated
Russian presence in the Alexander Archipelago, England, and perhaps
France or Spain, would have considered that part of the coast available. The
charter for the RAC had named 55° north latitude, effectively Dixon
Entrance, as the southern reach of the company's jurisdiction. But just as
the company might have extended that jurisdiction southward, as it sought
to do, so might it have had its area contracted had one of the major powers, or even the United States (if it had had a navy at the time), decided to
test Russian resolve and resources. Although the archipelago had tacitly

been conceded to Russia before 1800, it could not remain uninhabited by Europeans for long.

Projecting the consequences of Russian occupation of the archipelago for the Tlingit and Haida Indian people of the area is more difficult. As it was, the Tlingit would remain quite powerful and independent throughout the period of Russian occupation and would begin a process of selective adaptation of Western material culture and ideology. Little verifiable Indian testimony survives the period, though the oral tradition includes several versions of the Tlingit repossession of Mikhailovsk. Had the English occupied the archipelago, the history of Tlingit interaction with the British would likely have echoed the experience of the HBC along the coast north of Vancouver Island and in the Queen Charlotte Islands, where the European tread was light and fairly impermanent.

As it was, timing favored Russia remarkably. Europe had become embroiled in the wars of the French Revolution after 1793, distracting England from following up on George Vancouver's magnificent survey of the Northwest Coast. If logic had prevailed, England would have taken possession of the coast south of Yakutat all the way to San Francisco; England had the most powerful navy on the seven seas, as she was about to demonstrate to France and to history. And the British were poised to come by land also. While Vancouver was on the coast, Alexander Mackenzie of the Northwest Company of Montreal crossed over the mountains from Great Slave Lake in the Canadian Northwest to the Pacific Ocean. In subsequent years agents and traders of the Northwest Company would establish posts in the region. For the moment their ties ran back along the Saskatchewan River to Lake Winnipeg and across the Great Lakes to the St. Lawrence. Later, however, they would challenge the Russians by sea.

But the outbreak of the revolution not only kept the Mulovskii ships in Russia, it eventually drew all of Europe into conflagration. With the ascension of Napoleon the struggle became a contest for control of the seas and of world politics and commerce. Both English and French resources were exhausted by the conflict. During a short break in the war, from 1801 to 1803, Napoleon had to contend with a massive slave revolt in Haiti, which persuaded him to relinquish Louisiana in the interior of North America, which he had acquired forcibly from Spain in 1801 and hoped to develop as a granary for future control of the Caribbean. Had the hiatus been longer, either Britain or Spain might have moved to establish posts on the coast between the Columbia River and Yakutat. It was Russia's fortune that neither power had the resources, time, or energy to challenge the tsar or the RAC on the Northwest Coast, leaving a vacuum both Spain and Russia attempted to fill. Final settlement of the contest for sovereignty would await the end of the Napoleonic Wars, however, for neither Russia nor Spain could accomplish what they wished.

Spain actually made the first attempt, in the aftermath of Nootka and just as the wars of the French Revolution began. In 1794 the Spanish established a post at Neah Bay, Nuñez Gaona, on the south shore of the Strait of Juan de Fuca. The location served no purpose, however, for there were few Native villages in the vicinity to facilitate fur trading, and the viceroy in Mexico had insufficient ships or other resources to make the post a port for coastal patrol. North of San Francisco, it became clear, Spain was overextended.

This left the field to the Russians. From his new fort, Novo Arkangel'sk, Baranov sent out parties to find alternative sources of peltry and to learn what other resources might be exploited. But he, too, soon learned just how remote and problematic the North Coast really was. From the start the problem of supply became increasingly difficult, the colony now extending seven hundred miles beyond Kodiak. In addition, between 1799 and 1804 supplies expected from St. Petersburg did not arrive because of shipwreck and storm. No one would starve, for there were plenty of fish. But Baranov needed other essentials, including the trade goods for Natives.

Baranov's situation was complicated by the difficult Treaty of Nerchinsk with the Chinese. By that 1689 instrument, the Chinese limited the Russian fur trade to the interior mountain border town of Kyakhta, south of Irkutsk. This greatly complicated exploitation of the furs of Russian America, for they had to be carried over the Okhotsk-Iakutsk Trace, a trail of 683 miles between the coast and the lower Lena River, or over similar tracks from the coast to Irkutsk. The Okjotsk-Iakutsk Trace was one of the worst trade trails in the world, according to foreign visitors who had the opportunity to see it firsthand. The long journey over the Stanovoi Mountains and then up the Lena added a substantial burden to the cost of the trade. For example, a sea otter pelt cost four times as much at Kyakhta as in Kamchatka in the late eighteenth century, a price the Chinese were willing to pay rather than to risk having Russian ships at the wharves in Canton. The Russians estimated that taking furs by sea directly to Canton would cut their shipping costs by 40 percent. But the Chinese were unmoved. It was so expensive to ship sea otter pelts to Europe that Kyakhta was the only practical market for promyshlenniki and RAC peltry. This fact circum-scribed Russian policy in the Far East and Russian America, for the government had to take care not to antagonize the Chinese lest they close Kyakhta. Reacting to disagreements over customs duties, border crossings, and the return of fugitives from justice, the Chinese suspended trading a number of times between 1750 and 1800, sometimes for several years at a time.

Baranov brought both daring and creativity to bear in addressing this problem of supply and market. Beginning in 1788, increasing numbers of American trading vessels had frequented the coast. With the outbreak of the European war, the Americans found they had the trade almost to them-selves. In 1806 an enterprising young American, Joseph O'Cain, put in at Sitka on the ship *Eclipse* and offered to take Baranov's furs to the Asian markets at Canton, Batavia, or Nagasaki. There O'Cain would market both his own and RAC furs, taking half the profits of each; Baranov would pay O'Cain a freightage fee for transporting RAC furs. Baranov accepted the offer, and though the venture encountered problems that made it less prof-itable than he hoped, Baranov would enter into other contracts with visit-ing Americans in an attempt to obtain supplies he always needed and as a way to cut the costs on getting RAC furs to market. On this particular voy-age, O'Cain got very low prices at Canton because so many other Ameri-cans were marketing furs there. After purchasing tea, cloth, and wheat for Baranov, O'Cain sailed for Nagasaki. But the Japanese refused to deal with the Russians, or any foreign power, and ordered him quickly back to sea. O'Cain left the RAC goods at Petropavlovsk and sailed for Kodiak, appar-ently hoping to obtain more furs. But he shipwrecked near the west end of the Alaska Peninsula. He wintered over and built a small schooner in which he sailed for Unalaska in February 1809, but he wrecked again and drowned trying to reach the shore over ice. Future voyages would be more successful.

Difficulty in obtaining supplies exacerbated RAC treatment of its employees and Native subjects. Goods coming from European Russia took a minimum of seven months in transit, whether overland across Siberia or by the sea voyage. Many cargoes took more than two years to reach the col-ony, and when they finally arrived, anything even slightly perishable inev-itably had spoiled.[11] The hostile climate in the north prevented the company from growing its own crops. Attempts to establish plantations in the Pacific that could supply food, and trading arrangements with China or Japan, failed to materialize or when they did, were inadequate. The result was privation in the colony, more acute among the laborers and Natives than the officers and prekashchiks.

The Russians had already spent considerable time trying to persuade both the Chinese and the Japanese to open their ports to Russian furs. The voyage that brought Lisianskii and Krusenstern in the *Neva* and the *Nedezhda* to Hawai'i in 1804 was a major round-the-world expedition, Russia's first, which had multiple objectives. Planned partly by Krusenstern and partly by Rezanov, the Russians hoped the enterprise would supply Kamchatka and Russian America and would increase foreign trade by establishing relations with both China and Japan. To this end, the ships carried several RAC agents, most notably, Nikolai Rezanov himself. Now Chamberlain of the Court, Rezanov traveled as a Russian diplomat to China and Japan and as an agent of the RAC. Also, his wife had recently died in childbirth, and the voyage was an opportunity for solace. In addition to its other objects, the expedition would provide needed training for Russian seamen, and the ships would conduct a scientific examination of the coast north of the Alaska Peninsula.

After parting at Hawai'i, Krusenstern took the *Nedezhda* and Rezanov to Petropavlovsk and then to Nagasaki, Japan, where Rezanov expected to meet with court officials to discuss a commercial treaty. Instead, he was held under house arrest for six months while the Japanese debated whether to admit him to their country. In the end they declined to do so, and Rezanov was sent packing. Krusenstern, not particularly sympathetic to the mission's commercial objectives, deposited Rezanov back at Petropavlovsk and headed for Canton, where he was to rendezvous with Lisianskii. The tsar had instructed Krusenstern to try to persuade the Chinese to open the port to RAC ships. After reducing the Tlingit fort at Sitka, the *Neva* had sailed to Kodiak for the winter, returning the next summer to collect a cargo of furs that the company hoped to market at Canton.

The *Nedezhda* arrived at Canton first, nearly falling victim to Chinese pirates while entering the port. When the *Neva* arrived, the RAC agent sold the furs but at little profit once the Russians paid the requisite port fees, customs duties, bribes, and charges by government agents and pilots who could navigate safely past the pirates. In addition, Chinese officials were uneasy because the ships carried guns and flew the Russian imperial flag rather than the RAC flag. Messengers were sent to Beijing for instructions. As it happened, at the same time a Russian embassy was en route overland from St. Petersburg to Beijing. The government in Beijing instructed that the Russian ships at Canton be detained. But before that message arrived back in Canton, Krusenstern, anxious to return to Kronstadt before ice might complicate sailing in the Baltic, left without formal permission. In retaliation the Chinese government refused to accept the Russian embassy when it finally arrived overland in Beijing and refused to discuss opening the port of Canton or permitting the Russians to use the Amur River basin. They also threatened to close Kyakhta, although they did not actually do so. In sum the missions to Japan and China were utter failures, leaving the RAC with all the difficulties of moving furs from Okhotsk to Kyakhta that had obtained before the voyage.

Upon his return to Petropavlovsk, Rezanov, accompanied by Georg Heinrich von Langsdorf, a German physician and naturalist who had joined the expedition at Copenhagen, conducted a careful survey of RAC activities in Kamchatka, in the Eastern Islands, the Pribilofs, and at Kodiak before proceeding to Sitka, where he wintered with Baranov in the chief manager's new post that was being constructed there. Rezanov got on well with Baranov, and the two discussed plans for the future of the RAC in America, including establishing new posts at the mouth of the Columbia River, and in California and Hawai'i, which could relieve the supply problem in Russian America. Rezanov particularly hoped to find a way to drive out the American traders, or at least neutralize their effect on the trade with the coastal Indians. Along with nearly all Russians who assessed conditions in the colony, Rezanov recognized the deleterious effects of the American and British trade in arms and alcohol, which the Russian government would repeatedly but futilely protest to those governments. Rezanov's comprehensive concept, to make the Russian enterprise in America self-sufficient, was a departure from Tsarina Catherine's minimalist approach. Had it succeeded, the history of Russian America might have been quite different. But it was not to be.

When Rezanov arrived at Sitka in 1806, supplies were short. A ship coming from Petropavlovsk went down in a storm, and provisions had to be rationed. In August of that year a young American, "Nor'west" John D'Wolf, sailed to the post in his ship *Juno* with a cargo of food, manufactured goods, and furs he had collected along the coast. Baranov arranged to buy the ship and its cargo, less the furs, a purchase supported by Rezanov. Rezanov then sent the ship under the command of two young Russian naval lieutenants, Gavriil Davydov and Nikolai Khvostov, to Kodiak for a cargo of dried fish and probably also Aleut women, there being a shortage at Sitka. At about the same time, the Russians received a reminder of the precarious nature of their isolation. Traders brought news that at Novorossisk (Yakutat) a Tlingit attack party had destroyed the Russian post and killed all its inhabitants.

The cargo brought from Kodiak would only temporarily assuage the shortage at Sitka, so at the end of February, Rezanov took the *Juno*, commanded by Khvostov, with Davydov and accompanied by Langsdorf, on a voyage south along the coast toward California. Early in March 1806, Khvostov spent three harrowing days trying to get across the Columbia River bar, at one point jeopardizing the life of Langsdorf, who had gone ahead in a longboat, all to no avail. He abandoned the effort and continued on to San Francisco. As it happened, Captains Meriwether Lewis and William Clark, having been sent overland from St. Louis by U.S. president Thomas Jefferson, had wintered at the bar and had broken their camp just eleven days before. Had Khvostov succeeded in crossing the bar, Rezanov would likely have learned from the Indians of Lewis and Clark's recent departure and would have sent messengers upriver to fetch them. Rezanov certainly also would have founded the post that the Russians had for long wanted to establish somewhere on the coast north of San Francisco, the post that had been one of the objectives of the aborted Mulovskii expedition of 1789. Again, had Rezanov been successful, the history of the Pacific Northwest and the Northwest Coast might have been substantially altered.

As it was, the *Juno* proceeded on to California, where Rezanov sought a cargo of food to take back to Sitka. He approached San Francisco with considerable trepidation, for the Spanish had given strict orders that foreign vessels were not to be permitted in the bay. Previously the orders had provided the exception, normal for ports not at war, that ships could enter if in dire emergency. So many ships had dire emergencies when in the vicinity, however, that the exception had been canceled. The Spanish quite rightly still feared a Russian advance toward California, and aside from the missions and few presidios there, the Spanish presence was meager. In addition, on this far coast no one could be sure whether Napoleon and Spain were at peace or war back in Europe. Khvostov brought the ship in under cover of darkness and anchored close to the presidio. Fortunately for the Russians, both the governor of the region and the commandant of the fortress were on a visit to Monterey when Rezanov arrived. Rezanov charmed the vice-commandant as well the commandant's fifteen-year-old daughter,

Doña Concepción (Arguello). After a six-week stay he was able to return to Sitka with a cargo of wheat, beans, beef, and other food and a promise of marriage with the young Spanish lady.

Back at Sitka, Khvostov turned the *Juno* over to D'Wolf, who with Langsdorf set sail shortly for Petropavlovsk. After wintering there, they went on to Okhotsk and then traveled separately overland to St. Petersburg. Rezanov stayed at Sitka to await the construction of a small vessel, the *Avos*, which Khvostov and Davydov sailed to Okhotsk, in tandem with Rezanov in the *Juno*. From there Rezanov set off overland for St. Petersburg, but not before instructing Khvostov and Davydov in the *Avos* to sail to the Kuril Islands and sack some villages in retaliation for Rezanov's treatment at Nagasaki. These were impetuous orders, and they jeopardized future relations between Russia and Japan and the future of the RAC. In fact, Rezanov thought better of the project and sent word later to cancel it. But uncertain of his intentions, over the next two years the two young lieutenants burned villages in the Kurils and on Sakhalin. When they returned to Okhostsk, the commander there arrested and jailed them for acts injurious to the empire. They eventually escaped, however, and made their own way to St. Petersburg, where they were exonerated after a thorough investigation.

In the meantime Rezanov came to an untimely end. Traveling the Okhotsk-Iakutsk Trace and the Lena River during the fall rains, he contracted a fever. Rather than recuperate at Irkutsk, he pushed on. On the trail east of Krasnoyarsk, he was struck and killed by his horse's hoof. Rezanov was buried at Krasnoyarsk in March 1807. The RAC lost an invaluable advocate and enthusiast with Rezanov's death. He had known both Shelikhov and Baranov, and he had demonstrated his charm and competence at the imperial court. He had progressive ideas regarding conservation of the resources in Russian America and for relationships with the Natives, none of which was put in place until many years after his death. Most important, he envisioned a strong and aggressive RAC that would dominate the North Pacific and spread the Russian empire while enriching it. Had Rezanov lived, it is not unlikely that he would have continued to press for a Russian settlement along the coast of North America between Dixon Entrance and San Francisco, thereby conceivably changing the region's development.

In a strange twist of fate, Khvostov and Davydov also met premature deaths not long afterward. After returning from Russian America, Langsdorf had taken up residence in St. Petersburg to catalog and describe botanical collections he made during his travels. In October 1809, D'Wolf visited the city on a trading voyage and stopped to visit. The two summoned Kvostov and Davydov, who were then in the city, and the four veterans of America shared memories through the night and into early morning. Upon leaving for their apartments, the two lieutenants approached a drawbridge over the Neva River just as it began to open. Trying to cross anyway, they tried to jump from the bridge to a passing barge. But they missed the barge, fell into the icy river, and were never seen again.

Meanwhile in Russian America, Baranov pushed ahead with the plans he and Rezanov had agreed upon, to take advantage of the British absence on the coast because of the Napoleonic Wars to extend Russian occupation still farther south, beyond the Alexander Archipelago. Occupation of the coast anywhere north of San Francisco would greatly strengthen Russia's claims below Dixon Entrance, the southern end of the Alexander Archipelago. Baranov dispatched two vessels southward in 1808. The first was the *St. Nikolai*, commanded by Nikolai Bulygin, who was accompanied by his wife Anna Petrovna, three other women, and a hunting party headed by Timofei Tarakanov. The party sailed to the Columbia River, where they intended to establish a post.

They were unsuccessful trying to cross the bar, however, so they moved north to Grays Harbor but wrecked on nearby Destruction Island. The women were captured by Quileute Indians, while the rest of the party fled to the forest, going inland to escape the Indians and spending the winter in the foothills. In spring, returning to the coast by boat, they were captured by Makah Indians, who traded them as slaves through various villages south of the Strait of Juan de Fuca. Both Anna Petrovna and Nikolai Bulygin died during the ordeal. In May 1811, Tarakanov and a dozen of the others were liberated by Captain Thomas Brown of the *Lydia* and taken to Sitka. Seven of the original party had died, and one other had been rescued by Captain George Ayres of the *Mercury*.

The second vessel, the *Kodiak*, sailed to California and landed at a bight about ninety miles north of San Francisco Bay on the coast. There, Ivan Kuskov, Baranov's principal lieutenant, established a post that the Russians called variously Colony Ross or Ross Office; it was known to the Spanish and is now known as Fort Ross. Spanish resources in the area were too thin to support any effort to dislodge the interlopers. The Russian government took the post under its protection and pressured Madrid to formally recognize Russian possession, which Spanish officials would not do, for they understood too well the implications of giving the Russians a free foothold on the coast ninety miles from their northernmost occupied fort. For their part the Spanish adopted a policy of noncooperation and harassment, but the Russians forced an agreement from the local Pomo Indians to allow them to stay. After the Mexican Revolution in 1821, the Russians maintained an uneasy hold on the post and two nearby inland plantations.

The object of the Ross settlement was food production and whatever sea mammal pelts could be taken. But the post never produced the amount of goods that had been hoped. This was partly due to poor management and poor placement; the coastal fogs inhibited the production of healthy crops. In addition, much to their chagrin, the Russians found that they were as overextended in the region as the Spanish were, and the Russians eventually sold the post when they developed an alternative source of supply in the late 1830s.

At about the same time as he sent the *Kodiak* and the *Nikolai* south, Baranov received an enticing offer regarding his supply problem from another quarter, the American entrepreneur John Jacob Astor of New York. Having entered the fur trade in the Mississippi and Missouri basins after 1807, Astor sought to extend his operations to the Pacific Coast, capturing all the trade of the Pacific Northwest if possible. Neither of the Canadian fur trade giants, the Northwest Company of Montreal nor its principal competitor the Hudson's Bay Company, were yet firmly established in the region. Astor sought to make his headquarters at the mouth of the Columbia River. To avoid difficulty with the Russians, he sought to turn their need for supplies to his own advantage. Astor proposed to Baranov that in exchange for Baranov's grant of exclusive foreign access to the coast south of Sitka, he would supply the Russians with vessels of supplies annually; Astor's ships would then take furs to Canton to exchange for tea. Baranov liked the terms proposed and signaled that he would sign an agreement to this effect with Astor in 1812.

Meanwhile, Astor sent out the ship *Tonquin* with a party to found the post, Astoria, on the Columbia. After leaving a shore party at the mouth of the river, the *Tonquin* sailed to Clayoquot Sound on Vancouver Island, where Indians captured the ship and killed all but one man, who ignited the ship's powder magazine, killing himself and many of the Indian attackers. At the same time a supply party for the post Astor had sent overland from St. Louis experienced difficulty in the mountains and barely made it to Astoria. A ship Astor sent from New York, the *Lark*, wrecked in Hawai'i. Then the War of 1812 completely interrupted Astor's design. Fearing attack by a British war vessel, in 1813 the leader of the Astorians sold the post to an agent of the Northwest Company. By a peace treaty in 1815, the post was returned to the Americans, but by then Astor had lost interest in the project. Another potential solution for the RAC's supply difficulties went unrealized.

Also at this time the Japanese finally found a way to punish the RAC for Rezanov's rash decision to send Kvostov and Davydov on a retaliatory raid against the Kuril Islands. Vasilii Golovnin, a rising naval officer who, among other exploits, had daringly freed his ship from a thirteen-month captivity in Capetown, South Africa, undertook a survey of some of those islands in the sloop *Diana*. While ashore one day he was taken prisoner, along with two officers and four seamen. The Japanese held their captives for two years before finally releasing them. RAC operations in the Kurils, Okhotsk, and Kamchatka were under the general direction of the chief manager in Sitka, and the incident simply underscored the difficult circumstances that circumscribed RAC operations in Siberia and Russian America.

In the 1810s Baranov sent several other ships southward to trade for food at San Francisco and to poach along the coast south of the Juan de Fuca Strait and the Columbia River. One of these ships, the *Il'mena*, carried a large number of Aleut hunters under the command of a promyshlennik named Boris Tarasov. They landed eight baidarkas just inside the entrance to San Francisco Bay, on the north shore, among other places. The Spanish ordered the party off, but they later put back to shore again. The Spanish captured Tarasov and twenty-four Aleuts. Their captors took the prisoners south, where they were held at various of the missions for common labor. Several years later a party of Russians rescued one of the Aleuts, named Ivan Keglii (or perhaps Kykhliaia), who told of the torture of another Aleut by the mission's fathers. Petr, or Chungangnaq, had apparently refused Catholic entreaties that he convert from Orthodoxy, whereupon he was tortured, first his fingers being cut off, then his arms, and then his intestines opened, which of course killed him. Through the ordeal he refused to renounce his faith, thus becoming a martyr to Orthodoxy. Petr was canonized by the church in 1994. Although even the tsar believed Keglii's story, there is no corroboration in the sources, and historian Richard

Pierce has pointed out that such an act was contrary to the policy of the Franciscans at Santa Barbara and the other missions at the time.[12]

In 1815, Baranov tried again to address the supply problem, this time in a new way. Hawai'i had always been central to the idea of Russian American self-sufficiency, as food raised on a plantation there could be shipped easily to Sitka, Kodiak, and Unalaska. In 1808, Lieutenant Leontii Hagemeister, in Russian service, took the *Neva*, now back in Russian America, to Hawai'i to open negotiations with King Kamehameha I, who had unified all the islands except Kauai and Nihau under his rule. Hagemeister's voyage was in response to a proposal Kamehameha had sent to Baranov for an exchange of breadfruit, coconuts, pigs, rope, and other products for Russian textiles, timber, and iron. At the time Baranov had been unable to follow up on the offer because he lacked personnel. Help came, as it often seemed to, as the result of a fortuity.

In 1813 the Russian ship *Suvorov*, captained by M. P. Lazarev, arrived at Sitka. Georg Anton Schaffer, an Austrian surgeon and adventurer then in the RAC's employ, was on the vessel. Schaffer left the ship over a dispute with Lazarev. Baranov was happy to have Schaffer at Sitka. He soon asked the Austrian to go to Hawai'i to get help from Kamehameha in retrieving a Russian cargo of furs that had wrecked on Kauai while trading for food. Kauai and Nihau were then ruled by King David Kaumualii, a well-educated and cultivated rival of Kamehameha. Kaumualii wanted the Russian ship as protection against Kamehameha. Unfortunately for Baranov, and for the future of Russian America, Schaffer was the wrong man. Relations between Kamehameha and Kaumualii were tense, and the mission's success required careful, patient negotiations. Schaffer possessed neither of these qualities.

Schaffer went first to Oahu, where his activities generated Kamehameha's distrust. Then Schaffer made an alliance with Kaumualii, promising to secure for him an armed vessel and the protection of the Russian navy. He made Kaumualii an officer in the Russian Navy. For his part Kaumualii gave the Russians land for plantations on both sides of Kauai and permission to build a fort. Soon, however, encouraged by American traders who visited the islands regularly in their voyages to the Northwest Coast and Canton, Kamehameha began to threaten that he would invade Kauai if Kaumualii persisted in his Russian alliance. Kamehameha feared not only Kaumualii's growing strength, but the danger the Russians might mean to Hawaiian autonomy. Under this pressure, Kaumualii expelled Schaffer and his men, who fled to Oahu, where they were effectively Kamehameha's prisoners until taken back to Sitka by an American trader. Kamehameha had been quite favorably disposed toward Baranov, but the Schaffer episode led him to distrust the Russians. Captain Otto E. Kotzebue, on a round-the-world expedition in the *Riurik* in 1816, visited with Kamehameha and sought to set his mind at ease, assuring him that Schaffer had no authority to make the promises he made to Kaumualii, which in any case were not endorsed by the imperial court or the navy, even though a good deal of RAC resources had been invested in the project.

The Hawaiian debacle, however, helped to discredit Baranov with the board of directors in St. Petersburg.[13] The company's original charter, granted for twenty years, was due to expire in 1819. Baranov had been the RAC's only chief manager during all those years, and administration of the colony necessarily reflected his style of management and his assessment of potential and possibilities. In St. Petersburg the directors had, by the same token, a less than complete understanding of conditions and needs in the colony. The company's headquarters reflected the different worlds of noble Russia and the rustic colony. The company offices, spacious and situated in the city's best quarter, near the palace, were lavishly appointed. The directors' salaries were generous. Administration was efficient and orderly, but the office's principal focus, and that of the shareholders, was the annual dividend. Looking at the imposing, busy seat of power at St. Petersburg, it was easy to assume that the RAC was a well-managed, thoroughly modern enterprise.

But circumstances in the colony belied this. Working conditions for the common laborers and the Natives, mostly Aleuts, still were primitive and dangerous. Aleut hunters continued to be exploited and abused, despite repeated criticism by the Orthodox mission and negative reports from the various naval expeditions that visited. Rezanov and the founders of the company had taken an enlightened view of the colonial establishment; comfortable buildings were to have been built, as many managerial personnel as necessary were to have been assigned to the colony, relations with the Natives and the labor force were to have been humane and civil, and a fleet of RAC vessels was to have maintained regular supply and communication. In fact, there were never enough personnel assigned to Russian America to carry out all the responsibilities imposed by the company and the government, supply was always irregular, there was not enough housing and what there was continued to be inadequate, there was yet no physician in the colony, and schools and other institutions of culture were lacking. Far from the order of Europe, despite Baranov's will and ability, the colony was still a primitive, loosely ordered entity functioning reactively to successive crises, with none of the civility and urbanity assembled back in St. Petersburg.

Symbolic and symptomatic of these differences, Baranov had taken a mistress in the colony, Anna Grigor'evna, probably the daughter of an Aleut headman. When Baranov had come to America in 1790 to manage Shelikhov's enterprises, he had sent his Russian wife of some years to Kargopol to live and raise their daughter. A son had remained with Baranov's brother. Baranov's wife died in 1806, after which he married his Aleut mistress, who bore him a son and two daughters. Baranov and the colony did not manifest the enlightened, efficient reflection of modern Russia the elite administrators in St. Petersburg seemed to have had in mind. To have created in Russian America an efficient colonial administration on the order of Hudson's Bay Company in Canada would have required considerably more talent, commitment, and discipline than the RAC brought to bear on its activities, even though the company operated with more personnel than did the far western department of the Hudson's Bay Company. It would also have required the tsar and the board of directors to have given the RAC far more freedom than they ever did.

The approaching expiration of the charter provided an opportunity to address these circumstances and to decide whether to adopt policies to improve the situation, to let the colony continue to languish, or to liquidate it altogether. Clearly, the directors desired a more bureaucratized, tighter administration than Baranov provided, and some members of the government had identified a solution in the Russian Navy. The navy provided a logical alternative, and in fact, advocates of using the navy in the colony had been active in the RAC and at court for some time. The navy might be able to help meet the supply difficulty and also to discourage the American traders from their activities along the Northwest Coast at the same time. The service was organized as a modern bureaucracy and was rationally administered.

The navy had its own interest in Russian America, however. Naval ships with their officers and crews had insufficient area for training and outfitting exercises in the Baltic; the Pacific offered an opportunity to satisfy these needs and to demonstrate efficient, no-nonsense administration. This was an attractive alternative for the board of directors. Furthermore, the board did not feel as fully in control of policy in the colony as the directors thought they should be. Naval officers, used to the discipline of order and the hierarchy of command, could be counted on to be more effective in the implementation of policy, or so it seemed to the directors. But there were concerns. Throughout its brief history the company had offered naval officers lucrative posts, but few had taken advantage of the offer. Most naval officers came from the upper nobility and carried the traditional aristocratic prejudice against the merchant class. The idea of naval officers under the command of merchants was problematic at the very least.

In 1817 the directors appointed Lieutenant Leontii Hagemeister to go to the colony to investigate conditions and, if he thought necessary, to relieve Baranov. This was a broad grant of authority, one the directors knew the naval officer would take full advantage of. In fact, the navy had determined to take command of the company's supply and administrative functions, a move the directors were essentially powerless to oppose because they knew little of actual conditions in the colony and had been unable to solve the problem of supply. Tsar Alexander apparently agreed with senior naval officers that the government needed to exert greater control over colonial development, particularly in light of renewed interest in the Northwest Coast by both the British and the Americans. The war in Europe had ended in 1815 (the implications of which I return to shortly). Before Hagemeister left St. Petersburg, the board, succumbing to pressure from the government, named him chief manager of the company—that is, he was named to succeed Baranov.

Sailing with the ships *Kutuzov* and *Suvorov*, Hagemeister reached the colony in November and informed Baranov of his "retirement" almost immediately. The chief manager's lax management, together with a fall in RAC profits resulting from the Hawaiian venture and from declining numbers of furs no longer easily accessible, had suggested to some in St. Petersburg that Baranov might have siphoned off some of the company's resources to his own accounts. Hagemeister appointed himself manager and directed Kirill Khlebnikov, acting as agent of the company, to go through Baranov's business records to check the financial status of colonial affairs. That work took more than half a year; under Baranov's management the colony had produced three hundred million rubles from furs and other resources. When the auditing chore was complete, Khlebnikov reported that the company books were in balance, and that although Baranov could legitimately have profited at many turns, he instead had donated most of his personal funds to the company and to friends; he was in no way a wealthy man.

While Khlebnikov conducted his audit, Hagemeister set about to reform the colonial administration. He abolished the system of paying Russian hunters in shares of furs, held over from early promyshlenniki days, and instead put them on regular salaries, plus a monthly provisions allowance. He sent a vessel (the *Otkrytie*, captained by M. N. Vasil'ev) to Hawai'i to recover as much of Schaffer's supplies as possible and further to assuage Kamehameha. He also took an expedition north along the Bering Sea coast hoping to find new sources of furs, walrus tusk, and perhaps minerals. There was considerable resistance in the colony to the notion of naval administration. Partly to ease that anxiety, Hagemeister apparently encouraged one of his lieutenants, Semen Ivanovich Ianovskii, to pursue a romantic interest he had in Baranov's daughter, Irina, then fifteen. The two were married in January.

The government also sent an expedition to the colony, headed by Vasilii Golovnin, who was to gather information on the colony. In the ship *Kamchatka*, Golovnin stopped at Petropavlovsk, cruised in the Bering Sea and along the Aleutian Islands, visited Kodiak, and was at Sitka in midsummer, arriving on 28 July. Hagemeister had just departed on 22 July for Fort Ross and California, to obtain supplies. There had apparently been some discussion of Golovnin's replacing Hagemeister as chief manager, but no such appointment was made. Had it been, the future of the company might have been different, for Golovnin had a reputation for taking an aggressive, disciplined attitude toward his responsibilities. Instead, from Sitka, Golovnin went to Fort Ross, where he met Hagemeister in the *Kutuzov*, and then visited Monterey and Hawai'i on his return to St. Petersburg.

Returned from California, Hagemeister determined that he was not in good enough health to spend another winter in the colony and decided to return to Russia. In November he turned over administration of affairs to Lieutenant Ianovski as acting governor and to Khlebnikov as chief fiscal officer for the company. Taking Baranov with him, he sailed for Europe. Hagemeister apparently harbored considerable ill will toward the old manager, probably because Baranov was at root still a merchant, a class the nobility considered tainted by birth and by morals. Baranov had hoped to stop at Hawai'i to visit with Kamehameha, but Hagemeister ruled that out. He did stop at Manila, however, and for five weeks at Batavia, where Baranov contracted a fever and died soon after the ship's departure. He was buried at sea in Sunda Strait.

It was an ignominious end to a career, which if not glorious had been substantial. Baranov had established Russia and the RAC firmly in North America, had overseen the company's activities in such a way as to generate considerable profit, had directed the establishment of Kodiak, Sitka, and Fort Ross, and had exploited the resource in furs and other products from Kamchatka to California. He had continued the promyshlenniki's ruthless brutality with the Natives and added to it maltreatment of Russian laborers, policies that invited criticism from both the Church and from visitors, official and private, foreign and Russian. During his tenure conditions in the colony were probably not well understood; none of the directors had ever visited the colony. It had been easy to appoint Baranov, who was a merchant, after all, who identified more with Siberia and the promyshlenniki than with the protocols of European Russia; he was neither a bureaucrat nor a policy theorist. Rezanov would have done well to recommend the appointment of a trained manager in 1799 or in 1806 after his visit to Sitka. But he admired Baranov's spirit and determination as well as his adaptation to colonial conditions. Had Rezanov lived, the history of the company and its chief manager might well have been very different. If Baranov's end was tragic, in many ways so had been his long association with the Russian American Company.

6

Russian America

DURING THE SECOND and third charters of the Russian American Company (RAC), Russia's colonial experiment in America reached its fullest maturity. Although the number of Russians was always small, colonial administration was efficient and conditions both for company laborers and for Natives eased somewhat, though the Tlingit were still feared and the Aleut still subjugated, and common workers contracted to the company still labored in debt peonage. Nonetheless, treaties with the United States and England brought the contest for European sovereignty on the Northwest Coast to a resolution, establishing permanent boundaries for Russian America. As some populations of marine furbearers were depleted, the RAC's governors turned increasingly to land mammals and to walrus ivory to sustain company profits. Employing modest conservation measures, the company attempted to stabilize remaining sea otter stocks. In addition, exploratory expeditions were dispatched to find new areas for harvesting and for trade with Natives as yet beyond the Russians' purview. At the same time the colonial governors sought to develop untapped resources, such as mineral deposits and whales in the Bering Sea.

THE BOUNDARY TREATIES AND THE END
OF THE CONTEST FOR SOVEREIGNTY

Although the home government did not envision a new Russia in North America, it did support important scientific expeditions to learn as much as possible about the region. The colony's one cultural center, Sitka, grew into a Pacific port of visible if limited significance. Under the direction of a few of the governors and several extraordinary churchmen, the Orthodox mission carried on important pastoral and educational work. Had Russia determined to establish a new society in Alaska, it would have found in America in the mid-1840s a firm foundation on which to do so. But that foundation rested on significant changes in colonial administration in the second charter, promulgated in 1821. The full maturation of the colony came only slowly, through the efforts of a succession of new colonial governors.

The initial charter of the RAC, approved in 1799, included a twenty-year time limitation; the charter was renewable, at the discretion of the government. Although there was every expectation that the government would recharter the company, world circumstances in the late 1810s were dramatically different from twenty years earlier, and some of those changes would help to shape the new company charter. Britain had emerged from its great victory over France in the Napoleonic Wars as the primary world power with near total control of the seas and had effectively announced a new world order at the Congress of Vienna in 1815. Ideally, war no longer was to be an acceptable method of resolving international differences. England, Austria, Prussia, and Russia signed a quadruple alliance committed to "government by conference" rather than war, an ideal that was impossible to keep in the long run but that represented Enlightenment hopes for peace. As the contest for sovereignty was renewed on America's Northwest Coast after 1815, that hope would be tested.

At the same time an internal struggle over the future of the RAC developed in St. Petersburg. The directors had gathered much new information about Russian America from the voyages of Otto E. Kotzebue, M. P. Lazarev, Leontii Hagemeister, and Vasilii Golovnin. They accepted the proposition that the colony needed a more businesslike and organized administration, one in which control would rest more solidly with the board in St. Petersburg than with the manager in Sitka. Unfortunately, they were too sanguine about their own understanding of colonial conditions and necessities. They had no choice, given the tsar's backing, but to accept a controlling role by the Russian Navy. This was somewhat logical, for Russian America was in fact a maritime enterprise; the seagoing furbearers were the company's prime quest and asset, and they provided little incentive to move inland. In addition, disciplined naval officers could be counted on to execute the government's wishes more readily than could RAC officials, whose primary interest was the firm's profitability. And should the colony need to be defended, the navy's involvement would mean the presence of naval vessels in colonial waters most of the time.

As promulgated by the tsar, the new 1821 charter authorized company activities in the colony for another twenty years, and continued the RAC's privileges and labor conditions. However, merchants would no longer serve as the manager/governor. Instead, in the future only senior naval officers would serve in that position. Moreover, their tenure would be limited to five years, thus avoiding the cult of personality associated with Aleksandr Baranov and his long, twenty-year rule of the colony. The board was successful in insisting that a company officer would be in charge of the colony's financial affairs, stationed in the colonial capital. But the board was forced to accept Hagemeister's decision to pay salaries rather than shares to the Natives. Other new charter provisions changed the nature of the company, making it much more a government enterprise. Naturally, the board of directors resented being usurped by the navy and effectively declared incompetent to manage the company. But there was little they could do to prevent it. Senior naval officers had Tsar Alexander's confidence, and he was greatly concerned about the diplomatic situation in America.

When Golovnin returned to St. Petersburg as a naval hero from the Pacific in 1819, following his captivity in Japan, he announced to the directors that the colony was about to be taken over by the Americans. He referred to the large number of American traders on the coast. But he also noted an alarming new development: the year before, Britain and the United States had announced an audacious proclamation in which they took it upon themselves to solve the remaining questions of sovereignty on the Northwest Coast. Henceforth, they declared in the Convention of 1818 that Dixon Entrance (54° 40' north latitude) would be the southern boundary of Russian holdings in America. From there southward to 42° north latitude the coast and all the land east to the Continental Divide would be called the Oregon Country, under joint British and American protection. This was a daring, and for Russia and Spain, insulting declaration, for neither the British nor the Americans had sought agreement from either country before announcing their agreement. The British and the Americans argued that both Russia and Spain had squandered their opportunity—all during the French wars when England was enmeshed in Europe—to occupy the region south of 54° 40' north latitude. Now it was too late. But how would Russia and Spain react to such audacity?

The joint British-American claim rested on each country's separate history in the region. Both Captains James Cook and George Vancouver had surveyed the coast north from Nootka Sound on Vancouver Island, and Northwest Company and Hudson's Bay Company fur trappers had operated in the interior mountains since Alexander Mackenzie's land crossing in 1793. And in 1805 Simon Fraser had established a post on McLeod Lake and in 1808 had descended the Fraser River to its mouth (by present-day Vancouver, British Columbia). To the south the American Robert Gray had claimed all drainage of (i.e., all the land drained by) the Columbia River and its tributaries in 1792, and Captains Meriwether Lewis and William Clark had confirmed that claim with their epic trek of 1803 through 1806. The southernmost tributaries of the Snake, the Columbia's principal tributary, reached barely beyond 42° north latitude, while the drainage began at the Continental Divide. The important questions dealt not with the basis of the claims but with whether Russia and Spain would contest them.

In fact, Oregon was but one piece of a much larger territorial settlement in North America between Britain and the United States and between the United States and Spain. North America represented loose ends in the new balance of power following the Napoleonic Wars. Britain and the United States agreed on a boundary between Maine and New Brunswick, and along 49° north latitude between the Louisiana Purchase (the American Great Plains) to the south and Rupert's Land (prairie Canada) on the north, from the Great Lakes to the Continental Divide (making an adjustment for the Red River Valley). The Oregon declaration resulted from the failure of Britain and the United States to agree on how to distribute the territory west of the divide. One option would have been for the two countries to take no action in regard to the land between where the Spanish were, California, and where the Russians were, the Alexander Archipelago. But since John Jacob Astor's venture on the Columbia, fur trappers contracted to companies in both the United States and Canada had been working toward the American Pacific Northwest and the far Canadian West.

The land furbearers of the region were too valuable a resource to be left to countries that had not availed themselves of their opportunities to appropriate them (Russia and Spain); so both Britain and the United States thought a defining action of some kind was clearly warranted. But in the face of their failure to come to an amicable division of Oregon, they agreed to disagree. The joint declaration provided that neither country could exercise sovereignty in the region—that is, no army or navy, and no civil government or officers. The nationals of either country were free to operate within the area, however; the nationals both countries were concerned with were fur trappers. The arrangement was renewable every ten years and lasted until 1846.

Also at this time the United States began negotiations with Spain over the southern boundary of the Oregon Country. For many years Spain had recognized its impotence on the Northwest Coast and had more important needs regarding the United States. In 1819 in the Adams-Onis Treaty, Spain ceded the Oregon Country north of 42° north latitude to the United States. Spain also ceded the Floridas (from the Atlantic to the Mississippi south of 30° 60' and 31° north latitude) in exchange for an American renunciation of any claim to Texas. The Texas renunciation was especially important to Spain; the Northwest Coast was of no consequence by comparison. Spain, in other words, accepted the fait accompli represented by these diplomatic instruments of 1818 and 1819. A matter that had kept four countries in a state of uncertainty and occasional anxiety since 1768, and had nearly brought England and Spain to war in 1789 over Nootka Sound, was therefore summarily concluded by Britain and the United States with hardly an unsteady breath. Or so it seemed.

Russia was not to be so easily taken for granted, however. In fact, the tsar was highly incensed at the aggressive stance taken by Britain and the United States. Since the Billings expedition in 1790, Russia had claimed the coast south to the fifty-first latitude, the north end of Vancouver Island, and the government was not ready to concede such an expanse upon which no European settlements had been established. Russia's answer to the British-U.S. convention was an equally aggressive declaration of its own, announced in a *ukase* (the tsar's official decree), issued in 1821 at the same time as the promulgation of the second charter. Russia did not accept the boundaries declared by the United States and Britain. Quite the contrary, it considered its claim to the fifty-first latitude to be completely valid in the absence of settlement. As an antidote the tsar proclaimed that Russia was taking control of the coast above the fifty-first. Henceforth, the ukase declared, the waters north of that point were closed to foreign shipping. No ships were to approach within one hundred *versts* (roughly two-thirds of an English mile, or 1.06 kilometers) of any coast claimed by Russia. Moreover, Russia would patrol the coast to guarantee that the decree would be honored.

This was a decisive and provocative action. Britain and the United States had thrown down a gauntlet with the Convention of 1818, and now Russia had thrown down its own. Moreover, the American sea traders had to honor the Russian prohibition, for recovery of any cargoes confiscated would be very difficult. The stage was now set for a major confrontation. Although the American traders honored the tsar's ukase as a matter of practicality, the government response was irritation. Protests were entered at St. Petersburg by the Americans and by the British, as well as by other European powers.

In the meantime the United States and Britain confronted another challenge that had a significant bearing on the Russian problem. In 1820 and 1821, Spain's colonies in South and Central America, including Mexico, successfully revolted, throwing off the colonial domination of three centuries. Britain supported the dismantling of Spain's American empire for both practical and philosophical reasons, as did the United States. Spain had prohibited foreign trade in the Americas; the newly established republics represented a significant new trading market. As Spain contemplated a reconquest, U.S. Secretary of State John Quincy Adams persuaded President James Monroe to take a bold step. In 1823, Monroe published a new unilateral, hemispheric policy for the United States: henceforth, the United States would oppose the establishment of any further European colonies in the Americas.

Although aimed primarily at Spain, the policy included Russia as well, for the tsar's assertion of Russian territory south to the fifty-first latitude could be interpreted as an extension of the Russian colony, that is, the establishing of new colonial territory in the hemisphere. Moreover, Russian activities in California and Hawai'i over the previous fifteen years suggested that Russia might still seriously be contemplating a substantial extension of its American empire. With these considerations in mind, through the American ambassador in St. Petersburg, Henry Middleton, Adams sent a strong note to the Russian government declaring that the United States would ignore the Russian claim below 54° 40' north latitude, and south of that limit they would trade where they wished. Moreover, in a sharp warning, Adams told the emperor that the United States would "contest the right of Russia to *any* territorial establishment on this continent."[1]

This was a rash flinging of the gauntlet back at Russia, for the United States had dismantled its navy after the War of 1812 and was in no position to enforce its proclamation. But Adams calculated, correctly as it turned out, that Russia would not risk confrontation. In fact, Adams followed his stern letter with an invitation to the Russians to negotiate the matter of trade on the coast. As it happened, the Russians were very willing to discuss the matter and eagerly accepted Adams's invitation. Talks progressed quickly, and in 1824 the two parties announced a new treaty. Remarkably, the treaty opened Russian America to American trade and recognized that Russian territory ceased at 54° 40' north latitude, Dixon Entrance; colonization was prohibited below that line. In addition, the treaty declared that the area between Dixon Entrance and the forty-ninth latitude would be open equally to navigation and trade by both countries.

This was a stunning about-face. In three years Russia went from a complete prohibition of American trade to a nearly complete acceptance of it. What had caused this remarkable turn? For an answer we must look again at the bedevilment of settlement and economic development in northern latitudes: supply. In fact, no one in Russia who had not been to Russian America appreciated the magnitude of the problem of supply. The board of directors did not understand it and neither did the navy, as yet without much experience in the colony. The person who came to understand supply acutely, and to explain it to St. Petersburg, was Captain-Lieutenant Matvei Murav'ev, the first governor after Baranov to serve a full five-year term as mandated by the second charter.

Murav'ev had sailed with Golovnin on his inspection of the colony in 1817 through 1819, serving with distinction. Upon his return the board and the navy had appointed him to replace Lieutenant Semen Ianovskii, who had been left as acting governor in the colony when Hagemeister departed in 1819 to return Baranov to Russia. It fell to Murav'ev to implement the tsar's ukase (imperial decree) forbidding foreign shipping. The American traders could not afford to risk confiscation of their vessels and cargoes, and as each one called at Sitka in 1821 to learn the details of Russian policy, the governor told them they must leave the area and could not operate north of the fifty-first latitude. As ordered, the governor also refused to purchase their cargoes.

At first Murav'ev expected that supplies for the colony would come on the company ship *Elisaveta* and on the navy brig *Riurik*, both due to arrive in 1821. But the *Elisaveta* was badly damaged in a storm and had been salvaged at Capetown, and the *Riurik* was small, the navy said, and it had no room for cargo. The board in St. Petersburg had planned a third vessel but at the last moment, persuaded by one of the directors that there must be adequate supplies stocked in the colony, canceled the voyage. Then word came from California telling of crop failures there.

The situation at Sitka became desperate, and Murav'ev took matters into his own hands. He dispatched RAC lieutenant Arvid Etholen in the brig *Golovnin* to Hawai'i for food. Etholen stopped at San Francisco where he obtained wheat, and then in Hawai'i where he purchased an American trading vessel, the *Arab*, and her cargo, taking both ships to Sitka. Murav'ev then sent the *Riurik* to Hawai'i and California for still more supplies. With these cargoes he was able to relieve a critical situation at Sitka and elsewhere in the colony.

When the board of directors in St. Petersburg received Murav'ev's dispatches explaining his actions and the circumstances that prompted them, it finally began to appreciate the challenge of supplying a nonproductive, extractive outpost half a globe away, what one historian has called "the tyranny of distance."[2] They realized that old Baranov had actually been quite shrewd in establishing a colonial lifeline with the American maritime fur traders. The tsar understood this as well, so he ordered his commissioners to produce an understanding with the United States regarding trade in Russian America.

Britain moved quickly to make the settlement complete. The United States had ignored the British interest in the coast when negotiating privately with Russia for free access to the region, much to Britain's irritation. The Hudson's Bay Company (HBC), which in 1821 had forced a merger with the North West Company, particularly needed a clarification of England's status. In negotiations with the Russians, then, the British sought to bring finality to the question of territorial claims in the Northwest. As it had with the United States, Russia conceded the slim likelihood of expanding south of Dixon Entrance. The result was the Anglo-Russian Treaty of 1825, which not only opened the coast to British traders on the same terms as those for the Americans but for the first time established clear and permanent boundaries for Russian America. Russia's occupation of the Alexander Archipelago was formally recognized by setting the southern boundary of Russian America at 54° 40' north latitude; the line ran northeast up Portland Canal and then followed "the crest of the coast mountains" northward. A similar description was used for the area north of Lynn Canal and Glacier Bay and northward again along the coast to Mount St. Elias at 141° west longitude.

Above that point a different criteria applied. Negotiators assumed that within decades the HBC's new initiative in the northwest Rocky Mountains would bring its hunters within range of Russian trappers moving northeasterly from the coast. The two countries faced a rare opportunity to delineate each country's sphere of influence clearly before their colonial companies' apparent future expansion toward one another in Northwest America might lead to clashes over furbearing territory deep in the American interior. Moreover, the Russians had begun exploration along the Bering and Arctic coasts, though they had not yet penetrated very far eastward. With these considerations the diplomats selected 141 degrees as the boundary between Canada and Russian America from Mount St. Elias northward to the Arctic Coast. Thus were the boundaries of Russian America, later Alaska, established, and the four-nation contest for sovereignty on the Northwest Coast brought to a close, with the exception of the division of the Oregon Country by Britain and the United States in 1846. These boundaries have stood to the present day, though not without challenge and controversy.[3]

GOVERNING RUSSIAN AMERICA

The new naval governors and the reorganized RAC brought a more systematic, businesslike structure to colonial Russian America. Although they brought differing levels of competence and energy to the task, the governors through the middle decades of the century ran the colony responsibly and effectively. Their chief responsibility was to manage colonial affairs in such a way as to generate profit for the stockholders and avoid conflict, for the RAC was a quasi state-supported capitalist monopoly. As such it was highly exploitative, both of the Native populations and of its own personnel. It was also inefficient and wasteful. Nonetheless, the governors supported scientific and geographic exploration, expanded the area under Russian control, and endorsed education and the Orthodox mission.

But colonial administration presented several endemic challenges. Supplying Russian America adequately still remained problematic. Food and manufactured goods had to be purchased wherever they could be had, often in Hawai'i, California, or Chile. Neither could be brought economically or in a timely manner across Siberia or around the world by sea from Kronstadt. Labor also proved difficult, for there were few incentives (and many disadvantages) for workers to go to the colony. The Natives also presented a constant challenge. The Tlingit were never completely subdued and often attacked Russians when they were outside the fort at Sitka. The Tlingit greatly strengthened their position by regularly trading fresh deer meat to the Russians and by learning to grow potatoes on which the colony became heavily dependent. Russia never committed the resources necessary to completely sustain its colony, and it could not achieve self-sufficiency. But perhaps the most significant challenge for the governors was finding new resources to develop and new markets to absorb them.

The first permanent naval governor, Matvei Murav'ev, arrived at Sitka in the fall of 1820. He immediately set about organizing what the board considered a proper colonial establishment. He rebuilt the fortifications at Sitka and constructed many new buildings, including a spacious home on the mount overlooking Sitka Harbor, which came to be called "Baranov's Castle." He also ended the banishment of the Tlingit from Sitka proper. After the conquest of Sitka the Indians had been forced to live on islands north and south of the port, but Murav'ev invited them to make their homes adjacent to the Russian settlement, which they were happy to do. To protect the town, the governor constructed a stout palisade all around the perimeter, surmounted with cannon, and punctuated by a heavy gate. The Indians were permitted inside the compound on certain days but never at night, when sentries patrolled the streets, guaranteeing security by the exchange of passwords. He also divided the colony into administrative districts, with regional offices at Unalaska and Kodiak, in addition to the colonial capital at Sitka. Three additional districts would be created under later administrations: St. Michael (near the mouth of the Yukon River), Atkha, and Kuril. In an effort to find new resources the board of directors arranged for an expedition to cross the Alaska Peninsula and establish a post at the mouth of the Nushagak River, Novo Aleksandrovsk. Headed by Petr Korsakovskii and later Fedor Kolmakov, this effort was successful. On his own initiative Murav'ev sent an exploring expedition, with RAC lieutenants Arvid Etholen and Vasilii Khromchenko and assistant navigator Ivan Iakovlevich Vasil'ev, along the north coast of Bristol Bay and the mouth of the Kuskokwim River and Norton Sound. Murav'ev also discussed with the board the advisability of moving the colonial capital to Kodiak, discussions that were for the moment inconclusive.[4]

Meanwhile, in Russia, Tsar Alexander died suddenly while vacationing with his wife in the Crimea. The experience of Napoleon's invasion of Russia in 1812 had changed Alexander. Although Moscow had burned,

Alexander and the brilliant general Prince Mikhail I. Kutuzov had withstood the assault, contributing significantly to Napoleon's downfall. But after the victory Alexander became increasingly religious, verging on mysticism, and lost his zeal for rule. Confusion about the succession after his death in December 1825 led to a short-lived reformist revolt, the Decembrist Rising. Alexander was succeeded by his much younger brother Nicholas I. These changes had little effect in the colony, save that any officer suspected of sympathy with the Decembrists was regarded as tainted.

In 1825, Petr Egorovich Chistiakov replaced Murav'ev as governor of the colony. Honest and a liberal, Chistiakov attacked the unsanctioned liaisons between Russian employees and Native women, though with little long-term success, partly because he entered into such a union himself. Promoted twice during his tenure, he made a number of innovative changes, including introducing foxes to the Rat Islands and establishing a company post at Atka Island. He also sent Arvid Etholen, later himself to be governor, to the Kuril Islands, where the company lieutenant established a permanent, lucrative post on Urup. Chistiakov dispatched Ivan Iakovlevich Vasil'ev in 1829 on an expedition to explore the region west of Aleksandrovskii Redoubt on the Nushagak River. Over the next several years Vasil'ev explored the Nushagak and other rivers in the region and crossed over the divide to the Kuskokwim River. His work introduced the Russians to Natives of the area and clarified the geography of the Nushagak-Kuskokwim region. In 1829, Chistiakov sent Khlebnikov, still the chief civilian company officer, to California for grain. Khlebnikov found none there but obtained a cargo in Chile, a source unavailable before the South American revolution but too distant from Russian America to be very practical.

At this time the RAC began to build ships for Russian America at Okhotsk and at Sitka, and Chistiakov ordered construction of a series of smaller vessels for coastal work. Between 1827 and 1829 he saw six completed, including the three-hundred-ton *Urup*. The colony in America was active and expanding, though conditions for its employees were still in need of significant improvement, and the supplies of furs showed unmistakable signs of exhaustion. In 1830 the board appointed Ferdinand Petrovich (later Baron von) Wrangel to relieve Chistiakov. Wrangel was one of the most enlightened of all the Russian American governors. A veteran of several major expeditions, including one into the Arctic under his own command from 1810 through 1814, he brought his new wife with him to the colony. She would be an important ally in the reforms and organization Wrangel introduced to colonial administration. Among other changes, he improved relations with Natives, upgraded working conditions for laborers, and moved to stabilize resources by stringent conservation measures. In 1833 he attempted to start the company in the whaling industry, just then beginning to be heavily exploited by the Americans, but the RAC did not have the resources to pursue this initiative. Wrangel consolidated all ship-building in the colony at Sitka, closing ship works in Ross, Kodiak, and Resurrection Bay. He also established a sawmill at Ozerskoi Redoubt near Sitka, only the second sawmill on the Pacific Coast (the other was an HBC installation at Fort Vancouver on the Columbia River). Wrangel made extensive inspection tours around the colony and encouraged exploration. Building on the work of Vasil'ev, in 1833 Wrangel ordered Lieutenant Mikhail Teben'kov to proceed to Norton Sound to establish a post, which became Mikhailovskii Redoubt (St. Michael), near the mouth of the Yukon River. From there Andrei Glazunov ascended the Yukon (known to the Russians as the Kvikpak), turned up the Anvik River, crossed over to the headwaters of the Unalakleet, and descended that river to the coast. On another trek Glazunov crossed the portage between the Yukon and Kuskokwim Rivers and at one point attempted to find a passage through the Alaska Range to Cook Inlet. In 1836, Glazunov established a Russian post, Russian Mission, on the lower Yukon.

In the meantime Wrangel went to California to negotiate with Mexican officials for an expansion of Fort Ross. This led to establishment of a plantation inland near the mouth of the Russian River, which greatly improved the grain yields of the post. Also that year he sent Etholen to patrol the straits at the mouth of the Stikine River, having learned that the HBC intended to establish a post on that river just inside the British-Russian boundary. Although the British had the right of navigation to waterways crossing the Russian coastal

Baron Ferdinand Petrovich von Wrangel, governor of Russian America, 1830–35. Alaska State Library P20.027.

strip from the Interior, that right did not include the privilege of constructing fortifications. The reason for the planned British post was the intention of George Simpson, the western director (Columbia District) of the reorganized HBC, to strengthen British presence along the coast to force out the American maritime traders.

Wrangel was much concerned about the British plan, which he rightly interpreted as an invasion of now-recognized Russian territory. In response, Wrangell sent Captain-Lieutenant Dionisii Zarembo in 1834 to the straits to found a Russian post, Dionysius Redoubt, before the British could carry out their scheme. Later in the year, after the Russian post was completed, the HBC vessel *Dryad* arrived with men and material for construction of the British fort. Simpson had not anticipated Russian resistance, concluding that the Russians were too inefficient to be able to defend their colony against commercial interlopers. However, pursuant to Wrangel's orders, Zarembo warned the *Dryad* away by firing a cannon from the post. After several days of fruitless negotiations, the British gave up and headed back to Fort Vancouver, the HBC Columbia District headquarters. The British protested their treatment by the Russians at the Stikine River, and the incident generated negotiations between the RAC and the HBC that would eventually be fruitful to both. Wrangel also moved to reform the Orthodox mission in Russian America. He insisted upon the recall of a corrupt priest and the reassignment of a number of others. In particular, he requested that Father Ioann Veniaminov be transferred from Unalaska to Sitka, which he was in 1834. Veniaminov was a remarkable individual and his life and career warrant closer consideration, which I return to shortly.

In 1835, Wrangel left the colony for Mexico, where he hoped to negotiate a trade agreement that would help alleviate the supply problem in Russian America and also secure Russian title to the colony at Fort Ross. Mexico was willing to trade and to grant title to Russia's California post, but only if Russia would formally recognize the Mexican revolutionary government. Tsar Nicholas, a determined autocrat, would not do this, so the talks ended inconclusively. In 1839 the RAC asked Wrangel to go to Berlin for a conference with Sir George Simpson of the HBC. Originally distrustful of Wrangel, who had thwarted his plans to use the Stikine River, Simpson found himself drawn to and ultimately respectful of now Admiral Wrangel, and the two negotiated the important Stikine River lease.

By the terms of this remarkable document, the HBC would annually supply the RAC at Sitka with food and manufactured goods in return for the right to use the coastal area adjacent to the Alexander Archipelago as well as to man Dionysius Redoubt (renamed Fort Stikine by the HBC). The ten-year, renewable agreement confirmed the HBC's right to navigate the Stikine River. The lease did much to relieve, though not entirely solve, the problem of Russian American supply. As an indication of its importance, two years after the agreement was signed, Russia capitulated to growing settlement in California and to Ross's continuing cost and lack of productivity and liquidated the post there, selling it and the plantation to the Swede Johannes (John) Sutter.

Wrangel's successor at Sitka was Ivan Kupreianov, a full naval captain who had spent much of his career in the Baltic. During his tenure Kupreianov made annual inspection tours of the colony, including an important visit to Atka in 1837. The encroachment of American traders along the coast north of 54° 40' north latitude was a continuing problem for the RAC. The 1824 treaty opened the coast to the Americans for ten years; American ships could trade north of 54° 40' as long as they did not approach any area actually occupied by Russians. But the Americans had traded much more freely along the coast during the ensuing ten-year period than was comfortable for the Russians. As soon as the treaty period expired, the Russians closed the area above 54 degrees 40 to the Americans, notifying Washington through the Russian ambassador. Not only was this a problem for those ships trading with Natives in the archipelago, but the whaling ships in the Bering Sea often stopped at coastal villages to trade and to obtain local labor for the duration of their summer voyages. Not surprisingly, the United States sought continuation of the right of access, claiming that as long as they did not approach Russian posts, they were acting as free traders, an interpretation the Russians rejected. As always, however, the Russians needed American friendship as an antidote to British power in the north. The tsar's government was unwilling to extend the American privilege because of its economic cost to the RAC, but it did not want to push the Americans too hard.

An opportunity to test how volatile the expiration of the treaty-right might be came soon. In 1836 the American brig *Loriot* under Robert Blinn sailed from Hawai'i to the Northwest Coast for provisions and trade. The vessel anchored off uninhabited Forrester Island at Dixon Entrance, just north of the 54° 40' latitude boundary. But before a boat party could get ashore, an RAC ship appeared and forced the Americans to leave. Upon the ship's return to the United States, the vessel's owners protested, claiming financial loss. The incident forced both governments to assess their policies. Each country needed the other, and neither wished nor could afford war. The common element was Britain. Should Britain move against Russia in the Northwest, Russia would need the United States as an ally. The United States needed the coastal access and did not wish to see Britain secure any advantage in the region. Thus Kupreianov was instructed to monitor American activity, but not to be so confrontational as to cause further incidents. In the United States, in his annual message to Congress in 1838, President Martin Van Buren reiterated the American contention that the United States had the right to trade with Natives at unoccupied points along the coast. Both nations let the matter rest at that uneasy and unresolved point.

Kupreianov continued the exploration program in the north, the RAC hoping to locate new access to the Interior and find new fur resources. In 1838, Aleksandr Kashevarov, a Creole born on Kodiak, went to the Arctic Coast to explore the last portion of shore yet uncharted, running east two hundred miles from Point Barrow to the Return Islands. Kashevarov had graduated from the Kronstadt Navigation School and achieved the rank of sublieutenant and a considerable reputation as a navigator and cartographer. Kashevarov's father, Filipp Artamonovich Kashevarov, was one of the serfs who had come to the colony with the Orthodox mission in 1794 and was the progenitor of a very large family, many of whom rose to prominence in Russian America.

In separate expeditions in 1826, the British explorers Frederick Beechey and Sir John Franklin had reached Point Barrow (from the west) and the Return Islands (from the east) respectively, but the area in between had not been seen (the Return Islands are between Prudhoe Bay and the mouth of the Kuparuk River). Using a *baidara* (a large, open skin boat) and three *baidarkas* (single kayaks), Kashevarov reached Point Barrow but was only able to get thirty miles farther east before returning because of ice. Unknown to Kashevarov, an English (HBC) party working west from the Return Islands took to the shore and reached Point Barrow by foot just a few weeks after Kashevarov had been there.

In 1837 the Creole Petr Malakhov went up the Unalakleet River and crossed over the Yukon, where he ascended to the village of Nulato and discovered the Koyukuk River. He and his party wintered over on the Yukon and in spring became the first Europeans to float down the river to the sea, probably through Shageluk Slough and the Innoko River. Subsequently,

Malakhov twice attempted to establish a post at Nulato but was unsuccessful because of a smallpox epidemic that swept the country at the time. The Natives blamed the Russians for the epidemic, and Malakhov and his party were in considerable danger while in the country. Nonetheless, the region represented an important untapped source of furs. The Russians were persistent, establishing a station at Ikomiut (Russian Mission) on the lower Yukon in 1836 and a post at Nulato in 1839. Nulato was the deepest penetration by the Russians into the Alaskan interior. From there the Natives brought furs from farther upriver and from the low mountain country both north and south of the river.

Kupreianov was relieved in 1840 by Arvid Etholen, now a highly distinguished seaman and administrator with considerable experience in the colony and as assistant manager. He also pushed the northern initiative. He established a post at the Unalakleet River on Norton Sound and in 1842 encouraged the expedition of Lieutenant Lavrentii Zagoskin, perhaps the most important of Russia's northern expeditions in North America. Leaving from the Unalakleet post, Zagoskin and his party crossed the divide to the Yukon and working from Russian Mission, they established a new post at the mouth of the Koyukuk River, Nulato. From there they worked up the Koyukuk and then crossed eastward to the middle Yukon. The party's relations with the region's Natives were good, preparing the way for later hunting forays that continued into the 1860s but never with the success the RAC had hoped. Etholen also sent parties to explore the Susitna River drainage (Petr Malakhov) and the Copper River and Tazlina Glacier area (Spiridon Grigov'ev). The Copper River party encountered hostile Natives, however, and had to flee the country.

As the second charter of the RAC expired in 1841, the board of directors worked to make colony administration still more efficient in the third charter, which Tsar Nicholas granted in 1841 but which the government did not formally promulgate until 1844. The new grant made no substantive changes but did address much more fully the company's relations with and treatment of Natives. Bishop Innocent, patriarch of the Orthodox mission in Russian America who had traveled widely and whose career will be discussed later, was in St. Petersburg in the interim and may have contributed. The document categorized Natives based on the degree to which they were controlled by the Russians or lived in proximity to them. Some of the provisions stand out in comparison with the Russians' previous practice and with the habits of other Europeans in dealing with colonial indigenes. Those

Bishop Innocent, Ioann Veniaminov, a man of extraordinary talent with a reputation for effective pastoral support. Alaska State Library P20.031.

Natives who did not accept Christianity were to be left free to practice traditional rituals; no coercion was to be used to force conversions.

Etholen implemented these more enlightened principles immediately, improving relations with the Natives significantly. He improved the rates paid for pelts that had first been established by Wrangel, and in 1845 he issued an order that no company employee was to strike any indigenous person except in defense of his life. In fact, the Tlingit had never suffered as cruelly as the Aleut, and the new provisions represented as much recognition of the Tlingit's independence as it did liberal ideals. Highly organized into exogamous, competitive clans, Tlingit villages in the thickly timbered island archipelago were much more defensible than the unforested Aleutian Islands. Indirect and intermittent contact had probably eased the introduction of virgin soil epidemics among them, leaving their population of perhaps sixteen thousand reasonably intact until the smallpox epidemic of the late 1830s. Although the Russians established several posts in the archipelago, they always traveled the region in some jeopardy, for the Tlingit were unpredictable and quick to take offense. The arms they procured through trade with the Americans and the British made them especially dangerous. At no time during more than six decades in the archipelago could the Russians relax their guard.

The Tlingit women had charge of trade negotiations, and through their control of prices sometimes reduced the Russians to abject dependence on the food that the Indians supplied, including fish and later potatoes; when the women cut off the trade because they did not get the prices they demanded, or for any other reason, the Russians were left in dire circumstances. By this tactic the Tlingit kept the Russians close to their settlements and inhibited investigation or exploitation of the Interior, the access to which the Tlingit jealously guarded. In addition, a strong sense of retributive justice prevailed in Tlingit culture; any slight or injury had to be recompensed by the offender in like terms or a substitution acceptable to the offended party. The Tlingit did not forget or forgive behaviors or incidents that were offenses in their culture, and they might exact a revenge years or even decades after the event if the recompense were not paid. Only the smallpox epidemic weakened Tlingit ferocity, although not enough to eliminate them as a threat to the Russians.

In implementing the Stikine River lease, Etholen worked with the HBC to eliminate the trade in liquor north of fifty degrees. Dependent as they were on the Tlingit, the Russians had protested American and English use of liquor as a trade item both because of its volatility and because it drove up the prices for furs; if they could not get liquor, the Indians demanded much higher value in other goods. By the mid-1840s most of the American coastal trade had ceased because of a collapse in the fur market, and now that they had the agreement with the RAC, HBC officials found it in their best interests to cooperate. The two companies signed an agreement in 1842 that effectively eliminated liquor trade along the coast until after the sale of Russian America to the United States in 1867.

Sitka's significance on the Northwest Coast and the RAC initiative in the colony approached a high point with the tenure of Mikhail Teben'kov, who replaced Etholen as governor in 1845. Teben'kov continued exploration activities, sending the Creole Illarion Arkhimandritov to do additional charting in Cook Inlet (including the vicinity of present-day Anchorage), Prince William Sound, and along Kodiak Island.[5] In 1848, Ruf Serebrennikov, a Creole educated in St. Petersburg, went to the Copper River but with even more disastrous results than the failed 1843 expedition. The Ahtna Indians of the region sold furs exclusively to the Tlingit, despite Russian attempts to persuade them to trade with posts on Cook Inlet. Serebrennikov and eleven men ascended the Copper to Taral, the village at the mouth of the Chitina, where they wintered over. In the spring they ascended the Tazlina River to the Tazlina Glacier (visible today from the Glenn Highway). Returning to Taral, some sort of altercation with a Native headman prompted the Natives to kill all in the party, including one man who escaped but was eventually hunted down. The Natives later returned Serebrennikov's journal to the Russian post at Nuchek in Prince William Sound.[6]

At this same time relations with the Tlingit continued to be uncertain. In 1846 and 1847 large numbers of the Indians gathered at Sitka, probably combining several clan potlatches with the opportunity to carry on the potato trade. Large potlatches sometimes included the killing of slaves, and Teben'kov was disturbed to learn that eight females had been killed at the 1847 gathering. By persuasion and ransom he prevented the deaths of ten men and several additional women. Just several years later, however, relations with the Indians would sour over an incident with which the Russians had little to do. In 1852 a Stikine party from Wrangel came by invitation to a potlatch at Sitka, where they were all killed by their hosts. The killers placed all the bodies in a canoe that they floated onto Japonski Island in Sitka Harbor. Not long after, in retaliation, a party of Stikines attacked a small Russian settlement at a hot springs on the forest shore south of Sitka, burning all the buildings and killing one employee before the remainder fled into the mountains, eventually making their way overland to the town. Not surprisingly, the Stikine people held the Russians partly responsible for the Sitka massacre since it had happened in territory over which they exerted some control. To the Russians the incident demonstrated the continuing threat represented by Tlingit cultural forms and rituals the Russians little understood or appreciated. As well, it seemed to demonstrate that the Tlingit viewed interaction with the Russians as a significant element in interclan or intraclan rivalries within Tlingit society. In any case the incident reinforced the Russian perception that they could not take the Tlingit for granted.[7]

The great California gold rush occurred during Teben'kov's tenure and presented the colony with substantial new challenges. At first, Teben'kov sought to take advantage of the sudden new market developing at San Francisco and environs by sending whatever goods stored in Sitka he thought the argonauts might buy. He also sent mining engineer Petr Doroshin, newly arrived in the colony on a five-year mineralogical survey, to try his hand at prospecting. Working with four Russians and six Tlingit Indians, Doroshin was successful. From 174 tons of sand in the upper Yuba River they washed more than eleven pounds of gold. With the proceeds they purchased a ship for their return trip and delivered more than thirty-nine thousand rubles of gold and silver coin to the RAC office at Sitka.

Merchandising was less successful. Teben'kov's first two cargoes sold well; among them were included three prefabricated houses cut at Sitka and sent ready for assembly. But Teben'kov was hardly alone in trying to exploit the new market, and most could do it much more cheaply and efficiently than he because of the cost of transporting the product from the Far North; Teben'kov's agents were able to sell only a portion of the third Russian cargo. More serious was a shortage of grain occasioned by farmers abandoning their crops for the gold fields. Not only did Sitka's normal California supply atrophy, but so did the increasingly used alternative in Chile, distant but needed. Inconveniently, the HBC exacerbated the situation for the Russians by refusing to renew the Stikine River lease at this time. The United States had forced a division of the Oregon Country, and the HBC moved its headquarters to Victoria, British Columbia, leaving its Puget Sound agricultural lands to the Americans. Fortunately, Teben'kov was able to increase purchases from the Tlingit, whose supplies to the Russians of potatoes and also black-tailed deer and halibut reached their highest levels during these years.[8]

Teben'kov did much to refurbish the town itself during his tenure. Two additional sawmills were constructed and the original rebuilt, and one flour mill was repaired and another built. The town palisade was reinforced and the battery rebuilt. A dry dock for retimbering and fitting new masts was improved, and the foundation for a diocesan cathedral was laid. After three years of construction, Bishop Innocent consecrated St. Michael the Archangel church in 1850. Teben'kov's true monument, however, was the production of a major atlas of the coasts of Russian America and Siberia, drawn by the Creole navigator Mikhail Kadin and engraved on copper plates by Koz'ma Terent'ev, also a Creole, and then taken to St. Petersburg for printing. Years of careful surveys by Russian and Creole shipmasters and explorers had produced quite thorough and accurate data, which now could be summarized and presented. Teben'kov's atlas would be used for decades after the American purchase. Returned from California, Doroshin continued his colonial-wide survey of resources. In several trips to the Kenai Peninsula he found shows of gold in several creeks flowing into Kenai Bay (Cook Inlet) but did not have time to follow them to their sources. Coal deposits at several places, especially on the neck of the Alaska Peninsula near Lake Iliamna, excited his enthusiasm, but he dismissed deposits on Unga Island as of too low grade to support development.

In 1850 the board of directors sent Captain Nikolai Rozenberg to take over management of the colony. His appointment coincided with the board's decision to purchase and commission a number of large vessels for use in supplying the colony. At the same time, a U.S. firm in San Francisco, the American Russian Commercial Company, began a trade in lake ice between the colony and California. In 1852 the company bought 250 tons of ice at Sitka and in ensuing years bought ice both at Sitka and at Woody

Island near Kodiak. More significant, however, was the rapidly growing population of San Francisco. The new city boomed in the gold rush era, and while initial Russian attempts to develop a market there were not encouraging, growth was so swift that the RAC found modest but steady sales of both fish and timber. As long as real estate quadrupled in value in a year's time and shares in gold mines and prospects outpaced even real estate, San Franciscans found it cheaper in the 1850s to purchase fish and timber from the Russians than to develop their own stores of these same resources. RAC officials eagerly urged expansion of the California market. Ultimately, however, as gold fever subsided and more rational development replaced it, the California suppliers would easily undersell the Russians.

FORCES SHAPING RUSSIAN AMERICA:
WESTWARD EXPANSION AND THE CRIMEAN WAR

In fact, changed conditions in the Oregon Country and in California raised considerable concern in Russian America and in St. Petersburg at this time. Following the fur trapper era in the mountains of the American West, a few missionaries and settlers had filtered into the country. Beginning in 1841, however, this trickle became a flood as first about ten wagons negotiated what became known as the Oregon Trail in 1842, then nearly one hundred in 1843, and nearer to one thousand in 1844. These pioneers were motivated by what they perceived as economic opportunity. They came to harvest the land's natural abundance, to plant new crops, and to market these in the east, shipping them from ports in California and at the mouth of the Willamette River in Oregon Country. Stories of yields twice those in the fertile Ohio Basin and the Illinois Plateau drew them across the Great Plains, which they viewed as arid and worthless, to the lush valleys of the Pacific Slope. By the time of the U.S. presidential election in 1844, there were nearly five thousand Americans in Mexican California and about the same number living along the Willamette River in the Oregon Country, still governed by the terms of the 1818 agreement between Britain and the United States—which is to say, not governed, because by the convention neither country could exercise sovereignty within the region. Also by this time perhaps seven thousand Americans were living in Texas, which had successfully revolted from Mexico in 1836 and had since functioned as an independent country, denied entry into the United States by the slavery dispute building there.[9]

Sensing the inevitable, George Simpson had removed HBC headquarters to Victoria on Vancouver Island in 1843.[10] In the American presidential campaign in 1844, James K. Polk had run on a platform of aggressive, westward expansion. Since the western areas outside the United States had so many Americans living in them already, Polk reasoned, the United States ought to extend its borders to embrace them, so that all Americans could live on U.S. soil and be governed by U.S. laws. One of his campaign slogans was "54–40 or Fight!" suggesting a willingness, false but effective, to fight Britain for all of the Oregon Country. Polk won the election, and before a new Congress could be seated, the outgoing solons annexed Texas, despite Mexican warnings that such a move would be considered grounds for war. As soon as Polk was inaugurated, he notified Britain that at the end of the requisite year called for in the 1818 convention, he intended to terminate the agreement on Oregon. Britain recognized that war in the forested mountains of the Pacific Northwest would be impractical. Realizing that the United States would not yield the land west of the Columbia, they agreed in 1846 to an extension of the boundary along 49° north latitude, with the exception of Vancouver Island, which Britain insisted on having complete, even though it extends below forty-nine degrees. The Oregon Treaty brought Euro-American government and civil law to the vast region between 42° and 54° 40' north latitude for the first time.

In the same year, however, Mexico—doubly threatened by the United States in Texas and California—did not resist a war that the Americans seemed determined to launch. Although the Mexican War was highly divisive in the United States, as many Americans protested their government's willingness to fight a war of conquest and aggression, American forces prevailed, defeating the Mexicans at Buena Vista below Texas, at Vera Cruz and Mexico City, and at several places in California. By the Treaty of Guadalupe Hidalgo in 1848, the United States paid Mexico $15 million for the land west of Texas below forty-two degrees, south to a line running roughly from San Diego Bay eastward to El Paso on the Rio Grande. The area of land added to the United States by these actions, in just three years, was vast, nearly equal in size to the area that the nation's boundaries had encompassed previously. The Americans justified their actions by a notion they called "manifest destiny," a new term for an old idea, offered by a newspaper editor some weeks after Polk's election by way of explanation. It was the destiny of the United States, the idea ran, to extend its borders from the Atlantic to the Pacific Oceans; that destiny had been made manifest by the fact that by 1844 there were already five thousand Americans in the Oregon Country, five thousand in California, and seven thousand in Texas; this was incontrovertible evidence, advocates insisted, that the nation's destiny lay beyond its 1844 limits.

Europeans were astonished at this unabashed and lightning quick aggrandizement of national appetite but none more than the Russians who now, it seemed, had their own uncomfortable destiny to share the continent with an aggressive people who appeared unwilling to be deterred by any consideration in their lust for land and resources, certainly not by the national boundaries of other powers. Anxiety over the meaning of these events and uncertainty of American intentions would plague the Russians for the remainder of their vulnerable tenure in North America. Governor Rozenberg was unable to deal with these new circumstances, however, for he was not well. In 1853 the board replaced him temporarily with Captain Aleksandr Rudakov, who held the post for a year, pending the arrival of Captain Stepan Voevodskii, who would serve as chief manager until 1859.

Voevodskii quickly found himself in a precarious position, for the Crimean War loomed in Russia. Ostensibly, the conflict developed over Tsar Nicholas's insistence on the right to protect Orthodox believers in a group of small principalities on the Russo-Turk border, near the outlet of the Danube River into the Black Sea (Danubia). In the longer view, however, France and Britain, fearing Russian power in Southeast Europe, supported Turk resistance and when the Russian fleet destroyed a Turkish squadron at Sinope on the Black Sea southern shore, a joint Franco-British flotilla entered the sea. The war's major battles were fought on the Crimean Peninsula in the Ukraine, on the northern shore of the Black Sea. The battles near Sebastopol were particularly bloody, the Russians ultimately sinking Turkish ships and blowing up their forts. Nicholas contracted pneumonia while helping to lead the campaign; he died on 2 March and his son, Alexander II, succeeded him. Alexander was disposed to end the war and did so a year later, accepting terms dictated by the allies meeting in Vienna.

Although Russian America lay halfway around the planet from the Crimea, events there significantly affected the colony and its future. Concerned about Russian America's vulnerability, Nicholas's government had requested, and the English Parliament approved, a proposal from the RAC and the HBC that the Northwest Coast of North America be considered neutral territory during the war. The HBC feared for Victoria even as the

RAC feared for Sitka and Kodiak. But agreement regarding North America did nothing for Petropavlovsk, on the other side of the Pacific, and equally vulnerable to French and British attack from the sea. As the RAC feared, in 1854 a combined Franco-British task force approached the small colonial outpost and prepared to shell the defenses and sack the town. Much to their surprise, however, they were opposed by fire from shore batteries of which the attackers had no knowledge. The defenders held throughout the first day of bombardment and again through a second day. After several days for repairs the fleet attacked again, this time knocking out several batteries. Subsequently, marines made a landing south of the town but, unable to secure their position, withdrew. The allied attack had failed, and in humiliation the English commander committed suicide. The fleet retired south for the winter.

Petropavlovsk's savior was not Governor Voevodskii. Instead, two of the shore batteries were commanded by Prince Dimitrii Maksutov, the future and last governor of Russian America, and his brother Aleksandr. But the power behind these events was Nikolai Murav'ev, governor-general of Eastern Siberia (not to be confused with Matvei Murav'ev, who had been governor of Russian America from 1820 to 1825), a strong, intelligent, and determined leader. Appointed governor in 1847, Murav'ev at once determined that Russia must take back control of the Amur Basin, lost in the Treaty of Nerchinsk in 1689. He recognized the rich, undeveloped resources of the region, which could be much more easily defended than Russian America. He became persuaded that Russia should devise a new Far East policy around intensive cultivation of Siberia's agricultural, fur, and mineral potential, and he became an articulate, forceful, and effective advocate of such a policy. Officials in the tsar's government still feared that any Russian move toward Amuria would reverberate in Kyakhta, but Murav'ev successfully appealed to Nicholas's patriotism. Nicholas supported his new governor of eastern Siberia, but he made it plain that the policy should succeed. "Once the Russian flag has been raised," he averred, "it must not be lowered."

Over the next several years, through daring and negotiation, Murav'ev gradually opened the Amur River to Russian trade and established a number of Russian settlements, including Aian (Nikolaevsk) at the river's mouth in 1850. He was aided by the fact that the Chinese had evacuated much of the Native population from the upper river region so that they might not be corrupted or subjugated by bordering Mongolians. In fact, China no longer even patrolled the river's lower twenty-five hundred miles. At the outbreak of the Crimean War, Murav'ev used the Amur to supply and to fortify Petropavlovsk. This had strengthened the port enough for the Russians to defeat the allied fleet.

The combined British and French fleet returned to Petropavlovsk in early 1856, refitted and in a high state of pique. This time they were successful in bombing the remote port, for the Russians had chosen not to defend against what they knew would be a stronger and more determined force. They had even removed most of the furs cached at the town. The British and French admirals quickly realized that theirs was a Pyhrric victory. For the allies there was little point in occupying a remote post on the Siberian coast, particularly not with the negotiators about to decide the future half a world away in Vienna.

Alexander's acceptance of the allies' terms at Vienna was a harbinger of changes in Russia that would influence the future of Russian America. The outcome of the war demonstrated Russia's backwardness when compared with Europe's other powers. To move Russia ahead, Alexander embarked on a program of "great reforms" designed to modernize the country, release it from feudalism, and embrace Western culture and technology. He sought to reduce class privilege and encourage humanitarian progress and economic development. In 1861 he signed a legislative bill freeing Russia's serfs. Ultimately his reforms generated resistance among the old guard and impatience among reformers. In 1881 he was killed by a bomb planted by the terrorist reform group Peoples' Will.

In Siberia, Murav'ev continued to advance Russia's new Far East policy. In this he was significantly aided by political and economic turmoil in China. From the beginning of the century, the failure of the government in Peking to contain a series of internal revolts, aimed partly at extensive trade in opium through Canton, led England to impose a treaty in 1842 that opened five ports to English and eventually world trade. Then the Taiping Rebellion, beginning in 1850 and lasting until 1864, though unsuccessful in overthrowing the regime, badly weakened trade. During the rebellion the European powers forced further trade and territorial concession on the Chinese government.

Murav'ev seized on China's weakness. In 1858 in the Treaty of Aigun he brought China to agree to change the Russo-Chinese boundary as set down in the Treaty of Nerchinsk nearly two centuries earlier. Henceforth, the boundary would run down the Amur River north of Mongolia to the Ussuri

River and then south to the coast near the northeast extremity of Korea. This gave Russia the whole of the Asian coast north of Korea and land circling Manchuria. In addition, Murav'ev secured the right of navigation on the Amur and Ussuri Rivers and also on the Sungari, a major tributary of the Amur rising deep in Manchuria. The treaty also confirmed that the Chinese ports were open to Russian trade.

The Treaty of Aigun was a remarkable achievement with profound implications for Russian America. The freedom to move cargoes directly to Canton was momentous; Russia had been agitating for it for nearly a century. Remarkable as it was, however, it was overshadowed by the opening of Amuria, for the Amur Basin represented the first substantial new fur supply since the promyshlennik*i* (Russian fur trappers) had moved into the Eastern (Aleutian) Islands following Bering's 1741 voyage to America. Also in 1858, Murav'ev founded a new town at the confluence of the Amur and the Ussuri, Khabarovsk, named for Erofei Khabarovsk, who had led an attempt to settle on the Amur before the border was moved north by the Treaty of Nerchinsk. Two years later Murav'ev founded an entirely new city near the mouth of the Ussuri, Vladivostok, meaning "Ruler of the East."

But Murav'ev had been consistently critical of Russian America, which he regarded as a thoroughly impractical and senseless drain on Russian resources and the Russian treasury. Russian occupation in America defied logic, he argued. Russian America was far too vulnerable. Once they had mature settlements on the Pacific Coast, Murav'ev was certain, the Americans would turn north; they would need the northwest for its resources and for its bridge to Asian markets for their expanding and industrializing economy. The Aigun treaty brought Murav'ev's policy to fruition, for Amuria emerged as an alternative to Russian America, a replacement. It had what Russian America did, most especially resources and Natives, but more important, many things Russian America did not, most particularly accessibility and defensibility. And, Murav'ev thought, it would never cost Russia financially as Russian America had.

In the meantime the colony in North America fared reasonably well under the neutrality arrangement. Company ships handled most of the supply, and the HBC sold goods to the RAC. Voevodskii purchased additional vessels from the Americans. The ice trade contributed a modest but steady income. During the war, partly so the ice trade would not be disrupted, officials of the American Russian Trading Company suggested that the RAC draw up papers showing a sale of the company to the San

Francisco firm. The primary object of this idea was to prevent any RAC property from being confiscated by the French or British; but the maneuver would have been so patently transparent that company officials declined. Two hundred Siberian troops were posted in Sitka as a precaution, however. They were the first troops to be stationed in Russian America.

Voevodskii continued developmental activity despite the war. Most notably, a mining engineer named Enoch Furuhjelm (the younger brother of the future governor) arrived in the colony in 1854 to establish a coal mine at English Bay on the Kenai Peninsula, where Petr Doroshin had found deposits during his colonial survey. In San Francisco, Furuhjelm bought steam engines, pumps, and other mining equipment and inspected the California gold fields. Back at English Bay he supervised the construction of a plant and began to sink shafts. An American ship took eight hundred tons of Kenai coal to California the first season, but the quality was so low that further shipments would not have been able to compete with low-grade deposits available in California and in the Puget Sound region. Furuhjelm built up English Bay, or Coal Harbor, anyway. When he was finished, the village had a church, twenty various-sized dwellings, a large warehouse, two stables, an engine lathe, a sawmill, a blacksmith's shop, a kitchen, and a small foundry, in addition to the mine buildings. But without an economic raison d'être, there was no point. Furuhjelm returned to Russia in 1862.

Perhaps emboldened by news of the war, or perhaps because of Voevodskii's ineptitude, an ugly incident with the Tlingit at Sitka developed into a full-scale attack on the town in 1855. Stopped in the process of taking wood from the RAC supply, several Tlingits got into a scuffle with the Russian guards, and one of the Indians speared a guard. Voevodskii gathered the clan headmen together and demanded they surrender the culprit. They refused and quarreled with the governor. Subsequently, the Russians fired cannon over the village as a warning. The Tlingit took this as a provocation and began to chop down the town palisade. A full-pitched gun battle resulted, ending with seventy or eighty Tlingits killed or wounded and two Russians killed and nineteen wounded. Voevodskii immediately requested one hundred additional Siberian troops, who were quickly sent.

The board of directors replaced Voevodskii in 1859 with Johan Furuhjelm, the engineer's older brother and a naval captain who had served as port chief for Aian and Okhotsk during the Crimean War. The RAC's third charter was due to expire, so the government extended the company's privileges and contracts on a provisional basis. Furuhjelm restored good relations with the Tlingit, who resumed their sales of fish, deer meat, and potatoes. In the vicinity of Sitka they had become nearly as dependent on the Russians as the Russian were on them.

Soon Russian America faced another kind of threat. In 1861 prospectors found gold on the upper reaches of the Stikine River in Canada, and Furuhjelm feared the southern part of the archipelago might be overrun. But the strike proved minor and ephemeral. Far more important for the colony's future, however, was the government's last inspection and evaluation of colonial affairs. On that would hinge the fate of Russian America.

ACHIEVEMENTS IN SCIENCE AND THE
RUSSIAN ORTHODOX MISSION

Political and economic events, and international diplomacy, describe only part of Russian America's maturity as a colonial experiment, however. Russia's achievements in science in the early nineteenth century were considerable and have been underappreciated by historians. A number of important naturalists accompanied various exploratory and political maritime expeditions and collected many specimens of fauna and flora that provided great insight into the physical nature of northwest North America and that form basic referents for comparative study today. In addition, the Russians tested and demonstrated a variety of new technologies that became standards of maritime endeavor.

In 1741 the German naturalist Georg Wilhelm Steller had identified several species then unknown to science, including the Steller jay, the northern fur seal, and the Steller sea lion. Historian Barbara Sweetland Smith notes that Steller's most important work, however, was his documentation of species that are now extinct, including the northern sea cow and the spectacled cormorant, both native to the Commander Islands. Promyshlenniki headed for the islands further east during these years killed and preserved them for food until there were no more. But Steller was only the first of a long line of distinguished scientists who sailed for Russia. When Rezanov sailed to Russian America shortly after the tsar granted the first RAC charter, the two ships in his entourage were captained by Ivan von Krusenstern and Iuri Lisianskii. Both captains had served in the British Navy. The ships they sailed, the *Nadezda* (Hope) and the *Neva*, had been purchased in England. The Russians outfitted them with the best and newest British navigational and scientific instruments. Among these were a new chronometer (a kind of clock), a sextant, a reflecting circle (for helping to compute position), and a theodolite (for surveying on land).[11] In addition, the captains carried a deep water thermometer. The circumnavigation compiled important data on seawater density, on magnetism, and on world weather patterns.

While Rezanov waited in Japan for the imperial court to determine whether to receive him formally—that is, whether to enter into a commercial treaty—Krusenstern completed important hydrographic charts of the waters north of Japan. The two naturalists on the ship made more than one hundred illustrations of Japanese people and communities and fauna and flora. In the meantime Lisianskii made careful charts of Kodiak Island and the entrance to Kodiak Harbor. He also gathered scientific data on Native cultures in the Aleutians, Kodiak Island, and around Sitka.

In 1815 a wealthy Russian count tapped Otto E. Kotzebue, who had served with Krusenstern in 1805 and 1806, to head a new Russian maritime circumnavigation. Kotzebue charted the far northern coast of Northwest America, farther north than any European at that time. He included in his journal important descriptions (the first such descriptions) of his contacts with northern Eskimos, the Inupiat. Adelbert von Chamisso, an important naturalist, accompanied Kotzebue on the voyage. He collected unknown fauna and flora and published the first study of North Pacific whales. In California, Chamisso identified more than thirty new species, including what became the state flower, the California poppy. The ship's doctor, Ivan Eschscholtz, also collected numerous species. He returned to some of the same areas in 1824, again with Kotzebue, and later produced a superb zoological atlas. Another important contributor was Louis Choris, an artist on the 1815 expedition, who produced memorable portraits of Natives of California, the Aleutian Islands, and the earliest scenes of the Inupiat.

In 1827 the sloop *Seniavin*, captained by Fedor Litke and accompanied by M. Staniukovich, captain of the *Moller*, arrived in Sitka on a scientific expedition. The naturalist Friedrich Kittlitz accompanied this round-the-world voyage. Litke would survey the coast of Siberia to Bering Strait and the Pribilof Islands and St. Matthew Island. Both Litke and Kittlitz published important, informative accounts of affairs in the colony. On this voyage Litke used a new instrument to gauge the earth's actual shape. He also conducted studies on magnetism and barometric pressure. The expedition produced thirteen hundred illustrations and collected nearly four thousand specimens.

Il'ia Voznesenskii, regarded by some writers as one of the most important Russian scientists to work in the colony, arrived in 1839. Although he was not a particularly strong theorist, his contribution as a collector, cataloguer, and organizer was important. Originally funded for a three-year stay, Voznesenskii remained in the colony for nearly ten years. He collected flora and fauna in the Alexander Archipelago, in California (including Baja California), on Kodiak and in the Aleutians, on Kamchatka and in the Kurils. When he returned to Russia, he had mounted 3,687 specimens, including mammals, birds, and fish, and had preserved numerous amphibians, shells, annelids, mollusks, and zoophytes in alcohol. His dry state examples included crayfish, larval animals, shells, coelenterates, nests, birds' eggs, and more than ten thousand insects.

Voznesenskii also had the bones and skull of a sea cow (rhytina), mammoth tusks and teeth, the skulls of various people, and two thousand specimens of dried plants. He had a large amount of ores, fossils, soil samples, and rocks. He kept a large collection of weapons, garments, domestic utensils, adornments, models, and other objects acquired from the Natives of North America, the Aleutians, the Kurils, and Kamchatka. In addition, he had more than 150 drawings, views, and portraits, many in color, and notebooks and journals. Although his analysis of them was wanting, Voznesenskii collected more specimens than any of the other Russian scientists of the era.[12]

These and other Russian exploratory initiatives contributed importantly to the body of scientific knowledge about the North Pacific, Northwest America, and Siberia. Historians of Russian America have tended to undervalue the Russian contribution to science. This is explained less by the unavailability of historical materials than by insufficient attention to the sources, although new accessibility to Russian archives will surely encourage further study and interpretation. The Russians produced a great volume of data and very large collections of floral and faunal specimens for comparative and other study. They also compiled a rich trove of information on ethnography and ethnology that was highly significant in the eighteenth and nineteenth centuries and continues to be used today.

The role of the Russian Orthodox mission in Alaska is also highly significant. The colonial experience produced an unusual number of exceptional churchmen, foremost among them Ioann Veniaminov. Born Ioann

Popov in Irkutsk, he excelled in both theological and practical studies, and when he was seventeen he was given the name of a particularly well-loved Irkutsk bishop who had just died, Veniamin (Benjamin); Popov was afterward known as Ioann Veniaminov. In 1823 he accepted assignment to the missionary post at Unalaska, first spending a year in Sitka. At Unalaska he earned a deserved reputation as an exceptional pastor. He also taught the Russian laborers and Aleut residents brick-laying, stone masonry, carpentry, blacksmithing, locksmithing, and other basic skills, and with their help he built a home for himself and his family and a new chapel for the village.

Quickly learning Aleut, Veniaminov worked with the village headman Ivan Pan'kov to devise an alphabet for the language and translated the Russian Short Catechism and the Gospel of St. Matthew into Aleut. He was committed to literacy and opened a school. It is unlikely that a large percentage of the Aleut population became literate at this time, a long-term process in any case. However, his achievement in developing an Aleut alphabet was extraordinary, comparable to the work of the Cherokee scholar Sequoyah, who did similar work during these years in the southern United States. Veniaminov also kept daily weather records at Unalaska, the first such records kept in Alaska.

Veniaminov's pastoral tours became legendary in the colony. He routinely visited places near and remote, traveling by baidarka. He visited the Pribilof Islands in 1928 and also Akun Island at Unimak Pass and the new Russian post on the Nushagak River, beyond the neck of the Alaska Peninsula. Veniaminov's powers as a paddler also became legendary on these trips. He apparently was quite strong and indefatigable. He once wrote of paddling fourteen hours without a break. In 1828 he established a church at Atka village, appointing Iakov Netsvetov, a Creole priest from Attu, as its head. Netsvetov was the first Native (Creole) to be ordained in the Orthodox church. Raised on St. George in the Pribilofs, he had been sent to Irkutsk for theological training. The manager of the Atka post initially opposed his efforts, but when then colony governor Wrangel removed the manager, Netsvetov flourished, opening a school that produced a number of excellent students, including two priests.

In 1835, at Wrangel's insistence, Veniaminov moved to Sitka, where he continued, even expanded, both his practical and pastoral work. He made clocks, furniture, and an organ while ministering to the Aleuts and Creoles of the post. He helped to complete a new church that Wrangel had ordered be built. A smallpox epidemic in 1836 and 1837 gave

Veniaminov an opening with the Tlingit, most of whom refused vaccination offered by the priest. The resulting death toll encouraged survivors to credit Veniaminov's teachings and significantly discredited shamanism. In 1838 he traveled to Fort Ross and toured the northern California Catholic missions. Veniaminov returned to Russia in 1839 to work up his extensive notes on Native life and culture. While there his wife died, and church officials named him bishop of Kamchatka, the Kurils, and the Aleutians. As was religious custom, he took a new name, becoming Bishop Innocent, returning to the colony in 1841. From then until 1858 he traveled the length and breadth of RAC posts, from Sitka through the Aleutians to Kamchatka, the Kurils, and to Aian, the RAC post on the Siberian mainland opposite Sakhalin Island. Innocent's reputation for competence and piety continued to grow. In 1858 at his suggestion, the diocese was divided into three sites, Sitka, Iakutsk, and Amuria; Innocent was assigned to Amuria, where he continued to minister until 1865, when he was recalled to European Russia. In 1867 the bishop was appointed Metropolitan of Moscow, effectively the highest post in the Church. He died in 1879. In 1977 he was canonized as St. Innocent.

Netsvetov, meanwhile, continued his work and development at Atka. He collected specimens of flora and fauna for museums in Russia, and through correspondence with Veniaminov he developed an Aleut script that could accommodate all the Aleutian dialects. He translated numerous materials into Aleutian, including sermons, liturgical works, and secular articles. In 1844 Bishop Innocent assigned Netsvetov to begin a new mission on the lower Kvikpak (Yukon) River. There he repeated the work done at Atka, building a church, developing a script and translating materials, and creating an Orthodox community. Transferred to Sitka when ill, he died after a year's residence, in July 1867. Netsvetov was canonized by the Church in 1994.

The role of the Church in Russian America was significant and complex. Certainly its contribution in literacy and education can never be quantitatively measured. Countless individuals gained access to the world of universal ideas and the communication, knowledge and dignity that they convey. The Church's work in health care also was highly important, as was its care of orphans and widows. The advocacy of Alaska Native rights by Saint German, Bishop Innocent, and Saint Iakov and their continuing protests against the ill treatment of Natives and RAC employees doubtless eased conditions for these unfortunates. In its relations with Natives, the Orthodox Church sought not to replace existing cultures, as the Americans later would do, but rather to build Christianity on an extant cultural framework. The missionaries learned the Native languages to work within instead of against the cultural context.[13] Not all priests, monks, and servitors attached to the mission were of the stature of its most celebrated members, however. Nonetheless, the mitigating and nurturing work carried out by the mission represents an extraordinary and effective commitment to humanity and to the spiritual life of the adherents. At the same time the courage of many of the mission personnel doubtless helped form the conscience of the company and the government in regard to the inhabitants of Russian America.

Yet the colonial context of Russia's establishment in America limited its cultural significance. A small number of Russians interacted with a limited number of Natives, and in the end the Russians did not stay. Although the Orthodox faithful in Alaska today, mostly Native, represent a legacy of the Russian period, that legacy is itself limited as the cultural tread of the Russians on Alaska would ultimately be limited. Events in the 1850s in Europe and Siberia would change Russia's view of its colony enough that the costs and risks of maintaining a colonial enterprise so far away and so vulnerable would come to seem untenable.

The Sale of Russian America

I N 1860, PAVEL Nikolaevich Golovin was the senior adjutant in the inspector's department of the Russian Naval Ministry, a position of eminence and significance for which, because he was both competent and courageous, he was admirably suited and in which he had served since 1854.[1] Tsar Alexander II needed men such as Golovin, for careful judgment was demanded if the country was to hold together, its society and economy thoroughly stressed by the modernizing reforms Alexander felt duty-bound to implement. In 1860 the tsar sent Golovin, accompanied by a government official representing the finance ministry and other imperial agencies, to Russian America to conduct a complete and forthright survey of colonial conditions and prospects. Clearly, the future of the Russian American Company (RAC) would rest on what he found, though Golovin saw that future in terms of reform not liquidation.

In the colony Golovin rendezvoused with Governor Johan Furuhjelm and the new assistant manager, Prince Maksutov, now assigned to Sitka. Traveling to the colony by way of New York, Panama, and San Francisco, Golovin and his assistant spent the winter at Sitka and went to Kodiak the following spring before returning to Sitka, and then back to Russia over the same route by which they had come. Their work was thorough and revealing. Back in St. Petersburg in 1862, the inspectors submitted their report to a review committee of fourteen bureaucrats, stockholders, and scientists who were to make a recommendation regarding a new charter or some other alternative. Their findings were not encouraging. First, the company's financial condition was deteriorating. Worth five hundred silver rubles on the Russian stock market in 1850, company shares had steadily been falling in value and in 1862 sold for 150 rubles. The government had stepped in to guarantee the stock, subsidizing RAC operations so the directors could continue to pay a dividend.

The reasons for failing finances were not hard to discover: under navy management the company had erected an ideal colonial administration but could not sustain it with the meager colonial resources available. Development of those resources would cost more than the revenue they could generate. Without substantive change, the company would soon approach bankruptcy.[2] Contributing factors in the colony's long-range economic picture included the failure of Enoch Furuhjelm's coal venture, repeated failures to launch a Russian whale fishery, the failure to follow up on Petr Doroshin's gold prospecting survey, inadequate attention to conservation of furbearers, and insufficient support for the interior initiative along the Yukon River. In addition, Golovin and Kostlivtsev agreed that the Americans stood poised to turn their attention northward. President Abraham Lincoln had been elected in November 1860, and the American Civil War followed in April. But whether the union collapsed, American interest in the North Pacific seemed inevitable. Furthermore, the debacle at Petropavlovsk had demonstrated the colony's vulnerability and its abject dependence on naval protection, which clearly was inadequate.[3]

The fourteen-member committee wrote their own report based on Golovin's work. Not surprisingly, they were highly critical of company management and general conditions in the colony. In addition, monopoly presented a philosophical problem, increasingly seen as a relic of an unproductive past. In the interest of fairness, the board of directors commissioned Petr Tikhmenev, a naval officer and RAC employee, to write a history of the company. His study in two volumes—one narrative, the other documentary—won the prestigious Demidov Prize for literary accomplishment but was self-congratulatory and probably did little to influence the ensuing debate regarding the colony's disposition.

Golovin's inspection survey deepened the company's troubles, however, for it generated a crisis of uncertainty. Although senior officials enjoined everyone to secrecy, the survey and committee debate involved far too many people for that. In addition, there had been too many inquiries about the possibility of a sale between American officials and Edouard Stoeckl, the Russian ambassador in the United States, for word not to have traveled far. Investors had been hearing adverse information about the RAC for years, and during the Crimean War rumors of the false sale to the United States, as protection against a British-French attack on Sitka, led to a loss of confidence and resulted in a temporary fall in the value of company stock. Both the government and the board of directors had quickly stepped in to reassure investors and quickly squelched the panic. But the residual effect was harmful. In 1862 potential new investors and long-term contractors held back until they could be assured of the colony's health by the issuing of a new charter. This was the atmosphere when the contents of Golovin's report reached the public. Confidence sagged and the value of the stock fell as holders began to sell their investments. This time government and board assurances were insufficient, especially without a new charter being issued.

The financial crisis in the 1860s was not fully representative of the state of the colony's finances, however. Russian historian Semen Okun, writing in the 1930s, quipped that the company's first charter period was marked by much peltry and little order, the second by less peltry and more order, and the third by little peltry and still more order.[4] But the company generated considerable profit in the 1850s, concentrating on fish, timber, ice, and also tea, which the company imported from China and sold at a profit within Russia. Company factors also marketed furs from the Kurils in San Francisco, New York, and London.

But by the 1860s economics was not the principal issue. Russian America was a political as well as an economic entity. Russian presence in North America had limited British power beyond Russia's own territory, south of 54° 40' north latitude on the coast and east of 141° west longitude in the northern interior. And the RAC had functioned well in furthering Russian imperial expansion after 1800. But it could no longer do so. The Crimean War had demonstrated the colony's defenseless character, and leaders in Russian took it for granted that the United States would eventually take all of western North America. Although the idea of a strong United States directly across the Bering Sea from eastern Siberia was not the most attractive alternative for the future, it was better than a strong Britain in the same region, and in any case the Russians were convinced that there was nothing they could do to resist American expansion. The only strategy seemed to be to attempt to play the United States off against Britain. Otherwise, it would be a matter of desperately holding on to the colony as its circumstances became increasingly precarious until the United States demanded its capitulation.

The Crimean War had generated a protracted, comprehensive debate about the status and future of Russian America. Had not the HBC and the RAC instigated the agreement on neutrality, Sitka would almost certainly have been seized by the combined Franco-British fleet. Powerful members of the government began to question the wisdom of retaining the colony.

One of these was Alexander's younger brother, Grand Duke Konstantine. He joined with Siberian governor-general Murav'ev in advocating liquidation. As minister to the United States, Stoeckl argued the same. He had considerable experience in the United States, as he had served with Russia's legation there in 1839 and again from 1848 through 1853, serving part of the time as chargé d'affaires. Stoeckl also served a year as Russian consul general in Hawai'i before returning to the United States in 1854. Thoroughly familiar with American policies and styles of thought, he had married an American woman, Eliza Howard of Springfield, Massachusetts, in 1856. He agreed with Murav'ev that the United States seemed destined to occupy the whole of the North American West.

Persuaded by these views, in 1857, Konstantine submitted a memo to Alexander's foreign minister, Prince Aleksandr Gorchakov, urging the sale of the colony. Gorchakov was not enthusiastic about relinquishing Russian America, but he dutifully asked Baron von Wrangel to conduct an appraisal. Wrangel found the colony to be worth about $5 million. In the meantime, Konstantine's and Stoeckl's view seemed confirmed when, in 1859 following the discovery of gold on the Fraser River in British Columbia, more than thirty thousand Americans swarmed into the region. London quickly designated the area a crown colony, partly to prevent the development and spread of democratic ideas, which would lead to annexation to the United States.[5]

There were strong advocates of keeping the colony as well, among them Baron Fedor Osten-Saken, an official with the Asian Department of the Russian foreign ministry who had served in the United States. Sale to the United States would alter a delicate balance of power in the North Pacific, he argued, where the United States and Britain checked each other's ambitions to the benefit of Russia. But Konstantine and Stoeckl seized on Golovin's assessment and were joined by other influential figures in the government who felt certain that American "manifest destiny" would prevail sooner or later, and that Russia therefore should capitalize on American goodwill before it was too late.

American goodwill was plentiful. During the Civil War there had been considerable anxiety in the United States that Britain, because of the high amount of Southern planters' indebtedness to merchants in Bristol and Liverpool, might recognize the Confederacy's belligerency. In fact, this did not happen. But in 1863, soon after the Union victory at Gettysburg, sections of the Russian fleet put in to New York and San Francisco. In the United States the visit was widely interpreted in the press as a gesture of support for the Union cause. In reality, though, the fleet was at sea so as not to be caught and trapped at Khronstadt in the event of a European war. And in any case, as Russian historian Nikolai N. Bolkhovitinov has argued, Russia always sought to maintain amiable relations with the United States as an antidote to British power in America.[6]

The Americans actually had considerable knowledge of Russian America. A decade earlier, in the early 1850s, a promoter and American expansionist named Perry McDonough Collins associated with the American Russian Commercial Company in San Francisco had worked with California's Senator William Gwinn to interest the American government in a trade mission to the Amur River region. U.S. president Franklin Pierce was accommodating, and in Washington, D.C., Stoeckl had endorsed the idea enthusiastically and eased Collins's way with officials in St. Petersburg. With Murav'ev, Collins believed Russia could tap the trade of the Orient by opening the Amur River and building an easy connection to Lake Baikal and Irkutsk. Such a link would provide easy access to the Pacific; it would also facilitate commerce from America's West Coast ports, most particularly, San Francisco. Collins established an American trade office in Nikolaevsk at the mouth of the Amur, then returned to the United States.

From Collins's conversations with Murav'ev, he had developed the idea of a round-the-world telegraph line to facilitate trade and commerce, running north through British Columbia and Alaska, across Bering Strait and the neck of Kamchatka, marching up the Amur to Irkutsk, and then across central Siberia to Russia and Europe. While in the United States, Collins attracted the support of William Sibley, president of the Western Union Telegraph Company. In 1863 the imperial government granted Collins a charter for his line. Officials in London approved the project in 1864, and in 1865 Collins and Sibley obtained support as well from the U.S. Congress, which agreed to permit the use of engineer troops to survey and build the line in British Columbia. Although construction began in 1865, the line would not ever be completed. But work on it helped to educate America's intelligentsia on the true nature of Russian America, the future Alaska.

There could be no official consideration of the purchase of Russian America in the United States during the Civil War. However, soon after its conclusion, Stoeckl returned to St. Petersburg, where he met with the tsar. For Russia little had changed in the American equation. The Americans seemed poised more than ever to look north, for expansion first and ultimately for resources. By contrast, the promise of Amuria had begun to mature. Furs were available there, but more important Amuria succeeded politically where North America did not. Modest Russian settlement had begun soon after the Treaty of Aigun, and there would be little difficulty defending the region. After consultation, and acting with the grudging agreement of Prince Gorchakov, now chancellor in addition to his other duties, Alexander decided to sell the colony. The meetings were held at the Winter Palace before and after Christmas 1866. In attendance were Grand Duke Konstantine, Prince Gorchakov, Stoeckl, Finance Minister Mikhail Reitern, Minister of Marine (Navy) H. K. Krabbe, and Alexander himself. The tsar made the final decision on 28 December. He sent Stoeckl back to Washington, D.C., to try to establish and close the deal. Reitern told Stoeckl to accept not less than $5 million. The fateful turn had thus been made.

Some historians have suggested that Russia's need for currency explains the decision to sell the colony, but this is not tenable. The $7.2 million paid for the colony, 10.8 million rubles, would not have meant much to an empire with an annual income of half a billion rubles and debts of one and a half billion. As Osten-Saken noted in 1866, it would have been nice had the sale helped the Russian debt, but it could not be.[7] The reasons for the sale of Russian America were not economic, as historical geographer James R. Gibson has noted. Instead, the sale was Russia's response to a political policy for the Pacific region that had run its course, gaining for Russia as much from America as possible but now finished. In the final analysis, the central power in far northwestern North America would not be Russia, despite the victory represented by Spain's withdrawal, Britain's preoccupation with Napoleon, and the successful establishment of Sitka. It would instead be the United States. When all was said and done, Russia had been but a sojourner in America.

Prince Maksutov had returned to St. Petersburg in 1863. Once there he asked to speak on behalf of the RAC. A territory won at such peril ought not to be lightly disposed of, he protested. He criticized company directors for not doing more to develop the colony and called for still more exploration. His listeners probably did not agree, but in the interim nothing could be done, so they sent him back to the colony as governor, to replace Johan Furuhjelm. Maksutov's wife, Adelaide Ivanovna Bushman, the ex-wife of an English professor at the Russian Naval Academy, had died in Sitka, apparently of tuberculosis. Some say her ghost, clad in an elegant blue dress, still stalks the halls of the old Bishop's House. Policy required that company managers must be married, so like many of his predecessors, Maksutov quickly courted and wed again.

That the decision to sell the colony had not yet been made was clear in Maksutov's instructions. He was to continue to develop the export of timber and fish, to seek copper deposits on the Copper River, and to increase trade with California and the HBC posts in British Columbia. Relations with the Natives were to be improved, and deadbeat laborers to be returned to Russia. Maksutov was to prevent any further marriages between Russians and Natives, for the Russian men tended either to leave their spouses in Russian America or abandon them if they took them back to Russia. The company was to improve medical services, to provide more books for the colonial library, and to try to provide mail service from San Francisco and Victoria once every three months.

But in reality these plans were only a provision for business as usual pending the larger question of whether the colony actually had a future, and few of them were executed. In fact, in Washington, D.C., Stoeckl and U.S. Secretary of State William Seward entered into intense negotiations in the late winter of 1866–67. They came to agreement on terms without much difficulty and wrote up the treaty on 30 March 1867 (Seward's Day in Alaska). Both the American and Russian Senates ratified it in May. Maksutov's real challenge would therefore not be to govern Russian America but to liquidate the holdings of the RAC, not an easy task. The territory, the land and its undeveloped resources, was sold to the United States. But company property was not; it remained company property, including warehouses, ships, the various posts, furs (eighty thousand pelts), liquor (thirty thousand gallons), trade goods, employee houses in Sitka, and the like. Soon adventurers and entrepreneurs arrived from California to help. The American Russian Commercial Company bought the Ozerskoi Redoubt south of Sitka for $15,000. A fur merchant from Victoria, Leopold Boscowitz, bought sixteen thousand furs for forty cents each, which he sold in Victoria for $2 and $3 apiece. A veteran RAC skipper, Gustave Nie-baum, with four associates, bought a company brig for $4,000. And so it went.

The U.S. State Department, concerned that many Americans were crowding into Sitka, decided quickly to arrange a formal transfer of the territory before winter might make sailing conditions more difficult. On 10 October, Brigadier General Jefferson C. Davis (not the former president of the Confederacy) arrived on a steamer with two companies of U.S. troops, about 250 men. More than a week later, on 18 October, the formal transfer commissioners for both countries arrived on the same vessel, the U.S.S. *Ossipee*, General Lovell Rousseau representing the United States and Captains A. A. Peshchurov and F. F. Koskul representing the government of Russia and the RAC respectively. The troops, marooned on the steamer for eight days, officers and ladies included, were more than anxious to con-clude the formalities.

The dignitaries and a garrison from both the United States and Russia drew up before the flagstaff in front of the governor's residence on what has come to be known as Baranov Hill at about three o'clock in the afternoon. According to Mariette Davis, wife of the army commander, the ceremo-nies were not very imposing. Canons were fired and the Russian flag was run down. Or at least someone attempted to bring it down; it hung up in the halyard and a bosun's chair was rigged so a sailor could go aloft to free it. Perhaps misunderstanding directions, he tore it loose and then dropped it. The flag drifted down and at least a portion caught on the upraised bay-onets of the garrison. Princess Maksutova is said to have fainted at the sight. After the American flag had been run up, all retired to the residence for tea and spirits, and the Russian era concluded.

No one in the U.S. diplomatic service asked the Tlingit and Haida people of the Alexander Archipelago how they may have felt about the transfer of their lands from one alien sovereign to another. But they were not silent on what some of their leaders took as an elemental offense. As the American courts would confirm nearly a century later, the Tlingit had a concept of property ownership, and in any case, what the Russians had exploited and the Americans would continue to exploit were traditional Tlingit and Haida lands. Protestations in 1867 had no effect on the actions of the two powers who exchanged the claimed sovereignty over all the land identified as Russian America in the 1825 treaty between Russia and the United States.[8]

Few Americans know of the Russian American chapter in their history. Even though most know that Alaska was bought from someone, it is a surprise to most that the Russian Empire extended to North America in the eighteenth and nineteenth centuries, and that the history of not only the Northwest but of North America would have been quite different if Russia had not sold Alaska. Those who do know about Russia's presence in North America usually do not understand why Russia sold its colony, a decision that seems foolish in light of the subsequent history of Russo-American relations. Of course, Russia no more than the United States could foresee the development of twentieth-century geopolitics and the emergence of the United States and the Soviet Union as the titans of world power after World War II.

Russia's decision to sell Russian America was decidedly not a foolish one. The RAC and the government knew well the resources of the territory, its gold, furs, whales, timber, coal, fish, and ice. They also knew what it would mean in terms of material and personnel investment to develop these resources. Russia determined that such an investment was not worth the risk that would be lost, eventually, because of American intimidation or confrontation or even war. The United States, it seemed clear at midcentury, was indeed destined to dominate North America; Russia's statesmen understood that to contest that destiny could only lead to a Russian tragedy, as it had led to a Mexican one. Thus the decision not to invest men and money in a lost venture must be seen as prudent and wise, the kind of prudence and wisdom so often expected of statesmen and so seldom manifested by or attributed to them, it seems. Russia avoided a waste of resources and political embarrassment. Resources that would have been wasted in Alaska instead were invested in Amuria and in the Baikal region, in Russia's late-nineteenth-century Far East initiative, which culminated in the Russo-Japanese War that defined the limits of that initiative.

In the final analysis America was too far away, too difficult to supply and maintain, too vulnerable and too grudging in yielding its resources to development, and not directly connected to Asia. Russian America represented an interesting experiment, one that might not have developed in the same way had Amuria been available to the Russians at the beginning of the eighteenth century and whose development in the middle of the nineteenth century was altered much by the new availability of Amuria as an alternative. American expansion and the Crimean War combined to raise awareness in Russia that the experiment was in jeopardy, and in the end that it was over. The prolific scholar of Russian America, the Russian historian Andrei V. Grinev, has argued that more than these and other considerations, the stifling government limitations on the company's freedom of decision, which he calls politarism, explains the company's failure to expand and prosper, and in the end is the principal reason for the sale of the enterprise. The government effectively owned all the company's employees and required that everyone going to Russian America be issued a passport good for three to seven years, at which time the person could be recalled to Russia. This included nobility and military personnel. People were tied in one way or another to the land in Russia, and few owners relinquished their right to control their dependents. This, Grinev argues, was the principal reason the Russian population of the colony was so low. Moreover, the company provided few opportunities for advancement or even changes in the conditions of employment. Add to that the debt peonage in which the common employees lived, due to the high prices charged for all goods employees had to purchase, which charges were deducted from wages, and Grinev's argument is highly persuasive. Whether it be called mismanagement or state interference with free capitalism, it paints a dismal picture Russia's American enterprise.[9]

What is the final legacy of Russian America? Perhaps most tangible are the borders. Alaska's state/international borders are the same as those agreed upon by the negotiators in the Anglo-Russian Treaty in 1825, along 141° west longitude and on the mainland around the Alexander Archipelago. This is the detached, disembodied shape recognized today as Alaska on maps and letterheads. The Russian Orthodox Church in Alaska is another not insubstantial legacy, although the number of adherents is not large: today thirty-three clergy minister in about eighty villages and towns. The Church's role was critical in the survival of some Alaska Native languages, Orthodox missionaries adapting European liturgy and ritual to the local culture rather than seeking to replace it as did later American Protestant missionaries. Important lessons are contained within Russian American history as well, most particularly, the challenge of self-sufficiency and the concomitant reliance on external supply. This is less obvious at the beginning of the twentieth-first century, when the globalization of regional economies has become commonplace; it was more obvious in the eighteenth and nineteenth centuries, when embryonic global economic forces were more subject to national control. Coupled with this challenge is the reality that the only materials from which a modern economy can be created in Alaska are the region's natural resources.

Indeed, the most enduring lesson of the history of Russian America may be the colonial organization of the economy and politics of the area. Unlike materials that might be imported to the territory to support manufacturing or the personnel who might be imported to support a financial or electronic center of one kind or another, the natural resources are natural to the environment. It is those resources that will attract external investors, whose investment will sustain the region's culture. This, too, was less obvious in the eighteenth and nineteenth centuries when Alaska's Native cultures were still mainly self-sufficient; it was only the external culture that needed to be supplied and sustained from without. But at the beginning of the twenty-first century, all of the Native communities in Alaska have become dependent to greater and lesser degrees on an economy sustained from outside the region. The integrated modern culture that now characterizes most of Alaska, resting on a foundation of oil production and taxation, can only be sustained from outside the region. This is the historical link between Russian America and modern Alaska: Alaska is an economic colony and increasingly a political and social one as well. Its cultures and livelihood are characterized by dependence on forces outside the territory and largely outside the control of its residents. Despite protestations, mythologies, and even intimations of independence, this former and present colony is likely to remain dependent well into the future.

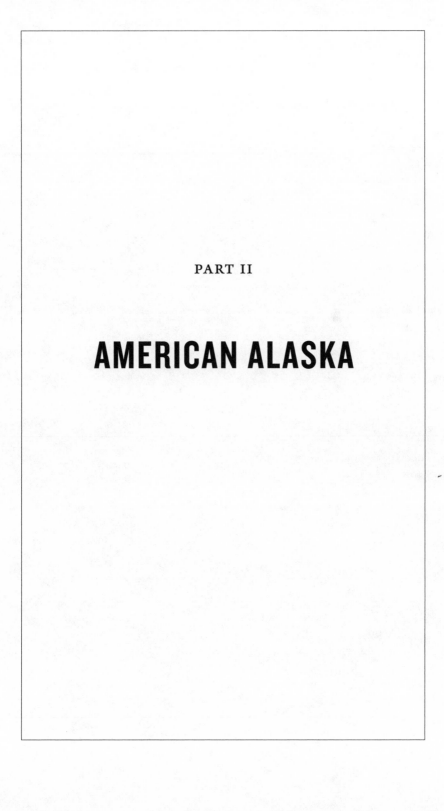

PART II

AMERICAN ALASKA

8

American Alaska, an Introduction

ALASKA WAS NOT an American design. Rather, it was an opportunity that the United States seized. Unlike Texas, Oregon, and California, where migration preceded American sovereignty and government, American citizens did not migrate to Russian America before its purchase by the United States. Alaska's Native residents were not considered U.S. citizens, as other Native Americans were not at the time; their claims to sovereignty and the right to be consulted were disregarded. Although several score of Americans had rushed to Sitka during the summer of 1867 when news circulated about the pending purchase, few contemplated moving permanently north. So few American citizens were in Alaska at the time of the purchase that Congress did not immediately extend its traditional basic policies for newly acquired lands there. Instead, it kept Alaska under military jurisdiction until the chief requisite for settlement, an economic base that would support the citizens' livelihood, was developed. This procedure was not unlike other territories in the American West, where military governorships had preceded civil government.

Many historians who have written about Alaska have embraced the notion of exceptionality. Because Alaska is not contiguous with the other states, and because it has a harsher climate than most, its exceptionality might seem obvious. Moreover, many commentators on Alaska have adopted a heroic and triumphalist interpretation of the state's history, one in which the tenacious argonauts trekking over the Klondike Trail, the intrepid builders of the Alaska Highway, the successful campaigners for Alaska statehood, and the determined engineers and laborers who constructed the Trans-Alaska Pipeline display a unique pioneer spirit not found in other regions of the country and that contemporary Alaska residents seek to emulate. A number of historians have argued that Alaska's past is sui generis: its history is unlike that of any other place.

Certainly Alaska is geographically and climatologically distinct from the contiguous states. To begin with, it is not contiguous to the rest of the continental states. Moreover, with the exception of the southern portion of the southeast coastal panhandle, all of Alaska is located in the subarctic and Arctic climate zones. Located in the high northern latitudes, the region is characterized by long, cold, dark winters and short, warm summers graced with near constant sunlight. Being noncontiguous and northern, Alaska is remote. It has a large Native population, one hundred thousand people or 16 percent of the state's total population, most of whom live in roadless, primarily wilderness locations in undeveloped and natural environments. The Native population includes Aleuts and Inuits as well as Indians. Although many of these people continue to pursue subsistence resources as a substantial portion of their diet, they do so with modern technologies. Alaska Natives fully participate in every aspect of Alaska's political, economic, and social life. Alaska has the only vast, unbroken areas of true wilderness left in the United States. In these aspects the region is genuinely unique.

But close analysis of the realities of Alaska history suggests that despite these valid exceptionalities, Alaska has always been economically, politically, and culturally like the United States as well as dependent on the United States. Its development has not taken place in a vacuum, and as a consequence, it is not broadly culturally distinct from the rest of America, except perhaps in the diversity of its Native cultures. As its history has developed, Alaska has been ever more closely drawn into and bound to the culture and life of the American nation. In fact, a primary drive of the majority of its people has been to reduce distinctions from the rest of America and to re-create U.S. culture as thoroughly and quickly as possible.[1]

In this respect Alaska has much in common with the history of at least one other region of the United States: the American West. Historians of the American West have revitalized the study of their region over the past several decades. In particular, they have emphasized the continuity of human experience in the West and have shown that its history did not begin with the arrival of American migrants in the 1840s. They have also stressed the dependence of the West on eastern capital and eastern culture.[2] Historian Clyde A. Milner II has summarized the major themes of these historians' work. First, Native Americans did not vanish in the twentieth century as many nineteenth-century Americans thought they surely must; they have persisted through the years and many Indian groups today manifest vitality and promise.

Second, settlement and development in the West were continually supported and subsidized by the federal government; internal and external navigation, exploration and survey, Indian wars, railroads, cheap timber, free grazing, cheap mineral leases, the treating of resources as a commons, conveyance of land for education and federal endowments for universities, military protection and expenditures, and construction of dams and management of water resources all represent only the most obvious subsidies of western development and life by the federal government. Most particularly, the government has sustained western economies. Third, it was extraction of the region's natural resources that drew Americans west, and in exploiting the minerals, forests, and arable lands, westerners failed to appreciate the fragility of the natural environment. Fourth, the societies of the West have always been multinational and multicultural; the region was never characterized only by Anglo-Saxon whites, however disabled minority groups may have been.[3]

Alaska's history manifests these same themes. First, Native peoples lived in the region for millennia before Euro-American contact. When the Europeans arrived, Alaska Natives did not succumb to the disease and dislocation brought by the Europeans, although they were severely affected in some places. Despite the pressure on their cultures brought by the Europeans, and the uneven balance of power that resulted, the Natives found adaptations that allowed them to survive in the face of new, externally imposed adversities.[4] Today they represent a vital and creative force in contemporary Alaska. Second, federal support has been a constant element of Alaska's development, from mapping and survey of the coast and the Interior soon after the purchase, through construction and operation of the telegraph line and the only federal railroad established to facilitate settlement in national history, to massive spending during the Cold War that created jobs and helped sustain the territorial and early state economies.

Third, non-Native settlement in Alaska awaited the development of natural resources by absentee investors who exploited first gold, then salmon, then copper, and most recently petroleum, providing the jobs on which residents depended for their livelihood; taxation of petroleum production and earnings on the state's investment of about 10 percent of petroleum tax revenue provide the principal public revenue stream in modern Alaska. Finally, Alaska society has been multicultural and multiethnic, including Native cultures, which were always present and often the focus of public policy. Alaska's Natives were settlers in the larger towns and often served as the labor force in gold, coal, and copper mining as well as in the salmon industry.

There are other historical aspects of culture that unite Alaska and the American West. Few non-Native settlers migrated to Alaska to pursue alternative lifestyles; few were interested in wilderness and subsistence living. Instead, as all across the West, migrants to Alaska sought to replicate the culture they came from. Early settlers established the towns and later settlers moved there, where cultural forms and institutions were familiar and where they had access to jobs and to the amenities of culture they did not wish to be without.[5]

Today 70 percent of Alaska's population is urban, only slightly smaller than the population of the American West. Alaskans share with many western residents a strong resentment of the federal government's presence in their region. When Congress created the western states, it provided for retention of federal title to large areas within the new states. Highly dependent on federal spending to sustain their economies, western states have argued that they are denied potential tax revenue from economic development of the federal lands in their states. In recent years they have bitterly fought stiffer environmental regulations on developmental use of those lands.

In Alaska few issues have generated as much anger as federal sovereignty, federal land management, and environmental regulation. Many Alaskans imagine themselves to be less dependent than other American citizens, and they view themselves as more individualist and more protective of their personal freedoms than other Americans. But this same conviction of self-reliance also characterizes most parts of the American West, where an imagined history of mythic proportions helps to authenticate belief in the existence of, and membership in, a heroic society. These and other commonalties suggest that Alaska is an extension of the American West, not an exception to it, and thus should be viewed as a part of it. Alaska history is thus another chapter in the history of the American West.

As with other residents of the American West, many Alaska citizens have misunderstood the history of public lands and the federal-state relationship, which have played a central role in Alaska's history. On the basis of the authority articulated in Article IV, Section 3, of the U.S. Constitution, which provides that Congress shall have jurisdiction over "the Territory or other Property belonging to the United States," Congress established basic policies for newly acquired lands and the people on them at the beginning of American national government. The Land Ordinance of 1785 provided that the territories would be surveyed and marked off into uniform units that would be sold to citizens on a first-come, first-served basis regardless of the characteristics of different land units.[6] The Northwest Ordinance of 1787 provided for a kind of civic apprenticeship for citizens who might migrate to the new lands; Indians were denied citizenship at this time.

Initially, Congress would name and define the territory's geographic limits (borders) and would appoint a governor, judge, and minor civil officials, such as marshal, clerk of the court, and so on. Appointment of the governor was often preceded by a period of military rule. Later, Congress authorized biennial election of a territorial delegate to the U.S. Congress, although at the time the delegate did not have a vote. When the Congress deemed it appropriate—when the population first reached five thousand free, white, adult males—the citizens could biennially elect a bicameral legislature. The Congress could disallow any law passed by this territorial legislature but did so infrequently because that would constitute abnegation of the right of self-governance proclaimed in the Declaration of Independence. Finally, when the population reached sixty thousand or when deemed appropriate, Congress could pass a statehood act bringing the territory into the union on an equal footing with all preexisting states, provided the new state's constitution was consistent with the U.S. Constitution. With variations, these two policies for land disposal and civil governance were implemented for all new U.S. territories, including Alaska.[7] In this legislation Congress acted as the agent of the American people and nation, who had acquired the new territory.

Congress's authority in governing the territories was regarded as superseding that of the people who lived there, the original inhabitants, and also those who might migrate there, who by so doing, might claim that right. In cases in 1803 and 1819, in the nullification crisis of 1832, and in the

Civil War, the Supreme Court confirmed the constitutional principle that federal sovereignty is superior to state sovereignty. That does not mean that state sovereignty does not exist; the Tenth Amendment provides that powers not delegated to the United States (federal government) are reserved to the states or the people. States have considerable sovereignty as limited self-governing republics, over standards of education, for example. However, superior federal sovereignty supersedes state sovereignty whenever the U.S. Supreme Court declares that it does, consistent with the federal Constitution. Because the notion of freedom is strong in the West, and particularly in Alaska, the supremacy of federal sovereignty has often been misunderstood, a misunderstanding that has often led to bitterness and to missteps in public policy.[8]

Alaska history also reflects American western history in one additional respect. Many residents of both areas imagine themselves to be substantially self-reliant, more individualist, and more committed to their personal freedom than people in other parts of the United States. Many Alaskans organize the rhetoric of self-reliance with the theme of exceptionality and explain their migration to the state in those terms: nowhere in the United States is as free as Alaska, they are likely to argue, which is why they moved there. Often the argument is cast in a declensionist context, as a lamentation for a past golden period when much greater freedom characterized American society, a freedom now repressed by modern culture and federal sovereignty. With many people in the American West, Alaskans often embrace an imagined history, a history of mythic proportions that describes such a golden past, one that produced people who manifested the values that such Alaskans claim as their own today. In this respect Alaskans are indistinguishable from residents throughout the American West.

The American period of Alaska's history is best understood in a colonial context, as is the Russian period. Alaska also shares this with the other states of the American West. Political and economic colonialism characterized Russia's tentative and impermanent grasp of Alaska, and it has also characterized America's relationship with the region. Dependence is the central element in Alaska's colonialism. Alaska's economy has been dependent on investors from outside the territory because the capital to develop regional resources has not resided in Alaska. But the only resources in the region are natural resources: hard rock minerals, fish, timber and forest products, and petroleum and natural gas. Economies of scale defeat both commercially profitable manufacturing and agricultural production. Only investment in exploitation of natural resources has provided jobs in Alaska, and the non-Native, immigrant population has come to Alaska for jobs, not for subsistence.[9]

In Alaska the immigrant population has not pursued alternative lifestyles; rather, over the years migrants have put in place as rapidly as possible all of the assumptions, institutions, behaviors, and material culture of mainstream America. These begin with jobs sufficiently lucrative to guarantee discretionary income and leisure time, which allows transplanted Alaskans to replicate the culture they left behind, the only culture they know and the only one they are interested in establishing in Alaska. Without these elements and the opportunity to create familiar forms of existence and activity, the early immigrants likely would not have tolerated the long, cold, dark winters and the remoteness. But the jobs that have created that familiar opportunity have been provided by sources of economy and power outside the region and have been controlled by the providers.

Absentee capital investment and federal support are the twin pillars on which Alaska's modern culture was built.[10] The dependency created by both led to Alaska's colonial character. But that dependence contradicts the images of rugged, self-reliant independence that so defines the American West, symbolized by videos and photos of empty landscapes (Monument Valley on Navaho land in northeastern Arizona is the most ubiquitous) and the lone horseman (e.g., the Marlboro Man). In Alaska familiar images of the prospecting sourdough and the solitary dog musher braving an empty snowscape carry the same symbolism of independence and rugged individualism. In Alaska's popular history the reader is most likely to encounter a heroic individual in a dramatic story of triumph over nature, rather than a tale of corporate investment or federal conservation. This book presents a more realistic history of Alaska, based in the documentary record of Alaska's past, interpreted by professional and other historians, and organized around the theme of colonial dependence.

The theme of colonialism requires some explication.[11] As detailed in Part 1 of this book, in the Russian period of Alaska's history the Russian American Company (RAC), a quasi-private investment venture, functioned as a semipublic entity, somewhat like the Hudson's Bay Company in Canada (Rupert's Land), standing in for the Russian government. The company's chief manager, always resident in the colonial capital, was also the governor of the civic and political creation called Russian America. In the age of mercantile capitalism, Russia sought to exploit any and all natural resources in the region that could be traded for profit in the world market system. The object of the exploitation was enrichment of the investors, not the construction of a new society in America. The Russian government owned at various times about 20 percent of the shares of the RAC and thus shared directly in the annual dividend along with the other investors. Despite complaints about too much colonial independence by the board of directors and the tsar's advisers during Aleksandr Baranov's tenure as governor, the locus of control was always in St. Petersburg.

Industrial capitalism was introduced into Alaska in the American period with lode gold mining, salmon canning, developing raw material for the forest products industry, and later petroleum production. The purpose of these enterprises has not been to build up Alaska; rather, it has been to enrich the corporate investors. The Alaska economy has expanded and contracted in response to the decisions of the managers of the absentee capital, decisions made in response to the vicissitudes of the world market system, not the perceived needs of Alaskans, their economy, or society. Recognizing Alaska's dependence on loci of control outside the territory and outside Alaskans' influence, Territorial Governor Ernest Gruening titled his keynote address to the Alaska Constitutional Convention in 1955 "Let Us End American Colonialism."[12] "The development of Alaska . . . cannot be achieved under colonialism," he wrote. He went on to say that "the whole nation will profit by an Alaska that is populous, strong and self-reliant." In this conviction Gruening's hope was misplaced, for Alaskans have yet today to establish their independence from investment and supply from outside the region. Not only has Alaska provided gold and copper for the mining industry, canned and whole salmon for the fishing industry, as well as natural resources for the forest products industry and the petroleum industry, the territory has also served as hinterland to the urban supply and transportation centers of Seattle and Tacoma. The region's history in the American period manifests Alaska's dependence clearly and repeatedly.

That history can be divided conveniently into several distinct periods. The first interprets events from the Alaska purchase itself to the gold rush of 1898. The territory's non-Native population was not appreciable until the Klondike and Alaska gold rush era, which may be dated from the Klondike discovery in 1896. Congress authorized military rule rather than civil government immediately after the purchase because the army did not clearly understand the disposition of the Natives and because of the low non-Native population. The first decennial census taken in Alaska, in 1880, reported only 435 non-Natives.[13] When San Francisco investors began development of lode deposits on Douglas Island after 1880, attracting working miners, the population increased to several thousand, and Congress responded with the first civil government legislation. Salmon canning rose from modest beginnings in 1878 to a major industry by the mid-1890s.

Both gold mining and salmon canning represented colonial investment, for the capital to develop those industries, or any industry or other economic activity, did not exist in the territory. Territorial economic development was dependent on outside investors. So too did the beginnings of civil government represent colonialism, for the governor and the territorial judge were appointed by the president with the advice and consent of the Senate.

The gold rush, the start of the next period, attracted tens of thousands of argonauts north; the 1900 census showed just more than thirty thousand non-Natives and slightly fewer than thirty thousand Natives. Congress again responded with a variety of measures intended to facilitate economic development and still more settlement. The era of Progressive liberal reform had just begun in the United States, and Progressive ideas and politics characterized the legislation, as did the enactments of the territorial legislature, authorized by Congress in 1912. This period ended in Alaska with America's entry into World War I in April 1917. Daniel Guggenheim and other corporate investors in Alaska increased the territory's colonial dependency, as did the operations of federal agencies in Alaska and the limitations on self-governance included in the 1912 civil government act.

The interwar period was deceptively quiescent in Alaska. Federal bureaus and agencies proliferated, and the territorial legislature sought to curb the governor's power by establishing a wide variety of Alaska boards. Falling prices during the Great Depression closed down the copper mines and depressed salmon prices, which led the salmon industry (which paid a small tax that generated most territorial revenue) to take still larger catches. Territorial delegate Anthony Dimond worked assiduously in Congress to bring all possible New Deal relief and reform programs to the territory, helping to assuage the impact of widespread unemployment. Congress set the price of gold at nearly double its market value, thereby spurring peak production before World War II.

Another period began in 1940, when the U.S. Army undertook the remilitarization of Alaska. The war transformed Alaska, as it had transformed the American West, through massive federal expenditures for bases, three hundred thousand personnel who served in the territory, and the campaign to retake Attu and Kiska from the Japanese. Then, astonishingly, the level of spending continued after 1945 as the United States entered the Cold War, and Alaska played a critical role in global strategic defense. Federal spending would be the principal base of the Alaska economy through the successful statehood campaign and the first decade of state administration. The federal government's role as a major economic player in Alaska's development during and after the war heightened colonial dependency, manifest in the private sector primarily in the salmon industry. Congress granted statehood to Alaska in 1958 (official on 3 January 1959), but because the area of federal land in the state was still substantial, and because so much of the war-era economy was federally based, statehood did not ease colonial dependence nearly as significantly as statehood advocates had hoped.

The current period of Alaska history began when an extraordinary congruence of forces in about 1970 brought together the chief elements that influence the nature and character of modern Alaska. The discovery of America's largest single deposit of petroleum at Prudhoe Bay in 1967 helped lead to Congress's settlement of Alaska Native claims in 1971, landmark legislation that simultaneously acknowledged the full equality of Alaska's Native people in the state's economic and political life and cleared the way for economic development. Congress included in that legislation environmental provisions inspired in part by the National Environmental Policy Act of 1969 and more broadly a manifestation of raised environmental consciousness in U.S. culture. Debate on those environmental provisions culminated in the Alaska Lands Act of 1980, hailed as one of the century's most important congressional environmental enactments.

Petroleum production began at Prudhoe Bay in 1977, and taxation of Prudhoe Bay oil created vast new wealth for the state. But many Alaskans interpreted the intrusion of national environmental legislation, which delayed state land selections provided by the statehood act, as a threat to further economic development. The creation of the Alaska Permanent Fund dividend program gave Alaskans a direct stake in oil production, while the elimination of the state income tax severed an important link between the people and public policy formation. The challenge of state government to find a policy to encourage petroleum production yet protect Alaska's interests formed a significant but largely unappreciated link with Alaska's past. At the end of the twentieth century, Alaska was as dependent on outside investment and on federal decisions regarding land and Natives as it had been a century earlier. Alaska thus continued to function as a colony of corporate investors and federal managers.

The statehood act, the discovery and development of oil at Prudhoe Bay, Congress's settlement of Alaska Native land claims, and the environmental provisions of the settlement act culminating in the Alaska lands act—as well as Supreme Court decisions on the meaning of the statehood act, on Native sovereignty, and on Native subsistence—all underscore the fact that Alaska's modern context, like its historical context, defined primarily by its political economy, is not generated in Alaska. Rather, what happens in Alaska is overwhelmingly a function of forces and decisions made outside Alaska. Organization and political activity by Native groups and investments by Native corporations, the taxing structure put in place by the legislature and the governor in a special session of the legislature in 1973, the creation of the Alaska Permanent Fund, lobbied through the legislature by Governor Jay Hammond in 1976, and successful resolution of state lawsuits dealing with royalties and taxes owed by the oil industry are all examples of actions within the state that have contributed to the modern context. But most actions within the state have been reactive. Alaska's history has developed in a specific world and national context, a basic fact of Alaska's cultural experience that helps explain the nature and meaning of that experience. This history of Alaska will investigate these and other developments that form the foundation on which contemporary Alaska society, economy, and politics are constructed.

9

Taking the Measure of Alaska

The Purchase of Alaska and the Politics of the Early Economy

SOME HISTORIANS HAVE credited Senator Charles Sumner with deciding to call America's newest territory Alaska.[1] Geographers and diplomats had long used that name to identify what is now the Alaska Peninsula and sometimes by extension all of the vast North American appendage that today is the forty-ninth state. Sumner was chair of the Senate Foreign Relations Committee in 1867. Because Alaska was purchased by treaty, which needed approval by Sumner and his committee before going to the full Senate for a vote, Sumner had a great deal to do with whether there would be an Alaska. The person who negotiated the treaty, Secretary of State William H. Seward, held his first negotiations with Russian minister Edouard Stoeckl in private because he was unsure of the politics of buying Alaska. When Sumner learned of the project, he was initially skeptical. But he read everything that had been published about Russian America that the Library of Congress and the Smithsonian Institution could assemble for him, and he soon became convinced that the purchase was in America's best interest.[2] In his argument to the Senate, Sumner cited all of Alaska's resources that the Russians had identified and suggested there were more. He urged that this area, which had been under the rule of imperial Russia, should in the future be graced with the republican institutions of American democracy. His arguments were convincing.

Seward, however, had a much broader view of Alaska's potential, so broad that it barely seemed to include Alaska at all. Similar to other

William Seward, U.S. secretary of state under Presidents Lincoln and Johnson, negotiated the Alaska Purchase Treaty in 1867. Alaska State Library, Alaska Purchase Centennial Photo Collection P20.023.

statesmen of the day, he believed that America's economic future depended on new world markets for the country's industrial and agricultural production. Cultivation of China and Japan, Seward thought—one opened by the Treaties of Tientsin and Aigun, the other by Commodore Matthew Perry and the Treaty of Kanagawa—would secure America's economy through the nineteenth century. "Commerce," he wrote in 1852, "is the god of boundaries."[3] Earlier still he had written that the American nation must inevitably "roll its restless waves to the icy barriers of the North, and … encounter oriental civilization on the shores of the Pacific."[4]

In this, Seward was an American imperialist, an architect of the expansion of American empire, which began with expansion westward over the Appalachian Mountains, then the Louisiana Purchase, followed by acquisition of the Oregon Country and through war, the American southwest and California. Americans generally do not imagine their country as an empire, but expansion west to the Pacific and then to Alaska and Hawai'i as well as the Philippines, Cuba, and Puerto Rico at the end of the nineteenth century carried American ambition and power well beyond its continental borders, usually to the detriment of the traditional residents of areas appropriated by the United States or brought under its control.[5]

Seward also understood that the shortest distance between two points was not necessarily a straight line, or at least not a straight line on a flat map. With others, he appreciated the economy of the "great circle" route between North America and Japan and China, shorter by nearly a third than the direct voyage across the central Pacific. Thus he had been an eager correspondent when Stoeckl began to talk of the possible sale of Russian America. In addition, with the conversion to steam already well begun, the Pacific merchant fleet would need coaling stations and provisioning ports in the north. In fact, Seward sought forward naval facilities for merchant and naval ships at all four corners of maritime America: St. Thomas and St. John in the Virgin Islands, Greenland and Iceland, which territories he attempted to purchase as secretary of state, Russian America, and Hawai'i in the Pacific.

Seward also sought to advance American interests relative to Britain, as had every American secretary of state before him. The potential purchase of Alaska not only seemed to cement ties between Russia and the United States but also appeared significantly to disadvantage their common rival England, entrapping British Columbia in a giant American pincer. U.S. possession of the Canadian West, American expansionists reasoned, would greatly strengthen the position of annexationists in eastern Canada and the maritime provinces. Britain had established crown colonies on the Pacific: Vancouver Island, where the Hudson's Bay Company had moved its western headquarters, and British Columbia, north of the mainland U.S. border (later to be combined as one). But the Canadian colonies were in no position to defend themselves, and the Americans had long coveted them. Many Americans had rushed to the Fraser River gold strike in British Columbia in 1859, and the home government had prohibited full democratic government in British Columbia lest the Americans gain a majority and seek to annex the colony to the United States. Now the Alaska purchase suggested that the United States might still force the annexation of British Columbia.

Many San Francisco businessmen shared Sumner's and Seward's interest in Alaska. During the summer of 1867, even before the formal transfer of the territory to the United States, they had purchased Russian American Company furs and ships from the last Russian governor, Prince Maksutov,[6] and soon would organize the Alaska Commercial Company to seek a charter to exploit the fur seals of the Pribilof Islands. California's U.S. senators readily supported these California interests, as they considered it their responsibility. These three distinct interests—Seward's, Sumner's, and the San Franciscans'—explain America's willingness to purchase Alaska when the Russians began to circulate the idea that they would like to liquidate their American colony. The trauma of the Civil War put off serious discussion of the issue until 1867, however.

When journalists first learned of the discussions between Seward and Stoeckl, there was considerable good-natured poking of fun at the idea. "Seward's Folly," "Walrussia," "Icebergia," and "The New National Refrigerator" were only a few of the quips printed in the press. For many years these phrases misled national historians who assumed that the purchase must not have been popular with the American people. But like Sumner, when the country's intelligentsia and journalists had an opportunity to study the question, they quickly concluded it made good sense. A survey of major U.S. newspapers in the summer of 1867 found that almost all of them editorially supported the purchase or were mute on the subject.[7] Only Horace Greeley's *New York Tribune*, the largest circulation paper at the time, vigorously opposed the treaty.

Seward and Stoeckl concluded their work on 30 March, but the treaty needed the approval of both the Russian and American Senates.[8] When the treaty came before the U.S. Senate in July 1867, where it would need a two-thirds majority to pass, there was little discussion. The country was then in the throes of a constitutional crisis that pitted the Congress and President Andrew Johnson against each other over how to handle reconstruction of the South after the Civil War. In March an extraordinary special session of Congress had passed an act designed to curb the president's authority, and the House Judiciary Committee spent the summer debating articles of impeachment. Alaska was not uppermost in the senators' minds. Nonetheless, Sumner had Spencer Baird, director of the Smithsonian Institution, and several scientists who had been in Alaska, testify before his committee, and he shared with his fellow committee members all of the data he was studying. When the full Senate took up the matter, Sumner made an impassioned, three-hour speech in favor of purchase.[9] There followed immediately a procedural vote to determine how members felt on the issue; this passed, 29 to 12, one more than the required two-thirds. Senators then passed the formal approval, 37 to 2, hardly an expression of unpopularity among those who were in the best position to understand Alaska's potential.

Embroiled in the impeachment debate, the House of Representatives did not appropriate the money for the purchase until the following summer, in 1868, while the Senate was conducting the president's trial. Even though Seward and his projects were identified with Johnson and the Johnson administration, there was no substantive opposition to funding the Alaska purchase. While the House debated Alaska, Seward dispatched another scientist, George Davidson, to make a quick survey of the region as a way of deflecting any further charges of its worthlessness. Davidson's favorable report has been credited by some with helping to bolster the case for Alaska.[10]

When the Alaska vote was taken on 14 July, the count was 114 to 43 to appropriate the funds. Forty-one of those who voted against Alaska had also voted to impeach Johnson. Some analysts later argued that senators must have been bribed to have voted so overwhelmingly in favor of purchasing Alaska. But investigations of such charges have shown that although Seward and others lobbied individual senators at dinners they held for that purpose, no bribery was paid.[11] In addition to the $7 million purchase price, the Russians requested an additional $200,000, which they used to reward Stoeckl, a common practice in many governments at the time. The check, U.S. Treasury Draft No. 9759 drawn against Riggs National Bank in Washington, D.C., is held today in the U.S. National Archives.[12]

A number of scientists also played an important role in the Alaska purchase. When Sumner schooled himself on Alaska's potential, the sources he found included the journal and reports of several, including Robert Kennicott, who had been in Russian America in the early and mid-1860s. Raised in Illinois and trained in natural history, Kennicott became the curator of the Northwestern University Museum of Natural History in 1857. When his collecting activities took him to the Red River of the North and into Canada, he resolved to explore and collect natural history specimens in Canada and Russian America. From 1860 through 1861 he worked his way north through the Lake Athabaska country, traveling with Hudson's Bay Company brigades, eventually getting as far as Fort Yukon, where he wintered over. A careful observer and tireless collector, Kennicott sent box after box of flora and fauna samples and Native artifacts back to the Chicago Academy of Sciences and the Smithsonian Institution, both sponsors of his trek. His work was astounding; he nearly single-handedly wrote the natural history description of the Canadian Northwest and overnight became an acclaimed specialist on the region.

In 1864 the U.S. government and the Western Union Telegraph Company sent Kennicott north again, this time to the mouth of the Yukon River. The American entrepreneur Perry McDonough Collins had interested Western Union in his idea for a round-the-world telegraph line (see chapter 6). Collins had secured government cooperation and sponsorship of his scheme, but Kennicott persuaded Congress that a "Scientific Corps" should accompany the construction troops to more fully justify the use of public monies. Seward had supported the scheme because it would place intelligent American observers in the heart of Russian America. As an "Alaskan expert" Kennicott won appointment as head of the Russian American division.

The corpsmen collected a wealth of specimens and information. Henry Bannister, for example, spent many months at St. Michael near the mouth of the Yukon making weather observations. William Healey Dall, as indefatigable a collector as Kennicott, named more than two hundred species of northern fauna and flora. The reports that the scientists filed with the Smithsonian Institution were an important source of accurate data on Russian America. The project was beset with tragedy, however, for the successful laying of a trans-Atlantic telegraph cable led to abandonment of the round-the-world project at about the same time Kennicott died from mysterious causes on the Yukon River not far from Nulato.

In 1869, William Henry Seward retired from public life and embarked on a trip around the world. One of his stops was at Sitka, Alaska. Although Alaska's own resources had not been primary in his thinking about the acquisition, Alaska was, he prophesied, a "great fishery, forest and mineral storehouse of the world." More in keeping with his specific interest in the territory, he suggested that the Aleutian Islands would be

Sitka, ca. 1886. View from Castle Hill, with the St. Michael Orthodox Cathedral at center. Anchorage Museum Rasmuson Center, Don Ingalls Collection B1988.003.001.

"hereafter ... the stepping stones between the two continents" of North America and Asia."[13] The Pacific, he argued, would be the principal future theater of American interest.

Seward recommended, and the president ordered, that Alaska should be temporarily designated as a military district and placed under the jurisdiction of the U.S. Army. Despite Sumner's intense, quick study, there was a great deal unknown about the territory. The Interior had not been mapped, there were few non-Native residents, and the character and intentions of the Native populations were not clear. Until more information could be gathered, official Washington, D.C., deemed it best to proceed with caution. Everyone expected that civil government would be established soon. "It is presumed that the transfer of this country will be followed by an organized territorial civil government with the extension over it of the general laws of the United States," wrote Major General H. W. Halleck, commander of the army's Division of the Pacific, a sentiment echoed by Seward in his speech to the citizens of Sitka in 1869.[14] Civil government would come but not for seventeen years after the purchase. During the interim first the U.S. Army, and subsequently the U.S. Navy, would have jurisdiction over the area. Although the military did not formally proclaim martial law, in effect the army and navy commanders were the sole arbiters of justice and order.

In 1867 when Seward and Stoeckl were discussing Alaska's future, and Sumner was studying all the reports that had ever been published about it, no one bothered to ask the Alaska Native people what they thought about the proposed purchase. Not only did both the United States and Russia ignore their sovereignty in the region, but no one officially asked the Natives' opinions about the transfer. U.S. officials were not in touch with most of the Native groups in Alaska, and for the most part they had little notion of who these Natives were. But some of Alaska's Natives had opinions, particularly the Tlingits in and around Sitka, and they were not bashful about expressing them. The U.S. Army commander at Sitka reported that many "frequently take occasion to express their dislike at not having been consulted about the transfer of the territory. They do not like the idea of the whites settling in their midst without being subjected to their jurisdiction."[15] This was in no way unusual. In this as in most other matters, experience in Alaska mirrored that elsewhere. Natives were viewed by the government and the military as a problem, one to be controlled in such a way as to facilitate white settlement and capitalist development. With the rise of the Native sovereignty movement in Alaska in the first decades of the twenty-first century, some Native leaders and historians have suggested that the American purchase was fraudulent because the true owners of the land did not sell it, and the Russians could not sell it because they did not own it. As is explained later in this book, the United States did not address the issue of aboriginal title, indigenous title to land in the United States, until well into the twentieth century and did not formally extinguish Alaska Native title to most of Alaska until 1971.

GOVERNING ALASKA

Following the transfer ceremony in October 1867, General Jefferson Columbus Davis occupied the military barracks in Sitka and dispatched companies of his 250-man garrison to Tongass, on the north side of Dixon Entrance, the international boundary, to Wrangell, the site of the Hudson's Bay Company post at the mouth of the Stikine River, to St. Paul in the Pribilof Islands, and to Kodiak and Kenai.[16] At headquarters, top brass undertook the establishment of a new Alaska Department of the western army, the Army of the Columbia. But while the wheels of bureaucracy slowly ground in Washington, Davis discovered that his troops were not really needed. There was little his contingent at Tongass could do except monitor the slight traffic that stopped by. A troop company did set up at Kodiak, but the squad that was sent to Kenai managed to smash their boat on Dangerous Cape at Port Graham (in Cook Inlet) and had to return to Kodiak for the winter. There and at Sitka the army realized that the Natives were peaceable and cooperative. Several Tlingit spokesmen announced that the Tlingit had never sold more than a few acres at Sitka to the Russians, but in the face of the army's show of strength, most determined that for the moment the best policy was accommodation with the United States.[17] By the time the new department became a reality, Davis and Halleck already were recommending its dismantling; it was scrapped in 1870.[18] But the army did have one chief responsibility: Congress charged it with maintaining order in the territory until other arrangements for government might be arranged.

By the terms of the purchase treaty, Russians could stay in the territory if they liked; if they did not, the United States would transport them to Russia, or to the American West Coast ports. Many Russians initially thought to stay but soon found themselves unable to cope with their changed circumstances. The army took no responsibility for the Russian civilians who were now on their own, many for the first time. In addition, confusion over what was public and private property exacerbated their distress. As soon as the transfer was completed, Davis evicted persons living in Russian American Company houses; many had no other place to live. The military court did not sympathize.

Several hundred Americans flocked to Sitka, hoping to get in on the ground floor of the West's latest boomtown opportunity. Historian Ted C. Hinckley estimates that together the army and the civilian population in the fall of 1867 did not exceed nine hundred.[19] The most important of them all was a group of San Francisco businessmen headed by Baltimore entrepreneur Hayward M. Hutchinson. Hutchinson had come west with his friend General Rousseau, the purchase commissioner. After visiting Portland, Hutchinson went to Sitka at the end of December. Working with Prince Maksutov, he purchased nearly the complete holdings of the Russian American Company: "buildings, boats, and paraphernalia." As Hutchinson later testified to Congress, "I bought everything they had."[20]

Organized as Hutchinson, Kohl and Company, the group later organized as the Alaska Commercial Company and secured a twenty-year monopoly lease on the Pribilof Island fur seal fishery. Congress approved a monopoly because the company insisted that competition would result in lower profits than the expense of carrying on the business.

The other go-getters who flocked to Sitka were not so fortunate. They soon discovered that the community that had been sustained by the Russian American Company since its founding had no independent economic base. Without a local resource of economic value, and without a continuing flow of outside capital, there was no way to make money, which is why they had come north. The easily accessible commercial furs had been effectively depleted. No minerals of value had been discovered. The timber of the forests could not compete with upper Midwestern and Pacific Northwest timber, which was much closer to the markets. There was some potential in fish, mostly cod, but the cost and difficulty of transporting fish to market militated against development. The canned salmon industry had not yet been developed. One combine developed guano deposits near Killisnoo, but despite the pristine nature of the resource, they soon exhausted it.

Without an economic base, something that would sustain the economic livelihood of would-be settlers, it was difficult for Congress to justify

THE KILLING-GANG AT WORK.

Method of slaughtering Fur-seals on the grounds, near the village, St. Paul Island.

The drove in waiting.   Sealers knocking down a "pod."   Natives skinning.

Killing Seals on St. Paul Island, Privilovs, by Henry Elliott, U.S. Treasury agent. The painting depicts the annual slaughter by Aleut workers under supervision of Alaska Commercial Company employees. Alaska State Library P20.058.

immediately extending the traditional land use and civil government policies. Potential migrants were not interested in going to Alaska to live a life of subsistence. As with migrants into the American West before and after the Civil War, settlement rested on profit, individual profit for farmers, miners, loggers, and ranchers. Without a resource to sell on capitalist terms, that is, for more than the cost of producing it, settlement had no incentive. People did not go west, nor were they interested in going to Alaska, for the spiritual qualities of broad landscapes; they went for economic improvement. The development of resources required major capital investment, for a mine or cannery cost tens of thousands of dollars to construct. Settlers did not have the necessary capital for such development, so it had to come from absentee investors and owners interested in long-term profit.[21] The jobs, and the services provided in towns that rested on the payrolls associated with the jobs, fueled the western economy along with federal aid.

In addition, Alaska was difficult to get to. Without an appreciable population, steamship companies had no incentive to service the territory. Furthermore, insurance rates were high because navigation aids were inadequate, and shipwreck was a constant danger. Infrequent transportation meant infrequent communication. Congress would have been irresponsible to have encouraged citizens to move to a remote region where there was no way to make a living and where they would be isolated and marooned. Congress authorized the Coast and Geodetic Survey to chart coastal waters and commissioned various surveys and reports to learn more about the territory. But without an economic base there would be no significant migration. Without civil government the several hundred citizens who did go to Alaska, mostly to Sitka, had no authorization for establishing town councils or undertaking any other actions of self-governance associated with new development. In place of civil government, the army handled routine drunkenness, petty theft, domestic strife, and other minor offenses to civil order, although at the peril of public criticism, because martial law was not authorized. Those who committed serious crimes were sent to the nearest federal court, which was at Port Angeles in Washington Territory.

The citizens discovered the realities of constitutional government when they attempted to govern themselves. Although they could not secure title to property, because the Congress had not implemented any land disposal provisions, they went forward anyway with what they conceived to be their rights and responsibilities. With General Davis's blessing they elected a city council and mayor, levied a subscription to build a school and hire a teacher, and generally settled down to administer their own affairs. However, when one of their number inquired of the military commander by whose authority they did these things, particularly when they levied taxes, the general had to reply that they were sanctioned only by his fiat. Purchased by the American people through Congress in the ratification of the treaty, the land, territory, and people were subject to the will of Congress. For the time being and until such time as it might provide for civil government, Congress willed that the military should govern Alaska. When that one citizen protested that the general did not have the authority to sanction elections and taxes, he was correct; only Congress did.

Military government sometimes had tragic results for the Tlingit Indians of the archipelago, for the army brought little sensitivity to its relations with them. The American government's refusal to recognize Indians as U.S.

citizens was confirmed in court cases after the Civil War.[22] Congressional legislation in 1871 banned any further treaty making with Indians, leaving the constitutional status of Indians uncertain. There were no treaties with Alaska Natives. This fact would have profound implications in the future, for without treaties there were no reservations. Thus the Natives' legal status and such claims they might make to land were uncertain. But at the time of the purchase this was a matter of no practical consequence. In 1869, Vincent Colyer, the secretary of the Board of Indian Commissioners, an advisory body, traveled to Alaska and prepared an enthusiastic report on the Native populations. He particularly cited their economic independence and their intellectual capability. Compared with what he interpreted as the lassitude of western reservation tribes' dependency on government rations, Alaska Natives seemed to Colyer energetic and confident.

In 1871 the board urged the Bureau of Indian Affairs to undertake a program of education and acculturation for Alaska Natives similar to what the bureau had designed for Plains and western Indians but without containment on reservations. The bureau briefly considered the prospect but ultimately rejected it because, they said, they were not equipped to deal with non-Indians, that is, Inuits and Aleuts. The actual reason, however, was that the agency was overextended and under severe criticism for corruption and inefficiency. Commissioner Francis Walker decided that if it was to survive congressional criticism, the bureau needed to get its continental house in order.[23]

After the Civil War the U.S. Army in the West generated a negative view of Indian legitimacy and capability among commanders and troops, a view many brought to the remote frontier post of Sitka in 1867. Individual army and later navy officers serving in Alaska often commented agreeably on the nature of the Natives, but neither institution was prepared to address the issue of acculturation or to accommodate Indian cultural traditions. Consistent with late-nineteenth-century American cultural assumption, the military imagined only two possible futures for the American Indian: extinction or assimilation.[24]

In Alaska the army and navy limited their activity to enforcing American justice, essentially without regard to Indian culture, Indian experience, or Indian dignity, generally responding poorly to the challenges of cross-cultural contact. When, for example, a Sitka settler killed two Indians on separate occasions, General Davis's response was to incarcerate the man after the second killing, but only until the settler community demanded his release. The Indians at Sitka continued to reside alongside the old Russian town, now occupied by the Americans and still surrounded by a palisade. They could enter the gates at nine in the morning but had to be clear of the village by six in the evening. On one occasion, when a Sitka clan chief appeared drunk on the parade ground after having visited with Davis and failed to stop when hailed by the sentry, a second sentry kicked him solidly. In an ensuing scuffle an Indian got hold of a sentry's rifle, which he took with him to the Indian village. Davis sent a detachment to the village to arrest and imprison the chief and the Indian with the rifle. In another incident, when two white men were killed in the village of Kake, Davis sailed to the island to apprehend the Indian murderers. By the time he arrived, however, the Indians had fled, so Davis burned their entire village. The military was determined to demonstrate that American law and justice would prevail. A decade later, after the U.S. Navy had replaced the army, a similar incident took place at the village of Angoon.[25] In 1973 the U.S. Indian Claims Commission awarded $90,000 to the village as compensation for clan property destroyed in the 1882 bombing.

Alcohol abuse by the military, the citizen civilians, and the Indians greatly exacerbated the army's problem and the Natives' circumstances. President U. S. Grant had issued an executive order in 1868 prohibiting the importation or sale of spirituous liquor, an order confirmed by the designation of the territory as "Indian Country" in 1873. But smuggling was rife, and the Indians soon learned to make their own alcohol from imported molasses.[26] Arrests for drunk and disorderly conduct were common. The major newspapers in the East covered all of these episodes with sympathy for the Natives and criticism of the military. In truth, such incidents bespoke more the inflexibility and cultural monism of American justice than military incompetence in dealing with the Alaska situation.

Historians have lamented and condemned the period of military rule. Writing in *The State of Alaska*, published at the height of the statehood movement in 1954, four years before Congress voted Alaska statehood, Territorial Governor Ernest Gruening (1939–53) called the military period "The Era of Total Neglect."[27] Many have noted the absence of codified law and lack of access to an organized judicial system as well as the fact that there was no mail delivery and there were no lighthouses and other navigational aids. In these circumstances it is not surprising that the population was sparse. On his visit in 1869, Seward argued that a show of military force was necessary with fewer than two thousand non-Natives living among more than twenty-five thousand Natives.[28]

But this was not a function of federal neglect. The real problem was the lack of an economic base in Alaska. Neither soldiers nor Natives provided sufficient business to sustain the merchants of Sitka, the only appreciable non-Native settlement, and the available capital soon migrated south to obtain necessary supplies. Even land disposal and title would not have created a marketable resource where there was none. In the face of this reality, Sitka atrophied. By 1873 more than half the boomers had left, and with the non-Native population barely more than two hundred, the city council held its last meeting. The U.S. Congress did not neglect Alaska. In fact, numerous department and bureau agents traveled the territory every year during the military period, gathering data and informing both executive agencies and congressional committees. Congress created the Alaska customs district in 1868 and special treasury agents and the commissioner of customs filed reports. Special army reports were filed as well.

At times there seemed too much information coming back from Alaska. Two scientists who did work in the territory, Henry Elliott and William Healey Dall, wrote contradictory analyses of Alaska in the early 1870s. Dall in particular contributed many papers on a variety of subjects, including hydrography, geology, zoology, botany, and ethnography. In 1870 he published a compilation of his notes, *Alaska and Its Resources,* and in the early 1870s still more scientific examinations. Historian Morgan Sherwood has called Dall "Dean of Alaskan Experts."[29]

Elliott went to Alaska in 1872, spending most of his time on the Pribilof Islands. Not only did he compile important information about the seal fishery and harvest, but he also painted more than one hundred watercolors of the islands. He worked with Alaska Commercial Company (ACC) personnel to gather data on the rest of the territory. The ACC established a number of posts on the interior rivers to collect furs and staked a number of prospector/traders to annual supplies. Elliott's work in no way matched Dall's but constituted a useful contribution. Elliott's view of the territory's potential was much more pessimistic than was Dall's, however. He thought the territory had no resources that could be readily developed. As a scientific laboratory it was wonderful, but beyond that it had little value, none for prospective settlers. He recommended withdrawal of the army but retention of a single customs agent at Kodiak. Indian reservations would not be necessary, he wrote; the only necessity was a general agent to keep the government well informed.

Elliott's view echoed the sentiments of Hutchinson's Alaska Commercial Company. The fur trade, as Sherwood has written, "thrives on vacant land unhindered by legal restrictions," and certainly the company opposed the creation of a territorial government.[30] But it did not do so consistently and often helped government employees and scientists in their work. Disgruntled ACC competitors kept up a drumbeat of criticism of the company's monopoly on the Pribilofs, but a congressional investigation could not substantiate charges of wrongdoing. Elliott worked closely with ACC personnel on the islands, but it is not clear that he was paid by the company. Nonetheless, ACC arguments against development would have been consistent with the prevailing national view at the time that corporate exploitation of natural resources should not be impeded by government action.

Dall rushed to counter Elliott's negative view and was joined by others. William Gouverneur Morris, special treasury agent, wrote that successful experiments with raising vegetables proved Alaska had some agricultural potential. Others looked toward mineral development. Marcus Baker, who had helped Dall in his hydrographic surveys, criticized Elliott's limited experience in Alaska. But in the face of no demonstrated economic viability, Elliott's voice prevailed. At a time when there were few non-Natives in the territory, Congress found it difficult to justify the expenditures necessary for civil governance. A governor and entourage, a judge and court system, together with marshals and jails, clerks and secretaries, all would have cost money. Congress had been willing to expend funds for development in the other western territories, but there had been settlers and miners who needed services. In Alaska such was not the case. And, as noted, much of the region's interior had yet to be mapped, and transportation was complicated by high insurance rates and lack of demand.

Some analysts have suggested that the situation in Alaska at this time represented a classic catch-22: on the one hand, the non-Natives had no support or title and without them could not remain in the region, and thus were few in number; on the other hand, the government would not provide support or title because the non-Natives were so few in number. But that argument also ignores the lack of an economic base. As the atrophying of Sitka indicates, would-be settlers did not go to Sitka or Alaska just to be there; they went to make money. As yet, there were few money-making opportunities in Alaska. Congressional restraint thus might better be understood as prudence than neglect.[31]

Just how much did Sitka atrophy when it became clear that would-be settlers had no way to make a living there? Determining the exact number of settlers presented a problem. The man placed in charge of compiling the first census taken after the purchase, in 1880, was Ivan Petroff, a Russian from St. Petersburg with a checkered history. Although a U.S. Army deserter, he had worked for respected San Francisco publisher Hubert Howe Bancroft. In gathering his data in Alaska, Petroff stated that he had traveled to places where in fact he had not. Historian Richard A. Pierce has called Petroff "a habitual liar."[32] Petroff satisfactorily explained the inconsistencies in his 1880 report and was retained again to compile the 1890 census, but while it was being prepared for publication, evidence came to light that he had falsified some translations he did for the State Department regarding a sealing controversy in the Bering Sea; the falsifications strengthened the American claims. He was dismissed from the census and his name expunged from it. Although he apparently could not refrain from fabricating data, Petroff retracted many of his false claims, and in the final analysis his work has been considered generally reliable and hugely influential.[33] It is possible that there were twice as many non-Natives in Alaska as he reported in the 1880 census. However, even if that were true, congressional reluctance to extend civil government seems reasonable, for not until after Petroff was gone from Alaska that year and editing his census report did economic circumstances in Alaska change significantly.

In 1877 army commanders in the Pacific Northwest withdrew the complete Alaska garrison. Ostensibly, the command needed the troops to pursue Chief Joseph and his Nez Perce band, who refused to settle on the reservation provided them, but in fact the army was glad for an excuse to dump a responsibility that could only lead to more negative publicity, criticism, and embarrassment. The removal left Treasury Department revenue cutters as the territory's only government policing arm. One week after the troops left Sitka, the local Tlingits came into the town, tore down a large portion of the stockade, occupied all the empty buildings, and took out doors, windows, and partitions for their own homes. Clan chief Annahootz told the few remaining whites that the Russians had stolen the country from the Tlingit and sold it to the Americans for a large amount of money. The Tlingits concluded that now the Americans were angry because they realized that the Russians had deceived them about the country's value to the Indians. "We are glad to say that after so many years hard fight we get our country back again."[34]

Such talk alarmed the townspeople and the collector of customs, now the territory's highest-ranking official. He wrote to the secretary of the treasury that "the Indians indulge in threats which no doubt they will put in practice when they find that no gunboat of any kind appears on the scene." But the Indians did not intend any bloodshed, for they had seen the nature of the American response. What the townspeople were hearing was competitive Indian bombast.[35] Calm prevailed until 1879, when an Indian murdered a white miner near the town. Other whites jailed the Indian, which the Indians said they could accept if the white government would compensate them for five Indians drowned the previous year while working for a white trader in the Bering Sea. When the Indians got drunk and rowdy, the whites sent off a petition to the British naval facility at Victoria, British Columbia. They were threatened with massacre, the whites claimed, and although they had sent word to their government, they were not confident when it would be able to respond.

Begging that "all forms of etiquette between governments" be set aside, the Sitkans pleaded for help. Securing permission to do so from Washington, a British warship, the HMS *Osprey*, immediately sailed for Sitka. Tempers and anxieties cooled when the ship arrived; eastern newspapers gathered that the Sitkans had exaggerated their danger, and in any case the revenue cutter *Alaska* arrived a month after the *Osprey*. The incident demonstrated some of the peril of the absence of authority and civil government. The U.S. Navy would take over policing duties, but experience had shown already that this could not be a permanent solution.[36] But Congress still could not justify the expenses of civil government for a handful of white settlers who might or might not stay in the territory.

Two influences would finally move the Congress to action in Alaska, however. The first was a Protestant missionary effort among Alaska Natives. Seventeen Russian Orthodox chapels and schools remained after the American purchase, most receiving some meager financial support from Russia but chiefly maintained by their parishioners. Most were in the Aleutians, on Kodiak Island, and in the Yukon delta region. Few of the eighteen Tlingit villages in the Southeast had resident Christian clerics.[37] In 1877, Dr. Sheldon Jackson, a Presbyterian church organizer then based in Denver and active in the Rocky Mountain region, traveled to

Wrangell with Mrs. Amanda McFarland, a missionary teacher. With Jackson's help McFarland established a church and school at the small town that had experienced a substantial boom when gold had been discovered two years earlier in the Cassiar district of northwest British Columbia, above the headwaters of the Stikeen River. Wrangell quickly became a service center for the Cassiar. The town's new residents included mostly miners and merchants. Some of the resident Indians were Christian, and one of them had written a letter asking for missionaries to help combat the deleterious effects of the gambling, drinking, and carousing that quickly came to characterize the new settlement.

SHELDON JACKSON

Jackson would leave his mark on Alaska. An energetic, able, and dedicated reform churchman, he dedicated the remainder of his career to building churches and schools in Alaska and to finding private and government funds to support them. Typically, he would travel to Alaska in the summer with building and curricular materials, and new missionary teachers, to supervise the erection of new mission sites. He spent his winters in the East, collecting funds in churches, lecturing to education conferences and Indian reform groups, writing volumes of tracts and portrayals of Alaska, and lobbying members of Congress and officials in Washington, D.C., and elsewhere. Jackson's dedication was unswerving and his talents were considerable. Soon missionary stations sprouted in most of the Tlingit villages and in Native communities across Alaska.[38] One story that has enjoyed wide circulation relates a meeting Jackson held in New York City with representatives of the various mission churches. At the meeting Alaska was divided into territories for each denomination. The story may be apocryphal; documentation for it is unclear. Jackson was a familiar speaker at almost every Protestant church conference in the 1880s. He urged all the Christian churches to get involved in Alaska, and the territory was so vast that there was no need for competition that in any case would have represented duplication and inefficiency. His primary interest was not the supremacy of his own church but rather the "civilizing" of the Native population.

Jackson's initiative in Alaska coincided exactly with the culmination of the drive to acculturate and assimilate American Indians and proceeded directly from it.[39] "Civilization of the Natives" was a common phrase and idea during the last half of the nineteenth century among missionary associations and within the federal government. Both the Bureau of Indian Affairs and the missionary reformers pursued the same policy, and the missionary societies were integrally involved in the generation of post–Civil War Indian policy.[40] What the missionaries and the Bureau of Indian Affairs meant by "civilizing the Indian" was acculturation, the supplanting of Native culture with mainstream, white, Protestant, American culture. And there was little doubt regarding what the reformers and the government policy makers considered American culture to be. Above all, they meant individualism.

Where the Indians were economically communal, Americanism meant economic individualism and self-reliance. Where clan, tribe, and fixed status characterized Indian social structure, Americanism meant social individualism and social mobility. Where Indian societies lacked permanent political leadership, Americanism meant a political system, democratic and free in nature, resting ultimately on individual choice. Where Indian mythology was dominated by animism and fatalism, Americanism meant freedom of thought based on science and individual choice. For the missionaries, thought was not entirely free, as Christianization was integral to their world view. Punctuality and hygiene also were integral, as were propriety and Western dress. Moreover, unlike the Russians before them, the American missionaries did not seek much to build on Native cultural norms but instead sought to replace what they found with their notion of legitimacy.[41]

Language was central to the acculturation process and in Alaska, Jackson instructed his teachers to speak, and allow to be spoken, only English. This was impractical at first; in actuality the teachers relied on Native interpreters, of which there were many, a significant number of Tlingit having adapted to the American purchase by learning the language. The teachers sought to suppress the tradition of the potlatch but initially did not have great success in doing so. In many villages the teachers distributed soap and alarm clocks, perhaps the most tangible instruments of their program. In Sitka the naval commander L. A. Beardslee issued an identity tag to all children stamped with their house number and fined or incarcerated parents who did not take the responsibility for getting the children regularly to school and on time. Beardslee also undertook to destroy stills and other paraphernalia associated with the domestic manufacture of liquor, even establishing an Indian police force, aping government efforts in the western continental states. Prostitution, slavery, and the torture of women accused of witchcraft were other affronts to official sensibilities that both Jackson and Beardslee sought to eliminate.

Against his better judgment, Jackson authorized the establishment of a boarding school at Sitka in 1879. The number of orphans taken in by the teachers there had grown sufficiently large that such a course seemed unavoidable. The school, named initially the Sitka Presbyterian Indian Industrial School, quickly became the regional seat of the mission and the center of the American acculturation effort in Alaska. Jackson met regularly with the major Indian reform groups of the period, the so-called Friends of the Indian, who posed assimilation as the only viable alternative to extermination and the ultimate vanishing of the Indian. In Alaska, Jackson's work was an extension of their philosophy. With them, Jackson was remarkably naively confident that the transformation could be accomplished in a single generation through education. He believed that one generation converted to American values would teach those who came after it, and the work would be done; Indian culture would be eradicated. The principal agent of acculturation would be the school, and to that end Jackson sought to establish Indian day schools in as many villages as the Presbyterian Board of Home Missions could support.

It is difficult today to appreciate the sincerity and authenticity of the Indian reformers of the later nineteenth century. Their commitment to acculturation seems not just naive but retrograde, for it can be interpreted as cultural genocide. Yet sincere they were; they were fully persuaded that without acculturation, Native Americans would become extinct and that they, the reformers, had a moral responsibility to prevent that in any way they could. The way they chose was forced acculturation. That the policy served others with nefarious interests—those who coveted Indian land—should not blind us to the genuine concern of the reformers. Their blindness should not be ours. It is not unusual in history for the motivations of one generation to be viewed by succeeding ones as misguided and destructive, or at very least a manifestation of the law of unintended consequences.

At the same time Jackson began to lobby Congress to allocate funds for Indian acculturation work in Alaska. In the early 1880s, he was a ubiquitous presence in Washington, D.C., arguing constantly his case for the government's responsibility for Alaska Natives. Moreover, he acquired a powerful ally in a fellow Presbyterian, Senator Benjamin Harrison of

Indiana, who favored Jackson's conviction that the government needed to embrace action in regard to Alaska. Nor did Jackson limit his lobbying to church groups. He also generated resolutions from the National Education Association and from a number of state education groups. In 1883 he arranged for the printing of one hundred thousand circulars urging "friends of education" to flood Washington with appeals for government action. Jackson was persuasive, and in 1884 Congress addressed Alaska in the first organic legislation adopted for the territory. But Congress's response was not due solely to Jackson's efforts, and it is doubtful that his remonstrations alone would have prevailed had not circumstances in Alaska changed dramatically. For at the same time that Jackson became enamored of the territory as virgin mission ground, others succumbed to a more tangible attraction. Alaska had begun its enduring fascination with gold.

Only the generation of a reliable economic enterprise in Alaska would give Congress the confidence to begin territorial development. Gold would be Alaska's early economic foundation, proving as irresistible to Congress as it was to businessmen looking for a lucrative investment. After the California gold rush of 1849, prospectors fanned out all across the North American West. Strikes of precious and valuable minerals followed one upon another from Arizona and Colorado to Idaho and Montana. In 1858 gold was discovered on the Fraser River east of Vancouver, British Columbia, and in the early 1860s in the Caribou district several hundred miles farther north. The opening of British Columbia's Cassiar district in the mid-1870s encouraged activity in Alaska and stimulated the development of the town of Wrangell. Already the brothers Francois and Moise Mercier, former Hudson's Bay Company trappers, had gone to work for the Alaska Commercial Company to organize trapping and prospecting along the Yukon River and its tributaries in both Alaska and Canada. The posts they established along the river system constituted the principal support network for trapper-prospectors in Alaska's interior. In 1873 three of the more important of these came into the country, men who would make their marks in the Alaska outback: Leroy "Jack" McQuesten, Arthur Harper, and Alfred Mayo.[42] But climate and distance in the Far North dictated a slow pace. In the 1874 trapping and trading season only thirty-two white men lived on Alaska's three major interior rivers, the Yukon, the Tanana, and the Kuskokwim.

Alaska's first major gold strike was not in the Interior; it was on the coast, along Gastineau Channel between the mainland and Douglas Island, north

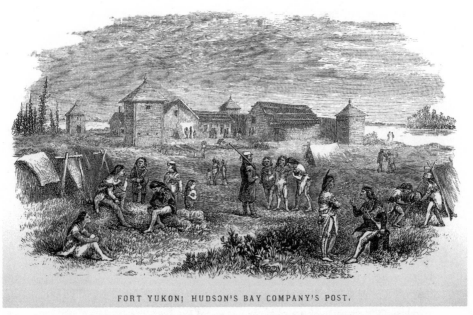

FORT YUKON; HUDSON'S BAY COMPANY'S POST.

Fort Yukon, Hudson's Bay Company Post, pained summer 1867 by Frederick Whymper, artist with the Western Union Russian American Overland Telegraph expedition. Anchorage Museum Rasmuson Center, Fort Yukon; Hudson's Bay Col post, from *Travels and Adventure in the Territory of Alaska* (London: John Murray, Albemarle Street, 1868).

of Stephens Passage. A mining engineer at Sitka, George Pilz, had staked two prospectors, Richard Harris and Joe Juneau, who persuaded several Tlingits from Auk Bay to show them potentially rich gold placers on creeks in the mountains above the channel. Gold is usually found in mineralized rock, the result of volcanic or other uprising from the earth's magma; such deposits are called lode gold. Often the rock closest to the surface has been eroded by temperature change and by the action of surface water. The resulting flecks, grains, and nuggets, usually washed into the bottoms of creeks, are called placer gold; it is the gold that can be most easily taken by individual prospectors, using a pan or a sluice. Lode gold, however, usually requires a considerable investment for tunneling, sinking shafts, blasting, and crushing. Development of lode deposits is capital and labor intensive, usually requiring significant investment and the contracting of a force of miners working for wages. Most of the gold in the creeks above Gastineau Channel was placer gold, which played out after a couple of years.

With news of the discovery in 1880, prospectors and adventurers from across the North and down the coast rushed to the area; by that fall there were perhaps two thousand people at what would become Juneau, Alaska. One of them, Pierre Brussard, had staked a claim on promising rock on Douglas Island. Needing funds to purchase supplies for a better prospect he had staked, he sold his claim for $5 to an experienced mining engineer named John Treadwell, who represented some San Francisco businessmen. In May 1882, Treadwell set up a five-stamp mill at the claim.[43] Treadwell's major contribution to Alaska's history was to organize the group of investors willing to pursue profit in the territory. In so doing, he established the model for modern Alaskan development.

Joe Juneau, who with Richard Harris "discovered" placer deposits in the mountains above Gastineau Channel when shown them by Auk Bay Tlingit Indians circa 1880. Alaska State Library P20.012.

This investment in equipment and transportation created jobs, jobs that drew immigrant settlers to Alaska from the contiguous states and territories as well as from foreign countries. The jobs paid sufficiently that workers had the discretionary income to re-create the cultural forms with which they were familiar. The workers would not have come if they had not been paid well enough. Soon business people set up trade shops to supply the workers with the goods and services they considered necessities and the amenities and entertainments they felt they deserved as modern Americans. By 1890 the growing towns of Juneau and Douglas boasted between them five hotels (with restaurants) and three lodging houses, two freestanding restaurants, thirty-six saloons, two drug stores, thirteen general merchandise stores, two grocery stores, two barbers, a steam laundry, two stove and tin ware stores, a shoe shop, two breweries, two jewelers, two fur and curio shops, two cigar factories, a slaughterhouse and a meat market, a newspaper, a photographer's studio, a confectioner, several blacksmith shops, and a lumber yard.[44] This same phenomenon of replication was repeated in the other towns that soon punctuated the southeastern coast and later, the wilderness interior. Alaska's modern evolution was now fully engaged.

Juneau, 1909, expanding up the foreslope of Mount Roberts. Alaska State Library P20.1124.

The Treadwell deposit was quite low-grade ore, that is, the amount of gold in the crushed rock was not great, a few ounces per ton of ore. But there was a lot of it, enough eventually to support four different mines. Because developing the deposit required no overland transportation with associated costs, it could be mined profitably. Much to the investors' delight, the site continued to produce large quantities of gold-bearing ore. By 1887 the Treadwell works, Alaska Mill and Mining Company, boasted a 250-stamp mill, the largest then operating in North America. By 1900 the mines had produced more than $17 million worth of gold. The complex continued to produce until a cave-in under Gastineau Channel flooded the mines in 1917. The Treadwell became Juneau's economic base, supporting a permanent population of twenty-five hundred or more. In subsequent years other investors developed lode deposits on the channel's mainland side. Seeing signs of permanence, political leaders in the new community began to agitate for civil government. In 1881 they called a convention of "all the towns in the region." Five delegates each from Wrangell, Sitka, and Juneau met in Juneau and organized an election in those towns for a territorial delegate. Again, citizen-initiated civic action had the support of the military, although the territory's official status had not changed, and thus the actions taken by the settlers were extra-constitutional. Mottrom Ball, the collector of customs and the principal convention organizer, received 234 votes, the majority. Ball traveled to Washington, D.C., where his petition on behalf of the Alaskans was dismissed by Congress but not before the legislators voted to reimburse him $4,665 for his efforts, which, Alaska historian Robert De Armond wrote, was probably more than he would have made wading around in a placer claim in the Juneau gold district.[45]

But development of the Treadwell works gave the region an appearance of substance that Congress could not long ignore. The workforce at the mines were wage earners, not prospectors. Within a few years increasing numbers of families began to settle in the town. The requisite merchants, bankers, lawyers, and other townspeople quickly accumulated and looked as if they intended to stay. Now supporters of government action in Alaska could point to more than an empty territory populated by unacculturated Indians, Inuits, and Aleuts befriended by dedicated but single-focused churchmen and churchwomen. Now Alaska began more to resemble the western frontier of committed pioneer settlers who needed their government's help to conquer the wilderness and plant the rudiments of civilization and American culture, a story becoming increasingly familiar in popular literature and historical imagery.[46]

Accordingly, by the organic act of 17 May 1884, Congress provided for the new region a skeletal territorial government. By its terms Alaska was officially designated a civil district with the external boundaries of the purchase, and the president was authorized to appoint a governor. The law established the entire territory as one judicial district with a judge, a district attorney, a clerk, a marshal, four deputy marshals, and four commissioners, that is, local justices of the peace, at Sitka, Juneau, Wrangell, and Unalaska. The court had the authority to appoint additional commissioners as they might be required. The laws of Oregon state were to be applied wherever applicable, and the federal district court there was to accept appeals from the Alaska court. The general mining laws of the United States were extended to the territory.

Responding directly to Jackson's representation of the needs of the Native population, the act made provision for a "General Agent of Education," responsible to the U.S. commissioner of education; the agent had the responsibility of establishing schools for school-age children "without regard to race." Otherwise, the Natives were "not to be disturbed in the possession of any lands actually in their use or occupation or claimed by them."

The act made no provision for land disposal, such to be addressed at a later time. It is highly significant that the act followed closely in time the discovery of an economic base and the setting in place of a permanent population of whites whose livelihood was linked directly to that base. With nearly all western territories in their earliest incarnations, that economic base lay in natural resource exploitation. Until there was a citizen population in the territory and some means for its economic prosperity, Congress refused to encourage settlers to move to Alaska and made only the most meager, and least expensive, provision for the aboriginal inhabitants. But once there was a citizen body to command their attention, and to legislate for, Congress acted with reasonable dispatch.

The postponement of land disposal, made much of by some historians, was not unusual and should not be surprising, particularly given the absence of accurate, scientific surveys of the territory's interior and of the Native populations. Not until 1885 did the army conduct a general reconnaissance of the Copper, the Tanana, the Koyukuk, and the Yukon River drainages under the able leadership of Lieutenant Henry Tureman Allen.[47] The provision for preservation of Native lands, however problematic of enforcement it might have been, showed Congress's intention to avoid in Alaska the creation of the dismal dependency of the plains and western Indians in the continental states. The education article, while it might sound enlightened on the matter of integration, in fact was not. The provision did not mean that Native and white children would attend the same schools. Rather, it meant that schools would be established for children wherever they were, in Native villages or white towns. In the few communities where there were both, there would be two schools, one for each race.

Senator (later president) Benjamin Harrison of Indiana, author of the bill, argued that he and his Committee on Territories understood fully the act's scope and limitations. He agreed, he told the Senate during debate on the bill, that the act constituted the most minimal civil provisions. It was an expedient, a temporary measure, something to serve the limited need and limited population until such time as greater settlement and development should warrant more. Again, it can be argued that Congress perpetuated in the act the catch-22 situation that had obtained under military rule: namely, settlers would not go to the territory without greater government support and security, but Congress would not provide more support and security until there were more settlers. But the extent of the gold deposits at Juneau was unclear, the fur gathering along the interior rivers did not represent economic support for more than a few permanent non-Native residents, and the growing canned salmon industry was almost a fully absentee operation, that is, it did not provide local jobs and produced little local revenue. Congressional prudence under those circumstances does not seem unreasonable. Moreover, when Congress became convinced that the economic base was permanent, members responded quickly with land disposal measures.

The act provided that Alaska Natives "shall not be disturbed in the possession of lands actually in their use and occupation," ostensibly an enlightened disposition of land resources and acknowledgment of Native rights. But Congress also confirmed in the Alaska act that the mining laws of 1872 extended to Alaska. That act allowed the staking of mining claims on all federal lands, unless otherwise expressly prohibited. All of Alaska was federal land, of course, and in 1884 it was all open to mining claims. The Native land provision of the 1884 act was enlightened to a degree; Congress could have ignored the issue of Native lands. But Sheldon Jackson, among others, had lobbied for some protection of Alaska Natives, and a number of former abolitionists were sensitive to Native rights. Without any pressing demand on Alaska land from whites, because they were so few, acknowledgment of the Native right of occupancy did not generate much congressional opposition.

The president and the Interior Department acted quickly to implement the act. The first governor appointed, John Kinkead, a former governor of Nevada, served only briefly, as President Chester A. Arthur was not reelected. But Kinkead had been in Alaska off and on from 1867 and had at least a passing familiarity with the territory. In his one report to the president he called attention to the need for more reliable transportation and for reconstruction of the few public buildings. In May 1885, President Grover Cleveland appointed Alfred P. Swineford, a Michigan newspaper editor, as governor. Swineford was an able administrator and observer who established a high standard of reporting on Alaska's conditions. Hardly a carpetbagger, he provided a realistic assessment of the territory's circumstances, petitioning Washington, D.C., with a long list of needs if settlers were to be attracted north. Inadequacies in transportation, public facilities, salaries, postal service, law enforcement, and education disadvantaged the settlers who were there, he argued, and inhibited more from coming.

Swineford did not, however, suggest what might sustain would-be settlers if they did go to the territory. He acknowledged that the growing salmon industry would not be useful, for the companies hired their labor force, mostly Chinese, later Filipino, in San Francisco and Seattle and transported them north for the short summer working season, where they labored in isolated locations with little economic impact on the territory.

Washington did less well in the selection of the first judges. Ward McAllister Jr. of California was an alcoholic whose indiscretions led to his removal after a year. His successor, Edward J. Dawne of Oregon, had embezzled funds and misrepresented himself as a physician before his appointment and was removed after only two months when he was found out. The third appointee, Lafayette Dawson of Missouri, proved satisfactory and would serve the remainder of Cleveland's presidency.

Probably the most significant early appointment in Alaska was the "General Agent of Education" provided by the act. The Bureau of Indian Affairs still was not interested in Alaska, so the secretary of the interior designated the responsibility for the appointment to the commissioner of education. The commissioner at the time was John Eaton, a Presbyterian friend and supporter of Sheldon Jackson. As commissioner, Eaton headed a fledgling agency, the U.S. Bureau of Education (BOE), whose responsibility was to collect statistics and publish an annual report on the state of education nationally. The bureau had no operating division. Eaton appointed Jackson as the general agent in Alaska. Jackson, who would serve as agent until 1906, was well qualified for the task, and he and Eaton quickly agreed that the bureau would implement in Alaska the same government acculturation policy to which the missionaries were committed and which national Indian reformers agreed was the only option for the survival of American aborigines. There would be one difference from the Bureau of Indian Affairs (BIA) program in the American West, however: in Alaska the BOE would not construct boarding schools but would rely on day schools in every village possible. The Presbyterian boarding school at Sitka, never a government enterprise, was an exception to this idea and not one about which

Jackson was enthusiastic, but it was already well established and provided a place for orphans and other children in unusual circumstances.

Upon taking up his duties as general agent, Jackson did not immediately resign his position as an officer of the Presbyterian Board of Home Missions. This was not unusual at the time. The BIA had for a time hired missionaries as Indian agents on western reservations on the theory that they would be less corruptible than other civilian agents. Christianity, particularly evangelical Protestant Christianity, was seen in this period of American history as an essential aspect of civil virtue, of citizenship. It was also a mark of social legitimacy. Such convictions blurred the doctrine of the separation of church and state, but critics' voices were lost in social and even official convention, at least for a time.

Although the congressional appropriation for his work was meager, Jackson immediately set out to expand the number of day schools in Alaska. He hired teachers, purchased building materials, and chartered a schooner to take them all to villages in southeast and south-central Alaska. To stretch funds, Jackson executed contracts with mission societies already conducting schools in Alaska, making up for their budget shortfalls for any given year. This practice, often called the "contract system," was also a clear constitutional violation, but one sanctioned by the Interior Department and borrowed by Jackson from the BIA's practice on the western reservations.[48] He would use the system until 1894, when criticism forced Congress to terminate the practice in all government agencies.

Jackson continued to spend the winter in Washington, D.C., and on the East Coast lobbying Congress and raising mission funds for his Alaska work, using his annual summer cruise to Alaska to check on existing missions and government schools and to establish new ones. On a trip into the Bering Sea on a revenue cutter in 1890, he noted that the annual whaling fleet had a detrimental effect on the coastal Eskimo villages. Not only did the whalers, numbering sometimes as many as two hundred ships in a season, take whales that normally the villagers would have taken for food, but they also hired Eskimo whale hunters from the villages to work on the ships, depriving the villages of the services of its most able hunters, thus reducing the amount of food the Eskimos could procure for the village.

Visiting on the Siberian coast, Jackson observed that the villagers there relied on reindeer for food, which they herded on the tundra throughout the year. The next year Jackson arranged to import more than a dozen Siberian reindeer into Alaska. The following year he brought nearly two hundred. Securing a modest congressional appropriation for the project in 1893, he brought not only more animals but also Lapp herders to teach the Eskimos how to herd the reindeer. In addition, Jackson established a central herding station at Teller on the Seward Peninsula. The BOE would administer the program into the 1930s when the herds would be privatized. The program did not work very well in the long run, for the Eskimos were not a truly nomadic people, preferring instead to spend much of the year in sedentary villages; the reindeer, however, needed to move constantly to find forage. Some Eskimos became successful herders, including a woman named Mary Antisarluk Adrewuk, "Sinrock Mary," who acquired one of the largest herds and helped to maintain others.

Jackson's overall missionary initiative in Alaska coincided with the passage in Congress of the Dawes General Allotment Act, often called the severalty act, which was an attempt to speed acculturation.[49] By its terms, Indian heads of households who formally terminated or severed their relationship with their tribe were given conditional title to land (40, 80, or 160 acres, depending on its character). If at the end of a twenty-five-year trust period the Indian was well acculturated—that is, lived apart from other Indians and manifested the rudiments of economic, social, political, and ideological individualism—he would be given full fee simple title to the land and would be declared a citizen.[50] Severalty applied to both reservation and non-reservation Indians but used the recognized tribe as the chief group from which the Indian needed to sever his relationship. With the exception of the Annette Island Indian Reserve, established in 1891 under special circumstances for the Coast Tsimshian of Metlakatla, British Columbia, there were no traditional Indian reservations in Alaska and no federally recognized tribes. But a general notion of what constituted a "civilized" Indian arose from the application of the act by the courts. By the "Dawes test," Indians living a life characterized by economic individualism, Western dress and hygiene, and Christian values often were accepted as citizens without an official conferring of citizenship by the government.

Assessment of the missionary and government education program in Alaska is a complex matter. Unquestionably, literacy, reduction of communicable disease, and acquisition of other Western values, behaviors, and mores broadened opportunities and extended life for many Native people. At the same time much of that change was forced, sometimes brutally, as in denying youngsters their cultural language. While all cultures are in a

constant state of change, from a combination of both internal and external forces, the brutality of the American assimilation of American Natives
included myriad injustices. Native populations throughout the non-
Western world developed accommodations with Euro-Americans that
permitted them to survive, however one-sided their relationships may have
been. Natives eagerly sought much in Western culture, and Native communities manifested many and varied selective adaptations to it. Certainly
by the end of the nineteenth century a growing number of Tlingits and Haidas were becoming literate and learning how to function effectively in the
dominant culture. At the same time a good many did not adjust well. For
all Natives the crisis of identity was significant, and sometimes left permanent psychological damage.

Generally speaking, American culture was intensely racist at the
beginning of the twentieth century; minorities were regarded by many
as not yet ready for "civilization," and by many more as unlikely ever to
be ready. In 1896 the Supreme Court in *Plessy v. Ferguson* found that
separate but equal public facilities for persons of different races were
constitutional. Native cultures were not regarded as equal in any way to
Western culture. In museums aboriginal artifacts, many of which were
collected on the Northwest Coast and in Alaska at this time, were considered objects of curiosity from people clearly considered inferior. This
led to widespread prejudice and discrimination, as much in Alaska as
anywhere else in the Western world. Nonetheless, a number of Natives
emerged as cultural brokers, seeking to serve as bridges between the two
cultures, as teachers primarily but also as interpreters and as commercial
entrepreneurs.[51]

Cross-cultural contact was less comprehensive and consistent in the
north than along the southeastern coast, but even among the coastal and
riverine communities contacts became increasingly frequent in the last
three decades of the century and were hastened by the publication of
official and popular accounts of U.S. Army exploration of the Interior. In
1869, Captain Charles Raymond, working up the Yukon River from
St. Michael, located the position of Fort Yukon, which the Hudson's Bay
Company had maintained at the confluence of the Yukon and Porcupine
Rivers since 1847. The post was well within American territory, of course,
and it was removed to a position on the Porcupine River that they said was
across the boundary. This was later found not to be the case, however, and
the post was moved a second time.

Not until 1883 would there be further recording of the geography and resources of the Interior. In that year the army dispatched Frederick Schwatka to provide a thorough mapping of the Yukon River from its headwaters in Canada above Skagway to the delta on the Bering Sea. Schwatka did not provide much new information, but the expedition recorded two achievements. First, the Chilkat Tlingit were persuaded that the United States intended to keep open and free the passes (Chilkoot and White) over the Coast Mountains, which the Indians had aggressively controlled. Second, full press coverage of the expedition popularized the idea that the United States was fully knowledgeable about and in control of the Alaska wilderness. The army justified the expedition by claiming that the security of prospectors could not be guaranteed because the Natives' disposition was unknown. This was not in fact true, but it was successful in securing funds for this and subsequent expeditions.

Lieutenant William Abercrombie failed in an attempt to ascend the Copper River in 1884, but the following year Henry Tureman Allen carried out his very significant reconnaissance of the Copper, Chitina, Tok, Tanana, and Koyukuk River drainages. Allen's expedition has been called the most difficult and most important exploration after Meriwether Lewis and William Clark's crossing of the continent from 1803 through 1806.[52] Allen was a careful observer who was able to keep his narrative unusually free of his own assumptions. There were other army expeditions in subsequent years, including that conducted by Edwin Fitch Glenn in 1898 in south-central Alaska from Portage Bay to Knik Arm and Resurrection Bay to Lake Louise. All of these facilitated development of the Interior.

Many of the army explorers published accounts of their travels in the circulating periodicals of the day, as had Dall and Elliott, and Jackson before them. Another publicist was the naturalist John Muir, the father of the aesthetic or spiritual movement in American environmentalism. Muir had already begun his agitation for national parks before he made his first trip to Alaska in 1879. Traveling with S. Hall Young, a young Presbyterian missionary whom Jackson had brought to Southeast Alaska that year, Muir discovered Glacier Bay on a canoe trip to the northern reaches of the archipelago. The glaciers there had receded remarkably, perhaps as much as seventy-five miles, in the decades between George Vancouver's 1794 expedition and Muir and Young's canoe trip.

Muir would make a number of trips to Alaska, and he became an inveterate popularizer of the beauty and pristine character of its wilderness. He was a "primitivist" in his thought about wilderness, holding that centuries of civilization had corrupted humankind, driving people away from harmony with nature. As historian Roderick Nash has written, the word "pure" occurred often in Muir's descriptions of wilderness.[53] For Muir, Alaska was the epitome of nature's perfection. As had Rousseau and Wordsworth, Muir saw God's hand in nature, writing a moral portrait of harmonious relationships where justice prevailed and that humans could only diminish.[54] His articles appeared frequently in every kind of publication, from *Leslie's Illustrated Weekly* and *Century* to esoteric scientific journals, and helped to encourage interest in Alaska and lamentably, from Muir's perspective, the beginnings of Alaska tourism.[55]

Muir would return to Alaska briefly in 1898, by then already an icon of American defense of nature. About this time the railroad magnate E. H. Harriman chartered a 250-foot passenger ship, the *George W. Elder*, for an Alaska trip. Harriman wanted to bag a Kodiak brown bear. He also wanted to investigate the possibility of building a railroad beneath Bering Strait to connect the two continents, an idea with extraordinary potential. Because there was so much room on the vessel, Harriman hit upon the idea of bringing along a group of respected scientists both to explain Alaska to his family and friends and to sponsor whatever scientific work they might be able to do on the voyage. Muir was invited along. Although several volumes of notes from the trip were eventually published, they contributed little to science. But they contributed much to a reformulation of Alaska in the American mind, according to Nash, replacing the popular idea of a wasteland with that of uncorrupted, untouched wilderness.[56] Several participants in the voyage wrote about Alaska's tourism potential, not having taken the lesson from Muir's experience that popularization of wilderness is logically inconsistent with the concept of wilderness.[57] Nonetheless, with the essayist and naturalist John Burroughs and others, the expedition provided Muir a last look at his beloved northern wilderness.[58]

In 1881 railroad magnate Henry Villard chartered the steamer *Idaho* for a scenic tour of the Alexander Archipelago and Glacier Bay, pioneering an excursion route that would take travelers over his Northern Pacific Railway to Portland and Tacoma and then by steamship through the Inside Passage to Glacier Bay. The following year, Jackson organized a similar excursion for members of the National Education Association, a tour that also allowed him to show off his new mission stations and the need for more. Muir hated the tourists. He called them "arm chair" wonders and decried their failure to wander beyond the decks of their ships in their pursuit of nature's mysteries and examples. He also despaired over the Kodak wrappers they left strewn about the moraine of the glaciers in the bay. But there was little to be done: Alaska tourism had begun; every year several tourist steamers invaded Muir's wilderness to disgorge their captives for a few hours' gambol in the magic Northland. All of these expeditions and tours increased the Natives' contact with Western culture while at the same time the reports and publicity reformed Americans' perceptions of the North.

Meanwhile, in the Interior, the miner-trader Jack McQuesten, working for the Alaska Commercial Company, established a trading post he called Fort Reliance on the upper Yukon River, upstream from the Canada-Alaska boundary, in 1874.[59] At one time or another he staked or traded with most of the non-Natives in the country, whose number increased slowly but steadily over the next decade. In 1886 some of these prospectors and trappers found placer gold on a tributary of the Forty Mile River, downstream from the border. The find was modest, but it brought many of the wanderers together and encouraged still more testing of the Interior's endless mineral prospects.

Ivan Petroff's Alaska census for 1890 was probably as accurate an account of the territory's population as could be made, given the difficulties of travel and climate. Petroff found 32,052 people: 4,298 whites, 23,531 Natives, 1,823 mixed, and a scattering of others. These figures suggested that the Native population continued to be devastated by virgin soil diseases and that the white population was truly increasing. Even if Petroff had been off by half with his number of 435 non-Natives for 1880, the 1890 total told at least a fivefold increase in the decade, due mostly to the continuing development of the Treadwell properties at Douglas but also to increasing numbers of prospectors working in the upper Yukon River valley.

The year before the census Southeast Alaska settlers again held a political convention to articulate and focus their feelings about self-government. Styled as a nonpartisan convention, reflecting the growing populist discontent in the continental states with mainstream politics, the delegates elected the popular steamship captain James Carroll to go to Washington, D.C., to present Alaskans' desire for an extension of land law to the territory so people could purchase property.[60] Historians have suggested that

Carroll was unsuccessful, but the evidence indicates the contrary, for Congress responded positively to the Alaska petition. Armed with the new census data and Carroll's firsthand report of settlement activity in the Panhandle region, at the end of the 1891 session Congress added two provisions to a major western lands act of that year, provisions that explicitly began the process of land disposal to Alaska. The act authorized the General Land Office to identify and name town sites and to survey and sell town lots to citizens; it also provided eighty-acre homesteads for trade and manufacturing.

This was a profound congressional action for Alaska; it was an important example of federal support for settlement and economic development of the territory. It is also an example of federal colonialism. In facilitating land title, Congress showed its willingness to support a resident colonial population as an adjunct of capitalist exploitation of the country's hinterland resources. In the provision of homesteads for trade and manufacturing, it showed its direct involvement in that colonial economic enterprise. The sale of town lots made possible private property ownership for the first time since the Alaska purchase. Now non-Native settlers could secure clear title to their homes and businesses in the few towns where they had chosen to make homes, in the few places where there were jobs. In Juneau and Douglas, where several thousand laborers now lived, many with families, the act encouraged home construction and purchase and the establishment of small businesses. It was important also in Wrangell, Sitka, and Kodiak, which each contained several hundred non-Natives.[61] The act facilitated the beginning of a permanent pioneer population in Alaska.

The homestead provision (i.e., free land) was intended primarily for the salmon canning industry but also for sawmills. Canneries represented an investment of tens of thousands of dollars, including wharves, barracks, warehouses, and mess halls, in addition to the cleaning and packing plant. Lack of land title jeopardized the security of that investment, and owners sought protection from the federal government, which was easily persuaded to provide it. Further discussion on the history of federal lands and resources policy in Alaska is detailed in a later chapter. For the moment it is useful to note that Congress became the willing partner of absentee capital exploitation of a resource treated as a commons: that is, fish.

These 1891 provisions manifest an important relationship between government and capitalism in Alaska that would be repeated frequently in the territory's history. With evidence to show the permanence of settlement, the growth of non-Native population and of economic enterprise, Congress responded with enabling legislation, both for settlement and for major capitalist investment. Far from neglecting Alaska early in its development, the government in fact supported exploitation of its resources. The 1891 measure was a land act and so did not provide any of the aspects of civil organization, including municipal government with its taxing and policing powers. However, these would follow before the decade concluded because of the development of new sources of economic support and an accompanying population increase.

10

National Currents in Alaska

The Gold Rush and Progressive Reform

I N AUGUST 1896, GEORGE Carmack, a longtime Yukon prospector with a dubious reputation for veracity, together with two Indian companions known as Skookum Jim and Tagish Charley, camped one night on Rabbit Creek, a small feeder stream of the Klondike River, not many miles up the Yukon from the Alaska boundary. Another Yukoner, Robert Henderson, who was camped on Goldbottom Stream, farther up the Klondike, had suggested that Carmack and his friends try Rabbit Creek, as Henderson had already done some prospecting there. Either Carmack or Skookum Jim found a layer of gold in soft rock near the stream and pried out a thumb-sized nugget, about a quarter of an ounce. At the price of gold then, it was worth about $4.

Along the Forty Mile River argonauts were staking claims and sinking holes to bedrock on the strength of pans worth five or ten cents! The Klondike turned out to be one of the richer strikes in the gold rush era, with hundreds of millions of dollars in gold along the little tributaries of the Klondike River, and nearly all of it placer. The Klondike rush would become an episode in western and northern history like none other, an extraordinary experience. Although Henderson never filed any claims, the Canadian government recognized him as the discoverer of the Klondike deposits and paid him a small life pension. The Canadian historian Pierre Berton endorsed the Henderson claim of discovery, but subsequent scholarship has shown that Carmack and his companions made the actual find.

Typical early gold miners' camp, near the mouth of the White River east of Alaska's Wrangell Mountains. Alaska State Library, Lorain Roberts Zacharia Photo Collection P178.017.

The Klondike discovery had been preceded in 1893 by a find on Birch Creek in Alaska, more than 250 miles downriver from the Yukon border. Circle City, the small community that quickly grew up to service the rush to Birch Creek, became the Interior's first gold town. Yukon River steamboats could easily navigate upriver from St. Michael through the Yukon Flats country around Fort Yukon to supply the region, and soon entrepreneurs established several saloons and an Alaska Commercial Company store. The residents used the traditional miners' meeting for self-governance. In 1872 the U.S. Congress had adopted the fundamental legislation governing citizens' rights to minerals on the public domain. On land that was open to entry, anyone could file a prospecting claim if they had reason to believe an eligible mineral might be present in commercial quantity. Staked claims needed to be registered and recorded, with a government official designated for that purpose, and usually a prospector's first chore after finding and staking a claim was to find the nearest government recorder, however distant that might be from his bonanza. The vagueness of the terms of the law encouraged ordinary citizens to prospect and make claims but at the same time permitted substantial and often abusive exploitation of mineral resources. Mineral law in Canada at the end of the century was similar.

Since the California rush in 1849, would-be miners had also used the miners' meeting as a mechanism for governance in new mineral districts where the government had as yet no presence or where it was not likely to penetrate because of the uncertainty of the extent of the find. In the absence of civil law or civil officials, all of the interested parties in a district would gather in a mass meeting to agree on fundamental rules for civil conduct and penalties for violation of them; they often also appointed a temporary recorder of claims. Prospectors at Juneau had used the form briefly until the U.S. Navy commander at Sitka dispatched an officer to impose official authority, and men in the Forty Mile and Circle City camps used it as well. Ignorance and disagreement often produced as much confusion as order in the meetings, but generally they functioned well, bringing a rudimentary but fundamental democracy to unsettled regions until there was more formal civil governance.

In the Klondike, however, no miners' meeting was necessary, for the government was already in the region. Dr. George M. Dawson of the Canadian Geological Survey had headed a reconnaissance survey of the Yukon basin in 1887 and 1888, while William Ogilvie, Dominion surveyor, had marked a tentative U.S.-Canada borderline. Responding to a report from the Anglican bishop of the region in 1892 and 1893, who noted more than two hundred prospectors in the area, the Canadian government sent Northwest Mounted Police to the Yukon in 1895 and a mining recorder and gold commissioner the following year. Everyone expected that some major strike would be made in the region, but no one imagined that its scope would be what the Klondike became.

There were about seventeen hundred men in the upper Yukon when Carmack and his companions made their discovery. Most of these headed for the Klondike that winter.[1] Word of the find circulated in Alaska and the Canadian Northwest, bringing another five hundred or six hundred to the district before spring. By May 1897 there were fifteen hundred people in the Klondike district, and more than one hundred at the town site William Ogilvie had surveyed at the mouth of the Klondike River and named for George Dawson. Ogilvie felt the need to get word of the strike to the authorities in Ottawa. Twice during the winter he sent official letters out over the Yukon River trail to Juneau and then Victoria. Captain William Moore, an experienced entrepreneur who had founded a town at Skagway because he expected a Yukon gold rush sometime, carried the first letter, a veteran dog sled driver carried the second. In Ottawa government functionaries failed to appreciate the significance of the find, and the information was duly filed on the appropriate shelf. Exasperated, Ogilvie send a third letter the following June. It too had no effect. There had been many, many notifications of gold discoveries, most of which had failed to meet even the slimmest expectations, and there was no particular reason why notice of the Klondike should have overcome experienced incredulity.

The Klondike excitement did not become a national phenomenon until the first ships to carry gold from the region came out in the summer of 1897. The *Excelsior* made San Francisco on 16 July 1897, with about $400,000 in gold aboard and plenty of prospectors to tell of their grand fortune. The *Portland* docked two days later in Seattle with nearly twice as much, the newspapers crying that she carried "a ton of gold"; actually the correct figure was closer to two tons. The news generated what Canadian writer Pierre Berton has called the "Klondike Fever."[2] By that fall there were more than five thousand people in the district. Still, the great rush to the Klondike did not come until 1898, again because of the problem of credibility. It was only with repeated news and magazine coverage of fabulous riches, in stories filed by reporters who had actually gone there, that the Klondike took on the ethereal character of glamour, greed, and glory that many came to attribute to the area. But by then all the gold-bearing ground had been claimed and staked.

By the summer of 1898, between one hundred thousand and two hundred thousand dreamers had started for the Klondike, most from the major West Coast ports of San Francisco, Portland, Victoria, and Seattle—none more than from Seattle because of a concerted and highly successful national advertising campaign touting that city as the jump-off point for the northern goldfields.[3] Most went by steamer up the Inside Passage to Skagway and Dyea at the head of Lynn Canal; many took passage across the Gulf of Alaska and through the Bering Sea to St. Michael and then up the Yukon. Not many more than forty thousand actually persisted all the way to Dawson, however. From Dyea the route lay over Chilkoot Pass, a punishing climb on foot sixteen miles to thirty-five hundred feet and then down to Lake Bennett, where the adventurers cut green timber for boats and barges that they floated five hundred miles down the Yukon to Dawson. Some chose the longer but lower and more dangerous twenty-four-hundred-foot White Pass. The White Pass Trail was so narrow in some

Prospectors ascending Chilkoot Pass on the Dyea Trail on their way to the Klondike, winter of 1897–98. Entrepreneurs built the tram line, on the right, to move the argonauts' "outfits" (but no people) up the mountain, for those who could afford it. Alaska State Library P20.044.

places and so boggy in others that many horses either slipped and fell or became inextricably mired.[4]

By October 1897 the trails were teeming with would-be argonauts. Photographers could set up their tripods and wait for a break in the normally gloomy weather to film, for the line up to the summit on Chilkoot Pass never ceased. Seeking to bring responsibility to the enterprise, the Canadian government soon instituted a customs policy, denying entry to those who had neither the money to purchase supplies nor the actual outfit, including food and extra clothing. Many argonauts made a half-dozen or more trips up the pass to assemble an outfit the Mounties regarded as likely to provide enough self-sufficiency. All along the trail before they got to Dawson, most heard repeatedly that all the gold-bearing ground had long since been staked, that the journey was long, and that the winters were unbearable.

Stories of the futility of the trek circulated also in Skagway, in St. Michael, at Dutch Harbor on the trip around by sea, and even in Seattle. The closer one got to the true North, an increasingly common response was to turn around and go immediately back to where one had come from. For those who carried on, the various reports proved true. Dawson was a booming, busy metropolis of twenty thousand in the summer of 1898, but the chances of a newcomer finding gold were nonexistent. Many drawn to the excitement, however, had not come looking for gold. They were adventurers and risk-takers who went north to test the climate for business opportunities and to make what they might from servicing the rapidly growing numbers of argonauts who would need everything from hotels to blacksmiths. The ethics of business activity in the wilderness setting inevitably were determined as much by what the traffic would bear as by traditions rooted in the carefully monitored laws and mores of the settled regions. Most of the gold seekers who brought substantial capital with them lost it to innkeepers, restaurateurs, bartenders, and dance hall girls, legitimate and illegitimate. Most who did not bring capital wound up working for those who did until they could book passage on the steamboats heading downriver in the fall.

Some argonauts did strike it rich in the Klondike. The region produced about $300,000 in 1896; $2,500,000 in 1897; $10,000,000 in 1898; $16,000,000 in 1899; and $22,275,000 in 1900, after which returns began to decline. But of the forty thousand or so who trekked to the district, the number that made legendary fortunes was small, not more than four hundred. Only four thousand seekers, a mere 10 percent, struck any gold at all. Those who turned back probably showed noteworthy prudence. Moreover, by 1900 the easily accessible placers had been panned and mined over, and heavy equipment and wage labor were necessary to take out what remained. Corporate investors began to buy up claims cheaply as their holders realized that they would never be able to get at whatever riches they might hold. Within a few years most work in the Klondike district was done by industrial mining, using both hydraulic and dragline technology to move huge quantities of earth, scouring the land and altering it substantially and permanently.

The writer Pierre Berton argued that even though most people who participated in the Klondike gold rush did not find wealth, and that the experience collectively was one of the most foolish enterprises of modern

Businesses on the lower part of the Chilkoot Trail, 1897–98. University of Alaska Fairbanks, Elmer E. Rasmuson Library 1975-0178-00017.

times, many of those who persevered felt later that the experience had been formative and positive. Many thought it the adventure of a lifetime. "I had thirty-five cents in my pocket when I set foot in Alaska, but I gave that to a mission church in Dutch Harbor," Berton quotes one Klondiker as saying. "I did not have so much when I left the country more than two years later. . . . I made exactly nothing, but if I could turn time back I would do it over again for less than that."[5] The trek and the surreal surroundings in Dawson and out on the creeks marked the Klondikers. What left the greatest impression were the hardships endured and survived, for these had tested the adventurers and had tempered character and judgment as few life experiences had done or could.

Many women made the trek over the passes as well, although it is difficult to estimate their number. Countless women accompanied their husbands and often enough proved stronger than their mates in meeting the challenges of the trail and the creeks. Others went not to dig for gold but to work in trades in Dawson, Nome, Fairbanks, and the other new towns. Still more went to work in the dance halls and as prostitutes.[6] None of these roles were new; women had been an integral part of American westward migration and the mining towns of the mountain West. But there may have been fewer women who came to the northern gold rush intending to stay; most of the argonauts were modern migrants, intending to return home after taking out their fortunes. Many women who came north moved easily into the demimonde, working for a percentage of the cost of the drinks they persuaded lonely miners to buy; for many it was a short step from there to part-time prostitution, where the profits were quicker and more substantial, but the physical and emotional dangers commensurably greater.[7]

Not all of the Klondike argonauts hiked up to the passes above Skagway and Dyea. In 1898 a group of London investors acquired the right of way over White Pass for a railroad. In an engineering feat of extraordinary proportions, Irish engineer Michael J. Heney built a mountain railway from seawater to the summit and on to Lake Bennett. He completed the line in February 1899; the following year he ran the line on into Whitehorse. At the same time other investors constructed elaborate trams and cableways up Chilkoot Pass, lining the route with tripods and other cable supports; the cables, driven by gasoline generators, were used only for freight, being too risky for large numbers of passengers. By 1900 travelers had a choice of methods for surmounting the coastal barrier, but by then the great stampede was over.

Many of the argonauts who made it to Dawson took one look and kept on going, into Alaska. Over the next several years gold strikes were made at many sites in the territory, at Candle, Sleetmute, Poorman, Ruby, Iditarod, Rampart, Ophir, Council, Placerville, and many others. Most of these strikes were not substantial, although enough gold was taken from most sites to leave a permanent print on the landscape. The two most significant finds were at Nome and Fairbanks, neither of which existed before their gold rushes. The Nome discovery was made by three Scandinavians— John Byrneson, Erik Lindblom, and Jafet Lindeberg—known in legend as the "Three Lucky Swedes," although Lindeberg was Norwegian. On a creek off the Anvil River on the south side of the Seward Peninsula they found $40 pans in late September 1898. They tried to keep the find secret through the winter, but by the following May there were several hundred northern-ers on the ground, two thousand by the end of the summer. The next sum-mer Nome was a town of twenty thousand, as Dawson had been the year before.

Among Nome's other distinguishing characteristics, it was easy to get to, relatively speaking. A would-be adventurer need only find his or her way to the wharf in San Francisco or any other port city, take booking on a steamer, watch the scenery float by along the edge of the Gulf of Alaska and on the Bering Sea coast, and upon arrival at Nome, wait to be lightered in to the beach (there was no harbor and no dock). There was no trekking over mountain passes and down rivers, with their unpredictable rapids and hoards of mosquitoes. Many gold seekers took advantage of these easy transportation circumstances. For example, the famous lawman Wyatt Earp came out of retirement to open a tent saloon in Nome, although within two years he had gone to newer fields in Tonapah, Nevada. The government dispatched a contingent of U.S. Army troops to Nome in the summer of 1899, which helped to maintain order, although the extent of their author-ity was unclear. Martial law was not declared, even though the deputy mar-shal assigned by the Alaska judge was clearly inadequate.

Perhaps the most remarkable phenomenon at Nome was the discovery of gold in the sands of the beaches. For forty miles in each direction, east and west along the Bering Sea coast, the sands themselves contained grains of gold, and gold-bearing bedrock was sometimes a mere foot beneath. Nor-mal mining law could not work under such circumstances. Instead of a given number of feet of stream bed, normally 1,320, on Nome's beaches a claim was the length of a shovel handle, as some said, stationary or swinging, and often only for as long as the claimant was in sight. Two thousand men and women took $2 million in gold from the sands in the first season alone.[8] Even at that, however, the quantity of gold found at Nome never equaled that in the Klondike, although the fields, spread over a larger geographic area, maintained their high productivity longer.

Of the other rushes that followed across the territory, the one called Fairbanks was the most significant. In 1902 a disreputable river boat cap-tain, E. T. Barnette, brought a steamer, the *Lavelle Young*, up the Tanana River and into Chena Slough, where he ran it aground, thereby discover-ing the head of navigation on the river. He decided to stay and opened a trading post to serve prospectors in the area, which became the earliest beginnings of Fairbanks. Soon afterward, Italian-American Felix Pedro

(Felice Pedroni) and his partner Frank Costa discovered gold on creeks flowing into the Chena River near its confluence with the Tanana. Although Pedroni staked his find, he could not find it again. A minor rush to the region ensued anyway, though it soon petered out. Later, however, Pedroni and others found more gold, and in 1903 a sizable rush developed again.[9] Although the placers were mostly buried, requiring heavy equipment and substantial capital to mine, the deposits were significant. Fairbanks became the principal service center for Alaska's Interior and for its first two decades was the territory's largest town. In 1906 gold production reached its peak in Alaska, the Fairbanks district producing 3.8 million ounces and the Seward Peninsula 2.7 million ounces. Only Colorado surpassed Alaska in gold production that year. But by then nearly all the accessible placers had been panned and sluiced out, and nearly all surviving gold operations were industrial.[10]

The impact of the gold rush on Natives, and on the environment, was substantial. Everywhere the prospectors went, they put pressure on the resident game populations, moose and caribou particularly. Moose became very scarce in populated areas, and it is likely that some caribou migration patterns were altered. The Chilkat Tlingit earned considerable income packing goods over the Chilkoot and White Pass summits. These Indians had jealously defended their control of the mountain trails before the early 1880s when Lieutenant L. A. Beardslee, the U.S. Navy commander at Sitka, forced them to guarantee free passage to prospectors. But increased numbers of prospectors reduced the game resources on which the Natives traditionally depended. Along the Interior rivers the demand for wood for the boilers of the steamboats had a similar impact; the riverbanks were denuded of trees, eliminating cover and forcing game away from the river. In the mining districts tailings soon inundated the landscape, crowding out vegetation, often polluting streams with mercury (used to separate gold from other minerals), and removing game habitat.

Many Natives initially made some profit at various jobs associated with moving supplies into the region. At Skagway and Dyea, for example, Indian packers carried goods and people from ships to the beach and charged handsome prices to move goods the sixteen miles to the summits. At St. Michael at the mouth of the Yukon, Eskimos formed the primary stevedoring force, transshipping goods from the oceangoing vessels up from Seattle to the Yukon River steamers. Along the river,

Tlingit Indians at Dyea at the start of the trail over Chilkoot Pass. Many worked as packers on the trail; others opened businesses along it or in Skagway or Dyea. Alaska State Library, William Duncan Photo Collection P171.067.

Athabaskan Indians cut wood for steamer fuel and piloted the boats through difficult and ever-changing channels in the great river. Steamer passengers also made a ready market for Indian arts and crafts. Indian women sold curios at all the river stops and learned quickly what the traffic would bear in terms of pricing.

But Natives were soon driven from such pursuits. They were inclined to leave off working when they received pay for services, purchasing the material goods they wanted and increasingly came to depend on, waiting to return to work only when they developed new needs. Whites quickly and easily replaced the Indians in nearly all aspects of the economic life of the rushes. Natives congregated around the new gold rush towns for access to the amenities available there and any jobs that might be had. But alcohol became a problem for many, and many Native women were drawn into prostitution. Missionaries helped to mitigate the impact of both issues but could not eliminate them. The missionaries themselves became powerful agents of cultural change, encouraging the eradication of traditional social and economic structures and their replacement by a social economy based on economic individualism. Natives in the towns, who were regularly subject to segregation and discrimination, became increasingly dependent on white goods and the white economy.

Moreover, cash income for them was always limited and unreliable, increasing their dependence and leaving them vulnerable to exploitation. Perhaps most disruptive was the Indians' tenuous hold on traditionally used and occupied lands. Wherever there was a gold or other mineral strike, prospectors and developers ignored Native land use patterns, appropriating land and water and forcing the Natives to relocate. In Nome, for example, prospectors dug and tunneled under dwellings in the Native village, causing the structures to collapse and the Natives to seek shelter on the tundra, where a number died of illnesses exacerbated by exposure.[11] Some Natives organized regional associations as a way of coping with these stresses.

Certainly the most devastating impact of the gold rush era on the Native population came from diseases carried north by the argonauts. The sixfold increase in the non-Native population meant expanded opportunity for contagion, a circumstance exacerbated by the congregation of Natives in white communities. Medical historian Robert Fortuine documented a "great sickness" of 1900 in western and northern Alaska that killed from a quarter to a third of the region's population. Apparently, simultaneous epidemics of influenza and measles raged across the area sometimes in concert, sometimes separately. First reports of influenza came from St. Michael, the Pribilofs, and Nome in the late spring of 1900. Measles struck at Gambell on St. Lawrence Island in June and moved on from there. Villagers died by tens and scores as U.S. Bureau of Education doctors and U.S. Army personnel watched helplessly, burying the dead, vaccinating those they could, and ministering to the sick. At Teller the missionary reported that a prominent Eskimo murdered the shaman there in an attempt to appease the evil spirit stalking the land.[12] In mid-August the government steamer *Nunivak* ascended the Yukon River from St. Michael. At every village they found death and devastation, people dying painfully without adequate shelter or supplies, many terrified by the specter. It was, Fortuine wrote, "probably the most calamitious [sic] event in the history of the Alaska Native people since the smallpox epidemic of 1835–40."[13]

Alaska's gold rush era lasted until the First World War, although most placer deposits gave out long before that. Gold mining would continue throughout the twentieth century, though in a limited number of places and most often with labor- and capital-intensive operations. The peak year was 1906. The Fairbanks fields accounted for a third of the Alaska total at that time. Gold would not be the mainstay of Alaska's economy, however. After

1912, taxes on exports of canned salmon quickly became the territory's principal revenue source, rising to 72 percent of general fund contributions by 1930.

THE IMPACT OF THE GOLD RUSH

The significance of the gold rush era left a lasting imprint on Alaska in three ways. It provided an enduring perception of Alaska as a last frontier and associated Alaska and the image of the grizzled sourdough firmly in the American mind. Second, it brought a non-Native population boom, which remained even after the rushes. The 1910 census showed 30,450 non-Natives in a population of 63,592, a sevenfold increase over 1890; ten years later, although there were important fluctuations between those years, the non-Native population was 36,400 of 64,356, nearly 8.5 times the 1890 non-Native population, an 18 percent increase over 1900. During the same twenty-year period the Native population was essentially stable: 25,354 in 1890, 29,542 in 1900, and 25,331 in 1910. Most important, however, the gold rush era and the consequent population increase generated a massive response on the part of the federal government. In kind, that response bore some similarities to that which followed the Juneau gold discoveries in 1880 and the census finding of increasing non-Native population in 1890. Congress extended civil governance in Alaska and provided for additional land disposal. But in quantity there was no comparison with what had preceded the broad expansion of self-governance and federal subsidization that had facilitated settlement and economic development of 1898 through 1900.

The government added a variety of new measures to ensure the safety and prosperity of the new population. The government's first step was reconnaissance, without which intelligent action could hardly be taken. The well-being and protection of the Americans in the region was the first priority. In late August 1897 the U.S. Army dispatched Captain Patrick Ray and Lieutenant Wilds Richardson to the Yukon River to investigate conditions stemming from the rush to Dawson. Traveling up and down the river, observing and talking to prospectors and others, Ray made a number of recommendations, nearly all of which his superiors would act on. Pursuant to his suggestions, Lieutenant Colonel George Randall established a post at St. Michael near the mouth of the river, garrisoned with twenty-five infantrymen, two officers, and a surgeon. Two officers were also sent to Dyea at the foot of Chilkoot Pass to monitor

Juneau Public School, teachers and students, 1909. Few schools in Alaska were integrated. This school served white families and was supported by local taxes, later by territorial funds. Alaska State Library P20.112.

conditions there. Ray also recommended two posts on the mid-Yukon, together with a cutter for patrol. In addition, he urged that two "all-American" routes from tidewater to the goldfields be surveyed, one from Cook Inlet, the other from Prince William Sound. He also called for construction of roads to assist mining and other economic development.[14]

Ray left the territory in February 1898, satisfied that order had prevailed and that additional military soon would be in the area. Within months, responding partly to a request from Governor John G. Brady, four infantry companies arrived in Southeast Alaska. A contingent was on hand in Skagway in July when a vigilante leader, Frank Reid, shot the notorious conman "Soapy" Smith. Most of Smith's gang were tracked down and arrested by army troops and ultimately prosecuted.[15] The troops developed a cordial relationship with the Canadian Northwest Mounted Police (NWMP), who manned the passes above the town, helping to locate a temporary boundary and otherwise police the region. They also helped mediate a dispute between some Chilkat Tlingits and Jack Dalton, an Oklahoman who had been in the territory since 1890 and who staked out a trail from Pyramid Harbor at the head of Lynn Canal (near present-day Haines) over Chilkat Pass to Fort Selkirk on the Yukon River, halfway between Whitehorse and Dawson.

The army also authorized new surveys of the country to facilitate the all-American passage to the Interior. Lieutenant P. G. Lowe and three men, using pack animals, ascended the Coast Mountains from Valdez and then took Henry Allen's route up the Copper River and over Mentasta Pass. After crossing the Tanana River, they made for Forty Mile on the Yukon. At the same time F. C. Schrader of the U.S. Geological Survey, working for the army, mapped out routes across the Valdez Glacier and through Keystone Canyon and Thompson Pass and the country between the Chitina and White Rivers. Lieutenant Edwin Glenn had charge of a team that surveyed the country east of upper Cook Inlet. His subordinates surveyed most of the routes in the south-central region, including from Resurrection Bay to Turnagain Arm and the Matanuska, Chickaloon, Susitna, and Chulitna River drainages.

One of Glenn's lieutenants, J. C. Castner, traveling with two men and some mules, made a harrowing trip across the pass above the Matanuska River, up the Copper River and over a pass to the upper Tok and Tanana Rivers, and then up the Goodpaster and over adjacent uplands to the Yukon River. Often out of food and mired in rough country, the small party was saved on several occasions by local Indians who guided them and gave them provisions. Another lieutenant, Joseph S. Herron, experienced similar danger on a trip up the Yentna River and across the Alaska Range on a route followed today by the annual Iditarod sled dog race. His Native guides abandoned the party while descending the south fork of the Kuskokwim River, and Herron and his men wandered for several weeks before finding a village where the Indians fed and nurtured them. Later the party worked north to a tributary of the Tanana, arriving finally on the Yukon. At one point a group of Herron's men were rescued by local Indians who had found bacon in the stomach of a bear they had killed, which alerted them to the presence of white men in the area; they backtracked until they found the soldiers.[16] Although most of the expeditions covered ground known already to Indians and miners, the soldiers described and recorded the country they traveled for the official record.[17]

The army quickly found itself drawn into more than reconnaissance, however, for the large number of prospectors and adventurers arriving in Alaska, attracted by continuing tales printed in the popular press, threatened to overwhelm the meager legal structure and traditional miners' meetings that functioned as agencies of civil order. In the summer of 1898, Richardson requested and stationed troops at Rampart and Circle City.

The court had appointed U.S. commissioners and deputy marshals for these places, the Treasury Department had dispatched customs agents, and the General Land Office had sent land agents. But Richardson found most of these officials to be corrupt, and he effectively declared martial law. In the fall he sent a detachment to Nome. The next year the army established frontier forts at the mouth of the Tanana River (Fort Gibbon) and at Eagle on the Yukon River (Fort Egbert).

Another significant army project was construction of a telegraph line to link Alaskan posts and towns together and Alaska to the contiguous states. In 1899, Captain William Abercrombie established a post, Fort Liscum, at the head of Valdez Arm, where several hundred argonauts had landed, thinking they would cross the mountains there and pioneer the all-American route northeasterly toward the Yukon. No route had been identified, and the hapless explorers soon found themselves trapped by the high mountains and treacherous glaciers spilling down their precipitous slopes. Abercrombie established a field hospital to treat would-be miners stricken by scurvy and snow blindness. He then dispatched a quartermaster clerk, John Rice, to survey the route. Rice returned before the end of the summer season, having reached the Yukon in forty days over Lieutenant Henry Allen's route to the Tok River and then crossing the Ketchumstuk Hills to the Forty Mile country.

While Abercrombie reconnoitered the Valdez Glacier, the veteran Arctic explorer General Adolphus Greely successfully lobbied Congress to appropriate funds to the Army Signal Corps for the telegraph. The Canadians already had constructed a land line linking Dawson to Whitehorse and across the wilderness to British Columbia and then to civilization. Not waiting for full funding, Captain Charles Farnsworth, in charge of the post at Eagle, pushed through construction of a link from Fort Egbert to Dawson, providing the first direct communication tie between Alaska and "Outside." In the meantime Captain Frank Greene oversaw erection of a line from Fort St. Michael to Fort Gibbon at the mouth of the Tanana River.

Finally securing his appropriation, Greely mapped out a plan to connect all the non-Native communities in the main part of the territory. The Corps would build a line from Valdez to Eagle on the Yukon over the route pioneered by Rice, and a link would be built from Fort Gibbon up the Tanana River to where the Valdez-Eagle line crossed the Tanana. The junction would be called Tanana Crossing, shortened to Tanacross. Greely planned a submarine cable from Valdez to Seattle with branches to Juneau, Haines, Skagway, Sitka, and Wrangell. Nome would be tied into the system with a wireless signal across Norton Sound to St. Michael. The hero of this work was Lieutenant William "Billy" Mitchell, who would go on to fame as a visionary in the U.S. Army Air Corps. The Alaska telegraph, dubbed the Washington-Alaska Military Cable and Telegraph System (WAMCATS), was operational by 1904.

The impact of the line was profound. Just at the time when significant numbers of non-Natives were flowing into the territory, Congress and the army reached out to link them to the rest of the country, using the most sophisticated technology available. The telegraph facilitated economic development by linking corporate agents to their directors in the world's capitalist centers. It put the government's field agents and administrators, including the governor and new judges just then being appointed, in touch with the government in Washington, D.C. One consequence of the connection was an instant newspaper industry in Alaska, for every editor and publisher could subscribe to the national wire services, gaining access to the same information used to fill papers from Emporia, Kansas, to Presque Isle, Maine.[18]

But the federal government did far more than simply authorize the army to assure protection and ensure order among the new population and link it to the "Outside" by telegraph. In 1898, Congress passed a homestead act for Alaska and appropriated funds for a program of agricultural experiment stations to determine the territory's farming potential. The legislation reflected a prevailing assumption among most representatives, and indeed most Americans, that a pioneer society needed to be built on a base of agricultural sufficiency. Many imagined that the American West had been settled by farmers and that Alaska would be also. Some knew better, though. "We are trying to deal with Alaska as if it were an agricultural district, which is far removed from the fact," one senator complained.[19] As enacted, the homestead act permitted eighty-acre sites. Along shorelines spaces were to be reserved between sites for access to the Interior and for wharves and docks, protecting salmon cannery interests. The act made no provision for surveys, thereby passing those costs to the filer. In addition, native-born Canadian citizens were to be afforded the same mining rights as American citizens. The act set forth conditions for obtaining rights-of-way and for constructing roads, trolley lines, and railways.[20] In practical terms the act did not mean very much, however, for the people rushing to Alaska were not interested in agriculture; they were interested in gold and the business opportunities it might provide. Investors were interested in mineral prospects and transportation. But the act reflected Congress's attempt to provide a foundation for Alaska settlement and economic development, however faulty its vision was of how that might proceed.

The agricultural experiment station program was more practical, although in the long run it did not contribute much to Alaskan self-sufficiency. The government established stations at Sitka, Kenai, Copper Center, Kodiak, and Rampart on the Yukon River. In time the stations would provide a wealth of information. Seventeen million acres of land in Alaska were found to be arable. Although many crops familiar in the eastern-central United States would not grow profitably in Alaska, some would. Barley did well, as did rye in some regions. Many traditional vegetables and legumes were usually successful, as were potatoes. Dairy proved feasible in nearly all locations, provided enough summer grasses could be put up as hay for winter feeding. Flowers, of course, abounded.

But agriculture would be defeated not by the climate but by economies of scale. Those who have attempted to farm in Alaska have discovered that except for some very small and specialized operations, the high costs of shelter, equipment, labor, utilities, necessary feeds and supplies, transportation, processing, and marketing defeat the attempt to get products to the Alaskan consumer at a competitive price. Ironically, this would be especially true as transportation facilities would improve, for the same roads and railroad that allowed would-be Alaskan farmers to move crops to market allowed Pacific Northwest and California shippers access to that same market. None of this had been adequately demonstrated in 1898, however, when Congress passed the homestead act and authorized the station program. The homestead act represented an attempt, at least, to expand land disposal in Alaska and thereby encourage settlement.

By far the most important congressional response to the gold rush population increase was new civil governance legislation, a multifaceted extension of organic law to facilitate elementary organization of the body politic. By separate acts in 1899 and 1900, Congress created commissions to draft criminal and civil legal codes for Alaska, increased the number of judges in the territory from one to three, authorized the moving of the capital from Sitka to Juneau, and provided for the incorporation of towns. At the same time the Carter Act repealed prohibition and put in its place a system of license fees, both for general commercial activity and for liquor sales, thus creating a revenue base for the territory. The legal codes were critical, for the laws of Oregon, applied to Alaska in the 1884 act, were wholly inadequate. To administer the new codes, the three judges were to divide the territory as they thought most practical. Local magistrates, the U.S. commissioners, would be selected by the judges from the local population they were to serve and would be paid from fees they collected, a provision meant to avoid the long delays experienced in securing appointments from Washington, D.C., which sometimes took years. The judges were to hold court at places and times they deemed expedient, a recognition of the fluid state of the gold rush population.

The incorporation of towns did the most to bring the beginnings of self-governance to the territory. Sixty residents of any community of three hundred or more could apply to the district judge to organize an incorporation election. Once incorporated, townspeople could elect a city council of seven members, which was empowered to collect poll taxes, dog taxes, such license taxes as deemed desirable, and most important, taxes on real and personal property. From these revenues the towns could fund school districts, hire constabulary, provide for sanitation, and establish such other services as the citizenry anywhere in the newly settled West had established for themselves. A three-member school board, selected in a separate election, would have exclusive jurisdiction over the town's schools.

Altogether the congressional legislation of 1898 and 1900 represented a massive federal response to increased non-Native population in Alaska. Although it resembled the pattern of response established by the 1884 and 1891 acts, it far surpassed them in magnitude, as did the gold rush era population surge. The population increase persuaded Congress that more services and more latitude for popular democracy and absentee investment were appropriate, and without much ado the Congress provided that latitude in a manner both timely and efficient. In debating this enabling legislation, many representatives in Congress understood fully where their enactments fit into the history and pattern of administration of the western territories. "We are beginning to practice now," said Representative

William Moody of Massachusetts, "upon the government of the colonies."[21] Some historians have vigorously criticized the scheme of civil organizing legislation put in place by Congress with the Northwest Ordinance of 1787 and applied to Alaska in the new congressional legislation at the end of the nineteenth century.[22] Ernest Gruening, in his representation of Alaska's victimization at the hands of the federal government, used the theme of colonization effectively as a political device.

In truth, the territorial system that was appropriate for 1787 may have been outmoded by 1900, particularly once the telegraph line was completed and Alaska was in instant and constant communication with the rest of the world. The populace was generally educated and familiar with the traditions of political practice that prevailed throughout America. Yet a case can be made for some caution on the part of Congress. Even in 1900 thirty thousand non-Natives was not considered a large population. Mineral rushes had traditionally attracted modern migrants, that is, people who went west not to build a new society but to accumulate capital that could be transferred back to the country's settled regions. The concept of democracy assumes an active citizenry supporting legislation intended to benefit society's long-term interests. That is one important reason why representative democracy, republicanism, works better than direct democracy.

On the one hand, it is not unreasonable that Congress might wish to be satisfied that the new population was permanent and thus should be entrusted with the civic responsibility of continuity. On the other hand, civic power in the form of a territorial legislature might complicate investment opportunities through increased taxation and regulation. There was high corporate interest in Alaska, and some in Congress might have acted to maximize capitalist profit by impeding the establishment of democracy. A review of congressional debates and hearings on Alaska legislation does not support the latter interpretation, but that is hardly conclusive. There is much discussion of whether the territory's new population was permanent, which can be interpreted either way.

What is clear is that within four years the Senate sent a subcommittee to Alaska, headed by Senator Knute Nelson of Minnesota.[23] Spending two months in the territory, the senators heard from witnesses in Juneau and Fairbanks on the effects of the Carter Act and other congressional legislation. Many emphasized the need for roads and for more schools. Roads would help to get freight into the mining districts. Schools were needed because the Bureau of Education, which from 1885 had the responsibility to provide schools for all children, could not keep up with the demand brought about by the sixfold increase in the non-Native population. In addition, a number of new communities did not take advantage of the town incorporation provision of the 1900 civil government act because it was unclear whether there was enough gold in the various districts to justify the effort. Furthermore, senators heard demands for more self-government at every stop on their tour. Nelson and his committee returned to Washington, D.C., and persuaded Congress to adopt several more pieces of legislation to better facilitate settlement in Alaska.

The Nelson Act of 1905 addressed roads and schools. The business and liquor license fees authorized by the Carter Act were deposited in an Alaska Fund, 75 percent of which was expended by the newly created Alaska Road Commission, which shortly began construction of the Richardson Highway from the coast at Valdez to Fairbanks in the Interior. Congress mandated that the remaining 25 percent of the Alaska Fund be used to construct schools for white children living outside the incorporated towns, that is, in the new unincorporated gold rush communities of which the future was uncertain.[24] These schools, called Nelson Act schools, were open also to mixed-heritage children living a "civilized" life. In implementation, the territory applied an implicit Dawes test, admitting well-acculturated children while forcing others to attend Bureau of Education schools. The refinements implemented by the Nelson Act directly addressed migrants' articulated needs, manifesting again Congress's support for settlement and development in Alaska.

Soon Congress adopted still more legislation for Alaska. In 1906, responding to the nearly universal demand for more self-government, it provided that a nonvoting delegate to Congress from Alaska be elected biennially at the same time as other members of the U.S. House of Representatives. It also increased the number of judges to four, acknowledging the significance of the new town of Fairbanks.[25] The Delegate Act represented the beginning of internal politics in Alaska. The delegate would be elected biennially, using the four judicial districts as election districts, regardless of population. The seat of the first district was Juneau; of the second, Nome; of the third, Valdez; and of the fourth, Fairbanks.[26]

Also in 1906, Congress passed the Alaska Native Allotment Act, authorizing 160-acre allotments for Native heads of households. In 1903 a special inspector for the Interior Department, J. W. Witten, had conducted a survey of Alaska Native conditions. General Frederick Funston compiled an army report on Alaska Natives also in that year. In 1904 the Nelson sub-committee conducted investigations into Native conditions, and in 1905, President Theodore Roosevelt commissioned retired navy lieutenant George Emmons to submit a thorough report on Alaska Natives to Congress. The General Land Office also submitted a report. All of these reports noted that encroaching white settlement brought hardship to Natives through disease, alcohol use, and unfair game laws. Although the Interior Department surveyor concluded positively that an allotment act would help to break down traditional cultures and speed up acculturation, Lieutenant Emmons emphasized the diversity of Native culture and argued that an allotment act would help Natives protect their lands and cultures.

Though modeled generally on the Dawes severalty act, the Alaska measure recognized the different circumstances of Alaska Natives. There had been no Indian treaties in Alaska and there were no traditional reservations,[27] nor were there yet any formally recognized tribes. Therefore, Alaska Natives could not signify their intention to acculturate by severing ties with their tribe, as required by the original Dawes Act. Where the primary intent of the Dawes Act had been to force Indians to acculturate and to break up Indian lands for distribution to whites, the primary purpose of the Alaska allotment act was to "afford individual Alaska Natives the opportunity to perfect legal title to lands they used and occupied."[28] Few Natives availed themselves of the allotment act, probably because they were unfamiliar with bureaucratic methodology and intimidated by it and because the only network of federal officers across the territory consisted of school teachers.

The teachers were part of a structure dedicated to Native acculturation, and although they were not officially land agents, they advised and informed many Natives of their options, encouraging some and not others. A study of teacher letters and memoirs from the period confirms their central role at the point of contact between Native life and culture and the institutions, restrictions, and opportunities of modern, Western culture.[29] Their actions, and those of the few designated federal officials in Alaska, became an informal, implicit Dawes test, rewarding the acculturated and not others. When applicants came forward to take advantage of the allotment act, the department applied fairly rigorous tests of eligibility and the potential impact of the granted land on resources.[30]

Much congressional legislation for Alaska in this period can be explained by the national development of Progressive politics. Just before the turn of the century, America entered an era of extraordinary reform generated primarily by industrialization of the economy. Industrialization raised the material standard of living of most Americans, but it also led to the creation of business forms, particularly the trust, which helped to establish huge aggregates of corporate and personal wealth and power. This was the age of industrial and financial magnates, including such familiar names as John D. Rockefeller, Cornelius Vanderbilt, Leland Stanford, Andrew Carnegie, J. P. Morgan, and their like. Because of what many Americans at the time perceived as abuses of economic and political power, they empowered government to restrain big business, to curtail the abuses that a majority of citizens were convinced represented greed at the top and unjust suffering at the bottom of society. Government was the only force that could be made powerful enough to curtail the abuses of capitalism and restore order to a world that people felt was disintegrating around them.

There were opponents of reform, to be sure, but during the Progressive period government at all levels adopted an impressive array of reform measures, including antitrust and antimonopoly legislation, banking restriction, industrial safety mandates, pure food and drug regulations, child labor laws, maximum-hour and minimum-wage legislation, interstate commerce regulation, and others. Several constitutional amendments sought to restore, or create, democratic opportunity, including a change in the method of electing U.S. senators (by direct election rather than by state legislatures), authorizing the imposition of a graduated income tax, prohibiting the sale and manufacture of spirituous liquors, and enfranchising women. Although historians generally regard the reform era as having ended with, or been transformed by, America's entry into World War I, most of the reforms were permanent and remain an integral part of the system of government today.

Progressive reforms, ideas, and politics had an important impact on Alaska. Congress's willingness to provide for the territorial delegate and to increase the number of judges represents the principle of increased access to representation and to justice. The Nelson Act represented a quick and direct response to the will of the people. There would be additional examples as well. James Wickersham became a spokesman of Progressive

James Wickersham came to Alaska as a federal district judge in 1900. Committed to the Progressive politics of the time, he served as Alaska delegate to Congress 1908–20 and again 1930–32. Alaska Public Library, Wickersham State Historic Site Photo Collection P20.021.

politics in Alaska. Although he was an astute politician, he might have as easily become a Progressive critic. He was the territory's most important early politician, and he understood Alaska's colonial context well. Wickersham had migrated to Tacoma, Washington, from Illinois, where he studied law and had been admitted to the bar. After serving as Tacoma city attorney, he was elected to the Washington state legislature and in 1900 was rewarded for his party loyalty with the first appointment to the third district in one of the new judgeships created in Alaska. Wickersham resigned his judgeship in 1906 to run for territorial delegate. An able politician with a nimble mind and iron determination, he emerged as the territory's most effective advocate. Elected in 1908, he served six successive terms and continued as an active political force for another decade, at the end of which he ran for and was elected to a final, seventh term as delegate. Wickersham was a typically flamboyant nineteenth-century politician; his rhetoric was colorful, prejudicial, and often inflammatory, but he was intelligent and shrewd. His two most significant contributions to Alaska history were Congress's actions in 1912, establishing the territorial legislature, and in 1914, creating the Alaska Railroad.[31]

Soon after he began his work in Alaska's third district, the government asked Wickersham to travel to Nome to unravel a spectacular scandal involving the new judge of the second district.[32] Wickersham's work in the case established his reputation in Alaska as a friend of both justice and the common man. The Nome judge, Arthur Noyes, had made himself a willing participant in a scheme devised to defraud a number of miners of their claims and the gold they had extracted. The plan, developed by Alexander Mackenzie, a powerful Midwestern politician and friend of President William McKinley, was implemented in the summer of 1900. It involved "jumping" the claims (i.e., contesting the validity of a recorded claim and filing a substitute claim) and then having Noyes, who owed his appointment to Mackenzie, approve the new claimant, who then signed over the claim to Mackenzie. Wickersham quickly discovered the elements of the scheme and courageously recommended charges against the defrauders. Convicted on some of the charges, Mackenzie served three months of a one-year sentence, while Noyes was fined and removed from the bench.[33] The episode demonstrated that Alaska was not beyond the reach of American law. Thus it was in keeping with the Progressive concept of making the constitutional system work to protect the rights of ordinary citizens.

Progressive reform ideas, particularly antimonopoly sentiment, became a potent influence on national perceptions of remote Alaska when linked with a major Progressive Era agenda: new interest in the conservation of the nation's natural resources. Americans had begun to reassess public lands policy. Essentially, the nineteenth-century national public lands policy had been to transfer both lands and resources into private hands, through purchase, homesteads, railroad construction land grants, and later, mining claims, as a function of democratic opportunity. The public's resources were thought to be a legitimate resource for commodity development for those citizens who were willing to invest in them. But mechanization and industrialization hastened consolidation of large land holds and much waste of resources. Sometimes, for example, mining companies in the West would use what available forest timber they needed from a particular tract to construct a mine and then burn the remainder on the site to prevent its use by competitors. As petroleum became an increasingly important commodity, analysts became concerned that should the country need petroleum for strategic defense—to fuel its army and navy, for example—all the accessible and valuable deposits might already have been transferred into private ownership, and the government might have to purchase those resources at whatever price the owner demanded. These and other concerns gave the conservation movement considerable momentum.

The object of Progressive conservation policy was not primarily preservation of natural resources; it was rather to manage those resources efficiently.[34] The most effective champion of the new policy was Gifford Pinchot, a close friend of President Theodore Roosevelt and a dedicated reformer. Perhaps the most important change during this period was that instead of selling or giving away the public domain—that is, all the land the United States still owned that had not been transferred to the several states and that had not been withdrawn for military or other special use—the United States would retain such land and manage it rationally. New federal agencies were created just for that purpose. Congress adopted organic legislation for a forest management agency in 1891 and established the U.S. Forest Service in 1905; Roosevelt appointed Pinchot its director. In 1904, Congress passed the Newlands Reclamation Act, leading to establishment of the Bureau of Reclamation, to manage water resources on the western lands. In time a roster of acceptable uses of the public lands evolved, which included commodity development (such as saw timber for houses and grazing for beef cattle), protection of wildlife habitat, management of western water resources, recreation, and some preservation. Recreation and preservation inspired the creation of the National Park Service in 1925. Of all of these, however, commodity development was the dominant use, particularly in the national forests.

In 1906, Congress passed the Antiquities Act, authorizing the president alone to withdraw land from the public domain for whatever purpose he deemed necessary. Because of concern over the appropriation of petroleum and coal lands by mining conglomerates, Roosevelt used the act almost immediately to withdraw all coal deposits on the public lands until such time as Congress should devise a plan for protection of the government's interest and for orderly private development. In 1914, when it authorized construction of the Alaska Railroad, Congress ended the restriction on coal lands in south-central Alaska, along the route of the railroad. Congress would establish a leasing regime for coal, petroleum, natural gas, and some other minerals in the 1920 Mineral Leasing Act. But the initial 1906 prohibition hit hard in Alaska, for the largest private mining conglomerate in the United States, the Guggenheim Corporation, already had an idea for developing Alaska that hinged on plentiful coal deposits in the Bering River region and on the Pacific Coast south of the Copper River, and on copper in the Wrangell Mountains.

The Guggenheim Corporation had great plans for Alaska. At the turn of the century, corporate officers learned of a very valuable copper deposit in the Wrangell Mountains of south-central Alaska, near the headwaters of the Chitina River. This was an extraordinary mineral deposit; some of the copper assayed at 85 percent ore, a phenomenon nearly unheard of before or since. The Ahtna Indians knew of the deposits and had shown them to Lieutenant Henry Allen on his reconnaissance of the area in 1885. But a massive mountain barrier lay between the copper and the coast. The only way to get the ore out was to build a railroad through the mountains, which many engineers thought could not be done. If it could be built, financiers wondered if anyone could afford to build it. And if it was built, its terminus on the coast would likely be near the Bering River coal deposits.

In addition to coal and copper, the Guggenheims learned that there were also oil deposits in the Bering River region. They hoped that by developing all three minerals at the same time, they could make their investment in Alaska efficient and profitable. They also planned to construct a smelter on Prince William Sound to make the copper ingots there to save the expense of shipping raw ore south. The coal would be used to fuel the copper mine, the smelter, and the railroad; it would also be marketed in Alaska and on the world market. The railroad could be extended inland to the Yukon River, linking steamboat and barge service on the Interior rivers with the coast. This would make feasible the acquisition and development of additional mining prospects in Alaska's Interior. This integrated scheme represented colonial capitalism at its height. All the investment, and nearly all the labor force, would come from outside the territory and would be completely in the control of the investment group's few directors. The purchase of the Chitina district copper claims in 1906 was a first step in organizing this potential coordinated blueprint for Alaska development.

Roosevelt's 1906 withdrawal of strategic coal deposits around the country included the Bering River coalfield. This was a serious blow to Guggenheim prospects in the territory. It meant that Canadian coal would have to be imported to fuel their operations, at a much greater cost. Reflecting the democratic impulses of the time, Congress passed legislation in 1908 to open the Bering River field. But this legislation was calculated to exclude the Guggenheims: all claims were limited to 2,560 acres, and no claim could be developed in concert with another. That was not enough acreage for successful profitable development; it would support only small, home lot operations. And it was certainly nothing approaching the level of development the Guggenheims had in mind.

The Guggenheims were not entirely dissuaded, however. After assessing the legislation's impact, corporate officials decided to go ahead with the copper project and a railroad from the coast to the Chitina district.[35] But first they approached and gained partnership with New York financier J. P. Morgan. The corporation then formed separate companies for each of the different enterprises. The Kennecott Copper Corporation built and operated the copper mines at Kennecott, Alaska;[36] the Copper River and Northwestern Railway (CRNWRR) ran between Kennecott and Cordova in

Prince William Sound. The corporation also purchased the Alaska Steamship Company, whose ships would transport the raw ore to a Guggenheim smelter in Tacoma, Washington, in addition to carrying passengers. They also purchased the Northwest Fisheries Company, which owned twelve major salmon canneries. For the moment they decided not to invest in the oil deposits. All the companies were organized into a confederation called the Alaska Syndicate.

The Guggenheim-Morgan combination of investments in Alaska led many Progressives to conclude that the Alaska Syndicate intended to take over the territory and exploit all its resources in traditional nineteenth-century unfettered fashion. The railroad connection to the Interior exacerbated this image, for the Alaska Road Commission, which was building an alternative route known as the Richardson Highway from Valdez to Fairbanks, could not make its road reliable. For the moment the engineering challenges of Thompson Pass and Keystone Canyon defeated them. Muckraking critics of corporate power could argue that ordinary settlers, businessmen, and prospectors were at the mercy of whatever the syndicate might wish to charge for freight and transportation over its railroad and steamship line; by extension, the Guggenheims held all Alaska hostage to corporate greed. This was a distortion of Alaskan realities, for there were other absentee investors putting money into Alaska; the Guggenheims had no monopoly in the territory. But the questions raised by critics were germane.

Although the CRNWRR freight charges were not exorbitant, they were high. The Alaska Steamship Company did not have a monopoly, but maritime freight rates to Alaska were also quite high. Both the railroad and the mines provided a significant number of jobs, and Cordova was almost a company town. More important, the corporation was aggressively anti-union and understandably opposed government regulations that might drive up costs and cut into the profitability of the various companies. Corporate officials and attorneys were in a much better position to lobby Congress for legislation favorable to its Alaskan interests and to oppose legislation that was not favorable.

Investment by the Guggenheim–J. P. Morgan Alaska Syndicate, coming at the same time as the government's financing of the Alaska Railroad, generated great enthusiasm for Alaska among others with money to invest. It gave credibility to the notion that Alaska was the next great capitalist bonanza. In 1909, hoping both to encourage that perception

Alaska Steamship Co. freighter leaving Alaska for the West Coast. Such ships were the transportation link between the West Coast and Alaska until after World War II, when air transport became normalized. Anchorage Museum Rasmuson Center, Arnold Nelson Collection B1987.070.028.

and to profit by it, Seattle's Alaska Club, together with two Seattle newspapers, the *Seattle Times* and the *Seattle Post-Intelligencer*, organized a mini–world's fair in Seattle, the Alaska-Yukon-Pacific Exposition. Alaska gold and furs were showcased, and Alaska Natives exhibited, and Alaska was extolled as the next chapter in American development. The fair was consistent with Progressive Era thinking that the restoration of competition would bring widespread prosperity.[37]

James Wickersham made Progressive antimonopoly opposition to the Guggenheims the centerpiece of his political career. He used reform ideas and rhetoric in his many campaigns for Alaska delegate and afterward, when he directed political activity in his retirement. He routinely attacked "the Interests," as the press labeled monopoly corporations during the period, a more virulent form of the term "special interests" in today's political rhetoric. Wickersham used the terms "antitrust" and "antimonopoly" commonly in his stump speeches and habitually railed against Guggenheim power in Alaska, which he painted as opposed to the democratic rights and opportunities of the ordinary citizen. The Alaska Syndicate, he averred, intended to lock up Alaska as "its own plaything," its "private investment." Alaska would never be developed fairly and the common man would never have the freedom he sought and deserved, Wickersham argued, as long as the Guggenheim trust controlled Alaska.[38] He wrote anti-Guggenheim articles of his own for *McClure's* and *Collier's*, two of the more important muckraking magazines of the day.

Wickersham was somewhat disingenuous in his rhetoric, however, for when he resigned his judgeship in 1906, he offered his services as the Alaska Syndicate's attorney in Alaska. Corporate officers did not consider him reliable and rebuffed the offer. Had he been hired, he would not have been as vocally or aggressively anti-interest as he was. It is unlikely, however, that this completely explains Wickersham's commitment to Progressive reform over the whole of his long career. Alaska's transiency rate was high, and the nation's politics were increasingly Progressive in 1905 and 1906 and into the 1910s. Working men and women across America keenly felt their exploitation by corporate insensitivity, and in Alaska, Wickersham repeated a familiar message that resonated with conditions in the territory as mining became increasingly industrialized. Unions were popular in Alaska, if short-lived and essentially powerless. Wickersham's anti-trust rhetoric told his constituents what they wanted to hear, and they elected him repeatedly, despite the opposition of the territory's corporations and major newspapers.[39]

In addition to using "anti-Guggenheim" as a theme for his political career, Wickersham argued that Alaska must be developed by Alaskans, which was consistent with his attacks on absentee capital. The territory's entrepreneurs must have the freedom to develop Alaska as they saw fit. Only self-government would provide that freedom, he insisted. The federal government wanted to manage Alaska for conservation while the absentee capitalists wanted to manage it for their own profit. Wickersham was the first Alaska politician to articulate the understanding that Alaskans must look after their own interests, whatever those might be, and that they could not rely on the federal government or the absentee capital investors to do so, as each would likely pursue their own distinct interests.

In his articulation Wickersham established the fundamental paradigm for Alaska politics and in his own career became the model for Alaska politicians. Politicians in Alaska at the time had three basic options regarding public policy: (1) ally themselves with absentee capitalists who provided economic development, or with the federal government, which pursued resource conservation while nurturing additional non-Native settlement (and, some charged, facilitated absentee capital investment); or (2) argue for more Alaska control over one or the other; or (3) both. As the century progressed, most politicians would choose the third option, at least in their public statements. But Wickersham did not make clear how, without capital, Alaskans might act independently and simultaneously develop the region's economic potential, which lay only in exploitation of such natural resources as gold, copper, coal, oil, and fish. The capital did not exist in the territory and there was little likelihood that it would. Nor did he explain how more self-government would empower Alaskans to generate such capital or force the federal government to remove restrictions on resource development. These dilemmas, endemic to Alaska, are as challenging today as they were in Wickersham's time.

THE BALLINGER PINCHOT AFFAIR, THE TERRITORIAL LEGISLATURE, AND WOMEN'S SUFFRAGE

The competing forces of federal conservation and absentee capital development in Alaska spilled over into national politics during the Taft administration with the celebrated Ballinger-Pinchot controversy. The battle fit nicely into a growing split in the Republican Party and became one of a handful of issues in the presidential election of 1912, helping to elect Woodrow Wilson as president. The affair arose soon after William Taft's election. The new president appointed Richard A. Ballinger to be his secretary of the interior. Ballinger had been head of the General Land Office when Roosevelt had withdrawn coal lands in 1906; he was widely regarded as an opponent of conservation. Rumors began to circulate that a group of thirty-three claimants in the Bering River coalfield intended to combine their claims for sale to the Alaska Syndicate; this would have been a violation of the restriction against claims being developed in concert. Louis Glavis, an Interior Department investigator, became convinced that the charges were true and, moreover, that Ballinger approved. Glavis took his suspicions to Pinchot, the champion of conservation, who advised Glavis to tell Taft. But Glavis should have worked within channels, at least within his own department, as Taft subsequently fired him for insubordination. Glavis went public with an article in *Collier's* titled "The Whitewashing of Ballinger: Are the Guggenheims in Charge of the Department of the Interior?"

When the new Congress convened in January 1910, there were cries for Ballinger's resignation, and a special commission was formed to investigate. The attorney for the claimants admitted that there had been talks about collusion (i.e., a conspiracy to defraud), but there were enough ambiguities in the testimony that no charges were brought; the thirty-three claimants were forced to surrender their claims, however. After the investigation Pinchot wrote a letter to a senator criticizing Taft's handling of the affair and the president's support of Ballinger. The letter was read into the record on the Senate floor, and Taft immediately fired Pinchot. Further investigations exonerated Ballinger but kept the issue alive. In the press and around the country the controversy became for Progressives a symbol of Taft's betrayal of conservation and for opponents of reform, a symbol of out-of-control reform.

In Alaska, Taft became anathema for his opposition to congressional authorization for an elected territorial legislature, even though Progressive conservation reform was not popular. Taft's appointee as governor, Walter E. Clark, dutifully opposed the idea as well. Absentee investors opposed the notion on the familiar grounds that it would mean increased taxes and more regulation of their Alaska enterprises. Many Alaskans felt caught between opposing forces—on the one hand, investors who supplied jobs and payrolls, and on the other hand, reformers who, while they advocated greater self-government, also supported conservation that had "locked up" potentially valuable natural resources.

In the 1912 election Roosevelt formed a third party, known as the Bull Moose Party, to try to take back the presidency from Taft; his mascot was the Alaskan bull moose, partly to remind voters of Taft's and Ballinger's apparent betrayal of conservation in Alaska. Republican voters split between Taft and Roosevelt, however, and Democrat Wilson was elected with an electoral majority but only 40 percent of the popular vote. The Ballinger-Pinchot affair demonstrates that the battle between resource conservation and development was joined at the beginning of the twentieth century. It also focuses attention on the dilemma of Alaska development: Alaskans can do little to control either federal policy or absentee capitalist investment in the territory, and there can be no economic development in Alaska, and therefore no attraction for non-Native immigrants, without such investment. It also manifests the significance for Alaska of the advent of national Progressive politics, the implications of which were enduring.

As a delegate in Congress, Wickersham kept up a steady drumbeat of alarmist anti-Guggenheim rhetoric. He had introduced bills for an Alaska territorial legislature in 1909 and 1911, asserting that all conditions for establishing the body had been met in the territory. His argument was strengthened by the 1910 census report; it showed that the non-Native population had remained fairly steady, falling to 25,331.[40] Wickersham reminded his colleagues that the original 1787 organic act had authorized creation of a territorial legislature when the non-Native population reached only five thousand. The citizens of Alaska, he insisted, deserved at least the level of self-government their counterparts in the territories had enjoyed a century earlier. As the country became more Progressive, Congress was susceptible to any assertion that citizens were being denied their democratic rights without a reasonable level of self-government.

Roosevelt's Progressive Party convention in Chicago included an Alaska "home rule" plank, for example, calling for "the same measure of local self-government that was given to other American territories," a line written by Wickersham. The House and the Senate passed separate bills on the matter in the summer, but the territorial governor and Seattle business interests were able to keep a conference committee from meeting until after the November election. In Alaska, Wickersham ran again for delegate, as a Progressive "Bull Moose" Republican. The election was held in August and the national press interpreted his win as a victory for Roosevelt's presidential campaign. Congress immediately passed the "home rule" bill, and Taft, conceding the inevitable, signed it on Wickersham's birthday, 24 August.

The act provided for a bicameral body to be elected in even-numbered years and to sit for sixty days, in March and April, in odd-numbered years: eight members in the Senate, two from each election district, half to be elected for four years at every election, and sixteen members in the House of Representatives, two each from four election districts, all to be elected at each election. There were a number of significant limitations in the act, which reflected Congress's intention to maintain firm control over the limited citizen population, many of whom were transient and thus perhaps not appropriately cognizant of their legislation's effect on future generations.[41] The limitations rightly irritated Alaskans. The territory could not borrow money without congressional authorization, and it could not levy taxes in excess of 1 percent of the assessed valuation of property, 2 percent for municipalities. The governor could veto specific legislative

appropriations. The act made explicit Congress's reserved right to legislate on such matters as divorce, gambling, liquor sales, and town incorporation. Public funding of religious education was prohibited, as was county
organization. More important, the legislature could not enact fish and
game regulations, except to tax and license harvest activity. As with other
territories, Congress could override any law passed, a power it did not use.

Historians have criticized these limitations, particularly that on natural resource and land regulation. But in addition to Congress's lack of confidence in the permanence of the population, restraint on the matters of
indebtedness and tax liability was probably prudent, particularly given the
dependence of economic activity on absentee investment, which could be
influenced by turns in the economy, by political changes, or by the perception of corporate management of the degree of risk involved in their
Alaska investments at any moment in time. As it was, the exception for taxation empowered the legislature to force the salmon industry to contribute to territorial development, while the retention of the federal
government's management authority was consistent with the fact that
Alaska was still a territory. In addition, the territory probably did not have
the capability to administer 375 million acres of wilderness.

Wickersham considered the act a success, a vast increase in Alaska's
powers of self-government. He immediately capitalized on this success to
strike a blow for another anti-Guggenheim measure and, as he said, for
Alaska freedom: congressional authorization for a federal railroad in
Alaska. With the only effective transportation link between the Interior
and the coast still the Guggenheim railroad from Cordova to Chitina,
and then over the Richardson Highway to Nenana and Fairbanks, the
corporation still held Alaska development hostage. It was clear that the
corporation's monopoly could only be broken by a competing transportation link, and the only feasible link would be another railroad. But it was
also clear that no private company, or even combination of companies,
could afford to build a railroad in Alaska. In fact, several railroad ventures
had failed because of the great cost and the meager return. Only the
Guggenheim-Morgan combine could afford to build a railroad in the
remote and rugged wilderness, and then only to service their own investment, namely, the Kennecott mines.

Progressive reformers supported the idea of publicly owned utilities,
arguing that public entities could be established with strictly limited profit
margins, thus eliminating corporate greed and its associated abuses while

Baseball field at the Kennecott Mines, owned by the Guggenheim Corporation and J. P. Morgan's Alaska Syndicate. Alaska State Library, Burns Photo Collection P425.12.146.

providing essential services at lower consumer cost. Wickersham initially opposed the idea of a federal railroad for Alaska, but as he grew to understand the impossibility of any other alternative to the Guggenheim transportation monopoly, he changed his position. The change may have represented new thinking, a surrender to political realities, or the depth of his anti-Guggenheim feelings; there is support in his diary entries for all three motivations. In any case Wilson included the idea in his 1912 platform, and after the election Wickersham moved quickly to ally himself with the new president. Support for the idea of the railroad continued to develop in Congress, and the bill reached the House floor in mid-January 1914. Wickersham gave a five-and-a-half-hour speech in which he outlined Alaska's resources and potential and argued that only freedom from monopoly, from the Guggenheims, would facilitate realization of the potential. After votes in the House and the Senate, Wilson signed the act in March.

This was truly an extraordinary achievement. Congress had subsidized construction of the transcontinental roads with generous land grants, increasingly more generous as the rails moved west, but those lines were constructed and run by private enterprise. Congress had provided for the fifty-mile Panama Canal Railroad to pull ships, move passengers, and guarantee the security of the canal. But the Alaska Railroad was the only railroad built and operated for the purpose of developing a territory, developing the country's western lands. It represents again federal support of settlement and economic development in Alaska, at a level surpassing federal support in the other western territories, which was considerable. The cost of constructing the Alaska Railroad amounted to 5 percent of the federal budget.

The act left the choice of a route up to Wilson. There were only two choices, for there are only two portals through the Coast Mountains, the Copper River and the combination of a path over the Kenai Peninsula to the Susitna River.[42] The Guggenheim railroad ran up the Copper River from Cordova, and the corporation hoped to sell its road to the government. But they asked too high a price, and the purchase would have raised cries of collusion.[43] Private investors already had started a line north from Seward, which had gone bankrupt. A group of Canadian banks had taken over the investment and later sold it to a combine that included the Guggenheim-Morgan syndicate. Wilson chose the Kenai-Susitna route. John Ballaine, one of the original investors in the Seward line, still owned land at the Seward town site and hoped to sell his holdings to the government for their main railroad facility. But he too asked too much money, and the Alaska Engineering Commission, the agency created to build the federal road, established their construction and operations headquarters at Ship Creek landing, the future Anchorage, instead of at Seward, even though the line would continue on to Seward. Construction began in the summer of 1915.

The continuing federal response to Alaska's circumstances and development during the Progressive Era, particularly after the initial excitement of the Klondike and later discoveries had passed, manifests again the thesis that the government persistently supported Alaska settlement and economic advance. The magnitude of the response disposes of the idea of federal neglect of Alaska. It is also inconsistent with the argument that the federal response was mild or unenlightened.[44] As it did in 1884 with the first civil government act, and in 1891 after the eleventh census, Congress responded to the initial surge of population in 1898 through 1900 with immediate measures to facilitate settlement, then over the next decade and a half continued to pass fundamental legislation that recognized both the stability and the rights of the territory's pioneer population. This pattern of response to changes in Alaska would be repeated in Alaska's future.

The congressional response also manifested concern over conservation of Alaska's natural resources. In denying the territorial legislature control over land, fish, and game in the territory, Congress was not concerned with the actions of the thirty-six thousand non-Native residents; it was concerned about territorial politicians becoming pawns of the absentee corporations that were ready to invest in exploitation of those resources. Roosevelt's sensitivity to efficient use of those resources in 1906 had become the country's sensitivity by 1912, as the Ballinger-Pinchot controversy demonstrated. This was not an unreasonable concern. In discussing the political power of the canned salmon industry in Alaska, for example, Ernest Gruening is said to have quipped once that the Alaska legislature could be purchased for the price of a case of good Scotch whiskey.[45]

Progressive thinking influenced Alaska in still other ways. The character of territorial legislation in the early years can be said to have been Progressive in nature, aimed at protecting individual rights in the face of private economic power and potential corruption. The first bill passed by the first Alaska legislature, for example, was a law enfranchising women. Socialist Party organizer Lena Morrow Lewis and others traveled in the territory after 1910 helping to develop local party groups, and a number of Socialist Party candidates stood for election to the first legislature.[46] Many western states enfranchised women before the national suffragist amendment. Historians disagree about the reasons for this, but the fact that Progressive reform sentiment overtook the country at this time may be a sufficient explanation. In some territories enfranchising women added to the population of voters, suggesting readiness for statehood. In some states there was a genuine reform sentiment, usually generated by Socialist and other new political movements. In still others, enfranchising women seemed to be a measure to prove the sophistication of the electorate. In Alaska, Socialist Party candidates supported candidates who supported women's suffrage, as did many labor unions. Corneiia Templeton Jewett Hatcher, managing editor of the Woman's Christian Temperance Union magazine, moved to Alaska in 1911 and established an Alaska chapter of the organization, of which she became president. She lobbied for women's suffrage and later for prohibition in Alaska, which became law in 1918, as did women's suffrage in 1913.

In 1915 the legislature passed an Indian citizenship act, establishing a complicated process by which Natives could achieve citizenship if they were living "civilized" lives and could find white citizens who would verify that fact before a judge. Like some other Progressive legislation, the act appeared to be liberal on its face, but its demeaning implications for Indians, that they could not be citizens unless whites approved, was in fact quite illiberal. The legislation was progressive for its time, however, coming nine years before the U.S. Congress granted citizenship to all American Natives.

Other early territorial legislation reflected the country's Progressive ideas: laws for mechanic's lien protection (indemnifying workers in industrial accidents), industrial safety, mine inspection, pure food and drug protection, maximum hours for laborers (an eight-hour day). Other legislation provided some powers of self-government for Native villages, made school attendance for all children compulsory through age sixteen, and established a territorial board of education. In 1918 the legislature voted a complete prohibition of the sale, manufacture, or possession of alcohol, a year before national prohibition.

There should be no surprise that the territorial legislature enacted laws that mirrored those of the rest of the nation. People coming into the territory brought with them the ideas they had assimilated elsewhere. They sought to create not an alternative society, but one as much like the one they had come from as possible. In addition, they had been enculturated to Progressive ideas simply by living in a culture that by the second decade of the twentieth century was overwhelmingly Progressive. Thus the history of the territory in this period reflected the major evolutionary changes in the American culture broadly and in the West particularly.

Congress selected three engineers to head the Alaska Engineering Commission: William C. Edes, a veteran civilian railroad engineer; Lieutenant Frederick Mears, who had built the Panama Canal Railroad; and Thomas Riggs, an engineer who had worked with the International Boundary Commission that had surveyed the Alaska-Canada border. As soon as Congress passed the legislation, laborers with an adventuresome spirit began to head north for jobs. Men and families from all across Alaska also flocked to the construction headquarters, for the placer mines of the gold rush areas had all played out, and those who wanted to stay in the North needed to go where they could get work.

In addition to choosing the route, overseeing the clearing of the right-of-way, engineering all the grades, bridges, and tunnels, and supervising the labor force, the commissioners had another especially unenviable task: town building. Anticipating that a substantial community would grow up around the railroad headquarters, Congress gave the commission a mandate to lay out a town, authorized the General Land Office to auction lots to homebuilders and businesses, and directed that the town be provided basic services and managed by the commission for five years. The legislation provided that after a five-year period, during which it was assumed construction would be complete, the town should become self-governing. As engineers, the commissioners did not welcome the task of founding a town.

By midsummer a tent city housed several thousand people at the mouth of Ship Creek on upper Cook Inlet. In June the regional officer of the land office held an auction for lots in the planned town, which the engineers had marked off on the bluff south of the creek. After several proposals for names for the new town, the settlers chose Anchorage in the first municipal election. Not wishing to impose their ideas on the future, the commissioners named the streets by letter (A, B, C) in one direction from the main north-south stem and by double letter (AA, BB, CC) in the other direction; the transverse streets were numbered (1, 2, 3). They assumed the designations would be temporary. (Only the double-lettered streets have been named; the numbers and the single letters remain today.) Purchasers began construction of houses and buildings immediately, and by the onset of winter many had moved in. The commission soon had the water, sewer, electricity, and telephone systems operational. Railroad construction proceeded rapidly, and by the end of the 1916 construction season, the line was open to Seward and moving north rapidly.

America's entry into World War I in early April 1917 nearly halted construction, however. Most of the labor force quickly joined the services and left the territory. The commissioners directed that laborers be recruited among the unemployed in Seattle. A number of men who might rather have spent their summer watching the calm waters of Puget Sound instead found themselves pushing the Alaska Railroad tracks along the Chulitna River and over Broad Pass toward Alaska's Interior. Most road construction was completed by the fall of 1918, although major challenges remained, including constructing bridges over Hurricane Gulch and the Tanana River at Nenana.

Meanwhile in Anchorage not everything went as planned. Wickersham's insistence on the right of greater self-government in his fight for the territorial legislature and the railroad rang somewhat hollow as the end of the five years of commission town site management neared. Commissioners tried to get the residents to make plans for taking over, and paying for, basic municipal services. To their surprise, however, they found a good deal of resistance. The townspeople had become used to government-supplied services and had some difficulty acclimating themselves to self-reliance. Repeated entreaties seemed to fall on deaf ears. At a mass meeting the commission accountant told the gathered townspeople that the government's role in their town was over. But his remonstrances were ineffective until someone asked if the commission would continue to provide fire protection if the town failed to incorporate. When he replied emphatically "no," the citizens seemed finally to understand.[47] Self-reliance on the last frontier often did not meet expectations.

Alaska would repopulate after the war; the 1920 census reported 55,036 people: 28,228 non-Native and 26,558 Native. The population was clearly stable. But in the "normalcy" that Warren Harding proclaimed during his presidential campaign and the prosperity of the ensuing decade, there was little interest in new reform. Harding traveled to Alaska in 1923 to drive the golden spike at ceremonies marking the completion of the Alaska Railroad and the Tanana River bridge. He was the first president to visit the territory. Returning to Seward from Fairbanks, the presidential party embarked on a naval ship for Cordova. Traveling across Prince William Sound, the president received telegrams informing him of pending revelations of major corruption in his cabinet. On the trip south he became ill, and during a speech at the University of Washington stadium in Seattle, he faltered and nearly fell. Rushed to a military hospital in San Francisco, Harding died within a few days.[48] It seemed a symbolic close to an era in the nation's, and Alaska's, history.

Pioneer Alaska

The Last Frontier

HISTORIANS HAVE CHARACTERIZED Alaska's economic history as a series of booms and busts. If this is an accurate analysis, the 1920s were a bust period; certainly there was no rush to take advantage of a newly discovered resource, as with the Juneau gold rush of 1880 or the Klondike and later rushes at the turn of the century and as would occur after the discovery of oil on Alaska's North Slope in 1968. But neither was there a downturn in the economy after the completion of the Alaska Railroad. The population reported in the 1920 census was comparable to that reported in 1900 and 1910; so would it be in 1930 and 1940.[1] A better characterization of Alaska's history might be that of an economy moving to successively higher plateaus, and the 1920s might be seen as one of these plateaus. The non-Native population in this period was probably less transient than at any other time in Alaska's history. Migrants who were in the territory after the war intended to stay, had found a way to make a modest livelihood, and enjoyed, or tolerated, the predictability of a stable economy.

THE ALASKA NATIVE BROTHERHOOD

There were important developments in this period. Aviation began to play a role in the territory's economic and social character, a role that would grow steadily. Congressional legislation brought structure to the fishing industry, although not without substantial criticism. The federal bureaucracy expanded significantly and became a focus of territorial complaints. Natives entered Alaska politics in a way that manifested the growing sophistication of Native organization and the racist nature of early twentieth-century Alaskan society, another commonality Alaskans shared with the West and other parts of the nation.

James Wickersham stepped down from the delegate's office in 1920. His last two elections had been contested; his opponents, Charles Sulzer in 1916 and George Grigsby in 1918, had filed legal challenges to the outcome, charging that there had been voting irregularities and questioning voting by Natives in some election districts. Wickersham won both cases in the House of Representatives, but he wanted time away from the political spotlight and he needed to make some money. He tapped as his successor Dan Sutherland, a miner and fisherman who had come north with the Nome gold rush, had served as a marshal for a time in Juneau, and worked in the Iditarod and Ruby gold districts. Sutherland was a confirmed "Wickite." He would win five successive terms as the Alaska delegate. Sutherland had help in several of his elections from the only viable Native organization in the territory before statehood, the Alaska Native Brotherhood (ANB). The ANB also supported other Wickite or Wickite-approved candidates for southeastern seats in the territorial legislature.

The ANB did not begin as a political organization, however, and its major role in Alaska's history was not in politics. Rather, it was an Indian self-help organization founded under the aegis of the Presbyterian church and the U.S. Bureau of Education. Founded in Juneau in 1912, its early objectives were to prepare Indians for citizenship and to provide models of acculturation. Later its primary goals would be the representation of Alaska Native rights, concerns, and programs to win recognition of Alaska Native equality and dignity. The ANB's evolution as a potent political and social force in Alaska manifested the conviction of most Tlingit leaders in Southeast Alaska that acculturation, mastering the ideas and forms of Western culture, would in the long run be the most effective and secure path to equality and freedom.[2] ANB leaders in the 1920s, 1930s, and 1940s hoped to utilize Western institutions in their fight for Native rights and justice while at the same time preserving Native cultural traditions and Native identity.

Most of the ANB leaders were acculturated men (and one woman) who had been educated at the Sheldon Jackson School, formerly the Sitka (Presbyterian) Industrial Training School. Eventually the organization would establish local chapters, called camps, in all eighteen of the southeastern Alaska Native villages. The ANB was a completely Indian organization, but it was structured in imitation of service auxiliaries then common in most Protestant churches in the United States. Its official song was "Onward Christian Soldiers." Initially, members had to speak English, support the suppression of traditional rituals, and pledge sobriety. In later years, however, eligibility requirements were made more flexible.

Soon after the founding of the ANB, women of the southeastern villages established the Alaska Native Sisterhood (ANS). The organizations elected delegates to annual jointly held conventions, which adopted resolutions urging program initiatives for the year and elected an executive committee to carry them out. Although in the 1940s they would attempt to found local camps in other parts of Alaska, neither the ANB nor the ANS had the resources to do so effectively. But while the ANB was always a Southeast Alaska and Tlingit-Haida body, because it was well organized and continually viable, federal and territorial officials sought its officers' views on policy issues affecting all Alaska Natives and addressed the annual conventions to explain policy initiatives and to hear comment.

The missionaries and the Bureau of Education teachers worked as a single establishment in Alaska, and many missionaries became government teachers. Both groups endorsed the founding of the ANB and the ANS. In fact, the ANB founding meeting took place while Indians were attending an education conference organized by the Bureau of Education, where Indians were invited to comment on the bureau's curriculum. The bureau and the missionaries taught not only that white culture was the best way to live but also that it represented the only alternative to extinction for Indians. Thus many Indians at the time aspired to lead acculturated "civilized" lives. In 1915 the ANB helped the Bureau of Education lobby the territorial legislature for the Indian citizenship act.

Two brothers emerged after World War I as the primary leaders of the ANB: Louis and William Paul. They and a third brother had been raised at the Sitka Presbyterian Indian School, where their mother, "Tillie" Paul Tamaree, had been a teacher and interpreter.[3] All the boys graduated from the Carlisle Indian School in Pennsylvania, where the curriculum was based on the idea of racial equality of whites and Indians and therefore the appropriateness of complete acculturation of Indians. Louis, the youngest brother, served in the U.S. Army in World War I and upon returning to

Alaska in 1919 was elected secretary of the ANB. He began to teach that Indians should take control of the acculturation process. In the meantime, William remained in the continental states, attending college and seminary, and earning a law degree. He returned to Alaska permanently in 1920 and was admitted to the bar, becoming the first Native attorney in Alaska. He also was elected an officer in the ANB.

The brothers William and Louis Paul soon took over ANB leadership and politicized the organization, redirecting its activities toward the Carlisle vision of Indian equality. They argued that Indians were already citizens by virtue of the Fourteenth Amendment: they had been born in the United States and therefore were citizens and thus had no need of the territorial citizenship act. This view was in some ways naive, for a majority of Indians were as yet unprepared to function effectively in white society without support, and they were subject to segregation, discrimination, and economic deprivation. But the idea nonetheless represented the commitment of the Indian leadership to equality, autonomy, and self-direction. Moreover, the brothers insisted, as U.S. citizens Natives had no need of mentorship by white leaders.

In 1921, William traveled to Washington, D.C., to testify on behalf of the ANB on the impact of fish traps on Indians in Southeast Alaska. At the time Congress was responding to requests from Alaska's canned salmon industry for help in regulating the fishery (a topic to be discussed shortly). By the very act of testifying as a spokesman for the ANB before a congressional committee, William gave form and credibility to the concept of organized, acculturated Indians in Alaska as well as to his own organization. In 1922 he decided to make the ANB a force in territorial politics by organizing the Indian vote in Southeast Alaska. There were about eighteen thousand Indian residents in Southeast Alaska at the time and perhaps as many as one thousand potential Indian voters, judging from official election returns in the previous decade. Some acculturated Indians (perhaps 20 percent of the Southeast Alaska Indian population) had voted in Alaska in the 1910s, even though technically Indians were not citizens and were not legally entitled to vote.[4] The law was not enforced by local officials. In fact, Natives had voted in elections for territorial delegates as early as 1916. William reasoned that if the ANB could use political power on behalf of Indians and their rights and concerns, control of a reliable bloc of voters also would make him personally and politically powerful.

Traveling to the various southeastern villages, William persuaded a large majority of Indian voters to support candidates of his choice and also drew many new voters to the polls. In several close elections in the southeast, his bloc of Indian votes was decisive. These victories made him a potent political force in Alaska. William had agreed to deliver his votes to Sutherland and to other "Wickite" candidates in return for their support of Indian issues and other matters William might favor. He overcame the illiteracy of many of the voters by supplying them with pieces of cardboard that fit over the ballot at the polling place in which he had cut out a space over the place on the ballot where the voter needed to make a mark. Neither organizing a bloc of voters nor supplying the cardboard guides was illegal, but critics objected to their use on moral and political grounds.

Some white politicians objected strenuously, resenting the new political influence of the ANB and William Paul's power. In 1923, William's critics introduced a bill in the legislature to require literacy as a prerequisite to voting in the territory. While the idea of literate voting was consistent with Progressive notions about responsible democracy, literacy had not previously been a prerequisite for voting. Although the bill was consistent with Progressive ideals, it was also an attempt to disfranchise Indians in Alaska. The literacy bill passed in the House and tied in the Senate, killing it for the session. William then decided to use his organized political power on his own behalf. In 1924 he ran for a seat in the territorial House of Representatives. In campaign statements he promised to work for the integration of schools in Alaska and to force the legislature to pay equal widows' and orphans' benefits to Indians. This prompted his opponents to run newspaper ads designed to raise voter anxiety over "Indian control of Alaska schools," revealing the racist character of their opposition. Despite these attacks, William won his seat, becoming the first Native elected to the territorial legislature; he was reelected in 1926. No other Native would be elected to the legislature until 1944.

Advocates reintroduced the literacy bill in the 1925 legislature. This time, despite William's opposition, it passed, but not before he rallied support for an amendment protecting the voting rights of anyone who had ever previously voted. Additionally, all Indians had become eligible to vote in 1924 when Congress had passed the Indian Citizenship Act. Alaska's literacy act was never actually enforced; it had been a ploy to destroy William's power and the political power of the ANB in the territory, but it failed to do so. When later a suit was brought to test the act, judicial review found that without adequate enforcement provisions, it was effectively null. Meantime, William's power and significance in Alaska and in Native affairs would be eclipsed in later years, even though he remained somewhat active until his death in 1979.[5]

THE ROLE OF SALMON AND ARRIVAL OF THE AIRPLANE

Delegate Sutherland opposed the territorial literacy act, and when similar legislation was introduced in the U.S. House of Representatives, he fought it unsuccessfully. He was more successful in supporting legislation dealing with the Alaska salmon fishery. From modest beginnings in 1878, the salmon industry had become the most important part of Alaska's economy before the turn of the century. By 1890 there were more than twenty canneries in Alaska; the pack that year approached eight hundred thousand cases. By 1895 there were thirty-seven canneries. Competition made consolidation desirable, and the Alaska Packer's Association (APA) emerged as the principal industry organization. The APA controlled 70 percent of the industry in that year. Their share would decrease to about 40 percent by 1900, but by then the total pack was more than two million cases, valued at nearly $10 million. Salmon canning would be the back-bone of the territorial economy until after World War II.

Each cannery operated during the runs of pink (humpback) and red (sockeye) salmon each June, July, and August. A ship would bring the workforce up from San Francisco at the beginning of the season. Labor in a large cannery consisted of 100 to 150 white fishermen and 150 to 200 mostly Filipino cannery workers. The fishermen used small dinghies and mostly gillnets. The canneries also began to use fish traps in about 1900. These were extremely efficient contrivances consisting of netting stretched from the surface to the floor of the ocean near the mouths of streams, extending perpendicular to the shore a thousand yards seaward where a large pen with a net floor caught almost all of the fish diverted from the stream mouth. If operated continuously, such traps caught nearly all the fish in a particular run and thus could deplete the fishery in a few seasons.

The cannery workforce was hired by contractors who exploited the workers, who knew little of their legal rights and were grateful for the promise of employment. Often many workers finished the season with little or nothing to show for their work after charges they had been forced to agree to pay—for waterproof clothing and boots, work tools, medical supplies,

Santa Anna Salmon Cannery near Wrangell, 1917. More than two hundred canneries operated in Alaska in the interwar period, often having appropriated Native fishing sites and using fish traps, which could catch almost an entire run of fish headed for their spawning grounds. Alaska State Library P20.156.

and food beyond a set minimum—had been deducted from their wages. This kind of contract labor was inevitably exploitative and was outlawed by state and federal legislation in the early 1930s.[6] The ships that transported the workers up in the spring and back down to San Francisco in the fall (along with the cases of salmon) were often old sailing vessels that were adequate because they needed to make only one trip a year. The APA acquired a fleet of old iron sailing vessels after 1900, which they named "Stars" (as in the *Star of Russia, Star of Falkland, Star of Alaska,* etc.) and used for annual trips to Alaska until the 1940s. The romance often associated with the ships belied the exploitative nature of the industry that used them.

Congress adopted legislation in 1906 that permitted the territory of Alaska to tax salmon at a fixed value per case, in the beginning, four cents. The territory consistently pressed to increase the tax, and the industry consistently argued that it could not afford to pay additional taxes. Through its lobbying association, Alaska Canned Salmon Inc., the cannery owners challenged the tax in court several times. During World War I, between April 1917 and November 1918, the U.S. Army and Navy purchased canned salmon for active duty personnel, and the canneries increased the amount of fish they caught and packed because they could sell nearly all the salmon they could put up. This led to a significant surplus after the armistice was declared. Aware that the fishery might be in danger of exhaustion, the operators took advantage of the surplus to discuss conservation measures.

Realizing their own inability to curtail fishing enough to ensure replenishment of the fishery, the cannery owners approached the government for help.[7] In 1922 the Commerce Department persuaded the president to create two limited-entry fish reserves in Alaska as a conservation measure, in Bristol Bay and around Kodiak Island. The government would issue only a limited number of permits annually. This was a revolutionary departure from traditional fisheries policy. Fish had been treated as a common resource, open to all fishers without qualification. Fishing seasons had been used to guarantee replenishment. Now the government assumed the responsibility of determining who got to fish and who did not.

Alaska fishermen, as independent operators, typically sold fish to the canneries each season, and many had come to depend on fishing as their livelihood. This included many Indian fisherman for whom other employment was severely limited. The 1923 territorial legislature protested the creation of the government reserves on the grounds that the established absentee operators would be given preference and the Alaskans would be denied the opportunity to fish in their own fishery. The Alaskans reasoned that industry lobbyists in Washington, D.C., would have a much better opportunity to make their case for permits than the local fishermen would. The Alaska Native Brotherhood also protested the creation of the reserves and absentee control of the fishery, as it would do until statehood in 1959. On the floor of the House of Representatives, Sutherland charged that the government was in collusion with the salmon industry to lock up the fishery for the absentee owners. He charged that Commerce Secretary Herbert Hoover knowingly allowed the industry to overfish the resource.[8]

The crisis led to landmark federal legislation in 1924, the White Act. Even though they had asked for help, the cannery owners fought passage of the act. But testimony demonstrated the need for measures to guarantee perpetuation of the resource. As finally passed, the White Act established the principle of open-entry for the Alaska fishery: anyone would be permitted to fish it. Conservation would be established by limiting the times during which fishing would be permitted and by monitoring fishing activities to guarantee 50 percent escapement of the available fish. Congress gave the Bureau of Fisheries inadequate resources to monitor the fishery, however, a continuing source of frustration in the territory. Nevertheless, the White Act would be the policy for governing the fishery, however ineffective, until statehood.[9]

The absentee-owned cannery companies were permitted to continue to use their large, efficient traps, despite continuing Indian and other protest that they threatened the fishery's existence. This led many Alaskans to conclude that Sutherland was right, that the federal government colluded with the industry to keep Alaska in corporate bondage. It certainly underscored the colonial nature of Alaska's economy, and all the Alaskans who depended on it, which increasingly included Natives who sold fish to the canneries. Even though more than six hundred traps operated during the 1930s, many Native fishermen made their summer livelihood selling to the canneries, whose operators were eager to can as many fish as they could get. As noted earlier, until 1940 about 75 percent of territorial revenue came from the cents-per-case tax on the salmon industry. Territorial dependence on the fishery in the 1920s and 1930s was similar to Alaska's dependence on oil after 1970.

As congressional legislation for Alaska declined in the 1920s, so did congressional appropriations. Funds for the agricultural experiment stations were eliminated, as were those for a mine experiment station established at Fairbanks in 1917. All but one U.S. Army post in Alaska closed in the 1920s, the Chilkoot Barracks at Haines, limiting the army's role to manning the telegraph line (the Washington-Alaska Military Cable and Telegraph System) and new radio-telephones that came into service. Congress reduced funding for the Alaska Railroad and forced the manager to raise freight rates. The budget for the Bureau of Education was clearly inadequate, given its mandate to provide schools for all Native children not enrolled in other schools. The bureau had added several new branches to its Alaska work, including a medical and dental service, a marketing agency for Native arts and crafts in Seattle, and, after the devastating influenza epidemic of 1918 and 1919 that killed thousands of Natives on Alaska's west coast, several orphanages.[10] Alaska was a long way from Washington, D.C., and in an age of conservative politics, an easy place to cut the federal budget.

The Progressive Era had led to a major expansion of the federal bureaucracy, for regulation created the need for government inspectors, agents, and bureaus. In addition, the new policy of natural resources conservation generated new agencies, several of which had units in Alaska. Congress established the Tongass National Forest in 1905, for example, and the Chugach National Forest in 1909, Katmai National Monument after a spectacular volcanic eruption there in 1912, Mount McKinley National Park in 1917 to preserve the variety of species of wildlife, and Glacier Bay National Monument in 1925. Many traditional bureaus and agencies also had offices in Alaska, numbering thirty-eight by 1920, such as the Customs Bureau, the General Land Office, the Commerce Department, the Department of Agriculture, and many more. Often different agencies had partial jurisdiction over the same activity or geographic area, sometimes leading to confusing and contradictory policies. Alaskans referred to the many officials in these bureaus, who were appointed in Washington, D.C., and often spent only a few years or even months in the territory, as the "federal brigade." The governor was ostensibly the head of the brigade, but many Alaskans considered his office but one more agency that often did not work in concert with the other agencies. Several attempts by Congress to create a three-person Alaska development board with authority over all of the agencies dealing with most federal activity failed in Alaska because cabinet officers were unwilling to surrender any of their jurisdiction.

Meanwhile, the territorial legislature had more success attempting to limit the power of the governor, who increasingly was seen as an unwanted representative of Washington, and as an absentee carpetbagger. The governors in the 1920s had been routine administrators. President Warren Harding had appointed Scott Bone, a former newspaper editor, and President Calvin Coolidge had appointed George Parks, a cadastral (land survey) engineer. President Herbert Hoover retained Parks. Wickersham regarded both men as weak and too favorable toward the salmon industry. Generally, territorial legislators seemed to agree. They restricted the governor by creating a number of elected offices, including a territorial auditor, treasurer, and highway engineer; there had been an elected territorial attorney general since 1917. The legislators also discussed creating an office called the territorial comptroller to which they would transfer any powers they had previously authorized for the governor. This bill, introduced in several legislatures, never became law, but it

Mount Katmai on the Alaska Peninsula erupted in 1912, spreading ash across Alaska, particularly on nearby Kodiak Island; exposed brass was tarnished as far away as Vancouver, B.C., and the sky darkened over New England. The upheaval formed a new mountain, Noverupta. Anchorage Museum Rasmuson Center, FIC Collection B1991.043.41.

demonstrated growing frustration in the territory with federal power and the "federal brigade."

After the 1928 election, Sutherland decided that he too had tired of the burden of the delegate's office and informed Wickersham that he would not run in 1930. Wickersham surveyed possible successors but found none of them adequate, so he decided to run again himself. Although he was now seventy-three, he was still in good health. The campaign focused on Wickersham. On the one hand, there was his record of achievements for Alaska, which the patriarch touted in every speech; but on the other hand, there was his long career of Progressive attacks on absentee capitalists, primarily on the Alaska Syndicate and the canned salmon industry, which his opponents raised at every opportunity. Wickersham won the election, defeating the territorial attorney general, a former "Wickite," in the primary and George Grigsby, a longtime territorial attorney and Wickersham's opponent in 1918 (and former territorial attorney general), in the general election. Despite salmon industry support for his opponents, Wickersham and his Progressive antimonopoly, anti-absentee capitalist agenda still appealed to a majority of Alaska voters.

Wickersham won without a number of the Indian votes that Sutherland had been able to count on. In 1928, William Paul had run for a third term in the legislature but had lost his race. On the eve of the election Paul's opponents published information that he had received contributions from salmon cannery companies. For a high-profile politician who had made abolition of fish traps and attacks on the salmon industry part of his stock in trade, this appeared duplicitous, as it was intended to appear. After the election Paul lost some of his following in the ANB. Two Democrat brothers from Klawock, Frank and Robert Peratrovich, organized their own bloc of votes for Wickersham's opponents. That they were able to do so demonstrated not only their own ability but the growing acculturation and sophistication of Alaska's Tlingit and Haida Indians.

In the 1930 delegate race Wickersham's opponents used a new campaign device in Alaska: the airplane. In a region with almost no roads, made up almost entirely of undeveloped country, the airplane had a dramatic impact. In the mid-1920s mail in Alaska still moved by dog sled relay. In 1924 the U.S. Army's first round-the-world flight of airplanes—open cockpit biplanes—flew through Alaska on the first part of a military expedition to demonstrate that the machines had practical as well as entertainment value.[11] Pioneer bush pilot Noel Wien established the first scheduled air route in Alaska, between Fairbanks and Nome. The first airplane company began operation in Anchorage in 1926. The airplane reduced travel time from weeks to hours and could quickly take sick and injured people to medical help. The plane greatly aided Alaska's economic potential, helping prospective investors gather information and keep track of their agents' work. It could get supplies to locations on an emergency basis and could get them to difficult-to-access locations. In critical ways the airplane revolutionized Alaska as significantly as the telegraph line had at the turn of the century, and as radio would do in the 1930s and 1940s.

But not everyone was convinced by the round-the-world flight that planes were reliable. They had some severe limitations, particularly that they could not fly in bad weather. A crisis in Alaska in the winter of 1925–26 helped to underscore those limitations. Medical officials had become alarmed when they learned that several cases of diphtheria had broken out at Nome. The town did not have enough serum should the outbreak

The airplane *Anchorage*, representative of planes that initiated the air age in Alaska. Anchorage Museum Rasmuson Center, Lu Liston Collection B1989 016.735.3.

become widespread. Territorial doctors ordered serum to be shipped from the government hospital in Seattle. When it arrived at Seward four days later, they sent it by railroad to Nenana on the Tanana River. Newspapers carried the story, and while people waited for the serum to arrive in Nenana, where it would be taken by dog sled relay down the Tanana and Yukon Rivers to Kaltag and then across to Norton Sound and on to Nome, several airplane pilots sent a telegram to Governor Bone, offering to fly the serum from Nenana. Under no circumstances, Bone wired back, would he entrust so precious a cargo to flimsy, unreliable, and unsafe airplanes. Thus the serum was carried downriver by dog sled, by Leonard Seppala and his lead dog Balto, across the sound's frozen ice to the anxious town—an effort that would be commemorated in the epic annual Iditarod sled dog race.

THE NEW DEAL IN ALASKA

The quiescence of the 1920s gave way to anxiety, privation, and fundamental change as Alaska experienced the Great Depression with the rest of the nation. Soon after the stock market crash in October 1929, unemployment began to rise across the country. President Hoover moved to shore up weak spots in the economy, most particularly in farming, and he canceled reparations payments owed by European countries from World War I to try to strengthen their economies. But the problems were more systemic than could be solved with short-term measures. In 1931 the national banking systems failed in Austria and Germany, then in Japan, and finally in England. The pressure on the U.S. economy was enormous, and it also collapsed. Prices fell as precipitously as the value of stocks had. Unemployment soared as production sank to the lowest levels on record. As a national average unemployment reached more than 20 percent. Farmers destroyed crops that they could not market for as much as it had cost to produce them. Self-help organizations collected and distributed surplus food and clothing in major cities, but it was not enough to meet the growing need. People began to question whether the Depression had revealed capitalism's fatal flaw.

Alaska conditions ran parallel to what was happening elsewhere. Seasonal unemployment became yearlong as employers could neither hire nor purchase. The price of copper plummeted along with other basic commodities, and in 1934 the Kennecott mines closed for the winter. In 1938 the corporation closed them permanently and sought to liquidate the property. They also hoped to sell the Copper River and Northwestern Railway to the government, but their asking price was too high. In their own cost-saving program, the Alaska Syndicate took up the railroad tracks, which they moved to operations in the American West. The government tried to absorb some of the labor force on the Alaska Railroad. Gold mining in Alaska had already reached its lowest level since the Klondike era, and the Depression held it there, despite the government artificially raising the price from $20.77 an ounce to $35.00. Soon there were no surplus inventories in the territory, and when several dock strikes in Seattle threatened basic food supplies, the government shipped needed staples to Cordova, Seward, and other towns on Interior Department vessels.

Incoming president Franklin Roosevelt's New Deal, the collection of programs that he and his advisors persuaded the Congress to adopt to deal with the crisis, included a number of general relief measures and some new liberal reforms. The Federal Emergency Relief Administration distributed surplus food directly to the needy. The Civilian Conservation Corps (CCC) employed young men in the national forests and on other public lands in quasi-military camps where they built cabins and cleared trails; they were compelled to send most of their meager monthly checks home to their families. Generally, the administration worked to get prices up so

Anchorage, 1930. Established in 1914 as the headquarters of the Alaska Railroad, Anchorage depended on railroad employment until World War II, after which it grew from about 3,000 people in 1940 to over 10,000 in 1950. Anchorage Museum Rasmuson Center, Arthur Eide, Pratt Museum Collection, B1984.047.4.

that producers, both industrial and agricultural, could stay in business and continue to offer employment. When the Supreme Court declared portions of the two primary congressional enactments of this initiative unconstitutional in 1935 because they restrained free trade, Roosevelt worked with Congress to reenact them in a form palatable to the Court. One such measure, the Wagner Act creating the National Labor Relations Board, provided federal guarantees of the workers' right to unionize and bargain collectively (and strike) for the first time in the United States.

The government undertook a number of programs designed to create jobs so that people could continue to feel they were earning their own keep, being economically self-sufficient. The Civil Works Administration (CWA) and the Public Works Administration (PWA) funded major construction projects, such as courthouses, docks, bridges, and dams, where unemployment was highest; both the CWA and the PWA also made low-interest loans for similar projects. The Works Progress Administration (WPA) funded smaller, short-term projects where·conditions had reached crisis proportions. Banking legislation imposed tighter rules on bank organization and functions. The new Securities and Exchange Commission (SEC) regulated stock and bond transactions. The Federal Deposit Insurance Corporation (FDIC) insured bank deposits. The most important systemic change was the creation of Social Security (Supplemental Security Income, or SSI), including old-age insurance, unemployment compensation, and support for the physically and mentally disadvantaged. Social security represented the creation of "welfare capitalism," a system that helps to support those without resources while maintaining free enterprise within limited regulation. Because its political economy is organized around the idea of personal, individual economic responsibility (providing for oneself), the United States was the last of the industrial democracies to establish a (limited) social safety net for its citizens. These and other New Deal programs did not ultimately solve the Depression, however; World War II did that. But they permanently changed the character of the American economy and the government's responsibility for individuals in ways that most citizens did, and do, approve.

All of these New Deal programs were implemented in Alaska in one form or another, representing significant federal aid that allowed the non-Native population to continue to live in the territory in the manner it demanded. Alaska's delegate to Congress during these years was Democrat Anthony J. Dimond, an attorney who had served a number of years in the territorial legislature. Elected in the Democrat New Deal sweep in 1932, he remained in office until 1944. Dimond made one of his chief activities bringing the New Deal to Alaska, often persuading Congress or the administration to adjust programs so Alaska would be eligible to take advantage of them.

Anthony Dimond was elected Alaska delegate to Congress in the Democrat sweep in 1932, serving until 1944. Anchorage Museum Rasmuson Center, Lu Liston Collection B1989.016 DimondAnthony2.

In addition to the government raising the price of gold, the Alaska Railroad increased its purchases of coal from mines in the Matanuska Valley and near Healy. The Commerce Department stimulated purchases of platinum, mercury, antimony, and gypsum, which helped some mine owners. CWA and

PWA grants and loans helped to build a bridge across the Gastineau Channel between Juneau and Douglas, construct a hotel at the entrance to Mount McKinley National Park, build a new city hall and federal building in Anchorage, pave streets in Anchorage, and construct fire stations, schools, waterworks, and playgrounds across the territory. U.S. Army engineers constructed small-boat harbors, breakwaters, and harbor improvements.

The WPA funded artists to travel the territory to paint Alaska's natural wonders and its people. When a fire destroyed most of Nome in 1934, the government provided emergency relief funds for the rebuilding. During Seattle dock strikes in 1934 and 1937 the Alaska Railroad distributed supplies at railheads free of charge. The U.S. Forest Service organized a number of CCC camps employing hundreds of young men on a seasonal basis to build forest cabins, construct trails and signs, and clear rights-of-way for roads and airfields. The CCC camps were supposed to be integrated, but when a Senate subcommittee gathering information on Indian conditions in Alaska conducted an investigation of the camps, they found that the Forest Service would not hire Indians. The camps were integrated shortly thereafter.

The most unusual New Deal program in Alaska was the Matanuska Colony project, an extension of a program that was attempted in a number of the lower continental states. With continuing mechanization and consolidation of agriculture, many former farm people had moved to cities to take jobs in the industrial sector. Many such marginalized people found themselves unemployed and in dire straits as the Depression progressed. Congress established the Rural Rehabilitation Administration to move them back to abandoned farmland where they could raise some of their own subsistence and perhaps begin to earn a living. Roosevelt advisor Harry Hopkins suggested bringing the program to Alaska, where its objectives would be to move Alaska toward agricultural self-sufficiency, a romantic idea associated with the frontier, and to encourage new migrant population for the territory.[12]

Program administrators selected two hundred families from economically depressed counties in north-central Minnesota and Wisconsin to start new farms in the Matanuska Valley; all were to have had farming experience.[13] One of the agricultural experiment stations had been located in the valley under the 1898 act, and work there had demonstrated the suitability of the valley for some grains and vegetable and dairy production. The valley was regarded as the most promising area for Alaska agricultural development. Colonists for the 1935 project came across the country by rail and to Anchorage by ship. Journalists followed every step of the process, celebrating the new settlers who were again carrying out "America's tradition of pioneering on the last frontier."[14] Feted by the townspeople of Anchorage, the colonists chose 160-acre parcels by lot. They were to make payments on the land at low interest rates once the farms became productive. First, however, the land had to be cleared of mature growth timber (birch and spruce). Colonists were paid for clearing the land. They were also extended credit for durable goods, seed, and other farm necessities as well as for some perishable goods.

The winter of 1935–36 was unusually harsh, and about half of the original families returned to the States. Replacements were quickly found. The Alaska Rural Rehabilitation Corporation, headquartered in the new town of Palmer, controlled the project, providing agronomic advice and helping to organize the social life of the colony. But most of the farms were not successful on a sustained basis. Historian Orlando W. Miller has concluded that the colony failed to achieve its goals.[15] The U.S. military undertook the remilitarization of Alaska in 1940, and from that time on discouraged farmers could find work in construction at the new army base in Anchorage, making reliable and high wages instead of investing strenuous and constant labor in a government scheme that might not work. Miller also concluded that there was a flaw in the selection process for participants in the project. Many were not actually farmers but had worked in auxiliary trades, such as farm implement sales or itinerant labor. Success in the valley would have been a challenge under the best of circumstances. Miller suggested that some participants did not have the perseverance to invest concerted labor in an enterprise whose profits would be delayed.

Perhaps more important, little agricultural or dairy production resulted from the project. Most analysts have argued that the costs of production are too high for the small size of the market in Alaska, making agriculture noncompetitive with agriculture in the lower continental states. The economies of scale prevent successful Alaska agriculture. Miller calculated that the government invested about $200 million in the project between 1935 and 1941 for roads and railroad trackage, payments for land clearing, credits that were never repaid, and general administration. This was an extraordinary infusion of dollars into south-central Alaska at the height of the Depression.

That the Matanuska Colony project failed to meet its objectives does not mean that there were no successful colonists. A number of farms produced vegetables and dairy products for the Anchorage market. Today there are a number of surviving colony farms and families in the valley. The Matanuska Maid Dairy, started as a colony enterprise, survived into the 1980s. However, almost all milk marketed by was imported from Washington State, as were most other dairy products. Economies of scale will likely continue to defeat profitable agriculture in Alaska until the population increases substantially.

In addition to other major reforms, the New Deal fundamentally revised American Indian policy. Culminating in a decade of reassessment of the Dawes policy of forced acculturation, in 1934 Congress passed the Indian Reorganization Act (IRA), establishing the policy of Indian self-determination. Based on the federal obligation to protect fundamental Indian rights articulated in Supreme Court decisions in the early nineteenth century, the IRA repealed allotment laws, committed the government to recovering Indian lands and restoring them to tribal ownership, and appropriated funds for this purpose; it also protected Indian access to subsistence resources. The act provided for government recognition of tribal governance through the creation of elected tribal governing councils. It established a revolving credit fund to capitalize Indian businesses. In addition, the act mandated preferential hire of qualified Indians in the Bureau of Indian Affairs. In its recognition of tribal sovereignty, inferior to federal sovereignty but distinct and actual, the act was truly revolutionary and represented an about-face in the history of federal policy.[16]

As passed, the IRA did not apply to Alaska. In fact, Dimond had worked carefully to be sure that it did not, for it was structured around recognized tribes as the basic organizing unit. But at this time there were only a few recognized tribes in the territory because there had been no treaties made with Alaska Natives. Dimond feared that including Alaska in the act would have the effect of excluding most of them. William Paul traveled to Washington, D.C., to work with Dimond on Indian matters in 1935 and 1936, and together they fashioned amendments for Alaska's unique conditions. For Alaska they made the basic unit not a tribe but "groups of Indians . . . not heretofore recognized as bands or tribes, but having a common bond of occupation or association, or residence within a well-defined neighborhood, community or rural district."[17] This change made the IRA applicable in Alaska and with it some significant funding, especially for education.

In 1931, in another significant policy change that affected Alaska Natives, the Interior Department transferred all Alaska Native services from the Bureau of Education (BOE) to the Bureau of Indian Affairs (BIA). The BIA had responsibility for government services to Natives in all other parts of the United States, and the transfer was mainly a rationalization of government structure. The ANB resisted the transfer because leaders felt the BIA would be more paternalistic than the BOE; they feared the BIA would seek to exercise much more control over Native affairs. In subsequent years many villages adopted IRA constitutions, but a perennial question was how much control the BIA would have. Working as a BIA field agent in Alaska, Paul sought to assure village elders that they would retain direction of their affairs, but he could not quiet all anxieties.

While working with Dimond and Paul on the amendments for Alaska, Interior Department officials decided to craft a comprehensive Native policy for Alaska. In particular, Indians and federal officials both wanted to determine what lands belonged to Alaska Natives. One way to do that was to define Indian (or Native) reservations in Alaska. The IRA authorized the

Alaska Native Brotherhood leader William Paul Sr. (*center*) and his attorney sons, William Paul Jr. (*left*) and Frederick Paul (*right*). Alaska State Library, Alaska Native Organizations Photo Collection P33.31.

secretary of the interior to establish new Indian reservations, if Natives wanted them. The ANB opposed reservations on the same grounds that some villages in Alaska rejected IRA village constitutions: fear of BIA paternalism. The Interior Department went ahead anyway. Officials were encouraged to do so by a landmark legal decision by Interior Department solicitor (chief legal officer) Nathan Margold, who held that Indian tribes retained all their original powers, their internal sovereignty, unless such had been formally extinguished by the Congress. Once reservations were defined and tribal, or in the case of Alaska, once village governments were certified by the interior secretary, Native lands would be secure, protected by the federal government.[18]

In 1941 the U.S. Supreme Court expanded Margold's declaration in a case involving Indians in Arizona. *United States v. Santa Fe Pacific Railroad* found that Indians had "aboriginal title" to any lands they had ever used or occupied, unless the Congress had formally extinguished that title.[19] The Congress had extinguished title to most Native lands in the United States by treaty, even though many of the treaties were forced on the Indians. But there had been no such extinguishment in Alaska because there had been no treaties with Alaska Natives, Congress having persistently deferred addressing land title to the future. Interior Department officials decided that creating reservations in areas traditionally used and occupied was the best way to secure Native lands in Alaska. In 1942, Margold expanded his declaration to include traditionally used fishing waters in Alaska. Soon after, the department established a 1.4-million-acre reserve, the Venetie Reservation in northeastern interior Alaska, and the smaller 35,200-acre Karluk Reserve on Kodiak Island. The Karluk Reserve included waters adjacent to the village to protect Native fishing rights.

Ultimately the reservation policy in Alaska failed, however.[20] The reserves at Venetie and Karluk had been declared without any advance public notice, generating citizen outrage. Then, despite an internal report to the contrary, Interior Department Secretary Harold Ickes recommended three smaller reserves in Southeast Alaska, at Kake, Klawock, and Hydaburg, each to include traditionally used fishing waters. He also recommended an additional inland reserve, at Tetlin. The Natives there approved the reserve, needing protection for the furbearers they relied on for cash income. But Kake and Klawock voted not to have reservations. Hydaburg approved their reserve, but the Supreme Court ultimately disallowed it and the reserve at Karluk, holding that their establishment had been flawed. The Interior Department was unprepared for the Natives' rejection of the proposed reserves and for the vehemence of white protest to their creation. In the face of this resistance, the department gave up the policy. Natives would need to find another way to secure title and protection for lands they claimed as their own. One historian has argued that the New Deal Indian policy for Alaska created division between Natives and non-Natives that had not obtained previously.

In fact, another method already existed: a direct suit in federal court. Congress had halted any further treaty making with American Indians by legislation in 1871. At this time Indians were barred from taking land claims to the courts, unless specifically authorized to do so by Congress. Congress had occasionally passed so-called jurisdictional acts allowing tribes to take land claims cases to the U.S. Court of Federal Claims. In 1935, Congress passed such a jurisdictional act for the Tlingit and Haida Indians of Alaska. The act had its origins in Wickersham's decision to run for Congress for a seventh term in 1930. Wickersham had long believed that the Indians of Southeast Alaska were entitled to some remuneration for government appropriation of their hunting and fishing lands and waters to create the Tongass National Forest and, as noted earlier, that there was some question about whether the Russians had properly acquired those same lands. In 1929 he addressed the ANB convention at Haines, Alaska, promising that if elected delegate, he would pursue a jurisdictional act so these questions could be put before the federal court. During his last term Wickersham introduced the legislation, but it did not come to a vote on the House floor.

When they were working on the IRA amendments for Alaska, Dimond and Paul also wrote a jurisdictional bill, which Congress passed in 1935. Their bill provided that if the court should find that the Indians had owned the land, and that if Congress in future should award any compensation for taking the forest, the compensation should be paid to a "central council," not to individuals. The idea was to have the award (money) work for all the Indians, and if invested, over a long period of time. Paul wanted to be hired as the Natives' attorney to construct the suit, but soon after returning to Alaska from Washington, D.C., in 1936, he was charged with unethical behavior for several legal misrepresentations and a misappropriation of fees; a year later, having failed to answer the charges, he was disbarred in Alaska.[21] The disbarment resulted partly from a conspiracy by Paul's enemies and partly from his own carelessness in handling his affairs. He would continue to be active and eventually, after statehood, would be reinstated to the Alaska bar, but his political power was effectively ended.

The land suit was eventually filed in 1947, and in 1959 the court found that the Tlingit's and the Haida's aboriginal title to Southeast Alaska had not been formally extinguished by the Alaska purchase treaty, so that at the time of the purchase of Alaska from Russia, the Indians still owned the land. But their title had been extinguished by creation in 1905 of the Tongass National Forest, encompassing sixteen million of the eighteen million acres in the archipelago and, the court found, the Indians were entitled to compensation for that taking of their title. Finally, in 1968 the court awarded $7.5 million to the Central Council of the Tlingit and Haida Indian Tribes of Alaska, an amount based on the commercial value of accessible timber in 1905, the date of the taking. This was a meager award that Tlingit and Haida leaders found wholly inadequate. But the fact that the court based its finding on the validity of aboriginal title was very significant, for aboriginal title had not been extinguished in the rest of Alaska either. It might be that all of Alaska was subject to aboriginal title, a question that would arise in the not distant future.

While Alaskans struggled with unemployment and federal grants, and William Paul worked with Anthony Dimond in Washington, D.C., to bring the Indian Reorganization Act to the territory, a remarkable visitor to Alaska published a book about a season he spent in the small community of Wiseman on the Koyukuk River deep in the Alaska wilderness north of the Yukon River on the lower slopes of the majestic Brooks Range. Robert Marshall had lived in New York City as a boy and had dreamed of Lewis and Clark forging a path through the pristine wilderness of the American West. He feared he had been born too late to experience anything similar himself.[22] But then he discovered a blank spot on the map of Alaska. Marshall made four trips to the Alaska wilderness and spent months living in Wiseman.

Like the naturalist John Muir before him, Marshall exulted in Alaska, for here civilization was a matter of small pockets lost in a sea of wilderness, land unknown and unfettered. Historian Roderick Nash writes that Marshall was the first American to recognize that wilderness preservation could involve "whole watersheds, entire mountain ranges, and intact ecosystems," rather than small, isolated parcels. In 1934, with a few friends who also were wilderness enthusiasts, Marshall founded the Wilderness Society, an organization for the purpose of "fighting off invasion of the wilderness" and stimulating "an appreciation of its multiform emotional, intellectual and scientific values."[23] Testifying before a congressional committee investigating recreational resources in Alaska in 1938, Marshall suggested that all of Alaska north of the Yukon River, as yet free of any cultivated economic development, should be set aside as a permanent wilderness, with no roads, agricultural activity, or industry. This would preserve a place where the emotional value of the frontier could be experienced yet once again, and true pioneer conditions might prevail. Noble as his idea was, it was fundamentally flawed by its failure to recognized time-honored Native harvest of traditional subsistence resources on land throughout Alaska. Later environmentalists would persist in this failure until forced in the Alaska lands act of 1980 (Alaska National Interest Lands Conservation Act) to compromise with Native subsistence harvest.

After his 1932 sojourn in Alaska, Marshall wrote a sociological study of Wiseman's diverse population, Native and non-Native. He described the lives of all the people there, the dominant role subsistence played in their survival, how they coped with winter darkness, how they interacted with one another. The people in Wiseman, he concluded, were the happiest of any on earth because they were surrounded with the beauty and majesty of nature, with which they had learned to accommodate and live in harmony; they were free from the need to acquire collections of material goods. They lived with what they needed, and they found that in the wilderness their needs were reduced to very little: food, shelter, adequate clothing, and the opportunity to contemplate their natures. They had learned how to be content as human beings, a gift Marshall thought he had observed nowhere else.[24] The Wilderness Society would emerge in the 1960s as one of the most important and effective national organizations working on behalf of environmental legislation and the designation and protection of wilderness. Sadly, Marshall died at the young age of thirty-eight.

The history of Alaska through the 1920s and 1930s manifests continuing federal support for settlement and economic development in the territory, more evidence that notions of federal neglect or complacency regarding Alaska are wide of the mark. However happy the people of Wiseman may have been, as detailed by Marshall, the conditions that made this contentment possible were about to be shattered forever. The crisis of war was about to break on Alaska, bringing with it a frenetic level of human activity, another dramatic surge in population, and more money than anyone in Marshall's day would have thought possible. A new era in Alaska and the American West was about to explode.

War and the Transition to Statehood

WORLD WAR II drew Alaska into the economic and political structure of modern America at an unprecedented level. With the Japanese invasion of the far western Aleutian Islands, and the subsequent Allied reconquest, Alaskans felt directly their membership in the American union. Alaska might be remote, but the war that enveloped their country reached out to engage them even more acutely and threateningly than any other part of the United States. After the war Alaskans found themselves bound more tightly than ever to the country and the West, especially Seattle. New population meant expanded towns and the business opportunities and the responsibilities that went with them. Oil exploration reminded people of their dependence on outside capital. With the advent of the Cold War, Alaska became a critical element in the strategic defense of the United States and the free world and was thus tied to the nation still more closely. Finally, throughout the war and postwar periods, federal spending was the principal base of the Alaskan economy. If it had ever been previously possible to conceive of Alaska as isolated, it became impossible during the 1940s and 1950s.

DUTCH HARBOR AND THE ALEUT EVACUATION

When the Japanese attacked Pearl Harbor, Hawai'i, on 7 December 1941, there was widespread, if momentary, panic in Alaska. The people of the territory did not know what the American military knew, that the attack was a singular effort by the Japanese that had stretched their capability to the maximum. The attack was intended to occupy U.S. attention and to serve as a blocking maneuver against any plans the Americans might have had for an attack on the Japanese Kuril Islands.[1] The immediate Japanese objective at Pearl Harbor was to cripple the U.S. Pacific fleet. The Japanese goal in the Pacific was to protect raw materials (and territorial expansion) in Southeast Asia, to support the internal economy and the global economic independence of the home islands. To do this, they needed a ring of Pacific islands, including New Guinea and the Solomon Islands to the south and Midway Island, a thousand miles west of Honolulu, to ensure protection of their expansionist plans in Indonesia. Midway was an American possession. Japan expected that following the Pearl Harbor attack, the United States would sue for peace in the Pacific to concentrate on the European war or stay out of the conflict altogether.

The Japanese had signed the (Washington) Naval Disarmament Treaty in 1921, actually an arms limitation agreement that held the tonnage of capital ships (warships) to a ratio of 5:5:3 between the United States, Britain, and Japan. The compensation to Japan for agreeing to the treaty under these terms was the U.S. promise not to fortify the Aleutian Islands. In 1936 the Japanese announced their intention to abrogate this treaty to increase their naval strength without reference to other powers. This was part of a general military buildup and mobilization in Japan. With Japan's announcement the Aleutians became vulnerable to hostile actions from large Japanese navy and air installations at Paramushiro south of the Kamchatka Peninsula. A U.S. naval intelligence report submitted to the president in 1938 recommended that naval bases be constructed at Sitka, Kodiak, and Dutch Harbor.[2] At the same time several Army Air Corps reports called attention to Alaska's unique position on the "great circle route" between Asia and America, the shorter sailing or flying distance northward from Japan to the Aleutians and then south toward Seattle and San Francisco. In addition, Alaska was a logical refueling station on a transpolar route between Europe and Asia. Alaska would clearly play a strategic role in any future military confrontation.

With these considerations in mind, Congress authorized the remilitarization of Alaska in 1940. The navy wanted the three recommended bases along the coast from which it could fly reconnaissance missions across the North Pacific to watch for Japanese shipping. Aside from tenders and patrol boats, the navy did not plan to consign ships of the line (warships such as carriers, battleships, cruisers, destroyers) to the territory. The army, however, wanted air bases from which to use fighters and bombers to defend the territory from enemy air and naval attack.[3] Construction began in 1940 on both naval and army air bases. By late 1941 there were more than twenty-one thousand army and thirteen thousand navy personnel in Alaska. Few units were ready for combat, though. The Alaska National Guard was called into active service, and Ernest Gruening, who had been appointed Alaska governor by President Franklin Roosevelt in 1939, organized an Alaska Territorial Guard, whose chief responsibility was to watch the coast for signs of enemy ships or aircraft. Major M. R. "Muktuk" Marston organized the guard in western Alaska, enrolling many Inuit and Aleut Natives. The guard units were not always taken seriously by regular army commanders, but they facilitated organization within and communication between Native villages.

Some months before the bombing of Pearl Harbor, the U.S. military had solved the Japanese military communications codes through cryptanalysis. This does not mean, however, that anyone knew beforehand of the planned attack on the huge American naval base. The Japanese maintained radio silence in the days before the attack, and the Americans, not imagining the Japanese capable of such an attack, erroneously interpreted what little radio evidence they had. The attack was a complete surprise and destroyed perhaps 40 percent of America's Pacific naval capacity. Alaskans learned of the raid by way of shortwave radio. A civilian radio station operator in Fairbanks actually alerted the military, who had not yet heard.

There was considerable alarm in the territory, for many feared an attack on Alaska as well, not knowing what the Japanese objective might be. The army ordered blackouts (no lights permitted outside or allowed to show from inside buildings) in the coastal cities, ships were detained in port, civilian air traffic was grounded, and the railroad shut down temporarily. The army evacuated military dependents and some families of civilian employees of the military. Some civilian leaders sent their families south as an example of cooperation. In Juneau the governor and top officials in the "federal brigade" quickly established a tent encampment at Auke Bay north of the city where women and children were housed temporarily while the able-bodied men patrolled the town with National Guard rifles. Fortunately, no one was injured as the groups of anxious, uncertain, and untrained men wandered the streets with loaded firearms. Territorial officials soon realized the futility of such preparations. Lack of information helped to sustain modest panic in Alaska for several months.

After the Pearl Harbor raid, tens of thousands of military personnel and civilian laborers poured into the territory to construct facilities for Alaska's defense. Early in 1942 the U.S. Army ordered Japanese citizens and Americans of Japanese descent living in the western states and Alaska to be evacuated to internment camps inland, in eastern California and in Idaho, Utah, Arizona, and as far east as Wyoming. One hundred and seventeen thousand people were affected, two-thirds of whom had been born in the United States and thus were U.S. citizens and could not, according to the Constitution, be deprived of their life, liberty, or property without due process of law. In the camps these citizens learned firsthand about barracks surrounded by barbed wire and prison food and armed guards. In Alaska, Japanese Americans were ordered to gather at the shipping points of Anchorage and Juneau and transported south. Many lost much if not all of their property; many did not return to Alaska after the war. In 1944 the U.S. Supreme Court upheld the validity of the internment on the grounds of national security.

Alaska was unprepared and indefensible when the United States entered the war. Between January and June of 1942 scores of military installations were constructed in the territory. The army was particularly anxious to have inland fields where aircraft could be sequestered if the Japanese should launch harassing raids along the coast. By war's end three hundred separate facilities had been built, although many were temporary and decommissioned once Alaska ceased to be an active theater of war.

On 3–4 June 1942, Japanese fighters and bombers attacked Dutch Harbor in the eastern Aleutians. The army had established a garrison, Fort Mears, and the navy had communications facilities there. In bombing and strafing raids, the Japanese attack killed twenty-five or more army personnel and four navy. The overall damage was modest, however, and the U.S. military quickly rebuilt and further fortified the town.

The Japanese raid was a cover for an invasion of Attu and Kiska Islands far to the west. On Attu, forty-two Aleut Islanders and two navy radio operators were captured. They were interned at Otaru City on Hokkaido during the war. Seventeen died during the captivity. An American man operating a radio installation that reported on the weather was killed resisting the invasion. His wife, a nurse and school teacher, was taken prisoner. The Japanese fortified the island and also Kiska Island, which they had occupied at the same time as Attu. They would remain in the islands until defeated in the battle of Attu in May 1943.

In the same week the Japanese launched a carrier-based attack on Midway Island. The invasion of Kiska and Attu had been an attempt to divert some of the U.S. Navy away from the defense of Midway. Also, the Japanese hoped to be able to conduct harassing raids on Dutch Harbor, Kodiak, and perhaps even Anchorage from airfields they would build on the islands. They hoped to use the airfields to deter American raids on Paramushiro. Despite the casualties and a number of buildings at Dutch Harbor being burned in the Japanese raid, the American Navy did not divert any ships from Midway, and the Japanese attack there failed. Midway was one of the classic naval battles in the history of warfare.

Immediately after the Dutch Harbor raid, the navy evacuated all Aleut Islanders living west of Dutch Harbor and in the Pribilof Islands. The Natives were now civilians in a combat zone and were removed for their own protection. They were taken to several abandoned canneries in Southeast Alaska.[4] Earlier in the year, as a contingency, various federal agencies had attempted to work out an orderly evacuation of the Aleuts to sites on the south shore of the Alaska Peninsula, an area environmentally comparable to their home islands, but the Japanese attack forced emergency action. More than eight hundred people were evacuated to four different sites. Planning for the evacuation was so undeveloped that the destinations were not agreed upon until after the Natives were already aboard ship.

Conditions for the Natives in the temporary camps were deplorable. There was little privacy, the water supply was inadequate, quarters lacked sanitation facilities, and most significant, the government supplied little medical care. Military officials responded to many complaints about these circumstances with protestations that war conditions prevented their doing any more, but it is unlikely that white civilians would have been treated similarly, or if they were, that there would not have been repercussions. In the summer of 1943 and 1944, Aleut hunters from the Pribilofs were taken back to their islands to conduct the annual fur seal harvest for the government and then returned to the evacuation camps. A number of Aleuts found work in towns near the canneries, but for most there was little to ameliorate their prison-like circumstances until after the war. It is estimated that one in ten of the evacuees died during the internment, mostly from disease. When the Aleuts returned to the islands, they were not permitted to settle west of Unalaska. Furthermore, they found that many personal belongings had been stolen and their property vandalized or appropriated by the army.

Most dispiriting was the theft of religious artifacts from the Russian Orthodox churches.[5]

In 1978, President Jimmy Carter signed legislation establishing a commission to study the evacuations of the Aleuts and of Japanese citizens and Americans of Japanese descent. The commission heard testimony in several sites in Alaska and made a recommendation for compensation to be paid to survivors. In addition to noting the racial motivation, the deplorable conditions of their housing, and the destruction of personal and community property in their homes and villages during their absence, the islanders argued before the commission that the U.S. government had never provided adequate reparations for their treatment. The Congress finally made the awards to the Aleuts in 1992.[6]

THE BATTLE OF ATTU AND THE WAR IN ALASKA

In May 1943 a combined Canadian-American army and navy force began the reconquest of Attu and Kiska. The Japanese had attempted a major naval resupply of their troops in March, but the convoy had been interdicted in the Bering Sea north of the Commander Islands. The subsequent battle of Massacre Bay on Attu was one of the costliest of the war. Of 15,000 attacking Allied troops, 549 were killed and another 1,148 wounded. More than 2,000 suffered frostbite and exposure. Of nearly 2,400 Japanese troops, only 29 survived. A major force then assembled for the attack on Kiska. The Japanese, however, were able to evacuate more than 5,000 troops by ship under cover of fog and by drawing American reconnaissance away from the island with misdirecting radar signals. Americans therefore landed in force on an abandoned island. Nearly 100 Americans were killed by friendly fire and booby traps and when a U.S. destroyer struck a Japanese mine.

With the success of the Aleutian campaign, the war was over in Alaska. From then until August 1945, the Americans flew reconnaissance missions over the Bering Sea and the North Pacific and bombing raids on Paramushiro without air or naval resistance in the Pacific. Because of the unpredictable and dangerous weather on the islands, personnel mostly sat for the duration of the war. During this time Dashiel Hammett, author of the *Maltese Falcon* and other classic detective novels, edited the military newspaper *Stars and Stripes,* and a young Gore Vidal wrote his first novel, *Williwaw.*

In the meantime conditions were trying for the civilian population in Alaska. Military censors routinely opened mail and cut articles from magazines under the guise of suppressing espionage. Travel in and out of the territory was irregular and closely monitored. Frequent blackouts reduced mobility, and military officials did not supply information about the war's progress. Despite the best efforts of military and territorial planners, Alaska's towns could not provide the services needed by the large new civilian population. Everything was inadequate, including housing, public utilities, schools, and medical services. Only entertainment seemed to keep pace. American comedian Joe E. Brown traveled to Anchorage for a USO appearance in 1943 and pronounced the town's Fourth Avenue "the longest bar in the world."[7]

Merchants thrived on the expanded market, although certain materials, such as cement, were declared strategic and therefore were unavailable. Price rises kept pace with, and sometime rose faster than, federal wages. The commander of the Alaska Defense Command, General Simon Bolivar Buckner, cautioned small businessmen in Anchorage and Fairbanks against raising prices to a point that would force the military to seek government controls. "Do not kill the golden goose," he told them. Buckner also worried about fraternization between white soldiers and Native women. He demanded strict segregation of private clubs and theaters, and he encouraged bars to post "No Native Trade Solicited" signs.

Governor Gruening, a former editor of the *Nation* and a staunch advocate of civil rights, objected to the army's segregation policy. He pressed the territorial legislature to pass an antidiscrimination act in 1943, but it was defeated. Gruening then urged the Alaska Native Brotherhood, which had been out of politics since 1930, to run candidates for the legislature. In the 1944 election William Beltz of Nome, Andrew Hope of Sitka, and Frank Peratrovich of Klawock were elected, and in 1945 the legislature passed the bill, nine years before the revolutionary *Brown v. Board of Education* decision by the U.S. Supreme Court, finding segregation of public facilities to be unconstitutional. Historian Terrence Cole has written that although the act represented a noble sentiment, it did not mean that racism ended in Alaska. It was a harbinger of a new age, nonetheless.[8]

One of the largest projects of the war was construction of the Alaska Highway. Ostensibly the road was built to supply Alaska during the war. In fact, the military never relied on the road for supply, which was a burden a pioneer path through the wilderness would not have been able to assume.[9] There had been numerous discussions with the Canadian government

Ernest Gruening was Alaska territorial governor (1939–53) and after statehood, U.S. senator (1959–69). Alaska State Library P20.009.

about an Alaska highway for many years before the war. The Canadians steadfastly resisted the project on the grounds of national security despite entreaties from the premiers of British Columbia who hoped the road would open the northern section of the province to economic development.

With the outbreak of the war, however, the Canadian resistance collapsed. But the American military refused to commit any critical resources to construction of the road because they did not consider it necessary. The U.S. Navy maintained a supply route along the coast throughout the war. However, planners wanted to take advantage of Canadian willingness to permit construction of a road, which would eventually have to be built. So the U.S. Army used mostly its African-American engineer regiments to build the road. The American military still was segregated in World War II, and the army did not consider the black troops critical to the war effort. Working under white officers, the African-American and white engineers built a "pioneer road" through twenty-five hundred miles of wilderness in nine months, an extraordinary feat. Later, civilian contractors took four years to upgrade the road to a reliable state.[10]

The overriding significance of World War II to Alaska's history was its economic impact. World War II completely, profoundly, and permanently changed Alaska. About 300,000 military personnel served in Alaska during the war, about 150,000 at the period of greatest strength. The resident population then was about 81,000. The United States spent about $3 billion in the territory over the entire course of the war. Airfields, communications installations, and roads were built in various parts of the territory to facilitate military movement. These, as well as other improvements and large amounts of equipment, were left after the war to form the basis of considerable post-war economic growth. The civilian population grew dramatically, from about 60,000 in 1940 to more than 100,000 at the end of the war. By 1950 the territorial population was more than 150,000. Wages and rents were high, and there were contracts and profits for people in every line of business. Alaska would never return to the quiet and isolated days of the prewar period.[11]

THE COLD WAR IN ALASKA

There was a momentary lull in Alaska's economic activity immediately following the war, however, and residents wondered if the territory would return to its prewar population and snail's pace of growth. Territorial leaders welcomed any plans for economic development. One idea was to build pulp mills in Alaska to take advantage of the splendid stands of hemlock, spruce, and cedar in the southeast, in the Alexander Archipelago. The Forest Service had talked about this idea with industry spokespersons before the Depression, but after the war conditions seemed especially favorable: there was a national shortage of newsprint, and the industry seemed ready to invest in Alaska. There was a major hurdle, though: Native land claims. The matter of Indian title would need to be solved before pulp and paper industry investors could risk development in Alaska. When attorneys for the Indians filed the Tlingit-Haida land claims suit in 1947, they assumed that the Forest Service would await the outcome before proceeding with plans for a pulp industry in Alaska.

B. Frank Heintzleman, the Forest Service director in Alaska, was not disposed to wait, however. Heintzleman was a dedicated "scientific" forester who believed a national forest should be consistently harvested as a source of jobs and a source of lumber for the construction industry; consistent with the doctrine of "sustained yield," keeping the harvest within appropriate limits and replanting on a regular schedule would make the forest an economic engine in perpetuity. A Forest Service study projected that five pulp mills could be built in the Tongass Forest, providing direct and indirect support for sixty thousand people. Governor Gruening and territorial delegate E. L. "Bob" Bartlett, who had replaced Anthony Dimond in 1944, were convinced that before Alaska could ask the Congress for statehood, it must have sufficient economic development to generate a tax base adequate to support state government. Gruening, in particular, was willing to put economic development ahead of Native rights to advance statehood.[12] In fact, for Gruening statehood and economic development were inextricably linked: in his thinking, economic development was necessary

B. Frank Heintzleman, U.S. Forest Service regional forester for Alaska (1937–53) and Alaska territorial governor (1953–57), was a "wise use" scientific forester committed to developing a stable economy through systematic harvest of the Tongass National Forest. Alaska State Library P20.010.

to gain statehood, but only the independence of statehood would make economic development possible. Gruening never unraveled this illogical circuitry, however.

In 1947 friends of the Forest Service and potential investors in the Alaska pulp industry introduced a bill in Congress to authorize the agency to sell timber to logging companies on fifty-year contracts to guarantee a reliable supply of pulp timber from the forest. In addition, the bill authorized up to five pulp mills in the forest. The issue of Native claims was unclear, so the money from the timber sales was to be put into escrow pending the outcome of the Native land claims suit; should the Indians win, the money would then be given to them. The bill also guaranteed Indian "possessory rights" to lands their villages were actually situated on; otherwise, the Forest Service conceded no Indian land rights in the forest, which took up sixteen million of the eighteen million acres of land in Southeast Alaska.

Alaska Indians protested the bill, traveling to Washington, D.C., to testify against it and calling it a new "Teapot Dome," a reference to the corrupt oil development scheme on one of the government's strategic petroleum reserves during the Harding administration. The Indians argued that the escrow account was no compensation for what timber harvesting would do to the land's character and to subsistence. Moreover, the Indians wanted the right to sell the timber themselves. But in a postwar, post–New Deal atmosphere, "termination" fever had gripped the Congress; there was a new determination to end federal services and special status for Native Americans. The Tongass Timber Act passed the Congress handily, clearing the way for the development of the forest. Gruening wrote to Delegate Bartlett that Alaska had "dodged a bullet," in that Native claims had been sidestepped and the path for economic development cleared. That done, Gruening urged that now was the time for Alaska leaders to turn their attention to the land claims matter. In 1956 a mill opened in Ketchikan, and in 1962 a second mill, Japanese owned, in Sitka. Since 1960 the annual harvest in the Tongass forest has been about three hundred million board feet annually. The Tongass would continue to be a major controversial force in Alaska through the advent of environmentalism and the Alaska Lands Act.

The level of federal spending in Alaska during World War II had been massive and wholly unprecedented. No one could have imagined that it would continue following the war. But it did. With the onset of the Cold War after 1947, Alaska became strategically critical in a geopolitical context for the one time in its history. The principal weapons system for the United States and the Soviet Union from 1947 to about 1960 was nuclear weaponry carried by strategic air forces. Alaskan Air Force facilities were the last refueling bases for American forces that would enter Soviet air space over eastern Siberia. Construction of airfields, early warning radar, and a communications network brought significant military spending in the territory. In the 1950s Alaska was a free world military bastion. At the same time new transportation facilities and heightened national awareness led to an upgrade of other federal agency operations in Alaska, all contributing to establishing federal spending as the base of the Alaskan economy.

Gruening welcomed other sources of federal spending in Alaska. Without an adequate economic foundation, he knew, Congress would not approve Alaska statehood. The Bureau of Reclamation and the Army Corps of Engineers expressed interest in developing power projects in the territory. The largest of these seriously contemplated was Rampart Dam, a Corps proposal to dam the Yukon River in Rampart Canyon downriver from the Yukon Flats area. The project would have cost $1.3 billion and generated five million kilowatts; it was to provide cheap power for mining and logging development in interior Alaska and Canada. The environmental costs of the project would have been substantial, however. The Yukon Flats would have been submerged in the resulting reservoir that would become the world's largest artificial lake, at nearly five thousand square miles, the size of the state of Connecticut.[13]

The Yukon Flats are one of North America's largest breeding grounds for migratory waterfowl. After the war environmental groups such as the Wilderness Society and the Sierra Club turned increasing attention to Alaska. They mounted a substantial protest to the Rampart project. Because of the high cost and the magnitude of the environmental impact, the environmentalists' case was not as difficult as some of the era's other challenges. In addition, more than one thousand Natives living in the area would have had to be relocated. Coming as it did just at the beginning of the postwar civil rights movement, Native protest alone might have been enough to kill the proposal. But political and other leaders in the territory embraced the dam project. The state Chamber of Commerce advocated for it, and the University of Alaska president campaigned for it. The major territorial newspaper, the *Anchorage Daily Times*, argued persistently for the infusion of federal money associated with the project. But supporters had no success generating political support outside Alaska, due both to sensitivity to Native concerns and to the rising environmental movement, leaders of which condemned the project. When the Army Corps of Engineers projected there would be a limited market for the power produced, the government let the project die.

Another project that Gruening thought had great promise became a much bigger struggle. In 1957 the celebrated nuclear physicist Edward Teller, the "father" of the hydrogen bomb, proposed that the Atomic Energy Commission (AEC) use low-yield nuclear devices for major civil construction projects, such as redirecting rivers and clearing new harbors, to show the peaceful uses of nuclear power.[14] Dubbed Project Plowshare, a central criteria for selection was locating sites that would pose no damage to wildlife or humans, sites that were in "empty" land. For the first such demonstration the AEC chose Cape Thompson on the Chukchi Sea, just north of the Arctic Circle on Alaska's western coast. Here scientists planned to detonate two one-megaton and two two-hundred-kiloton devices just belowground to excavate a deepwater harbor.[15] The experiment was named Project Chariot.

As with the proposed Rampart Dam, most prominent Alaskans enthusiastically supported Project Chariot. They accepted the AEC's assurances that there would be no substantial environmental impact, and they were happy for the millions of dollars the project would bring to the state's economy. Few discussed the long-term benefits of the proposal, however, for there did not seem to be any; the ocean at Cape Thompson is only ice-free two months of the year, and there were no mineral prospects or other resources for economic development in the area. Environmentalists, however, questioned the idea that the region was "empty" land. Not only would fallout from the explosions be lifted to thirty thousand feet and then dissipate with the prevailing winds, but Inuits living at Point Hope, twenty-five miles from the site, would lose the use of adjacent land.

To allay these anxieties, the AEC commissioned environmental studies of the area, giving some of the research contracts to the University of Alaska. After careful study these scientists reported that the environmental impacts were likely to be dramatic, negative, and long-lasting. Most particularly, they established links between vegetation, animals, and people in the region: lichens were eaten by migrating caribou, of which the Inuit villagers consumed thousands of pounds annually as a major component of their subsistence diet. Contamination of the area's vegetation, then, would contaminate both people and animals. This was one of the first demonstrated examples of "biocentrism" in the modern era; environmental study showed a detrimental impact by trusted technology on a whole ecosystem. The evidence seemed conclusive. The study came to the notice of activists in the continental states, particularly the Committee on Nuclear Information headed by Professor Barry Commoner, a cellular biologist who later became one of the founders of the modern American environmental movement.

But both AEC personnel and Alaska officials, including the university president, downplayed these findings, supporting the AEC's desire to go ahead with the project. Environmentalists in Alaska organized the Alaska Conservation Society to help protest the project and to try to build public awareness and opposition. They contacted national environmental groups and nationally recognized scientists, who helped to generate opposition. Eventually, the AEC gave up the project. The Alaska Conservation Society would go on to become a major factor in environmental assessment and policy regarding Alaska.

One AEC project generated considerable money for Alaska contractors, however. In 1965, 1969, and 1971 the agency detonated underground nuclear test devices on Amchitka Island in the Aleutians; the projects were named Long Shot, Millrow, and Cannikin. Cannikin was a five-megaton device, the largest underground blast ever undertaken. Amchitka Island was a wildlife refuge, and environmental protest of the program raised larger questions regarding seismic impact and long-range leakage. The test shots also helped to fuel the antinuclear movement in the United States.

ORGANIZING FOR STATEHOOD

Altogether, federal spending became the most substantial element in the Alaskan economy after World War II, replacing salmon as the most important sector. Combined military and federal spending remained the base of the economy until the development of North Slope oil just before 1970. Throughout that period economists worried that Alaska needed to develop economic diversity to become independent of the political vicissitudes of federal budgeting. But suggestions on how this would be done were few. With increased spending, a growing population, and broader national awareness of Alaska and its potential after the war, the stage seemed right for a drive for statehood, and political leaders in the territory dedicated themselves to this end. From 1946 until 1960 statehood occupied most of the political energy in the territory.

A territory-wide referendum in 1946, initiated by the territorial legislature, found that 9,630 voters favored statehood while 6,822 opposed it, 60 percent to 40 percent. The margin was wide enough for statehood advocates to begin to organize a concerted campaign but close enough to suggest a need for considerable work within the territory. The referendum was a necessary beginning of the statehood campaign, for without a clear expression by the electorate in favor, opponents could argue that the sentiment of territorial citizens was either unknown or negative. There were plenty of opponents, and their arguments were both practical and political; the most common were the sparse population and the question of an adequate tax base to support the costs of a state government. On the other hand, statehood advocates used the same arguments that had motivated the Alaska territorial political consensus throughout the previous forty years: economic development and freedom from federal control by increased self-government. This was purely an article of faith on the part of the advocates, for there was no evidence that self-government could be linked to economic development. No one, for example, advocated eliminating taxation on industry. Statehood opponents, in fact, charged that statehood would necessarily mean higher taxes, which would discourage industry and development. But the conviction that statehood would bring an economic bonanza to Alaska was deep and would remain a persistent theme of statehood advocacy.

There were a number of significant opponents against statehood. The salmon industry, which organized the strongest protest, feared additional regulation and taxation but publicly used the argument that there was not adequate economic development in the territory to pay for the administration of state government, an argument that greatly concerned many members of Congress. A significant number of Alaskans opposed the increased population and economic development that the statehood advocates touted as a benefit of statehood; the opponents thought development would mean destruction of Alaska wilderness and excessive harvest of such renewable resources as fish and timber.

The military opposed statehood because senior officers found unattractive the prospect of having to deal with an additional level of bureaucracy while organizing strategic defense. During the Korean War (1950–53) the army and air force used Alaska as a logistics staging area, and after the Soviet Union detonated its first nuclear weapon in 1949, Alaska's location made the territory strategically critical. Finally, President Dwight Eisenhower was not enthusiastic about Alaska statehood, perhaps on military grounds. Although the Republican Party platform included statehood planks in 1952 and 1956, the president refused to speak out on the issue. Statehood advocates needed to overcome these arguments to convince Congress that statehood's time had come.

The territorial legislature created an Alaska Statehood Committee in 1949. State leaders also established a private group known as Operation Statehood. The two orchestrated the campaign for statehood with considerable political sophistication. They wrote articles for national magazines, invited editors to tour the territory, and took every opportunity to spread word of the Alaskan desire for equal statehood status. Gruening supported statehood enthusiastically, both because he believed that Alaska's citizens were ready for statehood and because he hoped to return to Washington, D.C., as a U.S. senator. But Gruening's style was often arrogant and abrasive. Territorial delegate Bartlett provided critical help for the cause in Congress. Bartlett was, as historian Claus-M. Naske has written, "quiet and persuasive." He worked "effectively and tenaciously," making friends easily and pressing the case for statehood with confidence and acumen.[16]

By 1956 statehood forces felt strong enough to hold a constitutional convention. A successful convention and progressive state constitution would demonstrate Alaskans' self-governing capabilities. While voters elected fifty-five delegates, the legislature hired consultants from around the country to advise the convention and draft position papers on the principal powers of state government. The delegates met for seventy-five days in Fairbanks over the winter of 1955 and 1956 and produced an uncomplicated document described by the National Municipal League as "one of the best, if not the best, state constitutions ever written."[17] Some of its noteworthy

E. L. "Bob" Bartlett, Alaska delegate
to Congress (1944–58) and U.S.
senator from Alaska (1958–68). Ward
Wells, Ward Wells Collection,
Anchorage Museum, B1983.091.
S3070.S2.17.

provisions were the creation of a unified court system, multilevel local government options for rural, underpopulated areas, and an appointed attorney general.

At the suggestion of a New Orleans newspaper editor, the territorial legislature then adopted an unusual lobbying strategy. Voters needed to
approve the state constitution, and at the same election they were asked
to elect the two U.S. senators and one congressional representative to
which Alaska would be entitled when statehood was granted. Gruening
had been replaced as governor by Frank Heintzleman when Eisenhower
was elected, so he ran for one of the seats, as did William Egan and Ralph
Rivers, both territorial senators. These men had no official standing as
members of Congress; their election was a public relations gambit, called
the "Tennessee Plan" because Tennessee was the first territory to use the
device when applying for statehood. The three traveled to Washington,
D.C., in a well-publicized caravan, and then as salaried territorial officials they worked with Bartlett in making the case for statehood. The

team did not work well together, however, and their effort was mostly ineffectual.

Far more effective was the work of Ted Stevens, who had been U.S. attorney in Alaska. Soon after the constitutional convention concluded, Stevens won appointment as legislative counsel in the Interior Department in Washington, D.C. There he worked persistently on Alaska statehood, sometimes in violation of statutes prohibiting executive branch lobbying of Congress. Secretary of the Interior Fred Seaton, who favored statehood, was a friend of C. W. Snedden, publisher of the *Fairbanks News-Miner.* Stevens hired Margaret Atwood, daughter of the publisher of the *Anchorage Daily Times* and chair of the private Alaska Statehood Committee. Among other things, Stevens worked with the chairman of the Joint Chiefs of Staff to devise a military contingency for Alaska that helped assuage President Eisenhower's Cold War anxieties. They wrote for the statehood act a provision authorizing the president to withdraw for military purposes all of Alaska north of a line roughly along the Porcupine, Yukon, and Kuskokwim Rivers. Years after statehood, Stevens would become U.S. senator from Alaska, serving from December 1968 to January 2009.

The private statehood committee devised several brilliant public relations ploys. The U.S. Chamber of Commerce annually selected several American communities for its "All America City" awards, calling attention to the winners' positive qualities. To win selection, a city needed to have created conditions that made it a desirable place to live and carry on

Ted Stevens, U.S. senator from Alaska (1968–2008). Steve McCutcheon, McCutcheon Collection, Anchorage Museum, B1990.0.14.5.Pol.4.473.

business, including good schools with a low teacher-student ratio, a reasonable tax base, a low crime rate, an appropriate number of churches, playgrounds and parks, other public amenities, and the like. In other words the city must be as desirable and "normal" as other attractive towns in the United States. Members of the statehood committee in Anchorage wrote a brief town history, then with a population of about seventy thousand, and compiled a statistical profile demonstrating the community's suitability for the award; they won it in 1956.[18] City fathers put a large "All America City" banner across Fourth Avenue in downtown Anchorage, which showed prominently in all the photographs accompanying the many magazine articles about Alaska statehood over the next two years.

In the final analysis statehood advocates had only one strong argument they could make in their campaigning and lobbying: all citizens of the United States were entitled to the same powers of self-government. This was essentially a moral argument. Alaskans should have self-government because other Americans in similar circumstances have state government. Bartlett and the "Tennessee" congressmen spent much of their time on the defensive, countering the opponents' arguments. There were two especially formidable obstacles. The first was opposition from Southern senators who worried about civil rights. Ending segregation had been an issue since the end of the war, and it became particularly contentious after the *Brown v. Board of Education* decision. There was a close balance between pro—and anti–civil rights senators, and two new solons might upset that balance. There was nothing the Alaskans could do but try to persuade enough senators that the moral right of statehood must prevail. In this they were aided greatly by national polls that found that more than 80 percent of Americans favored bringing in Alaska as a state.

The second issue was how to pay for statehood, and advocates worried that on this issue alone they might lose the battle. Oil had been discovered at the mouth of Swanson River on the Kenai Peninsula in 1956 on what would be state land if statehood were granted. This was a promising development, but the find was not big enough to generate the tax revenue needed. In draft statehood bills Bartlett had provided a grant of more than 150,000 acres (of the 375 million total) of Alaska land for the state, hoping the land would have potential for economic development. Many members of Congress balked at so extensive an area; it was the same size as the state of Texas. More important, growing environmental consciousness militated against taking that much land out of the public domain. The Alaskans countered that without substantial state lands on which they could grant mineral leases for revenue, they would be denied an important funding source.

In negotiation Bartlett hit on an idea that had logic and promise to recommend it. Historically, in compensation for retaining significant amounts of land in the western states, the federal government rebated to those states a portion of the federal mineral lease revenue generated on those lands. The Alaskans argued that their state should get appreciably more federal lease rebate if the federal government was going to retain a larger amount of land there. The outcome of Bartlett's negotiations was very favorable to Alaska and helped to resolve the funding question. The federal government would rebate 90 percent of its Alaska mineral lease revenue to the state and use the remaining 10 percent to pay for the cost of administering those lands. Although the percentage of federal land retained in Alaska by the statehood act, 72 percent, was very high, the so-called 90-10 split was an act of remarkable generosity to Alaska, another example of federal support for the region's economic viability.

Members of Congress also worried that to generate revenue a new state government in Alaska might transfer land title to mining and other companies willing to invest in the development of Alaska's natural resources. So advocates wrote into the statehood bill a provision prohibiting the state from alienating title to any mineralized lands (oil is classified as a mineral); such lands must remain the property of the state, that is, the people of Alaska. The state can lease these lands but cannot surrender title to them. Should it do so, such lands immediately revert to federal ownership. Later, Governor Walter Hickel would call Alaska an "owner state," basing the phrase on the state's ownership of these resource lands.

Delegate Bob Bartlett was the primary author of another critical element of the statehood act, which is called a disclaimer. In Section 4 of the act, the state disclaims any right or title to land that may be subject to Native title. At one point in the debates on the statehood bill, Bartlett responded to mining and other interests who objected to the disclaimer on grounds that it might inhibit their opportunity to develop mining prospects, since Congress had not yet determined which lands might be subject to Native title. Upon learning of the disclaimer's removal, the Alaska Native Brotherhood informed Bartlett that the ANB would not support any Alaska statehood bill that did not include the disclaimer. Understanding that no statehood bill without support from Alaska Natives could pass Congress, Bartlett put the disclaimer back into the bill. As explained later, the disclaimer would come into conflict with another section of the act that authorized the new state to select for state title 104 million acres of land within the state, about 28 percent of Alaska's land.

With the funding compromise in place, promised Native support, the military satisfied it would have free rein in the event of Cold War operations in the new state, and a Gallup poll showing 82 percent of Americans favoring the measure, powerful House Speaker Sam Rayburn, long opposed to the idea, dropped his opposition to Alaska statehood, as did Lyndon Johnson, majority leader in the U.S. Senate. Their support was needed to pass the bill. In June 1957 the House Interior and the Insular Affairs Committee reported the bill out to the full body with a "do pass" recommendation. The House deferred action until the following summer, but in 1958 both the House and Senate approved the statehood act, and Eisenhower signed it. The statehooders had won. The *Anchorage Daily Times* ran its largest headline ever, proclaiming simply, "We're In!" The euphoria was endemic. In November of that year Alaskan voters elected Bartlett and Gruening to the U.S. Senate and former territorial senator Ralph Rivers to the House of Representatives—all Democrats.

Modern Alaska

The Last Wilderness

ALASKA STATEHOOD, WHICH became official on 3 January 1959, was the first of several basic elements that established the political and economic context for modern Alaska. Statehood combined with these other elements to change Alaska profoundly and permanently. First, soon after statehood and the 1959 Tlingit-Haida settlement, Athabaskan Indians, Inuits, and Aleuts began to assert title to their ancestral lands. Second, Americans changed their view of the country's natural environment, leading to a fundamental shift in environmental policy, which ultimately had a dramatic impact on Alaska. Third, the discovery and development of America's largest oil deposit, at Prudhoe Bay, acted as a catalyst to bring these elements together in a remarkably short period of time. Alaska's new political leaders did not understand these elements of change in the beginning, however. Nor could they have predicted the maelstrom of economic and political change that would transform the state.

The state's leaders learned that statehood was no panacea for lack of control over the major forces that circumscribed economic development. There still would be no manufacturing and no agriculture in the state. The only foundation for the economy still lay in federal spending and in the exploitation of natural resources. There was potential in processing some of those resources, adding value to them before they left the state. But little of that potential could be developed without cooperation from absentee investors, who would look to the state to provide

Young Inuit women at King Island, near Nome, traditionally home to about two hundred Inuits who lived in houses built on stilts on the island's rocky cliffs. The island was abandoned in the mid-twentieth century after closure of the Bureau of Indian Affairs school. Alaska State Library, Kenneth Chisholm Photo Collection P105.027.

incentives, which the state was not yet in a position to do. Fish, timber, and oil comprised the viable industries. The salmon fishery attracted thousands of fishers who sold their catch to the canneries, but the canneries did not provide a great many on-shore jobs. Logging provided employment in the Tongass National Forest, as did the two pulp mills. With statehood the state gained ownership of the productive oil lands in Cook Inlet and promising lands on the Arctic Coast, and oil lease sales and taxation of production became an important new source of revenue for the state. But all of these enterprises were owned by absentee investors whose primary focus was the greatest return for the least outlay, and who would be likely to liquidate their operations if the costs of production exceeded their expectations. Federal spending in Alaska began to decrease after 1960 as satellite and missile technology replaced the strategic air forces as America's principal defense. Congress adopted a major "omnibus bill"

Executives of the Coastal Management Corporation. These village leaders from Yupik communities in the Yukon-Kuskokwim delta region plan the investments of six villages. Anchorage Museum Rasmuson Center, Coastal Management Corp. B200 013A s7 005.

to help pay for the transition to statehood (the creation of a new state bureaucracy), but this was only a temporary measure.

Alaska shared with other western states dependence for its economy on absentee investors and federal government spending. But statehood advocates made freedom from absentee exploitation of the territory's resources a central feature of their campaign. With territorial politicians, statehooders made the salmon industry's use of fish traps a potent symbol of corporate appropriation of those resources, leaving little or nothing of the profit from their exploitation in Alaska or for Alaskans. Demonization of the traps was so successful that the electorate voted for their abolition by a 4 to 1 margin. The idea, then, that the state of Alaska was not much more in control of its long-term destiny than the territory of Alaska had been, despite the new powers of self-government, was an uncomfortable prospect for many. State politicians continued to preach the theme of Alaskan independence even as national policy circumscribed the state's freedom of action in the ensuing decades.

Establishing a new state administration was at once an exhilarating opportunity and a formidable challenge. The machinery of state government,

William Egan (*left*), Alaska's first state governor, serving 1958–66 and 1970–74. Nick Begich (*right*), Alaska's lone congressman in the U.S. House in 1971–72. University of Alaska Fairbanks, Elmer E. Rasmuson Library 1985.0120.0131.

all the executive departments and state agencies, had to be created in a short period of time. John Rader, Speaker of the state House, and (later Judge) Thomas Stewart in the state Senate took the lead in organizing and writing the principal legislation. When the session concluded, Rader became the state's first attorney general. Voters elected William Egan, who had distinguished himself as chair of the constitutional convention, as the state's first governor. A self-taught student of government, Egan was a master of compromise and quiet negotiation.

But on inauguration day in 1959, Egan was dangerously ill with undiagnosed gall bladder disease. He went from the celebration to the hospital in Juneau and then to Seattle in critical condition. The acting governor, Secretary of State Hugh Wade,[1] was reluctant to take any important action because he thought Egan should have the prerogative of establishing executive department precedents. Soon the federal Ninth Circuit Court in San Francisco exacerbated the confusion by refusing to serve as an appellate court from the courts in Alaska, as it had when Alaska was a territory. The statehood act provided that the state had three years to design and implement a state court system, but the Ninth Circuit's decision meant the process had to be completed immediately. Buell Nesbett, the first Alaska Supreme Court justice, provided the leadership required to accomplish this task, which was done in six months; Alaska courts began functioning in February 1960.

No sooner was the new administration in place than state leaders confronted a massive and unexpected challenge that demonstrated the magnitude of the larger context in which Alaska development was taking place. Section 6 of the Alaska Statehood Act granted 103 million acres of land in Alaska to the new state. As noted, cognizant that Alaska did not have an adequate tax base for statehood, Congress wrote into the statehood act a prohibition of the state alienating its mineralized lands; it could only lease them for development. At the same time, Congress committed to developing mineral deposits on federal land in the state, writing into the act the transfer of 90 percent of federal mineral lease revenue to the state. With Section 6, framers of the statehood act expected that the state would select mineral-bearing lands and other parcels with economic potential. The 103 million acres represented 28 percent of Alaska's land total, but an area larger than all of California.[2] As soon as the act became official, the state set about selecting the lands it wished to be included in the grant. One of the first areas provisionally identified was along the Arctic Coast near Prudhoe Bay. There had been oil seepages on the North Slope since time immemorial, and in the 1950s the U.S. Navy had conducted an extensive, if unproductive, exploration of a part of the national petroleum reserve west of Prudhoe Bay. Oil companies had long thought the area worth the cost and effort of careful examination.[3] Congress set aside the Arctic National Wildlife Refuge east of Prudhoe Bay in 1960, the culmination of naturalist Robert Marshall's idea of the 1930s to make all of Alaska north of the Yukon River a closed wilderness. The state selected the area between the reserve to the west and the refuge to the east, about one hundred miles along the Arctic Coast. The state continued to make other selections over the next few years, and the federal government began to convey provisional title for the lands to the state. By 1965 the government had conveyed 12 million acres of the 103-million-acre entitlement.

The state selection process had implications that statehood advocates and the framers of the statehood act had not fully appreciated, however, for it clashed directly with another section of the act: Native lands.

Section 4 of the act was the disclaimer by the state of "right or title" to any lands that might be subject to Native title. This clause had been inserted into all of the post–Civil War enabling (statehood) acts, a function of the federal obligation to protect basic Native rights, poorly honored in the nineteenth century but constitutionally sound. Since Congress had executed no treaties with Alaska Natives to identify which lands might be subject to Native title, and Congress had not undertaken an integrated and comprehensive land disposal program in the state, no one knew in 1958 which lands might be subject to Native title. But in 1941, the U.S. Supreme Court, in *United States v. Santa Fe Pacific Railroad* (often called the Hualapai decision because it involved the Hualapai Tribe of Arizona), had confirmed the existence and legitimacy of aboriginal title. About 54 million acres of Alaska land had been withdrawn before 1958 in conservation and military reserves (Mount McKinley National Park, for example, and Eielson Air Force Base near Fairbanks), and now the statehood act provided for Alaska's 103 million. But none of these withdrawals were part of a coordinated scheme.

There are persuasive reasons why the framers of the statehood act missed the implications of the disclaimer. In the debate over the 1947 Tongass Timber Act, the U.S. Forest Service acknowledged the validity of what it called "Indian possessory rights." This was land on which the Indian villages were actually situated and immediately adjacent lands that Natives used for subsistence resources. This was an extension of the Euro-American concept of fee simple title to individuals. The Indians certainly had a right to the land their houses were on, many whites agreed, and to some additional lands as protection for those villages and for hunting and other uses. But traditionally many Indian groups in North America defined land use in terms of its harvestable resources and collective use, not in terms of personal control over small parcels. Depending on the group and the resources in question, this might be tens of thousands of acres, land traveled for hunting migrating caribou, or deer or moose, or it might be traditionally used fishing sites many miles from winter villages.

U.S. Interior Department solicitor Nathan Margold had upheld the validity of this concept of land use in his 1934 decision recognizing original Indian powers, as had the Supreme Court more directly in the 1941 *Santa Fe* (Hualapai) decision. The long policy of acculturation of Natives to Euro-American values implied that the Indian idea of land use no longer had currency, but the court's action contradicted that. Most of the framers likely did not know of the Hualapai decision and thought instead, as the Forest Service did, that possessory rights were all that was at issue.[4] Some Alaskans did know the law on Native land rights and on Native rights in general. One of them was Ted Stevens, the former U.S. attorney in Fairbanks and the solicitor in the Interior Department in Washington, D.C., the later U.S. senator from Alaska. As an attorney in Alaska after statehood, Stevens worked without pay to help Alaska Natives defend their rights and seek title to their lands.[5]

As the state began making its selections in 1959 and 1960, Natives grew increasingly alarmed, for many of the selections involved land that Natives had used for various purposes since time immemorial and was therefore subject to aboriginal title, which had not been extinguished by Congress. Natives began to protest the state's selections on the grounds that they violated the disclaimer in the statehood act. At this point national policy intruded into the process, for 1960 was the beginning of the modern civil rights movement in the United States. Attorneys in the Bureau of Indian Affairs (BIA) encouraged Native Alaskans to assemble and file land claims to areas they considered ancestral. Already becoming sensitized to the government's casual dismissal of their rights by Project Chariot and the nuclear testing regime at Amchitka Island, Natives readily responded. The Interior Department had to hire additional attorneys to process the claims, for there were so many they soon blanketed Alaska. Eventually, because a number of claims overlapped, the number of acres under Native protest exceeded the total acreage in the state.[6] State leaders began to express concern, for although most did not believe the courts would recognize more than Native possessory rights, that process could take many years. In the meantime economic development on any contested land would be out of the question, since no one would invest in property to which they might later be denied title. In Alaska the regional U.S. Bureau of Land Management (BLM) office routinely denied Native protests and Native land claims and prepared to convey title to the contested lands to the new state. But Stevens and others helped Natives file appeals to the regional BLM actions back to BLM offices in Washington, D.C. There, Newton Edwards, an assistant to an undersecretary of the interior, in whose office the appeals landed, decided not to act on them, arguing there was no statutory direction under which he might proceed. This bureaucratic roadblock, not understood by many, had the effect of delaying the state's selection of its land entitlement.[7]

Alarming as this prospect was, Alaskans' attention was distracted in 1964 by one of the greatest natural disasters ever recorded in North America. On 27 March 1964, soon after 5:00 p.m., a 9.2 earthquake struck south-central Alaska, near the town of Valdez, the largest-magnitude earthquake ever recorded on the North American continent. The impact was cataclysmic, and the ground continued to shake and roll for more than four minutes. In Anchorage clay underlying the outwash plain on which the inlet edge of the city was built liquefied. The land closest to the inlet slumped toward the ocean, not unlike a dirt bank after a heavy rain, but on a vastly larger scale. The line of the slump ran down the middle of Anchorage's Fourth Avenue, the main commercial thoroughfare; buildings on one side of the street suddenly dropped more than four feet, the liquefied clay no longer able to support them. Most buildings in downtown Anchorage suffered structural damage. In the Turnagain-by-the-Sea subdivision on the bluff of Cook Inlet southwest of the city, the ground became chaos as

In March 1964, a 9.2 earthquake, the largest ever recorded in North America, struck Prince William Sound. The fault ran through Fourth Avenue in Anchorage, where one side of the street subsided over four feet. Anchorage Museum Rasmuson Center, U.S. Army, Betty Bannon Collection B1970.015.74.

fissures opened and closed, block-sized pieces of land sank while others rose or tilted at wild angles. Houses, automobiles, yards, trees, everything was tossed and shaken in a jumble of wreckage. In Valdez the seashore sunk several feet. Fifteen people died in Anchorage, including some children in the subdivision houses and an air traffic controller at the international airport.

In Kodiak the harbor emptied as the ocean pulled water seaward and then refilled in a giant wave, throwing fishing boats and docks inland several blocks. In Seward the waterfront buildings and railroad terminal facilities caught fire; oil storage tanks exploded. Another giant wave washed over the Native village of Chenega in Prince William Sound, obliterating it. Throughout Alaska, 115 people were killed and thousands left homeless. Tsunamis generated by the shock rushed southward, striking beaches in Oregon and California, where more than thirty people were killed.

The federal government responded quickly and comprehensively to the disaster. Regular army and National Guard units rendered assistance and patrolled to prevent looting. Army medical personnel provided care and supplies. Engineer troops set up electrical generators and surface piping for emergency water supplies. Private airlines ferried tens of thousands of tons of goods into Anchorage and the smaller towns. Although some despaired of the region surviving, city fathers vowed to rebuild. In Washington, D.C., President Lyndon Johnson established a special commission, the Federal Reconstruction and Development Planning Commission, to coordinate the effort; the commission answered directly to the president, over the cabinet secretaries, so as to avoid jurisdictional strife. By October the public infrastructure—such things as major roads, sewer systems, water, electricity, the railroad, and government buildings—was repaired or replaced. The Small Business Administration made loan money available for private reconstruction. Recovery proceeded rapidly.

ORGANIZING ALASKA NATIVE LAND CLAIMS

In the meantime the state's Native associations coalesced around the land claims issue, forming a statewide organization called the Alaska Federation of Natives (AFN) in 1965. And while Native leaders and state officers debated the issue, Senator Henry M. Jackson of Washington State, chair of the Senate Interior Affairs Committee, secured the president's approval to redirect the reconstruction committee to study the land claims dilemma. Restyled the Federal Field Committee for Development Planning in Alaska, the body undertook a two-year comprehensive study of Native conditions in Alaska, including historical land use patterns. The study was remarkably complete, providing statistical measures of housing, sanitation, utilities, employment and subsistence use, educational attainment, and rates of contagious diseases. Published in 1968 as *Alaska Natives and the Land*, their report concluded that Alaska Natives collectively had the lowest national levels of nearly all these measures and were so disadvantaged as to be denied equal opportunity with the rest of America's citizens.[8]

But even before the Field Committee completed its work, it became increasingly clear to many both in and outside Alaska that as long as Native claims were unsettled, and no one could be secure in their title hold, there would be no new economic investment in the state. To underscore this perception, in January 1966 the Inuit living along the Arctic Coast collectively filed a land claim to 60 million acres of land they traditionally used, on the basis of aboriginal title. The regional BLM accepted the claim, but then, mindful of Congress's intention that the government should lease lands in Alaska to spur economic development, announced plans to lease by November of that year 4.3 million acres of the claimed land for oil exploration. This action placed Secretary of the Interior, Stewart Udall, squarely in the middle of the conflict between Sections 4 and 6 of the statehood act, dead center between Native lands claims and Alaska's economic future. Committed to Native justice, and cognizant of the economic conundrum facing the state, Udall took a bold step: he canceled the lease sale. Then he instructed the BLM not to transfer title to any Alaska land to the state until Congress legislated a resolution of Alaska Native land claims. This moratorium became known as Udall's "land freeze."

With the land freeze, people across Alaska finally understood the magnitude of the conflict between the two sections of the statehood act. Many Alaskans regarded the land freeze as a betrayal of an implied promise, that Alaska would choose its lands from all those in Alaska before any other land disposal would be made, and that Congress would not interfere with the process. The promise was implied by the fact that the statehood act was passed before Native protests were made and also by the notion that the statehood act represented a compact, a sacred promise that could not be broken, between Congress and the state.

In fact, however, there was no promise and no violation. Congress, which indirectly reflects the will of the national public in the election of its members, has the power to pass any legislation not in violation of the U.S. Constitution. It can pass a 55 miles-per-hour speed limit at one time and repeal it at another. The states were created by Congress; thus Congress can alter the terms of their creation at any time if it chooses. The primacy of federal sovereignty was decided in the Civil War and confirmed by the Supreme Court shortly thereafter. The limits of federal and state power are constantly being tested in the courts, which are the principal mechanism in U.S. constitutional government for discovering the exact balance between federal and state sovereignty at any point in time regarding any particular issue. Moreover, unless the Supreme Court decides otherwise in a particular case, federal sovereignty is superior to state sovereignty. Not all Alaskans understood these fundamental constitutional facts.

The Field Committee finished its work in 1967. Its report identified fifteen areas traditionally used by Alaska Natives. The committee advised that Natives should be given title to those lands, perhaps forty-seven million acres; Congress should extinguish Native title to the remainder of Alaska, and the federal government should be free to dispose of the remainder of Alaska's land without restriction. In compensation for Native extinguishment, Congress should make a compensatory award to all Alaska Natives. The committee recommended that the award should be $100 million and a percentage of the federal mineral lease revenue paid to the state as provided in the statehood act. State leaders initially rejected the notion that the state should pay for Native lands in any way.

Meanwhile, AFN leaders, representing all Alaska Natives, crafted their own plan for resolving their claims to Alaska's land. They should gain title to all documented areas traditionally used and $500 million in compensation, plus 2 percent of the federal lease royalties in perpetuity. This was an ambitious plan and judged a fair one by many critics. But the most remarkable part of the AFN proposal was a truly revolutionary innovation: Native economic development corporations should be established, they suggested, and receive the compensatory award. All Natives would enroll in a development corporation as stockholders and thus share in the assets of the corporation, most particularly, the profit made on the corporation's investments, paid as an annual or other dividend. The Natives, in other words, sought to use a capitalist device, the corporation, to protect Native land and culture, making it possible for those Natives who wished to, to stay on their land by virtue of their annual dividends, which would supplement their subsistence lifestyles.

This was a truly remarkable recommendation, for if carried out it would solve the claims problem, would recognize the right of Alaska Natives to ancestral lands, and through the financial award would provide financial resources for Natives in perpetuity. The proposal seemed an elegant resolution, clearing the way for Alaska's economic development. With Natives in agreement, attorneys for the state, the AFN, and the federal government could craft legislation for Congress and wait. But the history of Indian land claim settlements suggested the wait might be a long one, at least years.

Nature, with an assist from America's largest oil companies, entered the claims discussions on 27 December 1967, creating circumstances that would cut short the time negotiators would take to reach a final settlement. On that day the newly formed Atlantic Richfield Oil Company (ARCO) tapped its Prudhoe Bay State No. 1 drilling well into North America's largest single petroleum deposit yet discovered. Actually, the magnitude of the find became clear only after several months, for a confirmation well was necessary to verify its quality and extent. The confirming data came through in May 1968.

The discovery at Prudhoe Bay was not inevitable, and the state almost passed up the opportunity to own the land involved. Governor Egan was quite distrustful of large oil companies and not enthusiastic about inviting them into Alaska. Just when it seemed to many Alaskans that the state had freed itself from absentee capitalists, symbolized by the hated fish traps, it did not make sense to the governor to go courting another group of them. But since the discovery in upper Cook Inlet (Swanson River) in 1957, oil companies had been keenly interested in Alaskan prospects, and with statehood, urged that the state lease promising areas for exploratory drilling. Oil lease sales could bring needed revenue to the state, and in the face of declines in other revenue sources, Egan agreed to open some land. A state lease sale in Cook Inlet in 1961 brought $15 million, a figure that caught people's attention across Alaska.

In the beginning the state sold leases on a noncompetitive basis, that is, the Department of Natural Resources established a minimum price and awarded the lease to the first person to file on an offered tract. This allowed smaller investors to file alongside major companies; the smaller investors would usually sell their leases to the majors, keeping a 5 percent "override" interest, if the tract had oil or was near one that did, because they did not have the capital to develop the lease. The federal government still owned Alaska's North Slope in 1959, an area both smaller and major investors found very attractive. In the previous decade the Interior Department held several noncompetitive lease sales there, and by 1953 half of all leases in Alaska were on the North Slope.

After 1958 investors were very vocal about their desire that the state select the North Slope land. They would rather lease from the state than from the Interior Department because historically states offered better terms than the federal government. But Egan, reelected in 1962, was not persuaded that the selection would be in the state's best interest. He felt that because by the terms of the statehood act the state got 90 percent of any federal lease revenue, it made more sense to let the federal government retain the land.

Egan changed his mind when several of the majors told state lease officials that they would welcome competitive leasing with concessions or bonuses. In addition, the Interior Department expressed concern over how long it might take to survey North Slope lands. Non-competitive leases tended to be smaller to attract as many filers as possible. If the state would offer leases on a competitive basis on very large areas, oil companies would not have to buy up packages of small leases from many winners; rather, they could bid on combined larger tracts. This might cost more money in the short run, because the majors would be bidding against each other, but it would be more efficient and manageable in the long term. However, competitive leasing would leave the smaller investors, the "little guys," behind.

Egan had to weigh greater opportunity for smaller players against more millions of dollars in lease revenue for the state. He chose the millions.[9] Egan selected the North Slope lands, which included Prudhoe Bay (soon to make history but not yet the focus of attention on the Slope), and in 1964 the state held the first competitive lease sale on tracts within the selection.

Atlantic Richfield personnel were drilling on newly leased state land when just after Christmas 1967 they broke into the gas cap over the Prudhoe Bay deposit. By May, when the company completed its confirmation well, seven miles from the original discovery, the geologists knew that the wells would produce at more than three thousand barrels a day, a phenomenal rate. It was a bonanza that dwarfed the Klondike discovery in 1896. Responding to excited appeals from the industry, the state conducted a new, well-publicized lease sale on lands in the region in 1969. Proceeds for the state amounted to more than $900 million, more than three times the annual state budget. Egan need have no more concerns about sufficient state revenue. The only problem was how to get the oil out of Alaska, or rather, what to do about Native land claims, for the industry had long understood that a pipeline from the North Slope to a warm-water port on the south-central coast, probably Valdez, was the only feasible method. That knowledge was confirmed by the voyage of the S.S. *Manhattan,* a conventional oil tanker refitted with an icebreaker bow, which transited the Northwest Passage from Baffin Island to Prudhoe Bay in late 1969. The *Manhattan* was able to make the transit only with the help of a Canadian icebreaker, assisted at times by ships of the U.S. Coast Guard. The voyage demonstrated that the sea route was not feasible for transporting Prudhoe Bay oil.

But by this time Egan was no longer governor. Walter J. Hickel, the son of a Kansas tenant farmer who had made millions in construction, hotels, and real estate in Alaska, successfully challenged Egan in 1966 for the chief executive's seat. Soon after the election Hickel directed his attorney general to sue the U.S. secretary of the interior over the land freeze. *State of Alaska v. Udall* argued that the secretary did not have the authority to halt the state's land selection. Although the federal district court in Alaska agreed, the Ninth Circuit Court soon overturned the decision. That left congressional legislation as the only quick way to clear the obstacle of Native claims, now a matter of great urgency for all parties.

In 1968 president-elect Richard Nixon selected Hickel to be his interior secretary. Alaskans were delighted, for they hoped Hickel might be helpful working for a claims settlement in Washington, D.C. Often headstrong and impulsive, Hickel announced that what one secretary had done with a pen, another secretary could undo, referring to the land freeze that Udall had implemented during his authority as secretary. Environmental critics already viewed Hickel with suspicion, and such statements confirmed their opinion that neither Alaska nor other national public lands could be entrusted to the Anchorage developer. They mounted a campaign to prevent his confirmation by the Senate, but then, when Hickel promised that he would respect the freeze and otherwise appeared to support balanced policies, he won confirmation.

While Hickel prepared for his hearing, Alaskans learned that Bob Bartlett, who had been reelected as U.S. senator in 1964, had died of heart failure in a Cleveland hospital on 11 December 1968. Before leaving the governor's office, Hickel appointed Ted Stevens, now in private practice in

Walter Hickel, two-time Alaska governor (1966–68 and 1990–94). Anchorage Museum Rasmuson Center, Steve McCutcheon, McCutcheon Collection B1990 015.5 Pol 16.5.

Fairbanks, to fill out Bartlett's term. In the same election year in which Nixon was elected, Gruening, who had been reelected in 1962, lost his Senate seat to Mike Gravel, an Anchorage real estate developer and a member of the state House.

Industry, Native, and state representatives met soon after the 1968 election to devise a strategy for Congress. Washington state's Henry M. Jackson was a powerful ally in the Senate. All were familiar with the AFN's recommendation for a settlement. That proposal became the context for solving the dilemma. But because of the pressure of bringing North Slope oil to market, what might have taken many years, perhaps decades, was solved within four years of the great find. On 17 December 1971, Congress passed the Alaska Native Claims Settlement Act (ANCSA), using the formula and elements of the AFN proposal. The chief objective of the complex landmark act was to free Alaska's potential economic development from Native protest while simultaneously empowering Natives through economic capitalization and achieving justice in terms of aboriginal land claims. In Alaska the act was received by Natives and non-Natives alike as a great milestone in the history of the territory and its people. As one speaker in Congress commented upon passage of the act, it acknowledged the "birthright" of Alaska Natives.

ANCSA established twelve Native regional economic development (for profit) corporations, each associated with a particular geographic area of Alaska and the Natives who traditionally lived in that area. The act also established as many village economic development corporations as villagers might wish to found. Under the act Natives were to enroll as stockholders in one or another of these corporate entities; the act defined "Native" as a U.S. citizen with one-fourth degree or more Indian, Aleut, or Inuit ancestry. Congress paid $962.5 million in compensation for extinguishment of the Native title to all but forty-four million acres of Alaska's land. The money, used to capitalize the corporations, was paid over a twenty-year period from the federal Treasury and from the federal mineral royalties paid to the state. Individual Natives enrolled at large in any one of the regions with which they had an affinity or in a particular village corporation. Each Native received one hundred shares of stock in the corporation upon enrollment. Also, 208 villages were explicitly identified in the act; later the federal government would tacitly recognize 227 separate tribal entities in Alaska. Eventually more than 200 villages would form village corporations.

There was some confusion at the time of enrollment (1972–75), for many people were uncertain whether to enroll in their home village or in the corporation associated with the place where they actually lived. As Anchorage held the greatest single concentration of Alaska Natives, many Natives living there enrolled in the regional corporation for that region, Cook Inlet Region Inc. (CIRI). Thus CIRI became a polyglot collection of Natives from different parts of Alaska, while other corporations, such as Calista Corporation in the Yukon-Kuskokwim delta area, included almost exclusively people from the geographical area associated with that region.

Villages were to select lands in and around their locations, from one to several townships depending on the village's population. The village would control the surface estate (i.e., the landscape) in the land allotted to the village, but the regional corporation would gain title to the subsurface estate (i.e., whatever minerals or other resources might lie underground). Fifty percent of the capitalization provided in the act, $962.5 million, went to the villages, 50 percent to the regional corporations. Many villages allowed their regional corporation to manage their resources for them. The corporations created by the act, chartered under Alaska state laws, had all the powers of traditional investment entities, although there were some limitations. Shares in the corporations could not be sold for twenty years after the date of the act, and land would not be alienable (i.e., could not be transferred) for the same twenty years. Certain tax limitations also applied until 1991. Section 7(i) of the act mandates that 70 percent of the revenue from mineral or timber resources developed on corporation land must be shared with all Alaska Natives; the distribution is through the other Native corporations.

Much criticism of the act focused on the creation of the corporate entities. Those who became part of the corporate structure were often the most able Natives in a particular village or region; often they were from families that had traditionally exercised leadership in the villages. Planning for the future necessarily lay mostly in the hands of the leadership cadre, and those not involved felt left out and sometimes victimized. For-profit corporations created a cultural context that many regarded as alien to Native culture and in any case did not address adequately many of the villages' social problems, although increased resources often resulted in housing improvements, better general conditions, and some jobs. In addition, many critics felt that Alaska Natives should not have been called on to relinquish title to 330 million acres of Alaska land.

It is important to understand that the claims settlement is not something that was foisted on Natives externally, by a capitalist-driven white culture bent on creating satisfactory conditions for economic development in Alaska (i.e., construction of the oil pipeline) at whatever the cost might be to Native Alaskans. Rather, Native leaders participated at every level of the drafting of the claims settlement act, and their participation was substantive and meaningful. Writing in the *New Republic* before the act passed, Tanana Chiefs Conference president Alfred Ketzler wrote, "Native leaders of Alaska have given great attention to the structure of the settlement. . . . Indeed, the concept of the development corporation is ours."[10] That does not alter the fact that this most fundamental change in the nature of Alaska Native life did happen with unprecedented speed, and in response to forces essentially external to Native Alaska. But it does mitigate substantially the notion that Alaska Natives were victimized by the process and its result.

Education was not addressed in the settlement act. In the early 1970s, a major suit (the so-called Molly Hootch case) over Native educational access brought by the Alaska Legal Services Corporation resulted in an out of court settlement by which the state agreed to provide secondary schools in any village with fifteen or more high school–age children. This was a remarkable agreement, for the cost of constructing high schools in most of Alaska's more than two hundred villages was enormous. Natives had complained that the export of village children to boarding schools in the contiguous states, or to non-Native homes in Alaska's major cities, was an unfair imposition, damaging to Native children. In this complaint they were surely correct, although there were some benefits to the boarding school experience, including new and broader perspectives on American Native cultures, observation of mainstream American culture, and friendships with other Alaska Native children from Alaska's diverse regions. As a part of the Molly Hootch settlement, the state legislature provided for local school boards in most of Alaska's villages. Coupled with other forms of local control created by the claims settlement act, the Molly Hootch case transferred significant new power to village Alaskans.

ANCSA raised important questions having to do with the possible loss of land after 1991, when shares could be sold, development could be taxed, and land could be transferred. Other questions dealt with the lifestyle of Native villagers. Would Natives have the option of maintaining subsistence and village lifestyles in the future? And if so, under what conditions? Furthermore, after 1991 what should be done about people born after passage of the act? At the invitation of the Inuit Circumpolar Conference, a coalition of Arctic Native groups, Canadian jurist Thomas R. Berger wrote a major report on the impact of the settlement act that helped produce amendments to it in 1989 and 1991. Among other things, the amendments addressed the problem of the loss of land. A movement for greater autonomy for individual villages, to be achieved by using the Native sovereignty provisions of the 1934 Indian Reorganization Act, attracted many adherents. Interest in this movement was somewhat diminished, however, with the passage of the 1991 amendments.[11]

On the one hand, the pressure the act brought to Natives to become adept in corporate management and culture has been interpreted by some analysts as a hastening of cultural genocide; Native culture, they say, cannot withstand that impact.[12] On the other hand, some recent scholarship has made a case that the act has had unexpected benefits in some villages, providing a resource base that made it possible for people to live in villages again, where before, the lack of resources made that impossible.[13] The framers of the claims settlement act, Native and non-Native alike, understood that ANCSA would hasten acculturation, that it would encourage change. It is important to study the ways Native culture has been forced to change. Much recent scholarship on Indians in the United States suggests that Indian communities and cultures have been remarkably resilient in accommodating to change, finding methods and avenues of survival and even potential prosperity. Much analysis remains to be done on the impact of the claims settlement act on Native culture and communities. But clearly ANCSA empowered Alaska Native people and entities in unprecedented ways. Several of the corporations are among the largest and most prosperous in Alaska today. They have lucrative investments across America. They are led by Natives, by some of the most capable people in Alaska and in American economic circles. The election of Tlingit leader Byron Mallott as lieutenant governor of Alaska in 2014 was an important manifestation of the role of Alaska Natives in the political, economic, and social life of the state.

The Native claims act was the most important development that shaped modern Alaska. It established Alaska Natives as partners in the state's economy and confirmed their significance in its politics. By eliminating obstacles to pipeline construction, it facilitated petroleum development, which through taxation provided a budgetary foundation for state government and for the construction of infrastructure. In addressing the question of environmental preservation, it put in motion the completion of federal land disposal, which removed another possible barrier to economic development. Few legislative enactments have had such a profound effect on a society.

WILDERNESS, OIL, AND THE ALASKA ENVIRONMENT

In some measure, ANCSA owed its passage through Congress in 1971 to the modern civil rights movement. Many who voted for the act did so in the context of recognizing the equal claim of American indigenous people to the benefits of modern culture. But the civil rights movement was not the only fundamental policy change that affected Alaska in the

1960s and 1970s. Another was environmentalism. Although aware of the dramatic social changes taking place in American culture in the 1960s, many Alaskans did not appreciate the implications of these changes for the new state until confronted with the Native land claims following the state's initial land selections immediately after statehood. Many Alaskans also seemed not to appreciate the implications of the environmental movement until the debate over the conservation provisions of ANCSA began in the 1970s. Environmental historian Samuel P. Hays has outlined several revolutions in the twentieth century that brought wilderness within the reach of most Americans after midcentury.[14] Detailed information about wilderness areas, a highway system that allowed Americans easy access to them, and equipment that made using them easier and more comfortable encouraged people to do what naturalist John Muir had always hoped they would: immerse themselves in wilderness.

But more important than these developments was an intellectual revolution. Americans began to learn more about what wilderness was: an integrated system of naturally occurring geology, physiography, flora and fauna, and scenic wonder unaltered by humans, a setting that inspired spirituality through its natural qualities. Thoreau, Muir, Robert Marshall, and others considered the spirituality inspired by nature to be fundamentally in harmony with the true nature of being human; they believed nature was more valuable, because it was more "pure," than the achievements of industrialization and commerce and than cities and consumerism. Increasing numbers of Americans became familiar with these ideas through Sierra Club and Wilderness Society publications and through western and outdoor magazines. For many people the beauty of mountain, forest, and desert landscapes—previously known only to limited numbers of people but now displayed in the large format photographs of Ansel Adams and other "nature" photographers in mass distribution weeklies such as *Life*, *Look*, and *Colliers*—kindled a national respect for and sentimentality about nature and wilderness.[15]

In the 1950s wilderness enthusiasts succeeded in organizing sufficient national political pressure to block construction of a dam at Echo Park on the Green River, a spectacular canyon in Dinosaur National Monument on the Utah-Colorado border. The Echo Park proposal generated enormous public attention, a manifestation of the new interest in wilderness preservation. Political success led ultimately to a new environmental policy for America's public lands, one that replaced the conservation policy of the Progressive Era. An early indicator of the change appeared with the Multiple-Use Sustained-Yield Act of 1960, in which Congress mandated that all five identified uses of public lands—commodity development (such as saw timber for house building), wildlife habitat, water resource management, range protection, and recreation—should be viewed as equally important rather than commodity development dominating the other four. The implementation of Progressive Era conservation policy had elevated commodity development as the dominant use of most public lands, particularly the national forests. The new multiple-use policy had significant implications. Over the next several decades environmentalism would become associated with preservation of natural areas, especially wilderness.

Both wilderness and ecology became more familiar to Americans through two highly visible books published in 1962–63. In *The Quiet Crisis*, Stewart Udall argued that through population growth, development, and ignorance, Americans were losing the last wilderness areas in the country, a heritage he called "priceless." The book was read widely and helped wilderness enthusiasts, then waging a campaign for the withdrawal of wilderness land, to win landmark congressional legislation. The Wilderness Act of 1964 provided for setting aside fifty million acres of "untrammeled" land in the United States, the first act of its kind in history.[16]

Untrammeled was a word carefully chosen by Howard Zahniser, executive secretary of the Wilderness Society from 1945 to 1964, a chief writer of the Wilderness Act, and a leader of the modern environmental movement. It means unbound by and free from human manipulation, nature taking its own course without interruption or intrusion by humans. The language of the act captures this idea: "A wilderness, in contrast with those areas where man and his works dominate the landscape, is hereby recognized as an area where earth and its community of life are untrammeled by man, where man himself if a visitor who does not remain." As the environmental movement developed, many interpreted *untrammeled* to mean the complete absence of humans. Whether or not there may be any such places on Earth, when planners attempted to implement that idea on vast areas of undeveloped land in Alaska, they were confronted with the subsistence harvest of traditional resources by Alaska Native peoples who had been using Alaska land from time immemorial, as well as some non-Natives who had adopted a "wilderness" lifestyle of subsistence hunting and fishing.[17]

The other book that familiarized Americans with wilderness and ecology was even more widely read. Rachel Carson's *Silent Spring* became a classic almost overnight. A biologist who had previously published the respected book *The Sea around Us*, Carson argued in *Silent Spring* that the careless use of technology the agricultural industry employed to guarantee a common food supply free of toxic bacteria was causing widespread environmental destruction, especially to wildlife. Such pesticides as DDT, which had been shown to be carcinogenic subsequent to its introduction as a miracle of chemistry, frequently leeched into heavily used aquifers.[18] The book sent waves of environmental action spreading across the nation, resulting in federal, state, and municipal laws banning certain pesticides; it ultimately led to the adoption of federal and state clear water and air standards. A decade of environmental legislation culminated in the National Environmental Policy Act (NEPA) of 1969, which established the Environmental Protection Agency (EPA) and required the filing of an environmental impact statement (EIS) with the EPA preparatory to any significant environmental alteration of public lands. In NEPA Americans demonstrated their determination to regulate environmental impacts across the nation. Similar state and municipal regulation followed.[19]

But the shift from conservation to environmentalism did not go unopposed. In particular, commodity developers—loggers, cattle and sheep grazers, fishers—fought against changes in public land policy.[20] Throughout the 1970s and 1980s environmentalists and developers fought well-publicized campaigns over scores of public land areas. Three of these were in Alaska, where the Trans-Alaska Pipeline, the Alaska Lands Act, and the Tongass National Forest became fierce battlegrounds.

With the passage of ANCSA, oil industry executives and state and Native leaders anticipated the start-up of construction of the Trans-Alaska Pipeline, which would run nearly eight hundred miles from Prudhoe Bay on the Arctic Coast to Valdez on Prince William Sound. Expectations for industry profits and for state revenues ran high. Industry engineers had conducted some studies of the pipeline corridor and drew plans for a line that would be buried over most of its distance. Construction crews stacked rows and tiers of forty-eight-inch-diameter sections of oil line pipe, purchased in Japan, at the former Valdez town site.

In January 1971, Hickel's office released a draft EIS of several hundred pages, declaring effectively that the design met environmental specifications. But Hickel's EIS generated a storm of protest and spirited debate.

Analysts criticized the engineering studies, showing that a line buried in permafrost would be unreliable. Others sought to demonstrate that the industry's estimates for spillage were too low. Still others attacked the industry's assurances that single-hull tankers would be adequate for navigating the sometimes ice-clogged waters of Prince William Sound. Wildlife biologists debated the impact of the proposed line on caribou, moose, and other animals. A dozen national environmental groups formed the Alaska Coalition to lobby against the project.

Some of the environmentalists brought a much broader scope to their comments. Repeating Robert Marshall's observation of four decades earlier, they pleaded that America's last unbroken wilderness should not be bisected by a pipeline, by the intrusion of modern technology.[21] Many supporters of the project did not understand such thinking. It seemed to them that there was no good reason not to use nature's resources to fuel the nation as well as the economy of Alaska and the oil industry. They considered the Prudhoe Bay field miraculous, a miracle of nature if not of heaven. In a telling demonstration of the ideological distance between some activists in the debate, Vide Bartlett, the senator's widow, stretched a thin black thread across a wide trail of newspaper she had spread on her dining room and living room floor; the thread, she said, was all the impact the pipeline would have on Alaska wilderness, represented by the spread of newspapers. But wilderness advocates commented that once a pipeline was laid across a wilderness, it wasn't wilderness any more.[22]

The debate had not ended when Congress passed the claims settlement act in December 1971. In fact, it had taken a more serious turn many months earlier, in March 1970, when five Native villages and then three environmental groups, the Wilderness Society, Friends of the Earth, and the Environmental Defense Fund, sued separately to prevent construction of the pipeline. The Native villages charged that the pipeline company had failed to honor promises to hire Native contractors and workers. The environmental suit asserted that the project as planned violated the Mineral Leasing Act and NEPA. In the same month a federal judge issued an injunction responding to Natives at Stevens Village who argued that they had not received adequate compensation for impacts on the village. These were formidable roadblocks to the project, but in an Earth Day (22 April) speech at the University of Alaska in Fairbanks, Hickel counseled patience. The pipeline was a massive project involving public lands; delay and negotiations were to be expected. But Alaskans held their collective breath.

The environmental suit dragged on for several years. The primary legal issue was whether or not the requirements of NEPA, the environmental protection act, had been met by improved pipeline plans that industry engineers had produced. New careful studies led to a complete redesign of the project, which industry spokespeople again assured was more than adequate. Environmental analysts were not mollified, however, and the impasse remained unbroken. Then fate again stepped in to alter circumstances. In October 1973, Egypt and Syria attacked Israel, and at a critical stage in the fighting the United States responded with massive material support for Israel, which then beat back the invasion. In response, the Organization of Petroleum Exporting Countries (OPEC) imposed an embargo on shipments of oil to the United States. Shortages led to gas rationing for the first time since World War II, more than an inconvenience to America's automobile culture. Politicians in the most populous states began to call for the Alaska pipeline to be completed to reduce the country's dependence on foreign oil in the future.

Supporters had already introduced legislation in Congress to waive the requirements of NEPA for purposes of construction of the pipeline. Debate on the bill was intense. Not only environmentalists but many centrist members as well argued that setting NEPA aside for this enormous construction project would make it unenforceable for any project. Opponents cited the danger of dependence on foreign oil, particularly when the Prudhoe Bay development was expected to contribute 20 percent of American consumption. The Senate took a dramatic vote on an amendment to the bill, the Trans-Alaska Pipeline Authorization Act, in July 1973. The final vote was 49 to 49; Vice President Spiro Agnew broke the tie, voting for the amendment, which prohibited further court challenges to the pipeline project. The final votes in the House and Senate took place after the Arab-Israeli War, and were never in doubt. President Richard Nixon signed the bill in November. The environmental suits had delayed construction of the pipeline beyond passage of ANCSA by three years. But at last, Alaskans could breathe a sigh of relief.

Crews began construction preparations as soon as the authorization permit was signed in late January 1974. The work took three years. At the peak of activity more than twenty-eight thousand personnel labored on various aspects of the project. It cost nearly $9 billion, far in excess of even the most generous initial estimates of $900 million. The line was built and owned by a consortium of oil companies; it is operated by a separate firm, the

Alyeska Pipeline Service Company. As with other high-latitude construction projects, Alyeska had to pay high wages and provide superior food and accommodations and a variety of amenities to maintain the labor force. The high wages resulted in typical boomtown conditions in Fairbanks and Anchorage. Unemployment dropped to near zero in both cities as Alaskans left their routines to take advantage of the pay and unusual circumstances. Lavish spending by off-duty workers was rife, not unlike the bizarre atmosphere in Dawson during the Klondike rush, when miners bought dance hall girls for pokes of gold dust.

In the meantime the governor and the legislature struggled with how to tax Prudhoe Bay production when it came on line. Voters elected Egan to a third but nonconsecutive term as governor in 1970. His distrust of the industry was legendary by now. He determined that this time, with the development of this newest Alaska natural resource, Alaskans would get a fair share of the wealth. Egan appointed as his attorney general John Havelock, a brilliant lawyer who had served as an assistant in the Department of Law during Egan's first administration. One of Havelock's first contributions was to insist that in negotiations with Natives and Congress over the claims settlement bill the state maintain flexibility rather than holding a rigid position. This policy helped immensely in getting the bill through the legislative process. Havelock would subsequently make several seminal contributions to Alaska's development, drafting a privacy amendment to the state constitution in 1972 and writing a limited entry fish law in 1974. Havelock took primary responsibility for developing the state's oil tax policy, which was embodied in two bills enacted in 1972. Alaska already claimed a one-eighth share as the state's royalty of all oil extracted there. The state paid the leaseholder to pump, transport, and market its oil.

The first of the new acts increased the tax rate on oil production and established higher minimum per-barrel tax obligations, subject to the royalty credit. The second bill established various conditions for pipeline rights-of-way across state lands, including substantial rentals as well as a requirement that pipeline owners' consent to state regulatory jurisdiction over the transportation of oil in interstate commerce. Not surprisingly, the industry opposed the new and higher taxes and filed suit to block them. The cases were resolved in a package that the legislature passed in a special session in fall of 1973. Havelock also wrote a bill, which the legislature adopted, creating an Alaska Pipeline Commission, and a measure providing strict liability for the discharge of hazardous substances including oil.

These measures positioned the state to capitalize on North Slope production. About 30 percent of the value of North Slope oil is paid in taxes to Alaska. Through the life of the pipeline this has annually accounted for about 85 percent of general fund revenue for the state. In 1976 voters created, by constitutional amendment, a permanent investment fund into which to annually place about about 25 percent of the tax revenue, rents, and royalties generated by oil production and transport.[23] Jay Hammond, who had defeated former Governor Hickel in the Republican primary and Egan in the gubernatorial election in 1974, was the champion of the Alaska Permanent Fund idea. A wilderness guide, commercial fisherman, and bush pilot, Hammond had opposed statehood on the grounds that it would bring new population and increased pressure on Alaska's environment. His gubernatorial campaign stressed "moderate" environmental protection. Hammond was as determined as Egan that Alaskans should have some share of the profits from oil production and equally determined that it should not all be spent as quickly as it appeared.

Hammond's original idea for the fund provided for a fixed dividend to be paid from its annual earnings to all Alaska residents, indexed to the number of years of Alaska residence. Anchorage attorneys Ronald and Penny Zobel filed a suit challenging this scheme, arguing that it discriminated against new residents. Press coverage of the Zobels' challenge generated widespread ire across the state, especially when the U.S. Supreme Court agreed. In 1980 the legislature adopted a modified plan for the annual earnings. The legislature agreed that dividends would be the most efficient way to deliver the benefits of North Slope oil to Alaskans. In addition, many believed a dividend program would create a vested interest in protecting the fund from use of its principal by the legislature.[24] The law requires that half the earnings be distributed as dividend. Also, as much as needed of the remainder of the earnings must be used to "inflation proof" the fund (i.e., an amount equal to the annual rate of inflation must be reinvested in the principal). Throughout the late 1980s and 1990s, with inflation at historically low levels, about 20 percent of the annual earnings were used for this purpose. Some of the earnings are kept in the earnings account to stabilize the dividend in case of a precipitous fall.

At the same time that the legislature adopted the dividend program, it also repealed the state income tax. With no state sales tax, and moderate local property taxes, *U.S. News and World Report* found that Alaskans had the lowest tax burden of all states in the nation.[25] Until 2016, constituent interest in the Alaska Permanent Fund dividend prevented the legislature from using the earnings for any other purpose and generated some debate about the obligations and responsibilities of public wealth. Several years of low oil prices before 2016 caused a significant budget deficit, to which the legislature reacted by changing the formula for use of fund earnings, resulting in some going to help balance the state budget. In 1990 voters created an additional fund, the Constitutional Budget Reserve (CBR), into which the legislature placed significant monies from negotiated settlements of suits brought by the state against the oil companies for payment of back taxes, improperly calculated by the companies. As Prudhoe Bay production began to decline in 1991, tax revenue began to decrease commensurably. In 1996, earnings from the Permanent Fund, whose principal stood at more than $24 billion, equaled and then surpassed revenue generated from oil taxes. Beginning in that year, the legislature began to use money from the CBR to balance the state budget. But as the CBR shrank, a major fiscal question facing Alaskans in the 1990s was how to depoliticize the Permanent Fund. By 2019 the principal of the Permanent Fund was valued at over $65 billion.

Although environmental protests failed to halt construction of the Trans-Alaska Pipeline, that did not mean owners ignored environmental considerations. Constant public scrutiny combined with industry sensitivity to produce a project with manageable impact on the production facility and pipeline corridor and minimal impact on adjacent lands. In the mid-1980s state review of construction records revealed discrepancies that led to some pipeline sections being rewelded, and considerable controversy surrounded the pipeline terminal through the end of the decade; analysts raised persistent questions about the discharge of uncleaned ballast into Valdez Arm in violation of regulations.

But in the 1970s Alaskans directed their attention to other environmental matters, most particularly the environmental provisions of the Native claims settlement act. With the rise of environmental consciousness in the nation and the shift in public policy from conservation to environmentalism, environmental groups began to focus on environmentally significant lands in Alaska. Some areas, Admiralty Island in the southeast and lands in the western Brooks Range, for example, had been studied for years. The claims settlement was a land disposal act, and to the framers it seemed appropriate to identify public lands in Alaska that Congress might wish to withdraw for preservation. Accordingly, Section 17, Clause d(2) of the act provided that within seven years Congress would set aside eighty million acres in several conservation categories. These would be parks, forests, and fish and wildlife refuges; in addition, some of each of these would be designated by the new classification, wilderness. To begin the process of determining which lands these would be, the act established a joint federal-state land use planning commission to study potential withdrawals and to make a recommendation.

The commission finished its work in 1974 with surprisingly little disagreement. The state wanted lands with economic potential, through mining, agriculture, forest, or urban expansion. The federal government, as environmental protector, wanted environmentally significant lands, including important wilderness acreage. Although there were areas of controversy, in large measure the two categories of lands were mutually exclusive. Reflecting the role of science in environmental thinking, planners sought to define environmental areas by whole ecosystems, that is, areas demarcated by integrated physiography and the interrelations of species of fauna and flora.[26]

Congress began work on a bill to incorporate the commission's recommendations in 1974. As various committees held hearings on the bill, national environmental groups campaigned for increases in the amount of acreage to be set aside and for stringent restrictions on how preserved areas might be used. Alaska's congressional delegation, Senators Ted Stevens and Mike Gravel, and Representative Don Young (R), who was elected in a special election in 1973 after Representative Nick Begich (D) went down in a small airplane while campaigning in Alaska, found the environmental designs unacceptable. Environmentalists considered Alaska a last opportunity for America to preserve significant acreages of wilderness in a truly natural state, a place where civilization and technology were dwarfed by wilderness, islands of human preoccupation in seas of unconstrained nature. These views reflected the majority opinion in American culture. Alaska's role in national consciousness had changed since the 1950s and the statehood battle; Alaska was no longer America's "last frontier"—now it had become America's "last wilderness." Alaska's delegation reflected the western states' typical resentment of the federal role in the West, their opposition to federal management of public lands, and the pioneer's desire to develop lands and resources into economically profitable enterprises.

The battle was joined in the Congress, where Representative Morris Udall of Arizona, the younger brother of former Secretary of the Interior

Stewart Udall, led the environmental forces. In hearings around the country citizens and scientists almost uniformly favored the environmentalist perspective; in Alaska residents often expressed vehement opposition. Many Alaskans fought proposed use restrictions and resented the fact that state land selections were still not complete. Not only had Natives gained title to forty-four million acres before the state got to take its land, but now the federal government was going to take many more millions of acres. Alaskans saw themselves as getting the leavings, and they considered the process a violation of promises they thought had been made in the statehood act, particularly that the federal government would use its lands in Alaska for economic development, not environmental preservation. More than once the hearings in Alaska threatened to become volatile.

For environmentalists the Alaska lands act was a cause célèbre because of its symbolic and actual value. One of the truly unique aspects of Alaska was the amount of undeveloped land. If those lands could not be protected, the whole concept of wilderness seemed diminished. Alaska represented the culmination of three-quarters of a century of environmental legislation in America. Preserving wilderness, wildlife, and ecology there would cap that campaign with the most "natural" wilderness in America, that is, the lands least associated with pressure from civilization. In addition, somewhat ironically, some environmentalists also celebrated the "frontier" value of Alaska wilderness, a place where one could go to experience the feeling of first entering "pristine" undeveloped areas.[27] For these reasons the environmental community understood the Alaska lands bill to be one of its most important battles ever. Noting that land and nature were essential to Alaska Native identity, culture, and history, some in the environmental community looked to Natives to be allies in their fight with developers. But while Natives did indeed hold land essential to life, their view of that land included the utilitarian: the harvest of traditional subsistence resources was as essential as the land itself. As noted, this view clashed with some environmentalists' concept of wilderness as unmanipulated by people.

The contest raged from 1974 to 1978, in between Americans' preoccupation with the Watergate scandal and Richard Nixon's resignation, the country's withdrawal from Vietnam, and the bicentennial of the American Revolution. Udall and his supporters continued to push for more acreage and a "pure" definition of wilderness. Then, as the deadline for congressional action neared, Gravel announced that he would filibuster the bill until the deadline expired. If he succeeded, this would force planners to start over, losing seven years of work.

Cecil Andrus, secretary of the interior under President Jimmy Carter, decided not to let that happen. Being from Georgia, Carter said he knew little about western lands; thus he had appointed Andrus, the former governor of Idaho and a skilled negotiator committed to environmental values, as a sort of western lands minister. Andrus had participated in the d(2) negotiations, and he went to Carter with an idea to trump Alaska's junior senator. He persuaded the president to use the 1906 Antiquities Act, the act Theodore Roosevelt had used to withdraw coal and oil lands, to withdraw all of the environmentally sensitive lands in Alaska.[28] Congressional action would supersede an executive withdrawal, but until such time as the Congress might act, the lands would be protected from development or any other disposal. Carter agreed, and in November 1978 he withdrew fifty-six million acres of Alaska lands, putting them in monument status. In addition, Andrus created forty million acres of new wildlife refuge. With another eleven million acres of forest withdrawals from mineral exploration by Agriculture Secretary Bob Berglund, all the lands environmentalists wanted were secure for the moment. Most Alaskans were livid, but national public opinion supported the president's action.

Andrus's ploy worked, but only in concert with an unexpected expression of national democracy. Congressional leaders continued to work on an Alaska lands bill, as Andrus anticipated they would. But by November 1980 they had not reached an agreement. Morris Udall's environmental forces pushed for a bill that would withdraw 122 million acres in new conservation withdrawals. Stevens, however, had introduced his own bill that provided for only 60 million acres, a vast difference. Negotiations effectively ended as politicians looked ahead to the coming presidential election.

In the end it was the American people who decided the nature of the Alaska lands act. Taking a cue from California's Proposition 13, which capped property taxes in that state, voters nationally imposed a conservative revolution on the country in the 1980 election. They elected Ronald Reagan as president and a Republican majority in the U.S. Senate. These results represented a watershed in American history; clearly, the American people wanted limitations on postwar liberalism. Environmental leaders realized this probably meant limitations on environmental protection as well. During the 1980s two applications of the 1973

Endangered Species Act, for a small fish called the snail darter and for the western spotted owl, had sparked intense debate on the relationship between wildlife protection and economic development and helped define the balance the American people would accept. While they embraced wilderness preservation, clear air and water, and creation of the Environmental Protection Administration, Americans were apparently less certain that the survival of an obscure, tiny fish should interrupt economic development.

Morris Udall and other congressional environmentalists knew that the incoming conservative majority in the new Congress would not accept many of the environmental protections that national conservation groups were hoping for in Alaska. Two weeks after the election they reluctantly accepted the political reality and quickly moved a compromise bill through both houses of Congress. The result was the Alaska National Interest Lands Conservation Act of 1980 (ANILCA).[29] The most comprehensive land and environmental enactment in history, ANILCA completed land disposal in Alaska. The act revoked Andrus's stopgap withdrawals and approved the state's own land selections, on hold since Secretary Stewart Udall's 1966 land freeze. The act set aside an additional 104 million acres (more than the 80 million called for in ANCSA) in permanent protection as national parks, fish and wildlife refuges, and forests, 56.7 million acres of which was designated as wilderness, bringing American national wilderness land to 100 million acres total.

The amount of national land in parks and refuges doubled with passage of the act. Alaska land was thus categorized: the state acquired title to about 105 million acres (the 103-million-acre grant plus mental health trust lands, university lands, and others); by ANCSA Natives had title to 44 million. In addition, 104 million acres of conservation reserves were added to about 50 million acres previously reserved by the federal government (Tongass and Chugach National Forests, Katmai National Monument, Mount McKinley National Park, Glacier Bay National Monument, Petroleum Reserve No. 4, various military reservations), for a total of 154 million acres of federally designated land; 72 million acres of undesignated federal land, public domain, was to be administered by the Bureau of Land Management. Sixty percent of Alaska land is held by the federal government; the state has title to 28 percent. The act renamed Mount McKinley park Denali National Park, and it renamed the petroleum reserve the National Petroleum Reserve–Alaska.

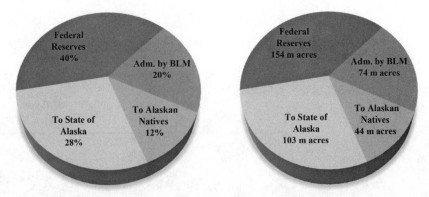

Disposition of land (375 million total acres). Alaska Department of Natural Resources.

There were a number of unusual aspects of the legislation. In a highly significant provision, the act recognized the right of Natives to use wilderness and other national areas for subsistence hunting, fishing, and gathering. In a departure from federal practice that represented a substantial compromise, non-Native bush residents also were permitted to use protected lands for subsistence. In fact, there were a number of important exceptions to national practice in the act. It sanctioned "frontier" use of the Tongass National Forest; that is, persons living in cabins and fishing and hunting for subsistence and livelihood were permitted to continue to do so for their lifetimes. Miners and hunting guides who had traditionally operated in lands now protected were permitted to continue to do so for their lifetimes. In addition, reindeer grazing and sport and commercial hunting were allowed in certain areas. Furthermore, the act included a $40 million annual subsidy for the Tongass Forest to guarantee that the Forest Service could continue to offer timber sales that would support the operation of the two pulp mills, at Ketchikan and Sitka. Alaska senator Ted Stevens said after the act passed that no economically valuable lands had been so circumscribed as to be labeled "locked up." The act was an environmental triumph nonetheless, for it provided permanent protection for the very wilderness that had come to symbolize environmentalism nationally. Now Alaska truly was America's "last wilderness." Upon leaving office, Carter called ANILCA his single most important act and legacy as president.

The exceptions included in ANILCA for economic development mollified Alaskan supporters of economic development somewhat. But rancor in Alaska did not die entirely. In 1980 the Alaska legislature established a

Arrigetch Peaks in Gates of the Arctic National Park, created by the Alaska National Interest Lands Conservation Act of 1980. Brooks Range Trust records, Archives and Special Collections, Consortium Library, University of Alaska Anchorage uaa-hmc-0076-b1-f26-38.

"statehood commission" to assess Alaska's relationship to the federal government. The commission was "to recommend appropriate changes in the relationship of the people of Alaska to the United States." In a sense the commission was a face-saving measure. It allowed Alaskans who supported wide-scale economic development harmlessly to trumpet their resentment of the exercise of federal power in the state. Assembled with balanced membership, the commission compiled a number of reports on Alaska's potential and on the likelihood of state viability should its citizens pursue secession. In the final analysis, however, unsurprisingly, the group had little to recommend.

Subsequently, Alaskans followed other western legislatures into the so-called Sagebrush Rebellion, an anti-environmental political movement of western commodity users of the national public lands directed at transferring title of those lands to the several states. Nevada led the movement, passing in 1979 an act asserting state control over BLM lands. The act had no constitutional validity, but it was a forceful way of expressing displeasure with the national shift from Progressive conservation to environmentalism.[30] In 1982, Alaska voters passed a similar "Tundra Rebellion" initiative, asserting state control over 56 percent of the BLM's seventy-two million acres. Again, the law had no standing, but it seemed to help dissipate some of the resentment over federal sovereignty.

Of all of ANILCA's compromises, the ones that disturbed environmentalists most were those in the Tongass National Forest. In addition to the $40 million annual subsidy, the act mandated that 450 million board feet of timber be harvested annually; the average cut on the forest from 1950 to 1980 was 300 million board feet.[31] Although the act designated 5.4 million acres of the forest as wilderness, permitted under the "frontier use" doctrine were hunting, sport fishing, trapping, motor boat, airplane, and snow machine use, subsistence harvest, commercial outfitting and guiding, commercial fishing enhancement, and trails and shelters. The only activity not permitted was commercial logging. The controversy over the western spotted owl in Pacific Northwest forests directed attention to the character of the Tongass.[32] The spotted owl nests in old-growth timber, trees five hundred years or older; it shuns second-and third-growth forest, which is most forest habitat in the Pacific Northwest. But the Tongass has the largest stand of old growth in the United States. In addition, much of the Tongass is true rain forest, as between forty-five and two hundred inches of precipitation annually produce an unusually lush vegetative cover that supports a wide diversity of flora and fauna. National environmental groups, particularly the Sierra Club and the Wilderness Society, decided that the Tongass Forest provisions of ANILCA needed to be revised.

As a part of the reevaluation of natural resource policy in the 1960s and 1970s, Congress had passed in 1976 the National Forest Management Act (NFMA), calling for the Forest Service to generate a land management plan for each forest in the system, to be renewed every fifteen years. Plans were to have the benefit of scientific analyses as well as public testimony by those likely to be affected by the forest's use and development. Alaskans concerned about the Tongass Forest organized the Southeast Alaska Conservation Council (SEACC) in 1969 to address forest issues and offered regular evaluations of management policy on the forest after the NFMA. SEACC found that buffers of trees along salmon-breeding streams, a requirement to keep the temperature of the water cool enough for eggs to survive, were missing or inadequate in much of the forest. SEACC also found that the amount of road building in the forest seemed on a pace with new road construction in Orange Country, California. More road mileage was constructed in the Tongass Forest in the decade after ANILCA than in all the years before the act. SEACC and other groups also alerted the EPA to discharge violations at the two pulp mills. Timothy Egan, the *New York Times* staff writer in Seattle, captured the environmental complaint about the Tongass when he pointed out in a Sunday edition story that a five-hundred-year-old old-growth Sitka spruce in the forest could be purchased for the price of a McDonald's Big Mac.[33]

In 1990 a decade of raucous debate culminated in the Tongass Timber Reform Act. That act removed the mandate to harvest 450 million board feet of timber each year, instead directing the Forest Service to meet "market demand" each year and to sell the timber at a profitable price. It reduced the $40 million annual subsidy to $4 million. And it protected an additional one million acres of the forest from timber harvest. One of the bill's sponsors in Congress asserted that the reform act ended "a decade of disgrace" in the forest. One result of the campaign and debate was to raise the Tongass National Forest to high national visibility. It is now widely viewed as a national treasure, a status that militates against its despoliation.

OIL REVENUE AND THE ALASKA PERMANENT FUND

In the meantime Alaska dealt with the oil boom. The vastly increased state revenue from oil production generated an orgy of state spending. With oil money, every legislator was able to bring millions of dollars in capital construction to his or her district. At the same time the legislature established numerous social service programs, most of which were badly needed. The legislature dedicated huge sums to revenue sharing, passing money through to municipalities to spend as they might wish. In particular, the state assumed most of the cost of public education in the urban centers and all of it in the bush. At times it seemed no one could figure out how to spend all the money that was coming in.

Although he was a moderate, Governor Jay Hammond was also a Republican, and he conscientiously tried to limit spending. But there was simply too much money to be controlled. When a small group seized control of the legislature (by organizing enough members to vote together on critical bills) and divided the annual revenue three ways, between the House, the Senate, and the governor's office, Hammond capitulated. A number of ill-advised programs resulted. One was a barley-growing project in the

Delta River region, where the grain grows quite well; the state subsidized a number of new farms and the recultivation of others. Hammond's advisors persuaded him that if the state grew barley and stored it, a market would develop; knowing there was a reliable, accessible source of the grain, world purchasers would include it in their supply profile. To this end, the state began construction of a grain terminal at Seward. Not to be outdone, however, the town of Valdez, closer to the Delta area and with the benefit of local taxation of the pipeline terminal facility, began construction of its own grain elevator. Not surprisingly, no market developed. So the barley simply sat. At the same time, bison, a nonnative species that had been imported into the Delta region in the 1920s to diversify the game population, found the barley fields to their liking and trampled thousands of acres.

A similar fiasco involved dairy farming at Mackenzie Point near Anchorage. The state subsidized land and cattle purchases for people willing to develop dairy operations, stipulating that they had to sell their milk to the state-owned Matanuska Maid Dairy in Palmer. The state then subsidized the dairy. This project was driven partly by the still circulating romantic conviction that a pioneer society needed agriculture to become self-sufficient and also by a miscalculation of the economies of scale involved in Alaska agriculture. The market for dairy products already was saturated by lower-priced milk from Washington state, and the farmers sank into bankruptcy. The state forgave a number of loans and bought back others, with damages. There were other projects, including three proposed dams to generate electricity. Two of these, one on the Kenai Peninsula and the other above Taku Inlet south of Juneau, were eventually built. The third dam, in a particularly rough and inaccessible location on the Susitna River, was abandoned.

Many state-funded projects benefited the general populace greatly, but the capital construction at the beginning of the oil boom of Alaska's material infrastructure, highways, public buildings, boat harbors, and so on was significantly underbuilt. No new major highways were built, but existing ones were improved, as the state was now able to meet contribution requirements to attract federal highway funds. In Anchorage four new public facilities were erected: a convention center, a sports arena, a headquarters library, and a state-of-the-art performing arts center. The schools built in Native villages allowed children to stay in their home villages. The state also helped construct urban schools, reducing the amounts needing to be bonded.

Where there was money, there was also corruption. On the North Slope, where local government also taxed Prudhoe Bay construction, politicians who hired on as government construction consultants steered hundreds of millions of dollars in contracts to favored clients in Seattle, who rebated or "kicked back" percentages of their contracts to the consultants. A state senator attempted to bribe at least one of his colleagues to pass a bill directing the legislature to purchase fire-fighting aircraft from a Canadian firm in which he had an interest. Another state senator purchased an abandoned pipeline construction camp and tried to sell it to the state for use as a highway maintenance facility at a usurious price.

In 1982, Alaska hotelier William Sheffield defeated conservative Anchorage insurance agent Tom Fink for the governorship. Sheffield promised to run government more like a business, by which he seemed to mean in a more cost-effective manner. Sheffield curtailed some state spending, abandoning the Seward grain terminal, for example, and liquidating the state's involvement in the agricultural projects. He was aided in this endeavor when world oil prices fell dramatically in 1985 and 1986, from more than $20 per barrel to barely over $9 per barrel. The state budget suffered accordingly, because much of the taxation of production is tied to the market value of the product. The urban real estate market, over-built with condos, collapsed in Anchorage and Fairbanks. For the first time since before World War II, Alaska experienced a significant out-migration, as more people were leaving the state than were moving in. When oil prices climbed back to $15 per barrel by the end of the 1980s, the economy stabilized.

Sheffield became the only governor in Alaska's history to be subjected to an impeachment proceeding. In 1985 the chief prosecutor in the state Department of Law, Dan Hickey, investigated rumors that the governor had illegally steered a lucrative state office building lease contract to a political supporter, Lenny Arsenault. When the state went in search of an office building to lease in Fairbanks, Hickey learned, Sheffield's chief of staff, John Shively, had structured the bid procedure so that only one building would qualify, the one partly owned by Arsenault. Hickey had already successfully prosecuted the state Senate bribery case and had brought to light the fraudulent pipeline camp sale. He was not intimidated by the implications of charging the governor; he took his evidence to the state attorney general and ultimately to a grand jury. In Alaska a grand jury can either indict, not indict, or issue a report. This grand jury issued a report recommending that the governor be impeached.

According to the Alaska constitution, the Senate conducts impeachment hearings and the House tries the case, the opposite of the U.S. Constitution. A subcommittee of the Senate conducted hearings. The critical issue was whether or not the governor had perjured himself before the grand jury. After a grant of immunity to secure his testimony, Shively said he had been present when the governor and Arsenault had discussed the building lease. But Sheffield twice told the grand jury that he could not recall ever discussing the lease with Arsenault. Both the Senate and the governor hired attorneys who had worked on Richard Nixon's impeachment. After two weeks the subcommittee found insufficient evidence to impeach the governor. But he lost the primary election the next year to Steve Cowper, a Fairbanks attorney, who went on to defeat Arliss Sturgulewski, the first woman to run for governor in Alaska, in the general election.

Oil money changed Alaska forever. It brought new population, as every resource development had done. It provided funding for a massive new construction of material infrastructure. It made Alaska one of the wealthiest states in the union. It transformed a modest, somewhat remote out-post of civilization into a thoroughly modern late-twentieth-century, technologically oriented, and literate society. But it did not reduce Alaska's dependence on absentee capital for development and sustenance; in fact, oil development exacerbated that dependence. Nor did it make Alaska agriculturally self-sufficient or generate diversity in the economy. Some analysts argue that it created a culture of greed, both through the high salaries and wages it had provided, and more particularly, by the establishment of the Alaska Permanent Fund dividend program. The fact of Alaska's near total dependence on oil, remembering that people did not go to Alaska to live subsistence lifestyles, raises questions about the relationship between the political, intellectual, and moral character of a society and the sources and nature of its sustenance, questions that, in the case of Alaska, cannot yet be answered with much finality.

At four minutes past midnight on 24 March 1989, the oil tanker *Exxon Valdez*, trying to navigate around floating glacial icebergs outside Valdez Narrows in Prince William Sound, ran up on Bligh Reef, a rock shelf on the edge of the ship channel. The ship was off course because a tired and inadequately trained third mate did not remember that the vessel was being steered by autopilot. Its hull ruptured and the ship poured a fifth or more of its cargo, generally estimated at 11.2 million gallons but possibly as much as 39 million gallons of crude oil, into Prince William Sound, an unusually

The tanker *Exxon Valdez* after it spilled at least 11 million gallons of crude oil in Prince William Sound in March 1989, off-loading its remaining oil to the smaller tanker *Exxon San Francisco*. Alaska State Library, U.S.C.G. Activities 17th Division Photo Collection P313.08.11.

beautiful, largely undeveloped natural area, a world-renowned ecosystem. It was the largest oil spill ever in North America before the blowout of British Petroleum's Macondo well (*Deepwater Horizon*) in the Gulf of Mexico in 2010. The *Exxon Valdez* went aground on Good Friday. The Great Alaska Earthquake of 1964 had also occurred on Good Friday, and people wondered at the coincidence.[34]

For several days the oil lay on the ocean's surface and continued to seep from the tanker itself. Oil response equipment, booms to contain the oil and skimmers to scoop it off the surface, required by state law to be in Valdez ready to respond to just this sort of emergency, were either out of commission or had been moved to other locations and not replaced. In addition, the U.S. Coast Guard, responsible for monitoring traffic in and out of the port of Valdez, did not know about the accident until notified by the tanker captain and failed to conduct a sobriety test of the captain and crew until twelve hours after the grounding. Then, before containment equipment could be assembled and deployed, a late winter storm developed with strong northeastern winds. It blew the oil across the sound and south along the shore of the Kenai Peninsula and eventually all the way to Kodiak Island, 470 miles from the spill site. Pollution on the shore-line was substantial, though not continuous, and varied in depth. Scientists estimate that 35 percent of the oil evaporated, 40 percent washed up on the beaches of Prince William Sound, and 25 percent was carried out into the Gulf of Alaska.

National media rushed to cover the story, and local reporters kept it before the Alaska public without a break for two months. All agencies involved in oil spill response had been negligent. The Alyeska Pipeline Company did not have the required equipment available and could not get it to the site quickly. The Alaska state Department of Environmental Conservation did not know that the equipment was not ready if needed. The U.S. Coast Guard did not know what was going on in the tanker channel and was slow and inadequate in its response. The Exxon Corporation had resisted the idea of double-hulled tankers, which might have reduced the effects of the spill, and was slow to accept responsibility. The tanker captain, although not in command of the vessel at the time of the spill, was probably legally drunk.

After several days Exxon announced publicly that the corporation would take responsibility for cleaning up all of the oil. Skimmers finally arrived and worked through the summer taking oil off of the water. Booms were stretched across the mouths of several bays in the path of the migrating oil to protect salmon hatcheries. Under the direction of the Coast Guard, Exxon hired thousands of temporary workers to clean up beaches using a variety of techniques, including hand wiping, washing with high-pressure hot water, and spreading fertilizer to speed up the activity of microbes that metabolize oil. Limited cleanup continued for the next five years. Exxon spent about $2 billion on the cleanup, but much oil remained, particularly in the beach substrata.

Marine wildlife suffered the greatest impact of the spill. Tens of thousands of sea birds died from ingesting oil while attempting to preen and from lowered body temperatures due to the inability of their feathers to hold heat. These included marbled murrelets, common murres, and pigeon guillemots; fewer ducks and eagles were affected. Harbor seals suffered also, but their populations had been in decline before the spill. Few killer whales seem to have been affected. Salmon population decline was not severe. Sea otters, so easy to anthropomorphize, became symbolic of the spill's victimization of innocent and powerless nature. Few otters that were cleaned survived, for the cleaning was apparently as traumatic as being oiled. Thousands of sea otters were likely oiled, but the sound's population of about thirty-five thousand recovered rapidly.

The spill also affected two Native villages, Tatitlek, very near the spill site but not in the oil's path, and New Chenega, directly in the oil's path; these villages were boomed for protection soon after the accident. Scientists and cleanup coordinators concentrated on protecting subsistence resources used by villagers, including various fish and mollusk species. Despite repeated assurances that resources were not contaminated, villagers attributed various physical maladies to pollution.[35]

The State of Alaska and the federal government both sued Exxon Corporation for violations of law. Civil suits for damages were settled out of court in 1992; Exxon paid $900 million. The settlement also provided for creation of the *Exxon Valdez* Trustee Council (EVOS), comprised of three federal and three state members, to disburse the settlement money. Mandated to use the money for restoration of Prince William Sound, EVOS has purchased Native inholdings (parcels of isolated land) and other lands and has consistently monitored recovery in the sound. Exxon also settled criminal suits, paying a fine of $100 million for the illegal discharge of oil. The criminal settlement went for disbursement to the secretary of the interior and the governor of Alaska. In addition, thirty-five thousand fishermen, property owners, business owners, cannery workers, and Natives filed a class action suit that went to trial in the spring of 1994. Finding the corporation guilty, the jury fined Exxon $5 billion. Exxon appealed the verdict, and the case went back and forth from Alaska federal district court to the Ninth Circuit Court of Appeals several times before the U.S. Supreme Court in 2008 awarded defendants about $50 million. By that time, many of the parties to the suit were no longer alive.[36]

The *Exxon Valdez* became a complex symbol of environmental despoliation and corporate greed. Even though Prince William Sound has largely recovered from the effects of the spill, many species of wildlife have not, and the event continues to symbolize for the American people the value of natural environment and the obligation of users to act responsibly. The 2010 Macondo blowout has added to the perception of the vulnerability of the environment. Yet the disasters have brought no reduction in oil consumption in the United States and no questioning of the validity of consumerism. Several thousand people sent cut credit cards to Exxon following the spill, but most of these likely simply changed gas stations. Continued reliance on fossil fuels, on petroleum and coal, makes more environmental pollution and more disasters a logical certainty. More significant, continued development cannot proceed without continuing loss of natural environment, because the technology that makes development possible, as well as the development itself in the form of houses, buildings, towns, and factories, depends on the exploitation of natural resources, particularly oil. This is one of the ironies of Alaska: it is a wilderness environment that must be developed to sustain the modern materialist culture that Americans, and increasingly everyone else in the world, consider necessary and regard as a right. Decrying the *Exxon Valdez* spill, then, is a cost-free way of expressing outrage at the wrong object, the developer corporation, unless the protest is against dependence on technology, about which few are willing to do much.

ALASKA POLITICS IN THE AGE OF OIL

As Alaskans approached the millennium in the 1990s, little had changed in the state's character. The state continued as an economic and political colony. Absentee-funded resource extraction, Native claims, and federal environmental protection continued to be the most potent influences in the state's development, and petroleum continued to be the state's principal preoccupation. The Prudhoe Bay oil field reached its peak of production in 1991; production will gradually decrease over the foreseeable future until it is not possible to extract more resource from the deposit with contemporary technologies. However, the field operators British Petroleum (BP), Exploration (Alaska), and ARCO have found, developed, and brought into production smaller ancillary fields adjacent to Prudhoe Bay. These have slowed the decrease in production significantly. At the end of the 1990s BP, which had already acquired Amoco Oil Company, purchased ARCO, giving BP a potential monopoly on North Slope production. However, the U.S. Federal Trade Commission (FTC) opposed the merger on the grounds that it would create an uncompetitive monopoly. To secure FTC approval, in 2000 BP sold about 30 percent of its North Slope holdings, essentially ARCO's Alaska holdings, to Phillips Petroleum Company. Phillips merged with Conoco in 2002 to create ConocoPhillips. Critics charged that BP's 70 percent control of Alaska's petroleum future still left the state too dependent on a single investor, but the final arrangement enjoyed the endorsement of state government.[37]

In 1994, Walter Hickel, who succeeded Steve Cowper in 1990, declined to run for reelection, citing age and a desire to spend more time with his family. Voters elected Democrat Tony Knowles as governor. A former mayor of Anchorage, Knowles ran a centrist campaign, promising responsible negotiations with the oil industry and fairness to Alaska Natives. Analysts in the press credited Knowles's victory to the Native vote. His running mate was Fran Ulmer, the first woman elected as lieutenant governor. Knowles faced a significant challenge generated by the success of the Alaska Permanent Fund dividend program. Throughout the 1990s the fund's worth exceeded $20 billion, approaching $27 billion by the end of the decade, more than the annual total budget of a number of small nations. Although the fund had been created by constitutional amendment in 1976, annual distribution of the earnings is left to the legislature.

As Prudhoe Bay production declined, so did the state tax revenue it generated. Yet as the state's population continued to increase, reaching 627,000 in 2000, the expenses of state government increased. By 1995 state expenditures exceeded state revenues. The state legislature took money from the Constitutional Budget Reserve, a windfall account, to balance the budget. In 2000 the reserve, invested for profit like the Permanent Fund, contained more than $3 billion. But the state operating budget was about $2 billion for most of the decade, and in the last three years of the decade the annual shortfall exceeded $500 million. Rather than exhaust the CBR, it might have been reasonable to divert some of the earnings from the $27 billion Permanent Fund to make up the budget shortfall. But voters made clear their unwillingness to use the earnings for that purpose by voting for Republican candidates who promised to "protect your dividend" and to cut government spending. Throughout the 1990s voters elected Republican majorities to the state legislature, often "veto-proof" majorities, electing enough members in each chamber to override a veto of their legislation by the Democrat governor. Thus Alaskans were faced with the strange anomaly of having $27 billion in the bank, having a $0.5 billion or more budget shortfall and no way to use the state's major bank account to pay for state government. Most people outside Alaska found this phenomenon unbelievable.

The governor convened a task force to address the issue, citing the state's most significant crisis as the "fiscal gap." The task force suggested that one option would be to reinstate a state income tax, which the voters had repealed in 1976 when they created the Permanent Fund. But statewide polls revealed that voters would reject that option overwhelmingly. Voters reelected Knowles in 1998, defeating John Lindauer who was found to have lied about the source of his campaign funds. But the budget stalemate continued, reaching resolution only when oil prices again rose.

In 1992, Undersecretary of the Interior Ada Deer formally recognized 226 Native tribes in Alaska. This was a significant administrative action, for it guaranteed such Native entities certain rights of self-governance and access to federal funds. Courts had long held that tribes could be formally recognized only by the U.S. Congress, but agencies of the government and Congress itself acted as if the Interior Department's recognition was formal and constitutional. The Hickel administration opposed the tribal designation, and the state likewise did not recognize the tribes. The governor argued that with the Native development corporations chartered by the state and operating according to state law, the federal recognition was inappropriate and potentially disruptive. Upon his election as governor, however, Knowles dropped the state's opposition, overtly acknowledging tribal status. The state entered into negotiations with a number of villages over the distribution of police and other local powers.

But the state's recognition of tribal status did not prevent a significant rift from developing between Native Alaska and state government. Two issues drove a wedge of distrust between them: Native sovereignty and subsistence. Many analysts took for granted that the Alaska Native Claims Settlement Act extinguished such Native sovereignty as might theoretically exist in Alaska at the same time that it extinguished Native title to all but forty-four million acres of Alaska land. However, in 1992 the Native Village of Venetie sued in federal court for recognition of its sovereignty. Although the village lost its case in district court, in 1996 the Ninth Circuit Court of Appeals reversed the lower court ruling, finding that the village retained its sovereignty.[38] The implications were portentous, for 226 tribal entities, if recognized by the courts, would constitute a significant diminution of state sovereignty, a bitter prospect in a state where the federal government already was widely perceived as a threat to state sovereignty. The state legislature appropriated $1 million to fight the suit in the U.S. Supreme Court, where in 1998 the court ruled that the village was not sovereign, settling the question for at least that particular village. But the state's appropriation of funds to fight Native sovereignty rankled Native leaders. Since the Supreme Court finding, the state has worked to accommodate Native village independence, if not full sovereignty, in many cases and circumstances. But the relationship between villages and the state is not settled.

As the state's fiscal gap widened, reflecting declining tax revenues from petroleum production, state legislators began to cut government services that had previously been considered immune. Among these were state funds for Native schools and for fuel costs to power electric generators in Native villages. Few Alaska Native villages can sustain themselves economically and thus have little or no tax base; they rely on the state for essential services. Native leaders fought the cuts vigorously, and with the governor's help, found some alternative funds. But these initiatives by the legislature further deepened the rift between Native Alaska and the legislature and the majority of Alaskans who elected the legislature.

Still another major issue exacerbated the rift and presented the governor with a major political challenge: subsistence. In all states, state governments manage fish and game on federal lands within the state's borders, unless Congress empowers a federal agency to manage the resources; the resources must be managed in a manner consistent with federal mandates. But in Alaska those mandates brought the state into conflict with the federal government once again. The Alaska state constitution provides that the natural resources of the state belong to all its people equally. However, in the Alaska National Interest Lands Conservation Act of 1980, the U.S. Congress included a provision mandating that the United States guarantee a preferential use of subsistence resources for rural residents in the state, a provision directed primarily at Native subsistence. Acknowledging the pending legislation, in 1978 the state legislature enacted a rural subsistence preference. However, in 1985 the Alaska Supreme Court struck down the rural preference as a violation of the state constitution.[39]

The legislature quickly passed another rural preference law, which the state supreme court also struck down.[40] Interpreting ANILCA as a mandate to guarantee the preference for Native Alaskans, federal courts ordered the state to come into compliance with the federal law. Successive legislatures in the 1990s, however, refused to take measures to do so, even when urged by the state's congressional delegation. And the legislature appropriated funds to fight the federal mandate. In 1998 and 1999, at the direction of the federal courts, federal managers took over the management of fish and game on federal lands in Alaska, and on state lands and waters through which migratory species move to and from federal land.

These actions by the legislature were interpreted by some Alaska Native leaders as an open attack. Byron Mallott, former executive of Sealaska, the Southeast Alaska regional development corporation, and former chair of the board of the Alaska Permanent Fund Trustees, wrote an opinion piece for the state's largest circulation newspaper under the heading "It's Not a Good Time to Be an Alaska Native." "I have come to the point of despair," Mallot wrote. "Having been born a Native, raised in my village and having my life in Alaska, I can say with conviction that there has not been a worse moment in Alaska's recent history for Alaska's Native peoples than now."[41] State political and civic leaders moved quickly after Mallot's assertion to build avenues for communication between urban and rural Alaska. But the continuing decline of state revenues, the legislature's recalcitrant refusal to amend the state constitution on subsistence preference, and the unwillingness of voters to entertain any other use of the Permanent Fund annual dividend except per capita distribution represented formidable challenges to such efforts. Over a decade later, however, as noted earlier, Mallot was elected Alaska's lieutenant governor, signaling an ease in tensions between Native Alaskans and state administration.

National environmental consciousness, manifest in executive policy and legislative action, continued to frame major public policy issues for Alaskans in the 1990s. In 1985, in a study provided for in ANILCA, the Interior Department reported its conclusion that there is a 20 percent chance that substantial oil resources, three to four billion barrels, underlie that portion of the Arctic National Wildlife Refuge (ANWR) immediately adjacent to Prudhoe Bay.[42] Since its creation the refuge had been closed to oil exploration and development. Oil companies were anxious for it to be opened, and state leaders supported opening of the refuge. Because ANWR is federal land, the state would not receive direct tax revenue from its development. However, the state would receive severance (for each barrel leaving the ground) and royalty payments and some economic benefit from construction.

American environmental leaders steadfastly opposed the opening of ANWR, as did the Clinton and later the Obama administrations, as well as a majority of the U.S. Congress, until the election of Donald Trump in 2016. ANWR is one of the few truly untrammeled areas of the state and home to one of the last vast migrating caribou herds in the North. It contains many unique species of flora and fauna. However, as American dependence on foreign oil sources continued and broadened, and as the composition of Congress changed, industry and state leaders hoped that the Congress would change its policy on the issue. Most Alaskans when polled support opening the refuge. This includes the Inuit on the North Slope who, through local government powers, have taxed production at Prudhoe Bay since the beginning of the oil flow there. However, Gwitchin Athabaskan Indians who live in villages at the southern edge of the refuge vehemently oppose its opening. They are dependent on the migrating caribou as a major subsistence resource and fear that oil production would disrupt the migratory patterns of the herds. They also fear destruction of their way of life. With the election of Trump and Republican majorities in both houses of Congress in 2016, Congress voted to open ANWR to exploratory drilling, and the Interior Department announced preparation of lease sales for that purpose.

In 2002, at the end of Governor Tony Knowles's (D) eight years, Alaska's U.S. senator Frank Murkowski (R) won election as Alaska's governor. It is unusual for a sitting U.S. senator to resign the seat, but that is what Murkowski did. That may have been partly because he and Alaska's senior U.S. senator, Ted Stevens (who had been appointed in 1968, on the sudden death of Senator Bob Bartlett, and subsequently elected in his own right) had, at best, a frosty relationship. Having resigned his seat, Murkowski had to choose someone to complete his six-year term in the Senate. Murkowski interviewed a number of people, some of whom came away convinced he had promised them the seat and also felt they deserved it; one of those was Wasilla mayor and member of the Alaska Oil and Gas Commission Sarah Palin. Instead, Murkowski chose his daughter, Lisa Murkowski, to complete his Senate term; she was then a member of the state House of Representatives and known as a moderate, centrist, conservative Republican. Two years later, Lisa Murkowski won election in her own right as U.S. senator from Alaska

During his term as governor, Frank Murkowski vigorously pursued funding and agreement with the oil industry for a natural gas pipeline from the North Slope to tidewater (Prince William Sound, most likely), to market Alaska's natural gas. Alaska has an extraordinary amount of natural gas, which, if sold, would be an economic bonanza for the state. Alaska politicians have been working on a development package for a natural gas pipeline for fifty years. The problem is that there is a glut of natural gas in the world, and most of it is closer to markets and cheaper to develop than Alaska's natural gas. That has been the holdup for decades and may well be for a long time yet. China has recently expressed interest in talking about Alaska natural gas, but many are skeptical that talks will lead eventually to a project.

Frank Murkowski also had a difficult relationship with the press and the public. He often seemed arrogant, uncommunicative, and belligerent, and his administration was not very transparent (people could not easily find out what was going on and what decisions were being made). Meanwhile, Alaska voters elected a large conservative majority in both chambers of the state legislature. Members of that majority favored less regulatory oversight and lessening the tax obligation of oil producers in Alaska. At the same time, Alaska politicians attacked the federal government for impeding economic development in the state by unduly restricting access to environmentally sensitive and protected lands, such as the Tongass National Forest and the Arctic National Wildlife Refuge.

When Lisa Murkowski was elected U.S. senator in 2004, Sarah Palin decided to run for governor. As a member of the Alaska Oil and Gas Commission (which has some regulatory authority over the operation of oil production), she revealed to the public that a fellow member of the commission, Randy Ruedrich, chair of the Alaska Republican Party, was using his state office to conduct party business, a violation of the law. Ruedrich was subsequently fined the largest ethical violation fine ever handed down in Alaska. This confirmed Sarah Palin's reputation as a "maverick," not a party team player. Two years later, Palin won election as Alaska's governor.

During her gubernatorial term Palin worked with Democrats in the state legislature to increase taxes on oil production in Alaska and to strengthen ethics regulations for legislators and public officials. This did not endear her to Republican Party loyalists. One potentially successful initiative was the Alaska Gas Incentive Act (AGIA), passed in 2007. An attempt to finally secure funding for a natural gas pipeline from the North Slope, the act committed $500 million to any company that would generate a successful funding scheme and design for a pipeline. In 2008 the state granted a license under AGIA to an international pipeline company, TransCanada. By 2013 the state had paid TransCanada $300 million. But the rise of shale oil and gas extraction in the continental states after 2008 produced a glut of natural gas and doomed Alaska's prospects as a natural gas supplier. Alaska terminated the license in that year.

Despite her legislative endeavors, Palin early emerged as a public official who seemed uninterested in details, who appeared not to like the

Governor Sarah Palin addressing the U.S. Army 1st Stryker Brigade Combat Team, 25th Infantry Division, at Fort Wainwright, Alaska, upon their deployment to Iraq in 2008. Alaska State Archive SR612 AS 33772.

tedious, day-to-day duties and responsibilities of administering a government, who had a short attention span, and who was mercurial in her interpersonal relationships with people in the government.

During Palin's time as governor, and unbeknownst to her, the FBI and the U.S. Justice Department began a quiet investigation of the owner of an oil exploration and production service company, Bill Allen. Allen had secured a number of contracts with Exxon for cleanup of the 1989 *Exxon Valdez* oil spill, had made a great deal of money, and through his campaign contributions and other activities had become a major player in Alaska Republican politics. Unschooled in politics and public service, and flamboyant and very self-confident, he had participated in bribing several state legislators and lobbyists, mostly on behalf of the oil industry, personnel who likely had some knowledge of Allen's activities but did not actively participate in them. The investigation ultimately led to the conviction of six sitting Alaska legislators and several lobbyists on bribery and corruption charges; several served prison time as a result. Allen himself served almost two years in prison, his sentence lessened by cooperating with prosecutors in the conviction of legislators. The state did not undertake prosecution of Allen or the legislators he bribed. The investigations and prosecutions of the offenders were conducted by the Public Integrity Section of the U.S. Justice Department, the FBI, and the Internal Revenue Service.

In 2008, Senator John McCain (R-Arizona) ran for president against Senator Barrack Obama (D-Illinois); McCain selected Alaska governor Sarah Palin as his vice-presidential running mate. Obama won the election. The McCain campaign had not vetted Palin very well, and during the campaign she emerged as a person who did not know much about national policy issues, who spoke off-the-cuff without knowing what she was talking about, and who otherwise embarrassed the McCain campaign with her lack of knowledge, understanding, or interest in public affairs. She was, however, a very effective campaigner, focusing on rhetorical presentations that emphasized the simplistic understandings of conservative issues that McCain's base supporters were interested in. Soon after the failed campaign, Palin, who had emerged as a media star, resigned as governor, an unprecedented action in Alaska. Her term was completed by her lieutenant governor, Sean Parnell, who was elected in his own right in 2010. In that same year, Lisa Murkowski was reelected U.S. senator.

Meanwhile, beginning in 2006, the FBI had begun to investigate Senator Ted Stevens, who was subsequently charged with violating U.S. Senate ethics laws by failing to report gifts barred by law. One such gift involved improvements to a house Stevens owned in Girdwood at Alyeska ski resort; the improvements were paid for by Bill Allen. Stevens was charged. Stevens was one of the most powerful people in American politics; he had served in the Senate nearly forty years, one of the longest-serving senators, and he had a reputation as a tough but fair negotiator and as someone totally committed to Alaska (as explained earlier, he had served in the Interior Department during the campaign for Alaska statehood). He had been chair of the Senate Appropriations Committee, which, with the companion House committee, manages the federal budget. He was likely targeted by the U.S. Justice Department to show that even the powerful are not above the law. With a reelection campaign coming in 2008, Stevens insisted that his trial be accelerated so that it would conclude before the election; he was confident of acquittal. Normally such a trial would take many months, but Stevens's legal team rushed the proceedings. Unexpectedly, he was convicted, just weeks before the November election. He subsequently lost his reelection bid to Democrat Mark Begich.

In subsequent months, irregularities came to light in the Justice Department's preparation of the case against Stevens. These were caused by the accelerated pace of the the preparation. The irregularities were serious enough that the conviction was vacated, exonerating Stevens. No one was charged with any violations of law in the trial preparation. Tragically, Stevens himself was later killed in a small airplane crash in Alaska, 9 August 2010.

In 2010 Lisa Murkowski was reelected to the U.S. Senate. She lost the primary election to a far-right conservative candidate, Joe Miller, but decided to run a write-in campaign. With the help of money raised by Alaska's Native corporations, she won; in American history, only one other sitting U.S. senator had won a write-in reelection campaign. She would be reelected again in 2016.

In 2014 Democrat Mark Begich was defeated in his reelection bid by Dan Sullivan, who had served as Alaska attorney general and commissioner of natural resources under Governor Sean Parnell.

In 1972, as noted previously, Alaska's lone member of the U.S. House of Representatives, Democrat Nick Begich, went missing in a small plane traveling from Anchorage to Juneau. After a presumptive death hearing, Republican Don Young of Fort Yukon defeated Democrat Emil Notti in a special election. Young has been reelected to the seat every two years since that time, becoming one of the longest-serving members of the U.S. House.

One-third of Alaska's economic base has derived from oil, including taxes on production as well as money spent for exploration and operations. The tax Alaska collects from oil production and other sources related to oil production depends partly on the world price of a barrel of oil. In 2008, oil prices rose dramatically from a norm of $40 or $50 to $140; then just as dramatically the price fell, down by 2009 to under $40 a barrel. Alaska's annual budget is about $5.5 billion. To balance the budget (revenue equaling expenditures), Alaska needs a price of about $75 a barrel. As noted earlier, in 1991 the Hickel administration negotiated settlement of a tax dispute with the oil industry going back to the beginning of North Slope production in 1977; the several billion dollar settlement was placed in a special fund called the Constitutional Budget Reserve. In the years after 2009 the state legislature used money from the CBR and other reserves to balance the state budget. But the legislature failed to develop a comprehensive fiscal plan that would resolve the budget gap. In 2017 the legislature elected to use some of the earnings of the Alaska Permanent Fund. At the same time, Governor Bill Walker, elected in 2014 (running as an independent), used his authority to reduce the amount of the Permanent Fund dividend by about half for 2017 and 2018, dedicating the money to the state budget to help bridge the shortfall gap. Walker was defeated for reelection (along with Lieutenant Governor Byron Mallott) by conservative Republican Mike Dunleavy.

Most Alaskans fear that without new natural resource development, the state's dependent economy, exacerbated by recession accompanying the drop in oil prices and the state fiscal shortfall, may become weak and unable to support new or even existing jobs. This fear is exacerbated somewhat by the expanded British Petroleum Company (the merged BP-Amoco-ARCO entity): the near monopoly may limit its Alaska activities if it finds more profit in other world oil deposits. But many Alaskans find the federal government at the source of most of their discontent. They resent continuing federal control of potential Alaska economic resources and with that control, national environmental leaders who tout ANWR, again, as America's last wilderness. This same juxtaposition of interest, anxiety, and sentiment is manifest in debate over management of the Tongass National Forest, Glacier Bay National Monument, and the new conservation lands withdrawn by ANILCA. Little, it seems, is new in the new millennium

In the meantime the urban replication corridor along the coast and into the Interior along the railbelt continues to grow and prosper. At the end of the decade Wal-Mart opened two facilities in Anchorage, with plans for more stores there and in other urban centers. Urban Alaska resembles urban America more completely with each new single-story "box" store (Home Depot, Office Depot, Lowe's Hardware) and each new subdivision. The built environment expands inexorably into the wilderness, and few Alaskans, it seems, are willing to curtail that expansion in the name of wilderness preservation or environmental integrity. In 1907 at the height of the debate over whether to dam the Hetch Hetchy River in Yosemite National Park to provide water for San Francisco, a signal event in the history of American conservation, President Theodore Roosevelt wrote to naturalist John Muir that he did not think most Americans would take the side of wilderness in a showdown with the material needs of an expanding civilization.[43] In Alaska this sentiment, coupled with latent but potent resentment of federal power, remained at the end of the twentieth century and in the first decades of the twenty-first the dominant paradigm by which most residents understood their history and their whereabouts.

Epilogue

IN 1990, WHEN Alaska voters again elected Walter Hickel as their governor, the veteran Alaska booster campaigned on a theme of more development. He coined the term "owner state," which became a mantra of the campaign and of his public appearances as governor. Alaska, he said, must become an "owner state," taking control over the development of the state's abundance of natural resources. In calling for Alaska to define the terms of its economic future rather than, as he implied, to be the pawn of absentee investors such as cannery owners or the oil industry, Hickel stood firmly in the tradition of James Wickersham and Ernest Gruening. This was the anticolonial tradition of Alaska political life, the vision of an independent Alaska whose people have control over their region's destiny. Wickersham and Gruening had sought to gain control through greater self-government, a territorial legislature in Wickersham's time and statehood in Gruening's. But self-government turned out to be no panacea for the region's dependence on outside capital. Market forces and the capitalist considerations of outside investors determined whether Alaska's resources would be developed, not protestations or propositions from Alaska politicians. Additionally, in labeling Alaska an "owner state," Hickel was offering a positive interpretation of the section of the Alaska statehood act that prohibits the state from alienating any of its mineralized lands; the state may lease them, but not sell them.

Exactly how Alaskans might take more control of their economic circumstances remained unclear in Hickel's program. For a Republican such as Hickel it did not mean that the state should form its own corporations to mine gold or molybdenum, or to explore for new oil fields, or develop geothermal power sources. It probably did not mean increasing the tax

burden on the oil industry, because that was likely to result in less exploration and development. Hickel repeatedly called for diversification of the
economy, but investors' attempts to start new enterprises in Alaska were
usually defeated by the higher costs of labor and transportation. Only
small package transshipment by global air freight companies at the
Anchorage airport seemed to hold promise for new business beginnings,
and the state could do little more than offer standard tax incentives and a
new runway. The freight companies' decisions to expand or contract
their Anchorage operations lay not in runways, but in the volume of the
global freight business. Another business, tourism, grew at an annual rate
of about 4 percent. But because most of the visitors came as part of pre-sold,
package tours marketed by companies outside Alaska who kept tight rein
on where their clients might go and for how long, the bulk of the profit
from that business stayed outside Alaska. The state could do little beyond
purchasing television advertising at the annual Superbowl. In any case
with petroleum and the earnings of the Alaska Permanent Fund providing 85 percent or more of state revenue, the tourism industry contributed
only a small part of state general revenue.

Presenting an image of "cleaning house," Hickel began his term in office
with a flurry of activity, vowing to replace large numbers of commissioners and bureaucrats and to change the political character of a number of
advisory boards; in reality, he actually replaced very few. But Hickel did
undertake three actions that aggressively advanced the interests of the
state. First, he ordered his attorney general to bring to conclusion several outstanding cases for back taxes with oil companies. The negotiated
settlements led to a $1 billion deposit to the Constitutional Budget
Reserve. Because the agreements prohibited public release of the settlement details, however, voters had no way to determine if the state's
interests had been well served. Second, the governor pushed to early
resolution settlement of the civil and criminal suits stemming from the
Exxon Valdez spill. But the federal district judge with jurisdiction initially rejected the settlement, saying that $900 million in civil damages
and $100 million in criminal penalties were insufficient to inconve-
nience Exxon Corporation. On reconsideration the judge accepted the
agreement. At the same time, as noted, the class action suit filed by residents of Prince William Sound languished in the courts for over twenty
years, while the original jury-ordered settlement of about $5 billion was
reduced to $50 million.

In a third initiative, however, Hickel stumbled badly. The governor cherished the idea that the Alaska statehood act was a solemn compact between the Congress and the State that Congress could not change unilaterally. Because the statehood act had been approved by a vote of the people of Alaska, Hickel reasoned, any change would have to be agreed to by a vote of the people. But the governor misunderstood the nature of federal sovereignty and the federal-state relationship in the United States. Then–vice president John C. Calhoun had made this same argument in 1828 in his *South Carolina Exposition and Protest*. President Andrew Jackson and the courts had seen the fallacy in and rejected the argument that the states are equal to the federal government, as had the Constitutional Convention in Philadelphia in 1787 and Abraham Lincoln in the Civil War: state equality with the federal government would almost certainly eliminate cultural cohesion and lead to disunion, resulting in the ultimate failure of democracy.

Manifesting a profound ignorance of history, however, Hickel and his advisors, perhaps bolstered by Sagebrush Rebellion rhetoric, sued the federal government for violation of the statehood "compact," requesting $29 billion in damages. The state argued that if Congress had honored the "compact" by allowing the state to complete its land selections as provided in the statehood act before allowing Natives, under the Alaska Native Claims Settlement Act of 1971, to select 44 million acres of Alaska land, and before subsequently taking 104 million acres more for itself in conservation reserves under the Alaska National Interest Lands Conservation Act of 1980, the federal government could have sold mineral leases on all of that land and have paid the state the 90 percent of such revenue as provided in the statehood act; the state calculated that those payments would have added up to $29 billion. Constitutional scholars around the country thought the state had no chance whatsoever of winning the suit, and not surprisingly, the U.S. Court of Federal Claims dismissed it. The judge pointed out in his finding that "a statehood act cannot be analogized to a commercial contract"; Congress is bound by what it provides in a statehood act only if it says explicitly in the act that it intends to be bound. There is no such congressional intention expressed in the Alaska statehood act. Both the Ninth Circuit Court of Appeals and the U.S. Supreme Court confirmed the district court's finding, the Supreme Court by refusing to hear the case. Hickel apparently did not realize that Congress must be free to change its legislation to conform to changing public opinion, to changes in society's will.[1]

In his wish that Alaska be equal to the federal government in sovereignty, Hickel was at one with a long tradition in the American West, where the imagery and rhetoric of self-reliance and rugged individualism have always generated similar desires. Hickel was unusual only in acting so stubbornly in service to his wish, although not remarkably unusual, for in the history of federal litigation Hickel's proposition has been tested and found wanting many times. Hickel was also typically western in his wish that Alaska be in control of its economic destiny. Historian Bernard de Voto characterized the West as a "plundered province" decades ago, dominated by eastern capital and world capitalist conditions.[2] Increased population and the generation of local capital have been helpful in reducing the West's dependence on outside investment, as has been diversity in the economic enterprises of outsiders.

Alaska's dependence, its colonial status, is a function of its people's desire to replicate in the North the material and institutional nature of American culture. Such replication has been possible because the technologies of modern civilization have been imported to Alaska (from the automobile to the communications satellite) and because economic development has created jobs, wages, and profits with which to establish the services and import the consumer goods characteristic of that lifestyle. Dependence is exacerbated by the limited scope of Alaska's attraction to outside investors. Petroleum is Alaska's only resource greatly in demand on the world market. There is little demand for gold, the demand for Alaska fish is declining, and the demand for Alaska timber logs has slackened considerably. Since the discovery of oil at Prudhoe Bay, Alaska's destiny has been principally controlled by oil, not by its politicians' wishful thinking.

The federal government is the second dominant force in Alaska, as it has been historically, both in Alaska and in the American West. Without federal support settlement and development of the sort acceptable to non-Native immigrants would not have been feasible in Alaska. Today the federal establishment, the "federal brigade," in Alaska is vast, including the military, the various public lands agencies, Native service agencies, and general civic affairs, such as aviation. This, too, Alaska shares with the West. And as westerners have had to do, Alaskans have had to accommodate to federal protection of Native rights and lands. The federal trust relationship with Natives supersedes the state's rights in certain areas (such as access to subsistence resources) and not in others (such as Native village sovereignty). The inconsistency between the rhetoric of freedom and the realities of federal limitations on freedom have confused many people in Alaska and in the American West.

Alaska has been overtaken by the national will on several occasions, as has the American West. Between the Alaska statehood act and the passage of the National Environmental Protection Act in 1969, American culture underwent a sea change. The civil rights revolution prompted Americans finally to address the issue of discrimination against minorities, including aboriginal people. Anxiety over guaranteeing the purity of water and air resources, as well as a new understanding of the nature of wilderness, led to a new environmental sensitivity. Neither of these perceptual and substantive changes represent conspiracies by special interest groups against majoritarian sentiment. Rather, they represent a change in the thinking of the majority of Americans. As the Congress moved to implement the new policies, Alaska, like much of the American West, was caught in this change. Ostensibly, the interests of the Native minority and of the uninhabited environment were placed ahead of the interests of Alaskans. No federal laws were violated in this implementation, nor was the U.S. Constitution. And in fact, Alaskan economic interests were protected. Economically viable lands were exempted from the lands legislation in 1980 in such areas as the Tongass National Forest and the world-class lead and zinc deposit at Red Dog north of Kotzebue. The state is still left with more than one hundred million acres of its own land, for which it has yet to develop consistent management policies.

The idea of an exceptional Alaskan spirit continues to dominate representations of Alaska in fiction, nonfiction, and casual publicity (such as tourism advertisements), a spirit characterized by greater individualism, self-reliance, and initiative than in the rest of America. Alaska's noncontiguity, sparse population, vast quasi-wilderness areas, and long winters all reinforce this notion of difference. But in terms of social and institutional context, there is more similarity to the rest of American settlement, particularly western settlement, in Alaska than there is real difference. Settlement away from the coast and the railbelt, by Natives and non-Natives, is considerably different. It is characterized by greater subsistence use and by much higher costs and more primitive "frontier" conditions. The 75 percent of Alaskans living in urban places often lump their Alaska with the more "genuine" Alaska and acquire uniqueness by the association. But as Governor Hickel learned, wishing it so does not make it so.

Always subject to the vicissitudes of world supply and demand, oil prices in 2010, having reached an all-time high of over $140 per barrel, fell, as noted, to under $40 per barrel. They remained low in subsequent years, seldom reaching much above $55 per barrel.[3] The effect on Alaska was devastating, where to be balanced, the annual budget of over $5 billion needs a price of about $75 per barrel. Faced with a severe revenue decline, the state legislature drew on the various budget reserves, effectively draining them. In 2017 and 2018 Governor Bill Walker cut the amount of the annual Alaska Permanent Fund dividend payment to all residents to help offset the revenue shortage. At the same time, because of reduced revenue from oil production, which is linked to the price of oil, the Permanent Fund became the largest producer of Alaska state revenue. The pressure on the governor and the legislature to use some of the fund's annual earnings to balance the state budget was enormous and generated debate over whether such use constituted the best use of the fund's earnings. Anti-tax sentiment runs high in Alaska, and successive state legislatures refused to implement a state income tax, which analysts argued was, with use of some Permanent Fund annual earnings, the best way to balance the state budget. One university economist argued that oil had not in fact made Alaska richer, a claim many found counterintuitive.[4]

In the future Alaska's economy likely will continue to be based on resource extraction, and Alaska is likely to continue to function as a colony for corporate investment in its resources and in the transportation and supply networks that help to sustain its population. As the population continues to increase, Alaskans also will likely continue to struggle with the basic conceptual dichotomy between development and environmental protection, that is, between development and wilderness. The sparseness of the population will encourage Alaskans to continue to view themselves as unique, but for many this will also present greater opportunity for visibility and influence. The character of Alaskan society will reflect the residents' assumptions about themselves, their understanding of their circumstances and the choices they make. A better understanding of the history of Alaska would make those assumptions and choices more realistic.

NOTES

PROLOGUE

1. U.S. Department of the Interior, *Alaska at Mid-century* (Washington, D.C.: Government Printing Office, 1952); Herb Rhodes, "Why an Alaskan Reporter?" *Alaskan Reporter* 1 (January 1952): 4; John McPhee, *Coming into the Country* (New York: Farrar, Straus, and Giroux, 1977); Robert Hedin and Gary Holthaus, *Alaska: Reflections on Land and Spirit* (Tucson: University of Arizona Press, 1989).

2. Alaska Department of Labor, *Annual Report 1999* (Juneau: Alaska Department of Labor, 1999), 1–4.

3. Al Gibbs, "Boat from Tacoma," *Anchorage Daily News,* from the "We Alaskans" supplement, 24 March 1996, H6–H13; Will Swagel, "Alaska and the Pacific Northwest: A Century of Service," *Alaska Business Monthly* 13 (March 1997): 30–33.

4. Tom Kizzia, *In the Wake of the Unseen Object: Among the Native Cultures of Bush Alaska* (New York: Henry Holt and Company, 1991); A. J. McClanahan, *Growing Up Native in Alaska* (Anchorage: Cook Inlet Region Inc., 2000).

5. Robert Arnold, *Alaska Native Claims Settlement* (Anchorage: Alaska Native Foundation, 1974).

6. David Treuer, *The Heartbeat of Wounded Knee: Native America from 1890 to the Present* (New York: Riverhead Books, 2018); Rosita Worl, "Models of Sovereignty and Survival in Alaska," *Cultural Survival Quarterly Magazine,* September 2003, https://www.culturalsurvival.org/publications/cultural-survival-quarterly/models-sovereignty-and-survival-alaska, accessed 19 May 2019.

7. Svetlana Fedorova, *The Russian Population in Alaska and California, Late Eighteenth Century–1867,* ed. Richard A. Pierce and Alton S. Donnelly (Kingston, Ont.: Limestone Press, 1973).

8. James R. Gibson, *Imperial Russia in Frontier America: The Changing Geography of Supply of Russian America, 1784–1867* (New York: Oxford University Press, 1976);

Gibson, "Russian Dependence on the Natives of Alaska," in S. Frederick Starr, ed., *Russia's American Colony* (Durham, N.C.: Duke University Press, 1987), 77–104; Richard Mackie, *Trading beyond the Mountains: The British Fur Trade on the Pacific, 1793–1843* (Vancouver: University of British Columbia Press, 1997), 140–41, 180–83, 203, 238, 271, 316.

INTRODUCTION

1. Scott A. Elias, *The Ice-Age History of Alaskan National Parks* (Washington, D.C.: Smithsonian Institution Press, 1995).

2. In the territorial period, Congress created four judicial divisions, which also served as election districts: 1st Division: Southeast, with the judicial seat at Juneau; 2nd Division: Seward Peninsula, with the judicial seat at Nome; 3rd Division: South-central, with the judicial seat at Valdez until 1929, when it was moved to Anchorage; 4th Division: Interior, with the judicial seat at Eagle until 1903, then at Fairbanks.

3. Alfred H. Brooks, *The Geography of Alaska, with an Outline of the Geomorphology* (Washington, D.C.: Government Printing Office, 1905); Burton L. Fryxell, ed., *Blazing Alaska's Trails* (Fairbanks: University of Alaska Press, 1973).

4. Here I have relied heavily on Stephen J. Langdon, *The Native People of Alaska* (Anchorage: Greatland Graphics, 1993).

5. Environmental historians have used the phrase "second nature"—which in common parlance has meant the things we take for granted as a permanent part of the world as we understand it—to mean the products of modes of production that use technology to transform unaltered nature; see Don Worster, "Transformations of the Earth: Toward an Agroecological Perspective in History," part of the special issue "A Roundtable: Environmental History," *Journal of American History* 76 (1990): 1087–106.

6. In 1992, Undersecretary of the Interior Ada Deer recognized 226 Native tribes in Alaska. The Alaska Native Claims Settlement Act of 1971 recognized 211 Native villages. The discrepancy in this number stems from the fact that there is more than one tribal group in some of the villages and some tribal groups are not in named villages.

7. Morgan B. Sherwood, *Big Game in Alaska: A History of Wildlife and People* (New Haven, Conn.: Yale University Press, 1981), 108–20.

8. William Dietrich, *Northwest Passage: The Great Columbia River* (Seattle: University of Washington Press, 1995), 154–56; Richard White, *Organic Machine: The Remaking of the Columbia River* (New York: Hill and Wang, 1995), 90–92.

9. Margaret Szasz, ed., *Between Indian and White Worlds* (Norman: University of Oklahoma Press, 1994); James Clifton, ed., *Being and Becoming Indian:*

Biographical Studies of North American Frontiers (Belmont, Conn.: Wadsworth Publishing Company, 1988).

10. Robert F. Spencer, *The North Alaskan Eskimo: A Study in Ecology and Society*, Smithsonian Institution Bureau of Ethnology Bulletin No. 171 (Washington, D.C.: Government Printing Office, 1959). I have relied heavily on the material in Langdon, *The Native Peoples of Alaska*, for the description of physical characteristics, material culture, and other Native Alaskan attributes.

11. Sergei Kan, *Symbolic Immortality: The Tlingit Potlatch of the Nineteenth Century* (Washington, D.C.: Smithsonian Institution Press, 1989).

12. Robert Fortuine, *Chills and Fever: Health and Disease in the Early History of Alaska* (Fairbanks: University of Alaska Press, 1989). Tuberculosis, although not a virgin soil epidemic in Alaska, afflicted vast numbers of the Alaska Native population in the 1930s, 1940s, and 1950s, partly as a result of the concentration of people in larger villages where, ironically, government services were available.

CHAPTER 1: RUSSIAN AMERICA, AN INTRODUCTION

1. George V. Lantzeff and Richard A. Pierce, *Eastward to Empire: Exploration and Conquest on the Russian Open Frontier to 1750* (Montreal: McGill-Queen's University Press, 1973); Raymond H. Fisher, "Finding America," in Barbara Sweetland Smith and Redmond Barnett, eds., *Russian America: The Forgotten Frontier* (Tacoma: Washington State Historical Society, 1990), 3–19.

2. James R. Gibson, *Imperial Russia in Frontier America: The Changing Geography of Supply in Russian America, 1784–1867* (New York: Oxford University Press, 1976).

3. Ibid.; James R. Gibson, "Russian Dependence on the Natives of Alaska," in S. Frederick Starr, ed., *Russia's American Colony* (Durham, N.C.: Duke University Press, 1987), 77–104.

CHAPTER 2: RUSSIAN EASTWARD EXPANSION
AND THE KAMCHATKA EXPEDITIONS

1. Mark Bassin, "Inventing Siberia: Visions of the Russian East in the Early Nineteenth Century," *American Historical Review* 96 (June 1991): 763–94.

2. James R. Gibson, "The Significance of Siberia to Tsarist Russia," *Canadian Slavonic Papers* 14 (1972): 442–53.

3. James R. Gibson, *Feeding the Russian Fur Trade: Provisionment of the Okhotsk Seaboard and the Kamchatka Peninsula, 1639–1856* (Madison: University of Wisconsin Press, 1969).

4. George V. Lantzeff and Richard A. Pierce, *Eastward to Empire: Exploration and Conquest on the Russian Open Frontier* (Montreal: McGill-Queen's University Press, 1973); James R. Gibson, "Russian Expansion in Siberia and America:

Critical Contrasts," in S. Frederick Starr, ed., *Russia's American Colony* (Durham, N.C.: Duke University Press, 1987), 32–40; Mark Bassin, "Expansion and Colonialism on the Eastern Frontier: Views of Siberia and the Far East in Pre-Petrine Russia," *Journal of Historical Geography* 14 (1988): 3–21.

5. Lewis Hanke, *All Mankind Is One: A Study of the Disputation between Bartolome de Las Casas and Juan Gines de Sepulveda in 1550 on the Intellectual and Religious Capacity of the American Indians* (DeKalb: Northern Illinois University Press, 1974), passim and 3–17.

6. Raymond H. Fisher, *The Voyage of Semen Dezhnev in 1648: Bering's Precursor, with Selected Documents* (London: Hakluyt Society, 1981).

7. John R. Bockstoce, *Furs and Frontiers in the Far North: The Contest among Native and Foreign Nations for the Bering Strait Fur Trade* (New Haven. Conn.: Yale University Press, 2010).

8. James R. Gibson, "Colonial Russian America," in S. Frederick Starr, ed., *Russia's American Colony* (Durham, N.C.: Duke University Press, 1987), 32–40.

9. Robert K. Massie, *Peter the Great: His Life and World* (New York: Alfred A. Knopf, 1980).

10. Carol Urness, "Russian Mapping of the North Pacific to 1792," in Stephen Haycox, James Barnett, and Caedmon Liburd, eds., *Enlightenment and Exploration in the North Pacific, 1741–1805* (Seattle: University of Washington Press, 1997), 132–46.

11. Raymond H. Fisher, "Finding America," in Barbara Sweetland Smith and Redmond J. Barnett, eds., *Russian America: The Forgotten Frontier* (Tacoma: Washington State Historical Society, 1990), 17–31. The translation is by Fisher. See also Fisher's *Bering's Voyages: Whither and Why* (Seattle: University of Washington Press, 1977).

12. The map was drawn by Evreinov in 1722, printed by a German mapmaker, Johann Baptist Homann; Urness, "Russian Mapping of the North Pacific to 1792," 132–48.

13. Fisher, "Finding America," 17–31.

14. The voyage is usually recorded in Gvozdev's name because Fedorov was too ill to act as navigator or to command the vessel. However, both kept logs that were submitted to the officials at Iakutsk.

15. The European colonizers either ignored the property and sovereign rights of the aboriginal inhabitants or argued them away on the basis of their lack of organization (i.e., civilization) and their lack of European and Christian values.

16. John M. Naish, "The Health of Mariners: Vancouver's Achievement," in Stephen Haycox, James Barnett, and Caedmon Liburd, eds., *Enlightenment and Exploration in the North Pacific, 1741–1805* (Seattle: University of Washington Press, 1997), 79–87.

17. The island group would be named the Commander Islands, and the island on which he and his crew were marooned, Bering Island, in his honor.

18. Georg Wilhelm Steller, *Journal of a Voyage with Bering, 1741–1742*, ed. O. W. Frost, trans. Margritt A. Engel and O. W. Frost (Stanford, Calif.: Stanford University Press, 1988).

19. James R. Gibson, *Otter Skins, Boston Ships, and China Goods: The Maritime Fur Trade of the Northwest Coast, 1785–1841* (Seattle: University of Washington Press, 1992).

CHAPTER 3: EXPLOITATION AND THE ORIGINS
OF THE CONTEST FOR SOVEREIGNTY

1. Raisa V. Makarova, *Russians on the Pacific, 1743–1799*, trans. Richard A. Pierce and Alton S. Donnelly (Kingston, Ont.: Limestone Press, 1975), 209–17. This is a gross figure.

2. James R. Gibson, "Russian Expansion in Siberia and America: Critical Contrasts," in S. Frederick Starr, ed., *Russia's American Colony* (Durham, N.C.: Duke University Press, 1987), 32–42.

3. James R. Gibson, "Sitka-Kyakhta versus Sitka-Canton: Russian America and the China Market," *Pacifica* 2 (November 1990): 35–79.

4. Richard A. Pierce, *Russian America: A Biographical Dictionary* (Kingston, Ont.: Limestone Press, 1990), 38–39, 511; Vasilii N. Berkh, *A Chronological History of the Discovery of the Aleutian Islands*, trans. and ed. Richard A. Pierce (1823; reprint, Kingston, Ont.: Limestone Press, 1974).

5. Raisa V. Makarova, *Russians on the Pacific, 1743–1799*, trans. and ed. Richard A. Pierce (Kingston, Ont.: Limestone Press, 1975), 38; *To Siberia and Russian America: Three Centuries of Russian Eastward Expansion*, vol. 2, *Russian Penetration of the North Pacific Ocean, 1700–1797*, ed. Basil Dmytryshyn, E. A. P. Crownhart-Vaughan, and Thomas Vaughan (Portland: Oregon Historical Society Press, 1988), xl ff.

6. James R. Gibson, "Russian Dependence on the Natives of Alaska," in S. Frederick Starr, ed., *Russia's American Colony* (Durham, N.C.: Duke University Press, 1987), 77–104.

7. Douglas W. Veltre, "Environmental Perspectives on Aleut Culture Change during the Russian Period," in Barbara Sweetland Smith and Redmond J. Barnett, eds., *Russian America: The Forgotten Frontier* (Tacoma: Washington State Historical Society, 1990), 4–5.

8. Svetlana Fedorova, *The Russian Population in Alaska and California, Late Eighteenth Century–1867*, ed. Richard A. Pierce and Alton S. Donnelly (Kingston, Ont.: Limestone Press, 1973).

9. Sir George Simpson, *Narrative of a Journey round the World, during the Years 1841–1842* (London: H. Colburn, 1847).

10. Lida C. Milan, "Ethnohistory of Disease and Medical Care among the Aleut," *Anthropological Papers of the University of Alaska* 16 (1974): 19, 20; Robert Fortuine, *Chills and Fevers: Health and Disease in the Early History of Alaska* (Fairbanks: University of Alaska Press, 1992).

11. Lydia T. Black, "Ivan Pan'kov: Architect of Aleut Literacy," *Arctic Anthropology* 14 (1977): 94–107.

12. Veltre, "Environmental Perspectives," 175–83.

13. Berkh, *Chronological History of the Discovery of the Aleutian Islands*; Pierce, *Russian America*; James R. Gibson, *Otter Skins, Boston Ships, and China Goods: The Maritime Fur Trade of the Northwest Coast, 1785–1841* (Seattle: University of Washington Press, 1992), 12–14.

14. Mari Sardi, "Early Contact between Aleuts and Russians, 1741–1780," *Alaska History* 1 (Fall/Winter 1975): 42–58.

15. So significant was the land that was not an island (i.e., the mainland) that the island next to it was called Unalaska, meaning "land which is not a land which is not an island."

16. Warren Cook, *Flood Tide of Empire: Spain and the Pacific Northwest, 1543–1819* (New Haven, Conn.: Yale University Press, 1973), 47–48.

17. Cook, *Flood Tide*, 86.

18. Benjamin Franklin, acting for several colonies as agent in England, wrote to ask that Cook's vessels not be interfered with, as they were on a scientific endeavor.

19. Andrew David, "From Cook to Vancouver: The British Contribution to the Cartography of Alaska," in Stephen Haycox, James K. Barnett, Caedmon A. Liburd, eds., *Enlightenment and Exploration in the North Pacific, 1741–1805* (Seattle: University of Washington Press, 1997), 116–31.

20. Cook Inlet Historical Society, "Legends and Legacies," www.alaskahistory.org /biographies/pennington-feodoria-kallander, accessed 5 March 2019; Wikipedia entry for Point Possession, Alaska, https://en.wikipedia.org/wiki/Point _Possession,_Alaska, accessed 19 May 2019.

21. Gannath Obeyesekere, *The Apotheosis of Captain Cook* (Princeton, N.J.: Princeton University Press, 1992), 3.

CHAPTER 4: GRIGORII SHELIKHOV AND
THE RUSSIAN AMERICAN COMPANY

1. Katerina Solovjova and Aleksandra Vovnyanko, "The Rise and Decline of the Lebedev-Lastochkin Company: Russian Colonization of South Central Alaska, 1787–1798," *Pacific Northwest Quarterly* 90 (Fall 1999): 191–205.

2. This interpretation, that war and diplomacy in Europe distracted Old World powers from making sovereign gains in the Americas, is generally summed up in a phrase often used by diplomatic historians: "Europe's distresses made America's successes." It is disputed by some historians but seems particularly apt for the contest on the Northwest Coast, at least in this early period.

3. Solovjova and Vovnhyanko, "Rise and Decline."

4. Ibid., 198.

CHAPTER 5: ALEKSANDR BARANOV

1. Ilya Vinkovetsky, *Russian America: An Overseas Colony of a Continental Empire, 1804–1867* (New York: Oxford University Press, 2011); Andrie Val'terovich Grinev, *Russian Colonization of Alaska: Preconditions, Discovery and Initial Development, 1741–1799*, trans. Richard L. Brand (Lincoln: University of Nebraska Press, 2018).

2. Svetlana G. Fedorova, *The Russian Population in Alaska and California, Late 18th Century, 1867*, trans. Richard A. Pierce and Alton S. Donnelly (Kingston, Ont.: Limestone Press, 1973).

3. *Creole* was a generic term referring to the mixed-heritage offspring of a Russian father and Native American mother, usually Aleut.

4. *To Siberia and Russian America: Three Centuries of Russian Eastward Expansion*, vol. 3, "Introduction," in Basil Dmytryshyn, E. A. P. Crownhart-Vaughan, and Thomas Vaughan, eds., *The Russian American Colonies, 1798–1867* (Portland: Oregon Historical Society Press, 1989).

5. James R. Gibson, *Otter Skins, Boston Ships, and China Goods: The Maritime Fur Trade of the Northwest Coast, 1785–1841* (Seattle: University of Washington Press, 1992); Winston Lee Sarafian, "Russian American Company Employee Policies and Practices, 1799–1867," Ph.D. dissertation, University of California, 1970.

6. Lydia Black, "The Creole Class in Russian America," *Pacifica* 2 (1990): 142–55.

7. Richard L. Dauenhauer, "Education in Russian America," in Barbara Sweetland Smith and Redmond J. Barnett, eds., *Russian America: The Forgotten Frontier* (Tacoma: Washington State Historical Society, 1990); Antoinette Shalkop, "The Russian Orthodox Church in Alaska," in S. Frederick Starr, ed., *Russia's American Colony* (Durham, N.C.: Duke University Press, 1987).

8. Shalkop, "Russian Orthodox Church."

9. Semen B. Okun, *The Russian American Company*, trans. Carl Ginsburg (Cambridge, Mass.: Harvard University Press, 1951).

10. George Thornton Emmons, *The Tlingit Indians*, ed. Frederica de Laguna (Seattle: University of Washington Press, 1991), 327ff.

11. Gibson, *Otter Skins, Boston Ships, and China Goods*, 137–203; James R. Gibson, *Imperial Russia in Frontier America: The Changing Geography of Supply of Russian America, 1784–1867* (New York: Oxford University Press, 1976).

12. Richard A. Pierce, *Russian America: A Biographical Dictionary* (Kingston, Ont.: Limestone Press, 1990), 397–98.

13. There are several interpretations of Baranov's removal, the most romanticized of which is by Hector Chevigny in *Russian America: The Great Alaskan Venture, 1741–1867* (New York: Viking Press, 1965), but more reliable accounts are in Semen Okun's history of the company, published in Russian in 1939 and translated into English by Carl Ginsburg (Cambridge, Mass.: Harvard University Press, 1951), and in Petr A. Tikhmenev's company history, written in 1868, translated by Richard Pierce and Alton Donnelly (Seattle: University of Washington Press, 1978). Kirill Khlebnikov's biography of Baranov was translated into English by Richard A. Pierce (Kingston, Ont.: Limestone Press, 1973).

CHAPTER 6: RUSSIAN AMERICA

1. William Appleman Williams, *American-Russian Relations, 1781–1947* (New York: Rinehart & Company, 1952), 8–18.

2. Geoffrey Blainey, *The Tyranny of Distance: How Distance Shaped Australia's History* (South Melbourne: Macmillan, 1982).

3. Stuart R. Tompkins, "Drawing the Alaskan Boundary," *Canadian Historical Review* 26 (1945): 1–24. See also Norman Graebner, "The Northwest Coast in Northern Diplomacy, 1790–1846," in David H. Stratton and George A. Frykman, eds., *The Changing Pacific Northwest: Interpreting Its Past* (Pullman: Washington State University Press, 1988), 1–22.

4. James R. Gibson, "Sitka versus Kodiak: Countering the Tlingit Threat and Situating the Colonial Capital of Russian America," *Pacific Historical Review* 67 (November 1998): 67–98.

5. Arkhimandritov had a remarkable career with the RAC and later with Hutchinson, Kohl and Company, the group of entrepreneurs that purchased much of the RAC's holdings following the purchase of Russian America by the United States in 1867. Born on St. George Island in the Pribylovs to a Tomsk teamster and a Pribylov Aleut woman, he attended Father Veniaminov's school at Unalaska and later a navigation school in St. Petersburg, having made his first voyage at about age eleven. Serving on a ship returning from California in 1842, Arkhimandritov took over the vessel when it was swamped in a sudden storm that killed the skipper and his assistant. He captained a number of colonial vessels and during the Crimean War served under an American captain when some colonial vessels were registered as American to avoid capture by the

British. In 1863 on a voyage to San Francisco he married an American woman, Caroline Otis Thompson Peters. After the American purchase he lived in San Francisco, and while working for Hutchinson, Kohl, he represented the people of the Pribylovs in their dealings with that company. Arkhimandritov likely died about 1872

6. Richard A. Pierce, *Russian America: A Biographical Dictionary* (Fairbanks: Limestone Press, 1990), 448; Fred John Sr., "Killing of the Russians at Batzulneta's Village," *Alaska Journal* 3 (Summer 1973): 147–48; Katherine Arndt, "Russian Explorations in North America," copy in possession of the author.

7. This story was related by Clarence Andrews in his history of Sitka and is included in Pierce, *Russian America*, 432ff, in the entry on Governor Nikolai Rozenberg.

8. James R. Gibson, "Russian Dependence on the Natives of Alaska," in S. Frederick Starr, ed., *Russia's American Colony* (Durham, N.C.: Duke University Press, 1987), 91, 92, 95.

9. Richard White, *"It's Your Misfortune and None of My Own": A History of the American West* (Norman: University of Oklahoma Press, 1991), 183–211.

10. Jean Barman, *The West beyond the West: A History of British Columbia* (Toronto: University of Toronto Press, 1991).

11. I am indebted to Barbara Sweetland Smith for information on Russian science in Russian America. Smith is curator of the exhibit *Science under Sail: Russia's Great Voyages to America, 1728–1867,* which opened at the Anchorage Museum of History and Art in 2000 and traveled to Calgary and San Francisco (California Academy of Sciences). Also see Katherine Arndt, "Consolidation and Expansion: The Russian American Co.," *Alaska Geographic* 26 (1999): 24–49; Pierce, *Russian America*; Richard Pierce, "Voznesenskii: Scientist in Alaska," *Alaska Journal* 5 (Winter 1975): 11–15; Terrence Cole, "Odyssey of a Russian Scientist: I. G. Voznesenskii in Alaska, California, and Siberia, 1839–49," *Pacific Northwest Quarterly* 80 (January 1989): 37–38.

12. A. I. Alekseev, *The Odyssey of a Russian Scientist: I. G. Voznesenskii in Alaska, California, and Siberia, 1839–1849,* trans. Wilma C. Follette, ed. Richard A. Pierce (Kingston, Ont.: Limestone Press, 1987).

13. Richard Dauenhauer, "Two Missions to Alaska," *Pacific Historian* 26 (Spring 1982): 29–41; but see also Stephen Haycox, "Sheldon Jackson and the Constitutionality of the School Contract System in Alaska, 1885–1894," *Pacific Historian* 28 (spring 1984): 18–28.

CHAPTER 7: THE SALE OF RUSSIAN AMERICA

1. Pavel Nikolaevich Golovin is not to be confused with naval captain Vasilii Mikhailovich Golovnin (1776–1831), the explorer and critic of the RAC.

2. James R. Gibson, "The Sale of Russian America to the United States," in S. Frederick Starr, ed., *Russia's American Colony* (Durham, N.C.: Duke University Press, 1987), 274. Gibson argues that the financial crisis of the 1860s was due to government interference more than from the economic failure of the colony itself. But the failure of various colonial enterprises, such as coal, gold mining, and whaling, suggests that Russian America could have been sustained only with a massive infusion of material and personnel resources such as the regime did not have and the government was loathe to condone.

3. P. N. Golovin, *The End of Russian America: Captain P. N. Golovin's Last Report*, trans. Basil Dmytryshyn and E. A. P. Crownhart-Vaughan (Portland: Oregon Historical Society, 1979).

4. As quoted in Gibson, "Sale of Russian America," 278; the original is in Semen Okun, *The Russian-American Company*, ed. B. D. Grekov, trans. Carl Ginsburg (Cambridge, Mass.: Harvard University Press, 1951), 225.

5. Barman, *West beyond the West*; Barry M. Gough, "The Character of the British Columbia Frontier," *BC Studies* 32 (1976–77): 28–40.

6. Nikolai N. Bolkhovitinov, "The Sale of Russian America in the Context of Russian American Relations," *Pacifica* 2 (1990): 156–71.

7. Gibson, "Sale of Russian America," 279.

8. Robert S. Cox, Rachel K. Onuf, and Lucien J. Frary, review of Andrei Grinev, *The Tlingit Indians in Russian America, Journal of the Early Republic* 28 (Winter 2008): 694–96.

9. Andrei V. Grinev, "Russian Politarism as the Main Reason for the Selling of Russian America," n.d., available at Academia, https://www.academia.edu/24762313/RUSSIAN_POLITARISM_AS_THE_MAIN_REASON_FOR_THE_SELLING_OF_ALASKA, accessed 19 May 2019.

CHAPTER 8: AMERICAN ALASKA, AN INTRODUCTION

1. As in other parts of the American West, Native leaders in Alaska devote considerable energy and resources to the revival of aspects of Alaska's Native cultures as a way of strengthening and clarifying Native identity and survival.

2. Patricia Nelson Limerick, *Legacy of Conquest: The Unbroken Past of the American West* (New York: W. W. Norton, 1987); Patricia Nelson Limerick, Clyde A. Milner II, and Charles Rankin, eds., *Trails: Toward a New Western History* (Lawrence: University Press of Kansas, 1991).

3. Clyde Milner II, *Oxford History of the American West* (New York: Oxford University Press, 1994).

4. Robert Fortuine, *Chills and Fever: Health and Disease in the Early History of Alaska* (Fairbanks: University of Alaska Press, 1989).

5. Richard White, *"It's Your Misfortune and None of My Own": A History of the American West* (Norman: University of Oklahoma Press, 1991), 184–86, 192–94. White has distinguished between types and patterns of migration to the American West. These include (1) kinship based, in which migrants moved to areas where there were relatives or people known to them from their communities, and where they sought to recreate the culture they had left; (2) utopian, in which migrants sought to create a new kind of society; and (3) modern, in which migrants did not intend to establish a new society but sought to create wealth that could be transferred back to the more settled regions.

6. Although framed by the Articles of Confederation government, both the land and civil governance ordinances were adopted by the first Congress under the new U.S. Constitution in 1789.

7. Jack Eblen, *The First and Second United States Empires: Governors and Territorial Government, 1784–1912* (Pittsburgh: University of Pittsburgh Press, 1968); but see Paul Gates, "An Overview of American Land Policy," *Agricultural History* 50 (January 1979): 213–29.

8. Mark Dowie, Jon Christensen, Weston Kosova, and Margaret Kriz, "The War for the West," special report, *Outside* 20 (November 1955): 55–75; R. McGreggor Cawley, *Federal Land, Western Anger: The Sagebrush Rebellion and Environmental Politics* (Lawrence: University Press of Kansas, 1993), passim.

9. There are exceptions, of course: people who came to Alaska specifically for its wilderness and the opportunity to live on the land by their own hand. But these numbers are very small, mostly because the challenge is great. Alaska's climate is harsh: winters are long, dark, and cold. Getting supplies to a wilderness setting is difficult and very expensive. Many of those who have made a go of wilderness living often give it up when their children approach puberty to give them exposures and opportunities comparable to most American young people. See Sam Wright, *Koviashuvik: Making a Home in the Brooks Range* (Tucson: University of Arizona Press, 1988).

10. In the Alaska Native Claims Settlement Act of 1971, Congress capitalized 12 (eventually 13) Native regional economic development corporations and (to date) 176 village economic development corporations with nearly $1 billion ($962.5 million), paid over a twenty-year period. These corporations do not represent a challenge to the thesis of colonialism, however, because most of the money is invested outside Alaska. In addition, these entities are incorporated under laws of the State of Alaska and function as modern, Western investment companies (indeed, the fact that they do is a significant criticism of the act). Moreover, corporate dividends, which many of the corporations began paying in significant amounts in the 1990s, have been used by the Native stockholders to purchase many Western goods deemed necessary to a satisfactory lifestyle in the modern era.

11. See William G. Robbins, *Colony and Empire: The Capitalist Transformation of the American West* (Lawrence: University Press of Kansas, 1994), esp. 12–13 and 163ff.

12. Ernest Gruening, "Let Us End American Colonialism: Alaska, the United States Colony," Alaska Constitutional Convention, University of Alaska, 1955.

13. See the discussion of Ivan Petroff in chapter 9.

CHAPTER 9: TAKING THE MEASURE OF ALASKA

1. David Herbert Donald, *Charles Sumner and the Rights of Man* (New York: Alfred A. Knopf, 1970), 310; Frederick William Seward, *The Reminiscences of a Wartime Statesman and Diplomat, 1830–1915* (New York: G. P. Putnam's Sons, 1916), 422.

2. Margaret Shannon, "Charles Sumner and the Alaska Purchase," in Barbara Sweetland Smith and Redmond J. Barnett, eds., *Russian America: The Forgotten Frontier* (Tacoma: Washington State Historical Society, 1990), 109–20; Morgan Sherwood, *Exploration of Alaska, 1865–1900* (New Haven, Conn.: Yale University Press, 1965).

3. Seward, *Reminiscences*, 452.

4. Quoted in Walter A. McDougal, *Let the Sea Make a Noise: Four Hundred Years of Cataclysm, Conquest, War, and Folly in the North Pacific* (New York: Basic Books, 1993), 300; Frederick W. Seward, *Seward at Washington as Senator and Secretary of State*, vol. 3 (New York: Derby and Miller, 1891), 346.

5. William Appleman Williams, *The Tragedy of American Diplomacy* (New York: W. W. Norton, 1959); Daniel Immerwahr, *How to Hide an Empire: A History of the Greater United States* (New York: Farrar, Straus and Giroux, 2018).

6. The Russian government sold the land and government property to the United States by the treaty, but the Russian American Company was a private joint stock enterprise and its property needed to be sold separately. Maksutov was ordered to get what he could for it.

7. Richard E. Welch Jr., "American Public Opinion and the Purchase of Russian America," *American Slavic and East European Review* 17 (1958): 481–94.

8. The state holiday Seward's Day is celebrated in Alaska on 30 March.

9. Although the speech was not recorded when given, within several days Sumner set about to write out the remarks he had made in the Senate. The task took him six weeks of concerted effort. It was printed by the *Congressional Globe* in May 1868 and inserted into the official record of the Congress, forty-eight double-column pages.

10. Morgan Sherwood, "George Davidson and the Acquisition of Alaska," *Pacific Historical Review* 28 (1959): 141–54.

11. Paul S. Holbo, *Tarnished Expansion: The Alaska Scandal, the Press, and Congress, 1867–1871* (Knoxville: University of Tennessee Press, 1983).

12. In 1928, Alaska's longtime congressional delegate James Wickersham investigated an oft repeated story about two checks having been issued as payment for Alaska, offered as circumstantial evidence that some of the money was used to pay bribes. In Wickersham's presence in the National Archives the Treasury Department photographed the original check. Evangeline Atwood, *Frontier Politics: Alaska's James Wickersham* (Portland, Ore.: Binford and Mort, 1979), 397.

13. Oliver R. Seward, *William H. Seward's Travels around the World* (New York: Appleton, 1873), 35–36, as quoted in William R. Hunt, *Alaska: A Bicentennial History* (New York: W. W. Norton, 1976), 178–79.

14. As quoted in Ernest Gruening, *The State of Alaska* (New York: Random House, 1954), 34; William H. Seward, *Speech at Sitka, August 12, 1869* (Washington, D.C.: Phillip and Soloman, 1869), 16.

15. General Jefferson Davis to Assistant Adjutant General, Military Division of the Pacific, Oct. 25, 1869, Record Group (RG) 393, National Archives and Records Administration (NARA); see also the discussion in Donald Craig Mitchell, *Sold American: The Story of Alaska Natives and Their Land, 1867–1959* (Hanover, N.H.: University Press of New England, 1997), 31, 44.

16. Not the Jefferson Davis who was president of the Confederate States of America.

17. Ted C. Hinckley, *The Americanization of Alaska, 1867–1897* (Palo Alto, Calif.: Pacific Books, 1972), 129; Hinckley, *The Canoe Rocks: Alaska's Tlingit and the Euramerican Frontier, 1800–1912* (Lanham, Md.: University Press of America, 1996).

18. Bobby Dave Lain, "North of 53: Army, Treasury Department, and Navy Administration of Alaska, 1867–1884," Ph.D. dissertation, University of Texas, 1974.

19. Hinckley, *Americanization of Alaska*, 87.

20. House Report 623, 44th Cong., 1st sess.

21. In the post–Civil War West, absentee investment capital funded many very large, mechanized farms covering thousands of acres; cattle ranches often covered even more vast acreages of consolidated operations financed by eastern and British investors.

22. *Elk v. Wilkins*, 112 U.S. *Reports* 94; see Francis Paul Prucha, *The Great Father: The United States Government and the American Indians*, vol. 2 (Lincoln: University of Nebraska Press, 1984), 681ff.

23. Stephen Haycox, "'Races of a Questionable Ethnical Type': Origins of the Jurisdiction of the U.S. Bureau of Education in Alaska, 1867–1885," *Pacific Northwest Quarterly* 75 (October 1984): 155–63.

24. On American cultural assumptions regarding Indians, see Brian W. Dippie, *The Vanishing American: White Attitudes and U.S. Indian Policy* (Middletown, Conn.: Wesleyan University Press, 1982), 92–94, 141–51, and passim.

25. See the discussion in Mitchell, *Sold American*, 44ff.

26. Morgan Sherwood, "Ardent Spirits: Hooch and the *Osprey* Affair at Sitka," *Journal of the West* 21 (July 1965): 12–23.

27. Ernest Gruening, *The State of Alaska* (New York: Random House), 33–46.

28. As cited in Claus-M. Naske and Herman E. Slotnick, *Alaska: A History of the Forty-Ninth State* (Grand Rapids, Mich.: William B. Eerdmans, 1979), 60.

29. Morgan Sherwood, *Exploration of Alaska, 1865–1900* (New Haven, Conn.: Yale University Press, 1965), 37.

30. Ibid., 45.

31. There are two interesting contradictions in the argument that Congress's delay in conferring civil governance constitutes neglect. First, it is somewhat disingenuous to argue for broad government support for self-reliant pioneering. With the nineteenth-century American settlers of the West, some historians want to have their cake and eat it too: they seem to want the government to have supported settlement, but they want that settlement to have been characterized by self-determination, rugged individualism, and independence. In addition, to emphasize the notion of neglect, as Gruening did so brilliantly, makes Alaska a victim of the federal government right from the start. Gruening's thesis was that only statehood could free Alaska from arrogant, misguided rule from Washington, D.C., both at the hands of executive agencies and the Congress. As other westerners had throughout the nineteenth and twentieth centuries, Gruening blamed nearly all of Alaska's woes on the federal government yet freely criticized that government for failing to provide enough support; he also ignored much support that the government did provide, while at the same time criticizing it for providing support with strings attached. None of these arguments were unique to Alaska; Gruening may not have realized that nearly all the western territories had made the same complaints, asserted with the same contradictions.

See Patricia Nelson Limerick, *The Legacy of Conquest: The Unbroken Past of the American West* (New York: W. W. Norton, 1987), 78–96 (especially the chapter "Denial and Dependence"); and Robert Athearn, *The Mythic West in Twentieth-Century America* (Lawrence: University Press of Kansas, 1986). It is remarkable that Alaska politicians continue to successfully use the neglect and victimization themes; see Malcolm B. Roberts, *Going up in Flames: The Promises and Pledges of Alaska Statehood under Attack* (Anchorage: Alaska Pacific University Press for Commonwealth North, 1990).

32. Richard A. Pierce, "New Light on Ivan Petroff, Historian of Alaska," *Pacific Northwest Quarterly* 69 (1968): 1–10; Morgan Sherwood, "Ivan Petroff and the

Far Northwest," *Journal of the West* 2 (1963): 305–15. Petroff wrote most of Hubert Howe Bancroft's *History of Alaska, 1730–1885* (San Francisco: A. L. Bancroft and Company, 1886), which must be read accordingly.

33. Sherwood, *Exploration of Alaska*, 68–69.

34. As quoted in Hinckley, *Americanization of Alaska*, 129.

35. Ted C. Hinckley, *Alaskan John G. Brady: Missionary, Businessman, Judge, Governor, 1878–1918* (Columbia: Ohio State University Press for Miami University, 1982), 46.

36. Hunt, *Alaska*, 39–43.

37. Sergei Kan, "Russian Orthodox Brotherhoods among the Tlingit: Missionary Goals and Native Response," *Ethnohistory* 32 (1985): 196–223.

38. Ted C. Hinckley, "Sheldon Jackson, Presbyterian Lobbyist for the Great Land of Alaska," *Journal of Presbyterian History* 46 (1968): 175–96..

39. Prucha, *Great Father*, 2:609ff.

40. Francis Paul Prucha, *American Indian Policy in Crisis: Christian Reformers and the Indian, 1865–1900* (Norman: University of Oklahoma Press, 1964), 33–46 and passim.

41. Dorothy Jones, *Aleuts in Transition: A Comparison of Two Villages* (Seattle: University of Washington Press, 1976), 22; Mitchell, *Sold American*, 78–92.

42. Melody Webb, *The Last Frontier* (Albuquerque: University of New Mexico Press, 1985), 59.

43. Stamps are iron plates that crush the ore so that it can be sluiced to recover the larger gold-bearing particles of rock that are then processed to remove the pure gold, which is then poured into molds to make bars or bricks each worth $15,000 or more (in 1885). See the description of the Treadwell operation in Hinckley, *Americanization of Alaska*, 135–36; see also Earl H. Beistline, "Alaska's Mineral Bonanzas of Yesteryear," *Journal of the West* 20 (April 1981): 68–76.

44. U.S. Department of the Interior, Census Office, *Eleventh Census of the United States*, section title: *Economics* (Washington, D.C., 1891), 238.

45. Robert N. DeArmond, *The Founding of Juneau* (Juneau: Gastineau Channel Centennial Association, 1967), 122.

46. There was yet another influence operating on congressional perceptions. In 1878 the first salmon cannery in Alaska opened. The number of canneries grew quickly over the next few years, to a dozen in 1884 and thirty-seven in 1890. The total pack in 1884 was about one hundred thousand cases valued at about $400,000. From these modest beginnings the salmon industry would grow to dominate Alaska's economy and also much of the country's perception of Alaska. In the early 1880s, however, its political significance was to suggest yet another economic aspect of the territory, which shortly before had seemed to have none, save the seal fishery on the Pribilof Islands.

47. Sherwood, *Exploration of Alaska*, 106–18. Sherwood explains the army's response to the need for comprehensive, reliable information about Alaska's unexplored Interior.

48. Prucha, *Great Father*, 2:693–94, 707–11.

49. The Dawes Act also helped to assuage the western demand for more land for non-Native settlement: the size of reservations was contracted as land supposedly not needed for Indians was declared as excess and sold to settlers or land companies. From more than 155 million acres in 1881, the Native land base had shrunk to less than 78 million acres in 1900, a circumstance recognized as a tragedy by reformers and ultimately reversed under the Indian Reorganization Act of 1934 (IRA). See White, *It's Your Misfortune*, 115. The Dawes Act also eroded tribal organization, as it was intended to do, another policy reversed by the IRA. See Charles F. Wilkinson, *American Indians, Time, and the Law: Native Societies in a Modern Constitutional Democracy* (New Haven, Conn.: Yale University Press, 1987).

50. Prucha, *Great Father*, 2:666ff.

51. Victoria Wyatt, "Female Teachers in Southeast Alaska: Sarah Dickinson, Tillie Paul, and Frances Willard," in Margaret Szasz, ed., *Between Indian and White Worlds: The Cultural Broker* (Norman: University of Oklahoma Press, 1994), 179–96; Wyatt, *Images from the Inside Passage: An Alaskan Portrait by Winter and Pond* (Seattle: University of Washington Press, 1989).

52. Sherwood, *Exploration of Alaska*, 115, 106–18.

53. Roderick Nash, *Wilderness and the American Mind*, 3d ed. (New Haven, Conn.: Yale University Press, 1982), 127–29.

54. John Muir, *Travels in Alaska* (Boston: Houghton Mifflin, 1915); Stephen Fox, *John Muir and His Legacy: The American Conservation Movement* (Boston: Little, Brown, 1981).

55. Despite his discomfiture with tourists, which was sometimes acute, Muir wrote at least one brochure for the Northern Pacific Railroad, which linked with cruise ships to take passengers north along the "inside passage"; see William F. Kines, "John Muir: A Reading Bibliography," manuscript copy in possession of the author.

56. Nash, *Wilderness*, 282–83.

57. On this theme, see Morgan Sherwood, "The End of Wilderness," *Environmental Review* 9 (Fall 1985): 197–209.

58. William H. Goetzman and Kay Sloan, *Looking Far North: The Harriman Expedition to Alaska, 1899* (New York: Viking Press, 1982).

59. The post was less than seven miles below the mouth of the Klondike, although there was as yet no hint of gold in the Klondike region.

60. It apparently did not matter that Carroll was a notorious smuggler who had been convicted and fined after customs agents found more than six hundred pounds of

opium belonging to him at a warehouse in Port Townsend and another three thousand pounds cached at the Tlingit village of Kasaan. Carroll, a popular steamship captain, was a self-promoter who easily ingratiated himself with the small number of whites in the coastal towns of the Southeast. See Hunt, *Alaska*, 44.

61 Gruening, *State of Alaska*, 80.

CHAPTER 10: NATIONAL CURRENTS IN ALASKA

1. William B. Haskell, *Two Years in the Klondike and Alaskan Gold Fields, 1896–1898* (1898; reprint, Fairbanks: University of Alaska Press, 1997), 240–90.

2. During the gold rush Pierre Berton's parents went to Dawson, where the popular Canadian writer and journalist was raised. Berton, *The Klondike Fever: The Life and Death of the Last Great Gold Rush* (New York: Alfred A. Knopf, 1982).

3. The U.S. population in the 1900 census was just under seventy-six million. On the activities of Erastus Brainard and the Alaska Bureau of the Seattle Chamber of Commerce, see Berton, *Klondike Fever*, 124–26.

4. Haskell, *Two Years in the Klondike*, 459–74. Many horses that reached the summit were soon shot or abandoned, for without sufficient feed, particularly grain, they did not have the strength to carry a load and were thus useless to the trekkers.

5. Berton, *Klondike Fever*, 429.

6. Lael Morgan, *Good Time Girls of the Alaska-Yukon Gold Rush* (Fairbanks: Epicenter Press, 1998).

7. Ibid.; James Bledsoe, "Kathleen Eloisa Rockwell: Belle of Dawson, Queen of the Yukon, Flower of the North," *Columbia* 25 (Winter 1998–99): 24–31.

8. William R. Hunt, *North of 53: The Wild Days of the Alaska-Yukon Mining Frontier, 1870–1914* (New York: Macmillan, 1974), 99.

9. Terrence Cole, *Crooked Past: The History of a Frontier Mining Camp, Fairbanks, Alaska* (Fairbanks: University of Alaska Press, 1991).

10. Terrence Cole, *E. T. Barnette: The Strange Story of the Man Who Founded Fairbanks* (Anchorage: Alaska Northwest Publishing Company, 1981).

11. Investigative memoranda relating to the Black Chief Mining Company at Nome, as reported in Donald Craig Mitchell, *Sold American: The Story of Alaska Natives and Their Land, 1867–1959* (Hanover, N.H.: University Press of New England, 1997), 154.

12. Robert Fortuine, *Chills and Fever: Health and Disease in the Early History of Alaska* (Fairbanks: University of Alaska Press, 1989), 218.

13. Ibid., 225–26.

14. Melody Webb, *The Last Frontier* (Albuquerque: University of New Mexico Press, 1985), 144.

15. William R. Hunt debunks the myth of lawless, chaotic Skagway in his account of the rush in *North of 53*, 37–43; see also Ken Coates, "Controlling the Periphery: The Territorial Administration of the Yukon-Alaska, 1867–1959," *Pacific Northwest Quarterly* 78 (October 1987): 141–51.

16. William S. Schneider, "Chief Sesui and Lieutenant Herron: A Story of Who Controls the Bacon," *Alaska History* (Fall/Winter 1985): 1–18.

17. Official firsthand accounts of the expeditions appear in *Compilation of Narratives of Exploration in Alaska*, Senate Report 1023, 56th Cong., 1st sess. Webb includes a comprehensive chapter on the army response in *Last Frontier*, 143–70.

18. William Mitchell, *The Opening of Alaska*, ed. Lyman L. Woodman (Anchorage: Cook Inlet Historical Society, 1982). Analyses that argue for the critical contribution of the U.S. Army in facilitating and stimulating development in Alaska include George W. Rogers and Richard A. Cooley, *Alaska's Population and Economy: Regional Growth, Development and Future Outlook*, vol. 2 (Juneau: Office of the Governor, 1962), 8; and Orlando Miller, *The Frontier in Alaska and the Matanuska Colony* (New Haven, Conn.: Yale University Press, 1975), 197.

19. Senator John L. Wilson of Washington, as quoted in Ernest Gruening, *The State of Alaska* (New York: Random House, 1954), 107.

20. Act of May 14, 1898, 30 U.S. Stat. 409.

21. 55th Cong., 3rd sess., *Congressional Record*, 2235, as quoted in Gruening, *State of Alaska*, 108.

22. Jack Ericson Eblen, *The First and Second United States Empires: Governors and Territorial Government, 1784–1912* (Pittsburgh: University of Pittsburgh Press, 1968).

23. Other members of the committee were Senators William Dillingham of Vermont, Thomas Patterson of Colorado, and Henry Burnham of New Hampshire.

24. Later 5 percent of the road fund was used to pay for the transportation and treatment of insane persons at a sanitarium in Portland, Oregon.

25. Cole, *E. T. Barnette*.

26. From 1899 to 1906 the seat of the third district was first Eagle and then Fairbanks. It covered all of Alaska that was not in the Nome area or in the Southeast. The seat of that district was moved in 1906 to the still newer town of Valdez. Then Congress created a new district, which, confusingly, was all of the old third district except coastal south-central Alaska; the seat of the new fourth district was set at Fairbanks, the seat of the old third district. Note also that until 1959, there were no courts in Alaska inferior to the Alaska (federal) district court. However, the judges of the four judicial divisions appointed magistrates, called

U.S. commissioners, for the towns in each division. The commissioners served as local judges for minor matters. See Stephen Haycox and Claus-M. Naske, "'A New Face': Implementing Law in the New State of Alaska, 1958–1960," *Western Legal History* 11 (Winter/Spring 1998): 1–22.

27. With the exception of the Annette Island Indian Reserve for the Metlakatlans.

28. David S. Case, *Alaska Natives and American Laws* (Fairbanks: University of Alaska Press, 1984), 135–38.

29. See, for example, Hannah Breece, *A School Teacher in Old Alaska: The Story of Hannah Breece*, ed. Jane Jacobs (New York: Random House, 1995).

30. Case, *Alaska Natives*, 138–39. Section 18(a) of the Alaska Native Claims Settlement Act repealed the Alaska Allotment Act.

31. Evangeline Atwood, *Frontier Politics: Alaska's James Wickersham* (Portland, Ore.: Binford and Mort, 1979), 79–97; Terrence Cole, "The History of the Nome Gold Rush: Poor Man's Paradise," Ph.D. dissertation, University of Washington, 1983.

32. Terrence Cole, *Nome: City of the Golden Beaches* (Anchorage: Alaska Geographic Society, 1984).

33. The story is told in the Rex Beach novel *The Spoilers* (New York: Harper and Company, 1906).

34. Samuel P. Hays, *Conservation and the Gospel of Efficiency: The Progressive Conservation Movement, 1890–1920* (Cambridge, Mass.: Harvard University Press, 1959).

35. The story of the construction of the railroad and the "Million Dollar Bridge" across the Copper River between Miles and Childs Glaciers was told in Rex Beach's novel *The Iron Trail: An Alaskan Romance* (New York: Harper and Company, 1913). See Elizabeth A. Tower, *Icebound Empire: Industry and Politics on the Last Frontier, 1898–1938* (Anchorage: E. A. Tower, 1996), which argues that the Guggenheims were the victims of reform propaganda and politics.

36. The mining corporation took its name from Kennicott Glacier, near the copper deposits in the Wrangell Mountains, named for the naturalist Robert Kennicott. A Geological Survey cartographer made the misspelling when labeling a map of the region.

37. Alan J. Stein and Paula Becker, *Alaska-Yukon-Pacific Exposition, Washington's First World's Fair: A Timeline History* (Seattle: University of Washington Press, 2009); Wikipedia entry for the Alaska-Yukon-Pacific Exposition, https://en .wikipedia.org/wiki/Alaska%E2%80%93Yukon%E2%80%93Pacific_Exposition, accessed 19 May 2019.

38. James Wickersham Diary (microfilm), Sept. 10, 1907, May 14, 1908, April 4, 1910, James Wickersham Papers, University of Alaska Fairbanks.

39. Atwood, *Frontier Politician*, 205–6; James C. Foster, "Syndicalism Northern Style: Life and Death of WFM No. 193," *Alaska Journal* 4 (Summer 1974): 130–41.

40. The Native population increased from 30,450 in 1900 to 36,400 in 1910, but some of this rise may have been a function of the definitions of Native and non-Native used by the enumerators.

41. The 1910 census showed a population of 64, 356, of whom 36,400 were non-Native.

42. Because of its enormously high tide, averaging over twenty-eight feet, Ship Creek (Anchorage) could not be used as a terminus for the road; Seward was the nearest ice-free, feasible port.

43. William H. Wilson, *Railroad in the Clouds: The Alaska Railroad in the Age of Steam, 1914–1945* (Boulder, Colo.: Pruett, 1977).

44. This was Gruening's characterization in *State of Alaska*, 103–56.

45. As related to the author by Robert Atwood, publisher of the *Anchorage Times*, interview, 24 April 1990.

46. Joseph Sullivan, "Sourdough Radicalism: Labor and Socialism in Alaska, 1905–1920," *Alaska History* 7 (Spring 1992): 1–16.

47. William H. Wilson, "The Founding of Anchorage: Federal Town Building on the Last Frontier," *Pacific Northwest Quarterly* 58 (July 1967): 130–41.

48. The cause of death was a pulmonary embolism.

CHAPTER 11: PIONEER ALASKA

1. The populations in 1900: 63,592, including 30,450 non-Natives; in 1910: 64,356, including 36,400 non-Natives; in 1920: 55,036, including 28,228 non-Natives; in 1930: 59,278, including 29,045 non-Natives; and in 1940: 72,524, including 39,566 non-Natives. U.S. Bureau of the Census, *Twelfth Census of the United States, 1900*, vol. 4 (Washington, D.C.: Government Printing Office, 1903); *Thirteenth Census of the United States, 1910*, vol. 4 (Washington, D.C.: Government Printing Office, 1914); *Fourteenth Census of the United States, 1920*, vol. 3 (Washington, D.C.: Government Printing Office, 1923); *Fifteenth Census of the United States, 1930—Outlying Territories and Possessions* (Washington, D.C.: Government Printing Office, 1932); and *Sixteenth Census of the United States, 1940—Outlying Territories and Possessions* (Washington, D.C.: Government Printing Office, 1944).

2. James Beverly, "The Alaska Fisherman and the Paradox of Assimilation: Progress, Power, and the Preservation of Culture," *Native Press Research Journal* 5 (1987): 2–25.

3. Victoria Wyatt, "Female Teachers in Southeast Alaska: Sarah Dickinson, Tillie Paul, and Frances Willard," in *Between Indian and White Worlds: The Cultural Broker*, ed. Margaret Szasz (Norman: University of Oklahoma Press, 1994), 179–96.

4. Indian voting had been one of the issues over which opponents had challenged Wickersham's last two elections. After investigation the U.S. House of Representatives found that, because their votes had been counted by territorial officials, they should be recognized as valid.

5. Donald Craig Mitchell in his study of Alaska Native land claims argues that William Paul acted dishonestly in a number of instances. Paul lost reelection in 1928 when, on the eve of the election, his opponents revealed in the press that he had accepted campaign contributions from the large fish canneries whose fish traps he had condemned. Paul was disbarred in Alaska in 1937 for retaining money paid him in the settlement of a case brought on behalf of several of his Indian clients. Admittedly a complex character, Paul unquestionably advanced Alaska Native rights materially and permanently. Mitchell, *Sold American: The Story of Alaska Natives and Their Land, 1867–1959: The Army to Statehood* (Hanover, N.H.: University Press of New England, 1997).

6. Chris Friday, *Organized Asian American Labor: The Pacific Coast Canned Salmon Industry, 1870–1942* (Philadelphia: Temple University Press, 1994).

7. Arthur McEvoy, in *The Fisherman's Problem: Ecology and Law in the California Fisheries, 1850–1980* (Cambridge: Cambridge University Press, 1986), calls attention to the challenge of fish conservation. Where a fishery is treated as a commons, open to all fishers, fish not caught by one fisher, as a conservation measure, will be caught by another fisher who is not seeking to conserve the resource. See Richard Cooley, *Politics and Conservation: The Decline of the Alaska Salmon* (New York: Harper and Row, 1963).

8. *Juneau Daily Empire*, 14 April 1924, 1; Herbert Hoover, *Memoirs*, vol. 2, *The Cabinet and the Presidency* (New York: Macmillan, 1951), 150–51.

9. Robert Henning, "Bristol Bay Basin," *Alaska Geographic* 5 (1978): 3–95.

10. Robert Fortuine, *Chills and Fevers: Health and Disease in the Early History of Alaska* (Fairbanks: University of Alaska Press, 1992), 209–26. Fortuine identified four major epidemics among Alaska's Native people: smallpox in the 1830s, influenza in 1918–19, tuberculosis in the 1930s and 1940s, and alcoholism at the end of the twentieth century.

11. The planes left from Seattle's Sand Point Naval Air Station on Lake Washington. Upon landing at Prince Rupert, one plane broke a propeller, which was then repaired. All four planes nearly floated out to sea on the stop at Sitka because they were not secured properly. Finally, one of the planes crashed on the Alaska Peninsula, although the pilot and navigator walked away safely. Three planes completed the flight, considered a remarkable feat in its day.

12. James Shortridge, "The Alaska Agricultural Empire: An American Agrarian Vision, 1898–1929, *Pacific Northwest Quarterly* 69 (1978): 145–58; Shortridge, "American Perceptions of the Agricultural Potential of Alaska, 1867–1958," Ph.D. dissertation, University of Kansas, 1972.

13. There were already some homesteads in the Matanuska valley dating from the construction of the Alaska Railroad; Wasilla was founded in 1916. But most land in the valley had never been broken to the plow.

14. Orlando W. Miller, *The Frontier in Alaska and the Matanuska Colony* (New Haven, Conn.: Yale University Press, 1975), xii.

15. Ibid.

16. Richard White, *"It's Your Misfortune and None of My Own": A History of the American West* (Norman: University of Oklahoma Press, 1991), 491–93; Francis Paul Prucha, *The Great Father: The United States Government and the American Indians*, vol. 2 (Lincoln: University of Nebraska Press, 1984), 940–68.

17. 49 Stat. 1250ff.; David S. Case, *Alaska Natives and American Laws* (Fairbanks: University of Alaska Press, 1984), 99ff.

18. Kenneth R. Philp, "The New Deal and Alaska Natives, 1936–1945," *Pacific Historical Review* 50 (1981): 309–27; Donald Craig Mitchell, *Sold American: The Story of Alaska Natives and Their Land, 1867–1959* (Hanover, N.H.: University Press of New England, 1997), 252–309.

19. 314 U.S. 399 (1941).

20. Philp, "New Deal and Alaska Natives."

21. Mitchell, *Sold American*.

22. Roderick Nash, *Wilderness and the American Mind*, 3d ed. (New Haven, Conn.: Yale University Press, 1982), 200–208, 287–88.

23. Ibid., 207; Harold C. Anderson et al., *The Wilderness Society* (Washington, D.C.: Wilderness Society, 1935), 4.

24. Robert Marshall, *Arctic Village* (New York: H. Smith and R. Haas, 1933), 375–79.

CHAPTER 12: WAR AND THE TRANSITION TO STATEHOOD

1. In 1875, Japan gave up its claim to Sakhalin Island in return for Russian cession of the Kurils to Japan.

2. Jonathan M. Nielson, *Armed Forces on a Northern Frontier: The Military in Alaska's History, 1867–1987* (Westport, Conn.: Greenwood Press, 1988), 125–78.

3. Until 1947 the American air force was part of the army, the Army Air Corps.

4. Dean Kohlhoff, *When the Wind Was a River: Aleut Evacuation in World War II* (Seattle: University of Washington Press, 1995).

5. Gary C. Stein, "Uprooted: Native Casualties of the Aleutian Campaign of World War II," University of Alaska Fairbanks Archives, 1976, p. 15; John C. Kirkland and David F. Coffin Jr., *The Relocation and Internment of the Aleuts during World War II* (Anchorage: Aleutian/Pribilof Islands Association, 1981), 78–89.

6. U.S. Congress, Public Law 100-383 (1988).

7. Joseph Driscoll, *War Comes to Alaska* (Philadelphia: J. B. Lippincott Company, 1943), 122.

8. Terrence Cole, "Jim Crow in Alaska: The Passage of the Equal Rights Act of 1945," *Western Historical Quarterly* 23 (November 1992): 428–46.

9. M. V. Bezeau, "The Realities of Strategic Planning: The Decision to Build the Alaska Highway," in Kenneth Coates, ed., *The Alaska Highway: Papers of the Fortieth Anniversary Symposium* (Vancouver: University of British Columbia Press, 1985), 25–35.

10. Heath Twichell, *Northwest Epic: The Building of the Alaska Highway* (New York: St. Martin's Press, 1992).

11. See Gerald D. Nash, *The American West Transformed: The Impact of the Second World War* (Bloomington: Indiana University Press, 1985). On military construction in Alaska, see Colonel James Bush, *Military Installations in Alaska* (Washington, D.C.: U.S. Army Corps of Engineers, 1944).

12. Stephen Haycox, "Economic Development and Native Rights in Alaska: The 1947 Tongass Timber Act," *Western Historical Quarterly* 21 (February 1990): 20–46.

13. Roderick Nash, *Wilderness and the American Mind*, 3d ed. (New Haven, Conn.: Yale University Press, 1982), 291.

14. Peter Coates, "Project Chariot: Alaskan Roots of Environmentalism," *Alaska History* 4 (Fall 1989): 1–31; Dan O'Neill, *The Firecracker Boys* (New York: St. Martin's Press, 1994).

15. Each of the smaller devices was ten times the strength of the bomb dropped on Hiroshima at the end of World War II.

16. Claus-M. Naske, "Governor Gruening's Struggle for Territorial Status: Personal or Political," *Journal of the West* 20 (January 1981): 32–40; Robert David Johnson, *Ernest Gruening and the Dissenting Tradition* (Cambridge, Mass.: Harvard University Press, 1998), 153–86.

17. As quoted in William R. Hunt, *Alaska: A Bicentennial History* (New York: W. W. Norton, 1976), 129.

18. Evangeline Atwood, *Anchorage: All America City* (Portland, Ore.: Binford and Mort, 1957).

CHAPTER 13: MODERN ALASKA

1. The name of this office was changed to lieutenant governor in 1970.

2. By comparison, the federal government retains 87 percent of Nevada, 66 percent of Utah, 64 percent of Idaho, and 45 percent of California.

3. Jack Roderick, *Crude Dreams: A Personal History of Oil and Politics in Alaska* (Fairbanks, Alaska: Epicenter Press, 1997), 135–44.

4. Author's interviews with John Rader, Warren Colver, and John Havelock for Stephen Haycox, *The Law of the Land: A History of the Office of the Attorney General and the Department of Law in Alaska* (Juneau: Alaska Department of Law, 1998).

5. Lael Morgan, *Art and Eskimo Power: The Life and Times of Alaskan Howard Rock* (Fairbanks, Alaska: Epicenter Press, 1988), 191, 195, 205, 223.

6. Robert Arnold, *Alaska Native Land Claims* (Anchorage: Alaska Native Foundation, 1974), 118.

7. Donald Craig Mitchell, *Take My Land, Take My Life: The Story of Congress's Settlement of Alaska Native Land Claims, 1960–1971* (Fairbanks: University of Alaska Press, 2001), 94, 123, 132.

8. Federal Field Committee for Development Planning in Alaska, *Alaska Natives and the Land* (Washington, D.C.: Government Printing Office, 1968).

9. Roderick, *Crude Dreams*, 123–92. The "little guy" versus the majors is one of the principal themes of Roderick's book.

10. Alfred Ketzler, "The Potential for Rational Land Use," *New Republic*, 11 September 1971, 15–18.

11. The amendments permit corporations to issue stock to "after borns"; only a few corporations have extended stock to "after borns," usually by issuing new stock, called "life estate stock," which is valid only during the lifetime of the holder and cannot be willed.

12. Thomas R. Berger, *Native Journey: The Report of the Alaska Native Review Commission* (New York: Hill and Wang, 1985); see also Tom Kizzia, *In the Wake of the Unseen Object: Among the Native Cultures of Alaska* (New York: H. Holt & Company, 1991).

13. Joseph G. Jorgenson, *Oil Age Eskimos* (Berkeley: University of California Press, 1990); Wendell H. Oswalt, *Bashful No Longer: An Alaska Eskimo Ethnohistory, 1778–1988* (Norman: University of Oklahoma Press, 1990).

14. Samuel P. Hays, "From Conservation to Environment: Environmental Politics in the United States since World War II," *Environmental Review* 6 (fall 1982): 14–29.

15. See also Roderick Nash, *Wilderness and the American Mind* (New Haven, Conn.: Yale University Press, 1967). Nash added a chapter on Alaska in the third edition of his immensely popular book, published in 1982.

16. Stewart L. Udall, *The Quiet Crisis* (New York: Holt, Rinehart and Winston, 1962).

17. Mark Harvey, *Wilderness Forever: Howard Zahniser and the Path to the Wilderness Act* (Seattle: University of Washington Press, 2005); William Cronin, "The Trouble with Wilderness, or Getting Back to the Wrong Nature," in William Cronin, ed., *Uncommon Ground: Rethinking the Human Place in Nature* (New York: W. W. Norton, 1995), 69–90.

18. Rachael Carson, *Silent Spring, 1907–1964* (Greenwich, Conn.: Fawcett Publications, 1962); Carson, *The Sea around Us* (London: Readers Union, 1953).

19. Nash, *Wilderness*, 387.

20. Charles F. Wilkinson, *Crossing the Next Meridian: Land, Water, and the Future of the West* (Washington, D.C.: Island Press, 1992).

21. Peter A. Coates, *The Trans-Alaska Pipeline Controversy: Technology, Conservation, and the Frontier* (Bethlehem, Pa.: Lehigh University Press, 1991), 175–216.

22. Ibid., 202.

23. Twenty-five percent of petroleum lease bonuses, royalties, and rentals are deposited in the Alaska Permanent Fund; none of the severance tax revenue is deposited.

24. Gerald A. McBeath and Thomas A. Morehouse, *Alaska Politics and Government* (Lincoln: University of Nebraska Press, 1994), 63–64.

25. As quoted in ibid., 65.

26. Coates, *Trans-Alaska Pipeline*, 308; G. Frank Williss, *"Do Things Right the First Time": The National Park Service and the Alaska National Interest Lands Conservation Act of 1980* (Washington, D.C.: National Park Service, 1985), 114.

27. See Morgan Sherwood, "The End of Wilderness," *Environmental Review* 9 (Fall 1985): 197–209.

28. Cecil D. Andrus and Joel Connelly, *Cecil Andrus: Politics Western Style* (Seattle: Sasquatch Books, 1998), 78–85.

29. Nash, *Wilderness*, 296–313.

30. R. McGreggor Cawley, *Federal Land, Western Anger: The Sagebrush Rebellion and Environmental Politics* (Lawrence: University Press of Kansas, 1993).

31. The amount of $15 million annually was dedicated to road building, $25 million to other operations. Before ANILCA the annual road-building budget for the U.S. Forest Service Alaska Region had been about $3 million.

32. William Dietrich, *The Final Forest: The Battle for the Last Great Trees of the Pacific Northwest* (New York: Simon & Schuster, 1992).

33. Timothy Egan, "Fighting for Control of America's Hinterlands," *New York Times*, 11 November 1990, iv, 18.

34. John Keeble, *Out of the Channel: The Exxon Valdez Oil Spill in Prince William Sound* (New York: HarperCollins, 1991).

35. Jeff Wheelwright, *Degrees of Disaster: Prince William Sound, How Nature Reels and Rebounds* (New Haven, Conn.: Yale University Press, 1994). Wheelwright argues that the 1964 earthquake was a greater disturbance to the sound than the oil spill and that there are few chronic (i.e., permanent) effects of the accident.

36. Stephen Haycox, "'Fetched Up': Unlearned Lessons from the *Exxon Valdez*," *Journal of America History* (June 2012): 219–28.

37. In August 2019, BP announced the sale of all its assets in Alaska to Hilcorp Energy Company of Houston, Texas.

38. 101F. 3d 610 (9th Circuit, 1996).

39. *Madison v. Alaska Department of Fish and Game*, 696 P. 2d 198.

40. *McDowell v. State*, 785 P. 2d 1.

41. Byron Mallott, "It's Not a Good Time to Be an Alaska Native," *Anchorage Daily News*, 3 May 1999, B8.

42. Gerald A. McBeath and Thomas A. Morehouse, *Alaska Politics and Government* (Lincoln: University of Nebraska Press, 1994), 60.

43. As cited in Nash, *Wilderness*, 164.

EPILOGUE

1. Stephen Haycox, *Battleground Alaska: Fighting Federal Power in America's Last Wilderness* (Lawrence: University Press of Kansas, 2016).

2. Bernard de Voto, "The West: A Plundered Province," *Harper's Magazine*, August 1934, 355–64.

3. Macrotrends, "Crude Oil Prices: 70 Year Historical Chart," https://www .macrotrends.net/1369/crude-oil-price-history-chart, accessed 8 March 2019.

4. "The Oil Boom Made Alaska Richer, Right? Economist Says 'No,'" *Anchorage Daily News*, 9 August 2018.

BIBLIOGRAPHY

RUSSIAN AMERICA

Books

Afonsky, Bishop Gregory. *A History of the Orthodox Church in Alaska, 1794–1917.*
    Kodiak, Alaska: St. Herman's Theological Seminary, 1977.

Alekseev, A. I. *The Odyssey of a Russian Scientist: I. G. Voznesenskii in Alaska, Califor-
    nia, and Siberia, 1839–1849.* Translated by Wilma C. Follette. Edited by Richard A.
    Pierce. Kingston, Ont.: Limestone Press, 1987.

Antonson, Joan M., and William S. Hanable. *Alaska's Heritage.* Anchorage: Alaska
    Historical Society for Alaska Historical Commission, 1985.

Barratt, Glynn. *Russia in Pacific Waters, 1715–1825.* Vancouver: University of British
    Columbia Press, 1981.

Berkh, Vasilii N. *A Chronological History of the Discovery of the Aleutian Islands.*
    Translated by Dmitri Krenov. Edited by Richard A. Pierce. Kingston, Ont.:
    Limestone Press, 1974.

Black, Lydia T. *Russians in America, 1732–1867.* Fairbanks: University of Alaska Press,
    2004.

Blainey, Geoffery. *The Tyranny of Distance: How Distance Shaped Australia's History.*
    South Melbourne: Macmillan, 1982.

Bolkhovitinov, N. N. *The Beginnings of Russian American Relations, 1775–1815.*
    Translated by Elena Levin. Cambridge, Mass.: Harvard University Press, 1975.

Dmytryshyn, Basil, E. A. P. Crownhart-Vaughan, and Thomas Vaughan, eds. *To
    Siberia and Russian America: Three Centuries of Russian Eastward Expansion:
    A Documentary Record, 1588–1867.* Portland: Oregon Historical Society Press,
    1988.

Divin, Vasilii A. *The Great Russian Navigator, A. I. Chirikov.* Translated and edited by
    Raymond H. Fisher. Fairbanks: University of Alaska Press, 1993.

Fedorova, Svetlana. *The Russian Population in Alaska and California, Late Eighteenth Century–1867.* Edited by Richard A. Pierce and Alton S. Donnelly. Kingston, Ont.: Limestone Press, 1973.

Fienup-Riordon, Ann. *Boundaries and Passages: Rule and Ritual in Yup'ik Eskimo Oral Tradition.* Norman: University of Oklahoma Press, 1994.

———. *Freeze Frame: Alaska Eskimos in the Movies.* Seattle: University of Washington Press, 1995.

Fisher, Raymond H. *Bering's Voyages: Whither and Why.* Seattle: University of Washington Press, 1977.

———. *The Russian Fur Trade, 1550–1700.* Berkeley: University of California Press, 1943.

———, ed. *The Voyage of Semen Dezhnev in 1648: Bering's Precursor, with Selected Documents.* London: Hakluyt Society, 1981.

Fitzhugh, William W., and Aron Crowell. *Crossroads of Continents: Cultures of Siberia and Alaska.* Washington, D.C.: Smithsonian Institution Press, 1988.

Gibson, James R. *Imperial Russia in Frontier America: The Changing Geography of Supply of Russian America, 1784–1867.* New York: Oxford University Press, 1976.

———. *Otter Skins, Boston Ships, and China Goods: The Maritime Fur Trade of the Northwest Coast, 1785–1841.* Seattle: University of Washington Press, 1992.

Golovin, P. N. *The End of Russian America: Captain P. N. Golovin's Last Report.* Translated by Basil Dmytryshyn and E. A. P. Crownhart-Vaughan. Portland: Oregon Historical Society, 1979.

Grinev, Andrei. *Russian Colonization of Alaska: Preconditions, Discovery, and Initial Development, 1741–1799.* Translated by Richard L. Bland. Lincoln: University of Alaska Press, 2018.

———. *The Tlingit Indians of Russian America, 1741–1867.* Translated by Richard L. Bland. Lincoln: University of Nebraska Press, 2008.

Hanke, Lewis. *All Mankind Is One: A Study of the Disputation between Bartolome de Las Casas and Juan Gines de Sepulveda in 1550 on the Intellectual and Religious Capacity of the American Indians.* DeKalb: Northern Illinois University Press, 1974.

Howay, Frederic William. *A List of Trading Vessels in the Maritime Fur Trade, 1785–1825.* Edited by Richard A. Pierce. Kingston, Ont.: Limestone Press, 1973.

Inglis, Robin. *Spain and the North Pacific Coast: Essays in Recognition of the Bicentennial of the Malaspina Expedition, 1791–1792.* Vancouver: Vancouver Maritime Museum, 1992.

Kan, Sergei. *Symbolic Immortality: The Tlingit Potlatch of the Nineteenth Century.* Washington, D.C.: Smithsonian Institution Press, 1989.

Khlebnikov, Kiril T. *Baranov: Chief Manager of the Russian Colonies in America.* Translated by Colin Bearne. Edited by Richard A. Pierce. Kingston, Ont.: Limestone Press, 1973.

Kisslinger, Jerome, trans. *Journals of the Priest Ioann Veniaminov in Alaska, 1823 to 1836.* Fairbanks: University of Alaska Press, 1993.

Kraus, David H., trans. *Russian Exploration in Southwest Alaska: The Travel Journals of Petr Korsakovskiy (1818) and Ivan Ya. Vasilev (1829).* Fairbanks: University of Alaska Press, 1988.

Langdon, Steve J. *The Native People of Alaska.* 3rd ed. Anchorage: Greatland Graphics, 1993.

Lantzeff, George V., and Richard A. Pierce. *Eastward to Empire: Exploration and Conquest on the Russian Open Frontier to 1750.* Montreal: McGill-Queen's University Press, 1973.

Mackie, Richard. *Trading beyond the Mountains: The British Fur Trade on the Pacific, 1793–1843.* Vancouver: University of British Columbia Press, 1997.

Makarova, Raisa V. *Russians on the Pacific, 1743–1799.* Translated by Richard A. Pierce and Alton S. Donnelly. Kingston, Ont.: Limestone Press, 1975.

McDougall, Walter A. *Let the Sea Make a Noise: A History of the North Pacific from Magellan to MacArthur.* New York: Basic Books, 1993.

Miller, David H. *The Alaska Treaty.* Kingston, Ont.: Limestone Press, 1981.

Okun, Semen B. *The Russian-American Company.* Edited by B. D. Grekov. Translated by Carl Ginsburg. Cambridge: Harvard University Press, 1951.

Oleksa, Michael. *Orthodox Alaska: A Theology of Mission.* Crestwood, N.Y.: St. Vladimir's Seminary Press, 1992.

Pierce, Richard A. *Notes on Russian America, Part I: Novo-Arkhangel'sk.* Compiled by Svetlana Fedorova. Translated by Serge LeComte and Richard A. Pierce. Kingston, Ont.: Limestone Press, 1994.

———. *Notes on Russian America, Parts II–V: Kad'iak, Unalashka, Atkha, the Pribylolvs.* Compiled by R. G. Liapunova and S. G. Fedorova. Translated by Marina Ramsay. Kingston, Ont.: Limestone Press, 1994.

———. *Russia in North America: Proceedings of the Second International Conference on Russian America, Sitka, Alaska, August 19–22, 1987.* Kingston, Ont.: Limestone Press, 1990.

———. *Russian America: A Biographical Dictionary.* Kingston, Ont.: Limestone Press, 1990.

Rennick, Penny, ed. *Russian America. Alaska Geographic* 26 (1999).

Shur, Leonid. *The Khlebnikov Archive: Unpublished Journal (1800–1837) and Travel Notes (1820, 1822, and 1824).* Translated by John Bisk. Edited by Marvin Falk. Fairbanks: University of Alaska Press, 1990.

Smith, Barbara Sweetland. *Russian Orthodoxy in Alaska: A History, Inventory, and Analysis of Church Archives in Alaska.* Anchorage: Alaska Historical Commission, 1980.

Smith, Barbara Sweetland, and Redmond Barnett, eds. *Russian America: The Forgotten Frontier.* Tacoma: Washington State Historical Society, 1990.

Starr, S. Frederick, ed. *Russia's American Colony*. Durham, N.C.: Duke University Press, 1987.

Steller, Georg Wilhelm. *Journal of a Voyage with Bering, 1741–1742*. Edited by O. W. Frost. Translated by Margritt A. Engel and O. W. Frost. Stanford, Calif.: Stanford University Press, 1988.

Tikhmenev, P. A. *A History of the Russian-American Company*. Translated and edited by Richard A. Pierce and Alton S. Donnelly. Seattle: University of Washington Press, 1978.

Vinkovetsky, Ilya. *Russian America: An Overseas Colony of a Continental Empire, 1804–1867*. New York: Oxford University Press, 2011.

Williams, William Appleman. *American-Russian Relations, 1781–1947*. New York: Rinehart & Co.

Znamenski, Ancrei A., trans. *Through Orthodox Eyes: Russian Missionary Narratives of Travels in the Dena'ina and Ahtna, 1850s–1930s*. Fairbanks: University of Alaska Press, 2003.

Articles and Book Chapters

Arndt, Katherine. "Consolidation and Expansion: The Russian American Co." *Alaska Geographic* 26, no. 4 (1999): 24–49.

———. "Russian Explorations in North America. " Unpublished paper in possession of the author.

Bolkhovitinov, Nikolai N. "The Sale of Russian America in the Context of Russian American Relations." *Pacifica* 2 (1990): 156–71.

Cole, Terrence. "Odyssey of a Russian Scientist: I. G. Voznesenskii in Alaska, California, and Siberia, 1839–49." *Pacific Northwest Quarterly* 80 (January 1989): 37–38.

Dauenhauer, Richard A. "Two Missions to Alaska." *Pacific Historian* 26 (Spring 1982): 29–41.

Dumond, Don E. "Poison in the Cup: The South Alaskan Smallpox Epidemic of 1835." *University of Oregon Anthropological Papers* 52 (1996): 117–29.

Fisher, Raymond H. "Finding America." In *Russian America: The Forgotten Frontier*, ed. Barbara Sweetland Smith and Redmond Barnett. Tacoma: Washington State Historical Society, 1990.

Gibson, James R. "Colonial Russian America." In *Russia's American Colony*, ed. S. Frederick Starr. Durham, N.C.: Duke University Press, 1987.

———. "Russian Dependence on the Natives of Alaska." In *Russia's American Colony*, ed. S. Frederick Starr. Durham, N.C.: Duke University Press, 1987.

———. "The Sale of Russian America to the United States." In *Russia's American Colony*, ed. S. Frederick Starr. Durham, N.C.: Duke University Press, 1987.

Kan, Sergei. "Russian Orthodox Missionaries and the Tlingit Indians of Alaska, 1880–1900." In *New Dimensions in Ethnohistory: Papers of the Second Laurier*

Conference on Ethnohistory and Ethnology, ed. Barry Gough and Laird Christie. Hull, Quebec: Canadian Museum of Civilization, 1991.

Lain, B. D. "The Decline of Russia's Colonial Society." *Western Historical Quarterly* (April, 1976): 143–53.

Znamenski, Ancrei A. "Sitka-Kyakhta versus Sitka-Canton: Russian America and the China Market." *Pacifica* 2 (November 1990): 35–79.

———. "Sitka versus Kodiak: Countering the Tlingit Threat and Situating the Colonial Capital of Russian America." *Pacific Historical Review* 67 (November 1998): 67–98.

Gough, Barry M. "The Character of the British Columbia Frontier." *BC Studies* 32 (1976–77): 74–92.

Graebner, Norman. "The Northwest Coast in Northern Diplomacy, 1790–1846." In *The Changing Pacific Northwest: Interpreting Its Past*, ed. David H. Stratton and George A. Frykman. Pullman: Washington State University Press, 1988.

John, Fred, Sr. "Killing of the Russians at Batzulneta's Village." *Alaska Journal* 3 (Summer 1973): 147–48.

Naish, John M. "The Health of Mariners: Vancouver's Achievement." In *Enlightenment and Exploration in the North Pacific, 1741–1805*, ed. Stephen Haycox, James Barnett, and Caedmon Liburd. Seattle: University of Washington Press, 1997.

Pierce, Richard A. "Voznesenskii: Scientist in Alaska," *Alaska Journal* 5 (Winter 1975): 11–15.

Shelikhov, Grigorii I. "A Voyage to America, 1783–1786." In *Alaska History*. Edited and translated by Richard A. Pierce. Kingston, Ont.: Limestone Press, 1981.

Solovjova, Katerina, and Aleksandra Vovnyanko. "The Rise and Decline of the Lebedev-Lastochkin Company." *Pacific Northwest Quarterly* 90 (Fall 1999): 191–205.

Tompkins, Stuart R. "Drawing the Alaskan Boundary." *Canadian Historical Review* 26 (1945): 54–68.

Urness, Carol. "Russian Mapping of the North Pacific to 1792." In *Enlightenment and Exploration in the North Pacific, 1741–1805*, ed. Stephen Haycox, James Barnett, and Caedmon Liburd. Seattle: University of Washington Press, 1997.

Van Stone, James W. "Russian Exploration in Interior Alaska: An Extract from the Journal of Andrei Glazunov." *Pacific Northwest Quarterly* 50 (1959): 77–92.

———, ed. "V. S. Khromchenko's Coastal Explorations in Southwestern Alaska, 1822." Translated by David H. Kraus. *Anthropology* 64. Chicago: Field Museum of Natural History, 1973.

Zagoskin, Lavrentii A. *Lieutenant Zagoskin's Travels in Russian America, 1842–1844*. Translated by Penelope Rainey. Edited by Henry Michael. Toronto: University of Toronto Press, 1967.

University Manuscript Collections

Alaska Conservation Society Papers, Archives, University of Alaska Fairbanks (UAF)

E. L. Bartlett Papers, Archives, UAF

Anthony J. Dimond Papers, Archives, UAF

Mike Gravel Papers, Archives, UAF

Ernest Gruening Papers, Archives, UAF

Robert Marshall Papers, Bancroft Library, University of California–Berkeley

Howard W. Pollock Papers, Archives, UAF

Ralph J. Rivers Papers, Archives, UAF

Dan Sutherland Papers, Archives, UAF

James Wickersham Papers, Archives, UAF

Government Manuscript Collections

Records of the Bureau of Indian Affairs. Record Group 75. NARA Washington, D.C. NARA, Alaska Archives Branch, Anchorage.

Records of the Department of Justice. Record Group 22. National Archive and Records Administration (NARA). Washington, D.C.

Records of the Office of the Secretary of the Interior. Record Group 48. NARA, Washington, D.C. NARA, Alaska Archives Branch, Anchorage.

Records of the Office of Territories. Record Group 126. National Archives, Washington, D.C.

Records of the Office of the Governor of Alaska. Record Group 239. Alaska State Historical Library, Juneau.

Government Publications

Alaska Department of Labor. *Alaska Population Overview.* Juneau: Alaska Department of Labor, June 1998.

Alaska Statehood Commission. *Draft Final Report.* Fairbanks: Alaska Statehood Commission, 1982.

U.S. Bureau of the Census. *Statistical Abstract of the United States 1998: The National Data Book.* October. Washington, D.C.: Government Printing Office, 1998.

U.S. Congress. Act of May 14, 1898, 30 U.S. Stat. 409.

———. *Congressional Record.* 55th Congress, 3d Session, 2235.

U.S. Congress, Federal Field Committee. *Alaska Natives and the Land.* Washington, D.C.: Government Printing Office, 1968.

U.S. Congress, House. House Report 623, 44th Congress, 1st Session.

———. House Report 1705, 79th Congress, 1st Session. *Alaska Highway.*

————. Hearings, Subcommittee on Territories and Insular Possessions. 85th Congress, 1st Session. *Alaska Statehood.*

————. Hearings, Subcommittee on Interior and Insular Affairs. 95th Congress, 1st Session. *Inclusion of Alaska Lands* (ANILCA).

U.S. Congress, Senate. Senate Report 1023. *Compilation of Narratives of Exploration in Alaska.* 56th Congress, 1st Session.

————. Senate Report 282. 58th Congress, 2d Session. *Conditions in Alaska.*

————. Committee on Interior and Insular Affairs, Hearings. 79th Congress, 1st Session. *Nomination of Walter J. Hickel to Be Secretary of the Interior.*

————. Committee on Interior and Insular Affairs, Hearings. 92d Congress, 1st Session. *Trans-Alaska Draft Environmental Impact Statement.*

U.S. Department of the Interior. *Alaska at Mid-century.* Washington, D.C.: Government Printing Office, 1952.

U.S. Department of the Interior, Census Office. *Eleventh Census of the United States: Economics.* Washington, D.C., 1891.

Newspapers

Anchorage Times
Cordova Times
(Juneau) *Daily Empire*
(Fairbanks) *News-Miner*
Ketchikan Chronicle
New York Times
Wrangell Sentinel

Legal Cases

Alaska v. Udall, 430F. 2d 938; cert. den., 397 U.S. 1076; 90 S. Ct. 1522 (1970)
Elk v. Wilkins, 112 U.S. *Reports* 94
In re Wickersham, 6 Alaska Reports 167 (1919)
Sturgeon v. Frost, 136 S. Ct. 1061 (2016); 587 S. Ct. 988 (2019)
Tlingit and Haida Indians of Alaska v. United States, 177 F. Supp. 452 (1959)
Tlingit and Haida Indians of Alaska v. United States, 389 F. 2d 367 (1968)
Wilderness Society et al v. Hickel, 325 F. Supp. 422 (1970)
Zobel et al. v. Williams, 457 U.S. 55 (1982)

Dissertations

Allan, Timo Christopher. "Locked Up! A History of Resistance to the Creation of National Parks in Alaska." Ph.D. dissertation, Washington State University, 2010.

Buske, Frank E. "The Wilderness, the Frontier, and the Literature of Alaska to 1914: John Muir, Jack London and Rex Beach." Ph.D. dissertation, University of California–Davis, 1976.

Cole, Terrence. "The History of the Nome Gold Rush: Poor Man's Paradise." Ph.D. dissertation, University of Washington, 1983.

Cuba, James Lee. "A Moveable Frontier: Frontier Images in Contemporary Alaska." Ph.D. dissertation, Yale University, 1981.

Jody, Marilyn. "Alaska in the American Literary Imagination: A Literary History of Frontier Alaska." Ph.D. dissertation, Indiana University, 1969.

Lain, Bobby Dave. "North of 53: Army, Treasury Department, and Navy Administration of Alaska, 1867–1884." Ph.D. dissertation, University of Texas, 1974.

Mangusso, Mary. "Anthony J. Dimond: A Political Geography." Ph.D. dissertation, Texas Tech University, 1978.

Morse, Kathryn. "The Nature of Gold: An Environmental History of the Yukon/Alaska Gold Rush." Ph.D. dissertation, University of Washington, 1997.

Shortridge, James. "American Perceptions of the Agricultural Potential of Alaska, 1867–1958." Ph.D. dissertation, University of Kansas, 1972.

Sisk, John B. "Charting Forest Policy on a Battleground of Conflict: A Case Study of the Tongass National Forest in Southeast Alaska." Ph.D. dissertation, Northern Arizona University, 1989.

Stearns, Robert Alden. "The Morgan-Guggenheim Syndicate and the Development of Alaska, 1906–1915." Ph.D. dissertation, University of California–Santa Barbara, 1967.

Wolfe, John Hilton. "Alaska Literature: The Fiction of America's Last Wilderness." Ph.D. dissertation, Michigan State University, 1973.

Books

Adams, George R. *Life on the Yukon, 1865–1867*. Edited by Richard A. Pierce. Kingston, Ont.: Limestone Press, 1982.

Adney, Edward Tappan. *The Klondike Stampede*. New York: Harper and Brothers, Publishers, 1900.

Allen, Lawrence J. *The Trans-Alaska Pipeline*. 2 vols. Seattle: Scribe Publishing Company, 1976.

Andrasko, Kenneth, and Marcus Halevi. *Alaska Crude: Visions of the Last Frontier*. Boston: Little, Brown, & Company, 1982.

Andrews, Clarence Leroy. *The Story of Alaska*. Seattle: Lowman & Hanford Company, 1931.

Andrus, Cecil D., and Joel Connelly. *Cecil Andrus: Politics Western Style*. Seattle: Sasquatch Books, 1998.

Arnold, David F. *Fisherman's Frontier: People and Salmon in Southeast Alaska.* Seattle: University of Washington Press, 2011.

Arnold, Robert. *Alaska Native Land Claims.* Anchorage: Alaska Native Foundation, 1976.

Athearn, Robert. *The Mythic West in Twentieth-Century America.* Lawrence: University of Kansas Press, 1986.

Atwood, Evangeline. *Anchorage: All America City.* Portland, Ore.: Binford and Mort, 1957.

———. *Frontier Politics: Alaska's James Wickersham.* Portland, Ore.: Binford and Mort, 1979.

Atwood, Fred N. *The Alaska-Yukon Gold Book.* Seattle: Sourdough Stampede Association, 1930.

Bade, William Frederic, ed. *The Life and Letters of John Muir.* Vol 2. Boston: Houghton Mifflin, 1924.

Balch, Thomas Willing. *The Alaska Frontier.* Philadelphia: Allen, Lane, and Scott, 1903.

Bancroft, Hubert Howe. *History of Alaska, 1730–1885.* 1886; reprint, New York: Antiquarian Press, 1960.

Barman, Jean. *The West beyond the West: A History of British Columbia.* Toronto: University of Toronto Press.

Barnett, James K., ed. *Captain Cook's Final Voyage: The Untold Story from the Journals of James Burney and Henry Roberts.* Pullman: Washington State University Press, 2017.

Barnett, James K., and Ian C. Hartman, eds. *Imagining Anchorage: The Making of America's Northernmost Metropolis.* Fairbanks: University of Alaska Press, 2018.

Beach, Rex. *The Iron Trail: An Alaskan Romance.* New York: Harper and Company, 1913.

———. *The Spoilers.* New York: Harper and Company, 1906.

Beaman, Libby. *Libby: The Alaskan Diaries and Letters of Libby Beaman, 1879–1880.* As presented by her granddaughter Betty John. Boston: Houghton Mifflin, 1987.

Berger, Thomas. *Village Journey: Report of the Alaska Native Review Commission.* New York: Hill and Wang, 1985.

Berry, Mary Clay. *The Alaska Pipeline: The Politics of Oil and Native Land Claims.* Bloomington: Indiana University Press, 1975.

Berton, Laura Beatrice. *I Married the Klondike.* Toronto: Little, Brown and Company, 1954.

Berton, Pierre. *The Klondike Fever: The Life and Death of the Last Great Gold Rush.* New York: Alfred A. Knopf, 1982.

Bockstoce, John R. *Furs and Frontiers in the Far North: The Contest among Native and Foreign Nations for the Bering Strait Fur Trade*. New Haven, Conn.: Yale University Press, 2010.

———. *Whales, Ice and Men: The History of Whaling in the Western Arctic*. Seattle: University of Washington Press, 1986.

———. *White Fox and Icy Seas in the Western Arctic: The Fur Trade, Transportation and Change in the Early Twentieth Century*. New Haven, Conn.: Yale University Press, 2018.

Bone, Scott C. *Alaska, Its Past, Present, and Future*. Juneau: Governor's Office, 1925.

Breece, Hannah. *A School Teacher in Old Alaska: The Story of Hannah Breece*. Edited by Jane Jacobs. New York: Random House, 1995.

Brewster, Karen, ed. *Boot, Bikes and Bombers: Adventures of Alaska Conservationist Ginny Hill Wood*. Fairbanks: University of Alaska Press, 2012.

Brooks, Alfred Hulse. *Blazing Alaska's Trails*. College: University of Alaska and Arctic Institute of North America, 1953.

Brown, Tom. *Oil on Ice: Alaskan Wilderness at the Crossroads*. Edited by Richard Pollak. San Francisco: Sierra Club, 1971.

Burroughs, John. *Harriman Alaska Expedition*. Vol. 1, *Narrative of the Expedition*. New York: Doubleday, Page & Company, 1902.

Bush, James. *Military Installations in Alaska*. Washington, D.C.: U.S. Army Corps of Engineers, 1944.

Cahn, Robert. *The Fight to Save Wild Alaska*. New York: Audubon Society, 1982.

Campbell, Robert. *In Darkest Alaska: Travel and Empire along the Inside Passage*. Philadelphia: University of Pennsylvania Press, 2007.

Carson, Rachael. *Silent Spring, 1907–1964*. Greenwich, Conn.: Fawcett Publications, 1962.

Case, David S. *Alaska Natives and American Laws*. Fairbanks: University of Alaska Press, 1984.

Cashen, William R. *Farthest North College President: Charles E. Bunnell and the Early History of the University of Alaska*. Fairbanks: University of Alaska Press, 1972.

Catton, Theodore. *Inhabited Wilderness: Indians, Eskimos, and National Parks in Alaska*. Albuquerque: University of New Mexico Press, 1997.

Cawley, R. McGreggor. *Federal Land, Western Anger: The Sagebrush Rebellion and Environmental Politics*. Lawrence: University of Kansas Press, 1993.

Chandonnet, Fern, ed. *Alaska at War, 1941–1945: The Forgotten War Remembered*. Anchorage: Alaska at War Committee, 1995.

Chasan, Daniel Jack. *Klondike '70: The Alaska Oil Boom*. New York: Frederick A. Praeger, 1971.

Chase, Will H. *Reminiscences of Captain Billie Moore*. Kansas City, Mo.: Burton Publishing Company, 1947.

Coates, Kenneth. *North to Alaska*. Fairbanks: University of Alaska Press, 1992.

Coates, Kenneth, and William Morrison. *The Forgotten North: A History of Canada's Provincial Norths*. Toronto: J. Lorimer, 1992.

———. *Interpreting Canada's North: Selected Readings*. Toronto: Copp Clark Pitman, 1989.

Coates, Kenneth, and Judith Powell. *The Modern North: People, Politics, and the Rejection of Colonialism*. Toronto: J. Lorimer, 1989.

Coates, Peter A. *The Trans-Alaska Pipeline Controversy: Technology, Conservation, and the Frontier*. Bethlehem, Pa.: Lehigh University Press, 1991.

Coe, Douglas. *Road to Alaska: The Story of the Alaska Highway*. New York: Julian Messner, 1943.

Coen, Ross. *Breaking Ice: The Epic Voyage of the SS Manhattan through the Northwest Passage*. Fairbanks: University of Alaska Press, 2012.

Colby, Merle. *A Guide to Alaska: Last American Frontier*. American Guide Series. Federal Writers' Project. New York: Macmillan, 1939.

Cole, Dermot. *Amazing Pipeline Stories: How Building the Trans-Alaska Pipeline Transformed Life in America's Last Frontier*. Fairbanks: Epicenter Press, 1997.

———. *Fairbanks: A Gold Rush Town That Beat the Odds*. Fairbanks: Epicenter Press, 1999.

Cole, Terrence. *Blinded by Riches: The Permanent Funding Problem and the Prudhoe Bay Effect*. Anchorage: Institute of Social and Economic Research, University of Alaska–Anchorage, 2004.

———. *Crooked Past: The History of a Frontier Mining Camp, Fairbanks, Alaska*. Fairbanks: University of Alaska Press, 1991.

———. *E. T. Barnette: The Strange Story of the Man Who Founded Fairbanks*. Anchorage: Alaska Northwest Publishing Company, 1981.

———. *Nome: City of the Golden Beaches*. Anchorage: Alaska Geographic Society, 1984.

Colt, Steve. *Salmon Fish Traps in Alaska: An Economic History*. ISER Working Paper. Anchorage: University of Alaska Anchorage, Institute for Economic and Social Research, 2000.

Cooley, Richard. *Politics and Conservation: The Decline of the Alaska Salmon*. New York: Harper and Row, 1963.

Cronin, William, ed. *Uncommon Ground: Rethinking the Human Place in Nature*. New York: W. W. Norton,1995.

Dall, William Healey. *Alaska and Its Resources*. Boston: Lee and Shepard, 1870.

Davidson, Art. *In the Wake of the Exxon Valdez: The Devastating Impact of the Alaska Oil Spill*. San Francisco: Sierra Club Books, 1990.

Dean, David M. *Breaking Trail: Hudson Stuck of Texas and Alaska*. Athens: Ohio University Press, 1988.

DeArmond, Robert N. *The Founding of Juneau*. Juneau: Gastineau Channel Centennial Association, 1967.

De Windt, Henry. *Through the Gold-Field of Alaska to the Bering Straits*. New York: Harper and Brothers Publishers, 1898.

Dippie, Brian W. *The Vanishing American: White Attitudes and U.S. Indian Policy*. Lawrence: University of Kansas Press, 1982.

Donald, David Herbert. *Charles Sumner and the Rights of Man*. New York: Alfred A. Knopf, 1970.

Drake, Brian Allen. *Loving Nature, Fearing the State: Environmentalism and Antigovernment Politics before Reagan*. Seattle: University of Washington Press, 2013.

Driscoll, Joseph. *War Comes to Alaska*. Philadelphia: J. B. Lippincott Company, 1943.

Drucker, Philip. *The Native Brotherhoods: Modern Intertribal Organizations of the Northwest Coast*. Washington, D.C.: U.S. Government Printing Office, 1958.

Dufresne, Frank. *My Way Was North: An Alaskan Autobiography*. New York: Holt, Rinehard and Winston, 1966.

Durbin, Kathie. *Tongass: Pulp, Politics, and the Fight for the Alaska Rain Forest*. Corvallis: Oregon State University Press, 1999.

Eblen, Jack. *The First and Second United States Empires: Governors and Territorial Government, 1784–1912*. Pittsburgh: University of Pittsburgh Press, 1968.

Ehrlander, Mary F. *Walter Harper: Alaska Native Son*. Lincoln: University of Nebraska Press, 2017.

Elliott, Henry Wood. *An Arctic Province: Alaska and the Seal Islands*. London: Sampson Low, Marston, Searle, and Rivington, 1886.

Fisher, Victor. *Alaska's Constitutional Convention*. Fairbanks: University of Alaska Press, 1975.

Fitch, Edwin M. *The Alaska Railroad*. New York: Frederick A. Praeger, 1967.

Fortuine, Robert. *Chills and Fever: Health and Disease in the Early History of Alaska*. Fairbanks: University of Alaska Press, 1989.

Fox, Stephen. *John Muir and His Legacy: The American Conservation Movement*. Boston: Little, Brown, and Company, 1981.

Frederick, Robert A. *Frontier Alaska: A Study in Historical Interpretation and Opportunity*. Proceedings of the Conference on Alaska History. Alaska Methodist University, Anchorage, Alaska, June 1967. Anchorage: Alaska Methodist University Press, 1968.

Friday, Chris. *Organized Asian American Labor: The Pacific Coast Canned Salmon Industry, 1870–1942*. Philadelphia: Temple University Press, 1994.

Gallagher, Hugh C. *Etok: A Story of Eskimo Power*. New York: G. P. Putnam, 1974.

Gates, Paul Wallace. *History of Public Land Law Development*. Washington, D.C.: Government Printing Office, 1968.

Goetzman, William H., and Kay Sloan. *Looking Far North: The Harriman Expedition to Alaska, 1899.* New York: Viking Press, 1982.

Goldsmith, Scott. *Structural Analysis of the Alaska Economy: What Are the Drivers?* Rev. ed. Anchorage: University of Alaska Anchorage, Institute for Economic and Social Research, 2010.

Gressley, Gene M., ed. *Old West/New West.* Norman: University of Oklahoma Press, 1997.

Gruening, Ernest. *Let Us End American Colonialism: Alaska, the United States Colony.* College: Alaska Constitutional Convention, University of Alaska, 1955.

———. *Many Battles: The Autobiography of Ernest Gruening.* New York: Liveright, 1973.

———. *The State of Alaska.* New York: Random House, 1954.

Hammond, Jay S. *Diapering the Devil: A Lesson for Oil Rich Nations.* Homer, Alaska: Kachemak Resources Institute, 2011.

———. *Tales of Alaska's Bush Rat Governor: The Extraordinary Autobiography of Jay Hammond, Wilderness Guide and Reluctant Politician.* Fairbanks: Epicenter Press, 1994.

Hanrahan, John, and Peter Gruenstein. *Last Frontier: The Marketing of Alaska.* New York: W. W. Norton, 1977.

Harkey, Ira. *Pioneer Bush Pilot: The Story of Noel Wien.* Seattle: University of Washington Press, 1974.

Harrison, Gordon Scott, ed. *Alaska Public Policy: Current Problems and Issues.* College: Institute of Social, Economic, and Government Research, University of Alaska, 1971.

———. *Alaska's Constitution: A Citizen's Guide.* 5th ed. Juneau: Legislative Affairs Agency, 2013.

Harvey, Mark. *Wilderness Forever: Howard Zahniser and the Path to the Wilderness Act.* Seattle: University of Washington Press, 2005.

Haskell, William B. *Two Years in the Klondike and Alaskan Gold Fields, 1896–1898.* Fairbanks: University of Alaska Press, 1997.

Hawley, Charles Caldwell. *A Kennecott Story: Three Mines, Four Men, and One Hundred Years, 1897–1997.* Salt Lake City: University of Utah Press, 2014.

Haycox, Stephen. *Battleground Alaska: Fighting Federal Power in Alaska's Last Wilderness.* Lawrence: University Press of Kansas, 2016.

———. *Frigid Embrace: Politics, Economics, and Environment in Alaska.* Corvallis: Oregon State University Press, 2002.

———. *The Law of the Land: A History of the Office of the Attorney General and the Department of Law in Alaska.* Juneau: Alaska Department of Law, 1998.

Hays, Samuel P. *Conservation and the Gospel of Efficiency: The Progressive Conservation Movement, 1890–1920.* Cambridge: Harvard University Press, 1959.

Hedin, Robert, and Gary Holthaus. *Alaska: Reflections on Land and Spirit.* Tucson: University of Arizona Press, 1989.

———, eds. *The Great Land: Reflections on Alaska.* Tucson: University of Arizona Press, 1994.

Hellenthal, John. *The Alaskan Melodrama.* New York: Liveright, 1936.

Helmericks, Harmon, and Constance Helmericks. *We Live in the Arctic.* London: Hodder and Stoughton, 1949.

Hensley, William I. Iggiaguk. *Fifty Miles from Tomorrow: A Memoir of Alaska and the Real People.* New York: Farrar, Straus and Giroux, 2009.

Hickel, Walter J. *Who Owns America?* Englewood Cliffs, N.J.: Prentice-Hall, 1971.

Hilscher, Herb, and Miriam Hilscher. *Alaska: USA.* Boston: Little, Brown, and Company, 1959.

Hinckley, Ted C. *Alaskan John G. Brady: Missionary, Businessman, Judge, and Governor, 1878–1918.* Columbus: Ohio State University Press, 1982.

———. *The Americanization of Alaska, 1867–1897.* Palo Alto, Calif.: Pacific Books, 1972.

———. *The Canoe Rocks: Alaska's Tlingit and the Euramerican Frontier, 1800–1912.* Lanham, Md.: University Press of America, 1996.

Holbo, Paul S. *Tarnished Expansion: The Alaska Scandal, the Press, and Congress, 1867–1871.* Knoxville: University of Tennessee Press, 1983.

Hoover, Herbert. *Memoirs.* 3 vols. New York: Macmillan, 1951.

Hunt, William R. *Alaska: A Bicentennial History.* New York: W. W. Norton, 1976.

———. *Distant Justice: Policing the Alaskan Frontier.* Norman: University of Oklahoma Press, 1987.

———. *North of 53: The Wild Days of the Alaska-Yukon Mining Frontier, 1870–1914.* New York: Macmillan, 1974.

Huntington, Sidney, as told to Jim Rearden. *Shadows on the Koyukuk: An Alaska Native's Life Along the River.* Anchorage: Alaska Northwest Books, 1993.

James, James Alton. *The First Scientific Exploration of Russian America and the Purchase of Alaska.* Chicago: Northwestern University, 1942.

Jensen, Ronald J. *The Alaska Purchase and Russian American Relations.* Seattle: University of Washington Press, 1975.

Johnson, Robert David. *Ernest Gruening and the Dissenting Tradition.* Cambridge: Harvard University Press, 1998.

Johnson, Samuel, ed. *Alaska Commercial Company, 1868–1940.* San Francisco: E. E. Wachter, 1940.

Jorgenson, Joseph G. *Oil Age Eskimos.* Berkeley: University of California Press, 1990.

Kan, Sergei. *Symbolic Immortality: The Tlingit Potlatch of the Nineteenth Century.* Washington, D.C.: Smithsonian Institution Press, 1989.

Kaye, Roger. *Last Great Wilderness: The Campaign to Establish the Arctic National Wildlife Refuge*. Fairbanks: University of Alaska Press, 2006.

Keeble, John. *Out of the Channel: The* Exxon Valdez *Oil Spill in Prince William Sound*. New York: HarperCollins, 1991.

Kitchener, Lois D. *Flag over the North: The Story of the Northern Commercial Company*. Seattle: Superior Publishing Company, 1954.

Kizzia, Tom. *In the Wake of the Unseen Object: Among the Native Cultures of Alaska*. New York: H. Holt & Company, 1991.

———. *Pilgrim's Wilderness: The True Story of Faith and Madness on the Alaska Frontier*. New York: Crown, 2013.

Kleinfeld, Judith. *Frontier Romance: Environment, Culture and Alaska Identity*. Fairbanks: University of Alaska Press, 2012.

Knapp, Gunnar. *A Very Brief Introduction to the Alaska Economy*. Anchorage: University of Alaska Anchorage, Institute of Economic and Social Research, 2013.

Kohlhoff, Dean. *When the Wind Was a River: Aleut Evacuation in World War II*. Seattle: University of Washington Press, 1995.

Kollin, Susan. *Nature's State: Imagining Alaska as the Last Frontier*. Chapel Hill: University of North Carolina Press, 2001.

Jorgenson, Joseph G. *Oil Age Eskimos*. Berkeley: University of California Press, 1990.

Langdon, Steve J. *The Native People of Alaska*. 3rd ed. Anchorage: Greatland Graphics, 1993.

———. *Native Peoples of Alaska: Traditional Living in a Northern Land*. 5th ed. Anchorage: Greatland Graphics, 2014.

LaRocca, Joe E. *Alaska Agonistes: The Age of Petroleum, How Big Oil Bought Alaska*. Chapel Hill, N.C.: Professional Press, 2003.

Limerick, Patricia Nelson. *Legacy of Conquest: The Unbroken Past of the American West*. New York: W. W. Norton, 1987.

Limerick, Patricia Nelson, Clyde A. Milner II, and Charles Rankin, eds. *Trails: Toward a New Western History*. Lawrence: University Press of Kansas, 1991.

Lipset, Seymour Martin. *American Exceptionalism: A Double-Edged Sword*. New York: W. W. Norton, 1997.

Mackovjak, James. *Alaska SalmonTraps*. Gustavus, Alaska: Cross Sound Publications, 2013.

Marshall, Robert. *Arctic Village*. New York: H. Smith and R. Haas, 1933.

———. *Tongass Timber: A History of Logging and Timber Utilization in Southeast Alaska*. Durham, N.C.: Forest History Society, 2010.

McBeath, Gerald A. *The Alaska State Constitution*. New York: Oxford University Press, 2011.

McBeath, Gerald A., and Thomas A. Morehouse. *Alaska Politics and Government*. Lincoln: University of Nebraska Press, 1994.

————, eds. *Alaska State Government and Politics.* Fairbanks: University of Alaska Press, 1987.

McClanahan, A. J. *Growing up Native in Alaska.* Anchorage: Cook Inlet Region Inc., 2000.

McDougall, Walter. *Let the Sea Make a Noise: A History of the North Pacific from Magellan to MacArthur.* New York: Basic Books, 1993.

McEvoy, Arthur. *The Fisherman's Problem: Ecology and Law in the California Fisheries, 1850–1980.* Cambridge: Cambridge University Press, 1986.

McGinniss, Joe. *Going to Extremes.* New York: New American Library, 1980.

McPhee, John. *Coming into the Country.* New York: Farrar, Straus, Giroux, 1977.

Metcalfe, Peter, with Kathy Kolkhorst Ruddy. *A Dangerous Idea: The Alaska Native Brotherhood and the Struggle for Indigenous Rights.* St Paul: University of Minnesota Press, 2015.

Miller, Orlando. *The Frontier in Alaska and the Matanuska Colony.* New Haven, Conn.: Yale University Press, 1975.

Milner, Clyde, II. *Oxford History of the American West.* Oxford: Oxford University Press, 1994.

Mitchell, Donald Craig. *Sold American: The Story of Alaska Natives and Their Land, 1867–1959: The Army to Statehood.* Hanover, N.H.: University Press of New England, 1997.

————. *Take My Land, Take My Life: The Story of Congress's Historic Settlement of Alaska Native Land Claims, 1960–71.* Fairbanks: University of Alaska Press, 2002.

Mitchell, William. *The Opening of Alaska.* Edited by Lyman L. Woodman. Anchorage, Alaska: Cook Inlet Historical Society, 1982.

Morgan, Lael. *Art and Eskimo Power: The Life and Times of Alaskan Howard Rock.* Fairbanks: Epicenter Press, 1988.

————. *Good Time Girls of the Alaska-Yukon Gold Rush.* Fairbanks: Epicenter Press, 1998.

Morse, Kathryn. *The Nature of Gold: An Environmental History of the Klondike Gold Rush.* Seattle: University of Washington Press, 2010.

Muir, John. *The Cruise of the Corwin: Journal of the Arctic Expedition of 1881 in Search of De Long and the Jeanette.* Edited by William Frederic Bade. Boston: Houghton Mifflin, 1917.

————. *Travels in Alaska.* Boston: Houghton Mifflin, 1915.

Murie, Adolph. *A Naturalist in Alaska.* Devin-Adair American Naturalists Series. New York: Devin-Adair Company, 1961.

Murie, Margaret E. *Two in the Far North.* New York: Alfred A. Knopf, 1957.

Murray, Peter. *The Devil and Mr. Duncan.* Victoria, B.C.: Sono Nis Press, 1985.

Nash, Gerald D. *The American West Transformed: The Impact of the Second World War.* Bloomington: Indiana University Press, 1985.

Nash, Roderick. *Wilderness and the American Mind.* 3d ed. New Haven, Conn.: Yale
University Press, 1982.

Naske, Claus-M. *Alaska Road Commission Historical Narrative.* Fairbanks: State of
Alaska, Division of Transportation, 1983.

———. *Edward Lewis Bob Bartlett of Alaska: A Life in Politics.* Fairbanks: University
of Alaska Press, 1979.

———. *An Interpretative History of Alaskan Statehood.* Anchorage: Alaska Northwest
Publishing Company, 1973.

Naske, Claus-M., and William R. Hunt. *The Politics of Hydroelectric Power in Alaska:
Rampart and Devil Canyon—A Case Study.* Fairbanks: University of Alaska Press,
1978.

Naske, Claus-M., and Herman E. Slotnick. *Alaska: A History of the Forty-Ninth State.*
Grand Rapids, Mich.: William B. Eerdmans, 1979.

Naske, Claus-M., John S. Whitehead, and William Schneider. *Alaska Statehood, the
Memory of the Battle and the Evaluation of the Present by Those Who Lived It: An
Oral History of the Remaining Actors in the Alaska Statehood Movement.* Fairbanks:
Alaska Statehood Commission, 1981.

Nelson, Daniel. *Northern Landscapes: The Struggle for Wilderness Alaska.* Washington,
D.C.: Resources for the Future, 2004.

Nelson, Richard K. *Hunters of the Northern Forest: Designs for Survival among the
Alaskan Kutchin.* Chicago: University of Chicago Press, 1973.

———. *Make Prayers to the Raven: A Native View of the Koyukon Forest.* Chicago:
University of Chicago Press, 1983.

Neufeld, David, and Frank Norris. *Chilkoot Trail: Heritage Route to the Klondike.*
Whitehorse, Yukon Territory: Lost Moose, the Yukon Publishers, 1996.

Nichols, Jeannette Paddock. *Alaska: A History of Its Administration, Exploitation, and
Industrial Development during Its First Half Century under the Rule of the United
States.* Cleveland, Ohio: Arthur H. Clark, 1924.

Nielson, Jonathan M. *Armed Forces on a Northern Frontier: The Military in Alaska's
History, 1867–1987.* Westport, Conn.: Greenwood Press, 1988.

Norris, Frank. *Alaska Subsistence: A National Park Service Management History.*
Anchorage: National Park Service, 2002.

———. *Gawking at the Midnight Sun: The Tourist in Early Alaska.* Anchorage: Alaska
Historical Commission, 1985.

Ogilvie, William. *Early Days on the Yukon.* Ottawa: Thorburn and Abbott, 1913.

O'Neill, Dan. *The Firecracker Boys.* New York: St. Martin's Press, 1994.

Oliver, Ethel Ross. *Journal of an Aleutian Year.* Seattle: University of Washington
Press, 1988.

O'Neill, Dan. *The Firecracker Boys.* New York: St. Martin's Press, 1994.

———. *A Land Gone Lonesome: An Inland Voyage Along the Yukon River.* New York:
Counterpoint, 2006.

Oswalt, Wendell H. *Bashful No Longer: An Alaskan Eskimo Ethnohistory, 1778–1988.* Norman: University of Oklahoma Press, 1990.

Penick, James, Jr. *Progressive Politics and Conservation: The Ballinger-Pinchot Affair.* Chicago: University of Chicago Press, 1968.

Penlington, Norman. *The Alaska Boundary Dispute: A Critical Reappraisal.* Toronto: McGraw-Hill Ryerson, 1972.

Prucha, Francis Paul. *American Indian Policy in Crisis: Christian Reformers and the Indian, 1865–1900.* Norman: University of Oklahoma Press, 1964.

———. *The Great Father: The United States Government and the American Indians.* 2 vols. Lincoln: University of Nebraska Press, 1984.

Rakestraw, Lawrence. *A History of the United States Forest Service in Alaska.* Anchorage: Alaska Historical Commission, 1981.

Rawson, Timothy. *Changing Tracks: Predators and Politics in Mt. McKinley National Park.* Fairbanks: University of Alaska Press, 2001.

Ray, Dorothy Jean. *The Eskimos of Bering Strait, 1650–1898.* Seattle: University of Washington Press, 1975.

Remley, David A. *Crooked Road: A History of the Alaska Highway.* American Trail Series. New York: McGraw-Hill Book Company, 1976.

Ringsmuth, Katherine Johnson. *Alaska's Skyboys: Cowboy Pilots and the Myth of the Last Frontier.* Seattle: University of Washington Press, 2015.

Robbins, William G. *Colony and Empire: The Capitalist Transformation of the American West.* Lawrence: University of Kansas, 1994.

Roberts, Malcolm B. *Going up in Flames: The Promises and Pledges of Alaska Statehood under Attack.* Anchorage: Alaska Pacific University Press for Commonwealth North, 1990.

Roderick, Jack. *Crude Dreams: A Personal History of Oil and Politics in Alaska.* Fairbanks: Epicenter Press.

Rogers, George W. *The Future of Alaska: The Economic Consequences of Statehood.* Baltimore, Md.: Resources for the Future, and Johns Hopkins University Press, 1962.

———, ed. *Change in Alaska: People, Petroleum, and Politics.* College: University of Alaska Press, 1970.

Rogers, George W., and Richard A. Cooley. *Alaska's Population and Economy: Regional Growth, Development, and Future Outlook.* 2 vols. Juneau: Office of the Governor, 1962.

Rogers, Susan Fox. *Alaska Passages: Twenty Voices from above the Fifty-Fourth Parallel.* Seattle: Sasquatch Books, 1996.

Roscow, James P. *Eight Hundred Miles to Valdez: The Building of the Alaska Pipeline.* Englewood Cliffs, N.J.: Prentice-Hall, 1977.

Ross, Ken. *Environmental Conflict in Alaska.* Boulder: University Press of Colorado, 2000.

———. *Pioneering Conservation in Alaska*. Boulder: University Press of Colorado, 2006.

Sandberg, Eric. *A History of Alaska Population Settlement*. Juneau: Alaska Department of Labor and Workforce Development, 2013.

Satterfield, Archie. *The Alaska Airlines Story*. Anchorage: Alaska Northwest Publishing, 1981.

Service, Robert W. *Collected Verse*. Vol. 1. London: Ernest Benn, 1930.

Seward, Frederick William. *The Reminiscences of a Wartime Statesman and Diplomat, 1830–1915*. New York: G. P. Putnam's Sons, 1916.

———. *Seward at Washington as Senator and Secretary of State*. New York: Derby and Miller, 1891.

Seward, Oliver R. *William H. Seward's Travels around the World*. New York: Appleton, 1873.

Seward, William H. *Speech at Sitka, August 12, 1869*. Washington, D.C.: Phillip and Soloman, 1869.

Sheldon, Charles. *The Wilderness of Denali: Explorations of a Hunter-Naturalist in Northern Alaska*. New York: Charles Scribner's Sons, 1930.

Sherwood, Morgan. *Big Game in Alaska: A History of Wildlife and People*. New Haven, Conn.: Yale University Press, 1981.

———. *Exploration of Alaska, 1865–1900*. New Haven, Conn.: Yale University Press, 1965.

Shiels, Archie W. *The Purchase of Alaska*. College: University of Alaska Press, 1967.

Sodeberg, K. A., and Jackie DuRette, *People of the Tongass: Alaska Forestry under Attack*. Bellevue, Wash.: Free Enterprise Press, 1988.

Soos, Frank, and Ehrlander, Mary, eds. *The Big Wild Soul of Terrence Cole: An Eclectic Collection to Honor Alaska's Public Historian*. Fairbanks: University of Alaska Press, 2018.

Spurr, Stephen H., ed. *Rampart Dam and the Economic Development of Alaska*. Ann Arbor: University of Michigan, 1966.

Strohmeyer, John. *Extreme Conditions: Big Oil and the Transformation of Alaska*. New York: Simon and Schuster, 1993.

Stuck, Hudson. *Ten Thousand Miles with a Dog Sled: A Narrative of Winter Travel in Interior Alaska*. New York: Charles Scribner's Sons, 1915.

Sundborg, George. *Opportunity in Alaska*. New York: Macmillan, 1945.

Tomkins, Stuart Ramsay. *Alaska: Promyshlennik and Sourdough*. Norman: University of Oklahoma Press, 1945.

Tower, Elizabeth A. *Anchorage: From Its Humble Origins as a Railroad Construction Camp*. Fairbanks: Epicenter Press, 1999.

———. *Icebound Empire: Industry and Politics on the Last Frontier, 1898–1938*. Anchorage, Alaska: E. A. Tower, 1996.

Treuer, David. *The Heartbeat of Wounded Knee: Native America from 1890 to the Present.* New York: Riverhead Books, 2018.

Twichell, Heath. *Allen: The Biography of an Army Officer, 1859–1930.* New Brunswick, N.J.: Rutgers University Press, 1974.

———. *Northwest Epic: The Building of the Alaska Highway.* New York: St. Martin's Press, 1992.

Udall, Stewart L. *The Quiet Crisis.* New York: Holt, Rinehart, and Winston, 1963.
Underwood, John J. *Alaska: An Empire in the Making.* New York: Dodd, Mead & Company, 1913.

Webb, Melody. *The Last Frontier.* Albuquerque: University of New Mexico Press, 1985.

Weeden, Robert B. *Alaska, Promises to Keep.* Boston: Houghton Mifflin, 1978.

———. *Message from Earth Weeden: Nature and the Human Prospect in Alaska.* Fairbanks: University of Alaska Press, 1992.

Wharton, David. *The Alaska Gold Rush.* Bloomington: Indiana University Press, 1972.

Wheelwright, Jeff. *Degrees of Disaster: Prince William Sound, How Nature Reels and Rebounds.* New Haven, Conn.: Yale University Press, 1994.

White, Richard. *"It's Your Misfortune and None of My Own": A History of the American West.* Norman: University of Oklahoma Press, 1991.

Whitehead, John S. *Completing the Union: The Alaska and Hawaii Statehood Movements.* Anchorage: Alaska Historical Commission, 1986.

Whymper, Frederick. *Travel and Adventure in the Territory of Alaska.* London: John Murray, Albemarle Street, 1868.

Wickersham, James. *Old Yukon: Old Tales, Trails, and Trials.* St. Paul, Minn.: West Publishing Company, 1938.

Wilkinson, Charles F. *American Indians, Time, and the Law: Native Societies in a Modern Constitutional Democracy.* New Haven, Conn.: Yale University Press, 1987.

———. *Crossing the Next Meridian: Land, Water, and the Future of the West.* Washington, D.C.: Island Press, 1992.

Williss, G. Frank. *"Do Things Right the First Time": The National Park Service and the Alaska National Interest Lands Conservation Act of 1980.* Washington, D.C.: National Park Service, 1985.

Williss, Roxanne. *Alaska's Place in the West: From the Last Frontier to the Last Great Wilderness.* Lawrence: University Press of Kansas, 2010.

Wilson, William H. *Railroad in the Clouds: The Alaska Railroad in the Age of Steam, 1914–1945.* Boulder, Colo.: Pruett, 1977.

Wright, Sam. *Koviashuvik: Making a Home in the Brooks Range.* Tucson: University of Arizona Press, 1988.

Wyatt, Victoria. *Images from the Inside Passage: An Alaskan Portrait by Winter and Pond.* Seattle: University of Washington Press, 1989.

Young, S. Hall. *Alaska Days with John Muir.* New York: Fleming H. Revell Company, 1915.

Zaslow, Morris. *The Northward Expansion of Canada, 1914–67.* Toronto: McClelland and Stewart, 1988.

Znamenski, Andrei A. *Shamanism and Christianity: Native Encounters with Russian Orthodox Missions in Siberia and Alaska, 1820–1917.* Westport, Conn.: Greenwood Press, 1999.

Articles and Book Chapters

Ascott, Ivan L. "Comments: The Alaska Statehood Act Does Not Guarantee Alaska Ninety Percent of the Revenue from Mineral Leases on Federal Land in Alaska." *Seattle University Law Review* 27 (2004): 999–1034.

Beistline, Earl H. "Alaska's Mineral Bonanzas of Yesteryear." *Journal of the West* 35 (1979).

Beverly, James. "The *Alaska Fisherman* and the Paradox of Assimilation: Progress, Power, and the Preservation of Culture." *Native Press Research Journal* 5 (1987): 2–25.

Bezeau, M. V. "The Realities of Strategic Planning: The Decision to Build the Alaska Highway." In *The Alaska Highway: Papers of the Fortieth Anniversary Symposium,* ed. Kenneth Coates. Vancouver: University of British Columbia Press, 1985.

Coates, Kenneth. "Controlling the Periphery: The Territorial Administration of the Yukon-Alaska, 1867–1959." *Pacific Northwest Quarterly* 78 (1987): 141–51.

———. "Discovering the North: Towards a Conceptual Framework for the Study of Northern/Remote Regions." *Northern Review* 11 (Summer–Winter 1994): 15–43.

Coates, Peter. "The Crude and the Pure: Oil and Environmental Politics in Alaska." In *Politics in the Postwar American West,* ed. Richard Lowitt. Norman: University of Oklahoma Press, 1995.

———. "Project Chariot: Alaskan Roots of Environmentalism." *Alaska History* 4 (Fall 1989): 1–31.

Cole, Terrence. "Jim Crow in Alaska: The Passage of the Equal Rights Act of 1945." *Western Historical Quarterly* 23 (November 1992): 429–49.

Cravez, Pamela, "Revolt in the Ranks: The Great Alaska Court-Bar Fight." *Alaska Law Review* 13 (June 1996): 13–26.

de Voto, Bernard. "The West: A Plundered Province." *Harper's Magazine,* August 1934, 355–64.

Doig, Ivan. "The Tribe that Learned Capitalism." *American History* 24 (1974): 25–39.

Foster, James C. "AFL, IWW, and Nome, 1905–1908." *Alaska Journal* 5 (Spring 1975): 66–73.

———. "Syndicalism Northern Style: Life and Death of WFM No. 193." *Alaska Journal* 4 (Summer 1974): 130–41.

———. "Treadwell Strikes, 1907 and 1908." *Alaska Journal* 6 (1976): 2–11.

Egan, Timothy. "Tongass Timber Fiasco." *New York Times*, 22 August 1989.

Gates, Paul Wallace. "An Overview of American Land Policy." *Agricultural History* 50 (January 1979): 213–29.

Gough, Barry M. "The Character of the British Columbia Frontier." *BC Studies* 32 (1976–77): 74–92.

Gruening, Ernest. "The Plot to Strangle Alaska." *Atlantic Monthly* 216 (July 1965): 56–59.

Hartzog, George, Jr. "The Impact of Recent Litigation on Administrative Agencies." In *Wilderness in a Changing World*, ed. Bruce M. Kilgore, 172–80. San Francisco: Sierra Club Books, 1966.

Haycox, Stephen W. "Alaska and the Canadian North: Comparing Conceptual Frameworks." In *Northern Visions: New Perspectives on the North in Canadian History*, ed. Kerry Abel and Ken S. Coates, 141–58. Peterborough, Ont.: Broadview Press, 2001.

———. "Economic Development and Native Rights in Alaska: The 1947 Tongass Timber Act." *Western Historical Quarterly* 21 (February 1990): 20–46.

———. "'Fetched Up': Unlearned Lesson from the *Exxon Valdez*." *Journal of American History* (June 2012): 219–28.

———. "The Political Power of a Rhetorical Paradigm." In *Land in the American West: Private Claims and the Common Good*, ed. William G. Robbins, 164–89. Seattle: University of Washington Press, 2000.

———. "'Races of a Questionable Ethnical Type': Origins of the Jurisdiction of the U.S. Bureau of Education in Alaska, 1867–1885." *Pacific Northwest Quarterly* 75 (October 1984): 155–63.

———. "The View from Above: Alaska and the Great Northwest." In *The Great Northwest: The Search for Regional Identity*, ed. William G. Robbins, 145–57. Corvallis: Oregon State University Press, 2001.

———. "William Lewis Paul: Tlingit Advocate." In *The Human Tradition in America, 1920–1945*, ed. Donald W. Whisenhunt. Wilmington, Del.: Scholarly Resources, 2002.

———. "William Paul, Sr., and the Alaska Voters' Literacy Act of 1925." *Alaska History* 2 (Winter 1986–87): 17–37.

Haycox, Stephen W., and Claus-M. Naske. "'A New Face': Implementing Law in the New State of Alaska, 1958–1960." *Western Legal History* 11 (Winter–Spring 1998): 1–22.

Heintzleman, B. Frank. "Forestry in Alaska." In *Proceedings of the Alaska Science Conference*, 129–30. Washington, D.C.: National Academy of Sciences, 1951.

Henning, Robert. "Bristol Bay Basin." *Alaska Geographic* 5 (1978): 31–39.

Hinckley, Ted C. "The Early Ministry of S. Hall Young, 1878–1888." *Journal of Presbyterian History* 46 (1968): 175–96.

———."Sheldon Jackson, Presbyterian Lobbyist for the Great Land of Alaska." *Journal of Presbyterian History* 40 (1962): 32–46.

Kan, Sergei. "Russian Orthodox Brotherhood among the Tlingit: Missionary Goals and Native Response. *Ethnohistory* 32 (1985): 196–223.

Keithahn, Edward L. "Alaska Ice, Inc." *Pacific Northwest Quarterly* 36 (April 1945): 1–16.

Naske, Claus-M. "Governor Gruening's Struggle for Territorial Status: Personal or Political." *Journal of the West* 20 (January 1981): 32–40.

———. "The Shaky Beginnings of Alaska's Judicial System." *Western Legal History* 1 (Summer–Fall 1988): 22–36.

Nelson, Arnold, and Helen Nelson. "The Bubble of Oil at Katalla." *Alaska Journal* (a 1981 collection).

Norris, Frank. "Popular Images of the North in Literature and Film." *Northern Review* 8–9 (Summer 1992): 53–72.

———. "Showing off Alaska: The Northern Tourist Trade, 1878–1941." Alaska History 2 (Fall 1987): 1–18.

Peel, Ryan T. "Katie John v. United States: Balancing State Sovereignty with a Native Grandmother's Right to Fish." *BYU Journal of Public Law* 15 (2001): 263–79.

Pierce, Richard A. "New Light on Ivan Petroff, Historian of Alaska." *Pacific Northwest Quarterly* 59 (October 1968): 1–10.

Philp, Kenneth R. "The New Deal and Alaska Natives, 1936–1945." *Pacific Historical Review* 50 (1981): 309–27.

Purdy, Anne. *Tisha: The Story of a Young Teacher in the Alaska Wilderness. Anne Hobbs, as Told to Robert Specht*. New York: Bantam Books, 1976.

Rhodes, Herb. "Why an Alaskan Reporter?" *Alaskan Reporter* 1 (January 1952): 4.

Shannon, Margaret. "Charles Sumner and the Alaska Purchase." In *Russian America: The Forgotten Frontier*, ed. Barbara Sweetland Smith and Redmond J. Barnett. Tacoma: Washington State Historical Society, 1990.

Sherwood, Morgan B. "Ardent Spirits: Hooch and the *Osprey* Affair at Sitka." *Journal of the West* 4 (July 1965): 301–44.

———. "The End of Wilderness." *Environmental Review* 9 (Fall 1985): 197–209.

———."George Davidson and the Acquisition of Alaska." *Pacific Historical Review* 28 (1959): 141–54.

———. "Ivan Petroff and the Far Northwest." *Journal of the West* 2 (1963): 305–15.

Shortridge, James. "The Alaska Agricultural Empire: An American Agrarian Vision, 1898–1929." *Pacific Northwest Quarterly* 69 (1978): 145–58.

Sullivan, Joseph. "Sourdough Radicalism: Labor and Socialism in Alaska, 1905–1920." *Alaska History* 7 (Spring 1992): 1–16.

Vevier, Charles. "The Collins Overland Line and American Continentalism." *Pacific Historical Review* 28 (1959): 237–53.

Welch, Richard E., Jr. "American Public Opinion and the Purchase of Russian America." *American Slavic and East European Review* 17 (1958): 481–94.

Wilson, William H. "Ahead of the Time: Alaska Railroad and Tourism." *Alaska Journal* 7 (Winter 1977): 18–24.

———. "The Alaska Railroad and Coal: Development of a Federal Policy, 1914–1939." *Pacific Northwest Quarterly* 73 (1982): 66–73.

———. "The Founding of Anchorage: Federal Town Building on the Last Frontier." *Pacific Northwest Quarterly* 58 (July 1967): 130–41.

Wyatt, Victoria. "Female Teachers in Southeast Alaska: Sarah Dickinson, Tillie Paul, and Frances Willard." In *Between Indian and White Worlds: The Cultural Broker*, ed. Margaret Szasz. Norman: University of Oklahoma Press, 1994.

INDEX

Paramushiro, 277
Parks, Governor George, 261
Paul, Louis, 254–55
Paul, William, 254–55, 263, 273–74;
    election, 255, 263; and IRA, 270–71
Paul I, Tsar, 35, 90
Pearl Harbor, 276–79
Pedroni, Felice (Felix Pedro),
    220–21
Peratrovich, Frank, 263, 282
Peratrovich, Robert, 263
Permanent Fund, 339
Perouse, Comte de la, 70–71
Peshchurov, Capt. A. A., 159
Peter the Great, 35, 47–48
Petr the Martyr, 112
Petroff, Ivan, 191, 209
Petropavlovsk: in Crimean War, 143;
    founded, 52
Phillips Petroleum, 337
Phoenix (ship), 86
Pilz, George, 197
Pinchot, Gifford, 236, 242
Pipeline. *See* Trans-Alaska Pipeline
Plate tectonics, 4–5
Point Possession, 67
Politarism, 161
Portland (ship), 215
Potlatch, 17, 28–30
Pribilof Islands, 107
Pribylov, Gavriil, 76
Prince William Sound, 7; and *Exxon
    Valdez*, 333–34
Progressive reform, 234, 256, 261; and
    Alaska railroad, 245; and conservation,
    236; and literacy bill, 256; and
    territorial legislature, 243
Project Chariot, 287
Project Plowshare, 287
Promyshlenniki, 35
Prospecting, 214
Prudhoe Bay: discovery of, 133
Public Works Administration (PWA), 266,
    268

Quiet Crisis, The (Udall), 316

Rampart Dam, 286
Randall, Lt. Col. George, 224
Ray, Capt. Patrick, 224
Raymond, Capt. Charles, 206
Reagan, President Ronald, 325
Reid, Frank, 225
Replication in Alaska history, 171, 198
Rezanov, Nikolai Petrovich, 89–90, 106–10
Rice, John, 227
Richardson, Lt. Wilds, 224
Richardson Highway, 232
Riggs, Governor Thomas, 249
Rivers, Rep. Ralph, 291
Roosevelt, President Franklin D., 266, 268,
    278
Roosevelt, President Theodore, 236–37,
    244
Rousseau, Gen. Lovell, 159
Rozenberg, Capt. Nikolai, 141
Rural Rehabilitation Administration, 268
Russian America, xvii, 127, 160; and
    Crimean War, 143, 154–55; exploration
    of, 127; population, 58; sale of, 154, 160;
    supply problem, 125–27
Russian American Company (RAC),
    92–100, 112, 126; and Baranov, 105, 109,
    115; established, 91–92; and persecution
    of Natives, 96–100
Russian Orthodox mission, 88, 100;
    established, 92–93

Sagebrush rebellion, 328
Salmon fishery, 255, 257, 263; canneries,
    257–58; and Native lands, 272; origin of,
    257–60; White Act and, 259–60
San Francisco, 108, 178, 277; *Excelsior*
    arrives at, 215
Sarychev, G. A., 73
Sauer, Martin, 73
Schaffer, Georg Anton, 113
Schrader, F. C. (USGS), 226
Schwatka, Lt. Frederick, 207

Sea otter, 57; and Cook's voyage, 67, 69

Sealaska, 341

Seattle, 215, 268, 276–77

Securities and Exchange Commission (SEC), 267

Seppala, Leonard: and serum run, 264

Serebrennikov, Ruf, 136

Seward, William Henry, 158, 180–81; Alaska purchase, 176–77

"Seward's Folly," 178

Sheffield, Governor William, 332

Sheldon Jackson School, 253

Shelikhov, Grigorii, 64, 75–76, 89; and Baranov, 87; plans for North America, 77

Shelikhova, Natal'ia, 89

Sherwood, Morgan, 189–90

Siberia, 15, 42

Silent Spring (Carson), 317

Simpson, Sir George, 58, 131

Sindt, Ivan, 61

Sitka (Novo Archangelsk), 102, 191; 1840 development, 136

Sitka (Presbyterian) Industrial Training School, 253

Skagway, 215, 217

Skookum Jim, 212

Smith, Barbara Sweetland, 146

Smith, Jefferson ("Soapy"), 225

Social organization, 28

Social Security, 267

Socialist Party, 248

Solov'ev, Ivan Maksimovich, 59–60

Southeast Alaska Conservation Council (SEACC), 329–30

Spain, 103; and Krenitsyn expedition, 62; and Nootka affair, 83

Spotted (Northern) owl, 326

S.S. *Manhattan*, 69, 309

St. Michael, 221, 223

State of Alaska v. Udall, 309

Statehood, 289–90, 296; 1946 referendum, 289

Steller, Georg Wilhelm, 51, 53, 146

Stevens, Sen. Ted, 292, 302, 309

Stevens Village, 318

Stoeckl, Edouard, 153, 157, 176

Strange, Capt. James, 70

Subsistence, rural priority, 340

Sulzer, Charles, 253

Sumner, Sen. Charles, 176, 179

Sutherland, Del. Dan, 253, 256–57, 260, 262

Sv. (St.) Gabriel (ship), 49

Swineford, Governor Alfred P., 202

Taft, President William H., 242–43

Tagish Charley, 212

Tarakanov, Timofei, 110

Tarasov, Boris, 112

Taxation, oil, 320

Teben'kov, Governor Mikhail, 136

Telegraph, 1899, 228

Teller, Edward, 287

Tennessee Plan, 291

Three Saints Bay: Shikhov post, 76

Tlingit Indians, 17, 108, 263; and Alaska purchase, 183; and ANB, 253; and land claims, 273; precontact, 28–29; and Russians, 102, 128; and trade, 40, 135–36

Tlingit-Haida Jurisdictional Act, 273

Tolstykh, Andreian, 60

Tongass National Forest Timber Act (1946), 285, 301, 327, 329–30; and ANILCA, 261, 273–74, 284, 317; and Reform Act (1990), 330

Tonquin (ship), 111

Trans-Alaska Pipeline, 317

Trans-Alaska Pipeline Authorization Act, 319

Treadwell, John, 198–200

Trump, President Donald, 341–42

Tsarina Catherine, 64, 71, 76, 78, 90, 107

Udall, Rep. Morris, 323, 325

Udall, Stewart, 305, 316; *State of Alaska v.*, 309

Ulmer, Lt. Governor Fran, 338

Unalaska, 70